W9-ABT-536

Third Edition

The Structure of
Social Stratification
in the United States

Leonard Beeghley
University of Florida

Allyn and Bacon
Boston • London • Toronto • Sydney • Tokyo • Singapore

Series Editor: Sarah L. Kelbaugh
Editor in Chief, Social Sciences: Karen Hanson
Editorial Assistant: Jennifer DiDomenico
Marketing Manager: Brooke Stoner
Editorial-Production Administrator: Annette Joseph
Editorial-Production Coordinator: Holly Crawford
Composition Buyer: Linda Cox
Electronic Composition: Cabot Computer Services
Manufacturing Buyer: Julie McNeill
Cover Administrator: Linda Knowles

Copyright © 2000, 1996, 1989 by Allyn & Bacon
A Pearson Education Company
160 Gould Street
Needham Heights, MA 02494

Internet: www.abacon.com

All rights reserved. No part of the material protected by this copyright notice may be
reproduced or utilized in any form or by any means, electronic or mechanical, including
photocopying, recording, or by any information storage and retrieval system, without
written permission from the copyright owner.

Library of Congress Cataloging-in-Publication Data

Beeghley, Leonard.
    The structure of social stratification in the United States /
Leonard Beeghley. — 3rd ed.
        p.   cm.
    Includes bibliographical references and index.
    ISBN 0-205-27835-3
    1. Social classes—United States.   2. Social
stratification—United States.   3. Social structure—United States.
    I. Title.
    HN90.S6 B44   1999
    305.5'0973—dc21   99-26838
                                                                  CIP

Printed in the United States of America

10 9 8 7 6 5 4 3 2 1   04 03 02 01 00 99

For EHB

Contents

Preface

In this book, I have tried to distill out of the rich vein of sociological research some of what is known about the *structure of stratification* in the United States. This term refers to the distribution of valued resources, such as income, prestige, and power. The structure of stratification affects every aspect of life: where (and whether) one lives, who one marries, how (and whether) one earns a living, who one's friends are, and much more. In revising the book to explain these and other issues, my objective has been to make each chapter factually accurate, interesting to read, and relevant to readers' lives. In the process, the book has been completely reorganized, updated, and rewritten for this Third Edition. A new chapter has been added that places the United States in the context of stratification around the world.

In making these revisions, I have tried to keep in mind that science is the art of asking questions. But questions are always asked in light of an intellectual framework—which needs to be explicit. In Chapter 1, the ideas of the most important theorists of stratification are reviewed, and a coherent strategy for studying stratification is developed and used throughout the book. This strategy has three elements: First, as often as possible, I place data in a historical and international context. This information leads to important questions. For example, if the rate of poverty has fallen in all Western societies (and it has), one wants to know why. But if, even given the historical decline, the rate of poverty in the United States is much higher than in Western Europe (and it is), one again wants to know why. Second, I distinguish between social psychological explanations of individual actions and structural explanations of rates of behavior. Just as one obtains different insights from examining a painting up close and afar, these two levels of analysis provide complementary but different insights into social life. For example, the reasons individuals become poor (e.g., they lack skills) have nothing whatsoever to do with why so many people are poor (e.g., macroeconomic policy restricts the number of jobs that are available whenever it is necessary to control inflation). There is an enduring insight here: Regardless of the topic, the variables explaining why individuals act differ from those explaining why rates of behavior vary. This fact will be illustrated throughout the book. This distinction aids in understanding issues as diverse as poverty, mobility, voting, gender stratification, and racial/ethnic stratification. Third, I emphasize the importance of power for understanding the structure of stratification. The story of the last century is one of increasing choice in human affairs. For example, nations now control how much inequality and poverty exist. Hence, the periodic use of macroeconomic policy to restrict the number of jobs provides one example (there are others) of how poverty is created and maintained in this country. More generally, I argue that the level of inequality in the United States reflects the power of the rich and middle class to protect their lifestyles. Again, there is an enduring insight here: *The higher the social class, the greater the influence over access to valued resources in the society.*

This statement is called the Political Power Hypothesis. It is just one of many hypotheses and findings presented in the book. The importance of hypothesis testing is emphasized throughout. This is, in part, a pedagogical device. It illustrates for students (rather than merely asserting) the possibilities of scientific sociology by showing both how much we know and, by implication, how much remains to be learned. Most hypotheses and empirical generalizations (stable findings) are phrased as statements of covariance. This tactic shows students how a change in one phenomenon is associated with change in another. This point is typically made in methods and (less often) theory courses, but neglected elsewhere. Too frequently, I think, text writers give the impression that sociological knowledge depends on the assumptions observers make. Nothing could be further from the truth. In part, however, the emphasis on hypothesis testing is also a statement about the nature of social science. If science is the art of asking questions, then our answers must reflect knowledge based on observation.

Yet how observations are to be interpreted remains a vexing issue. In the study of stratification, for example, the relationship among class, race, and gender as systems of ranking has become controversial in recent years. Throughout this book, I try to show how they are interrelated. Minorities remain unequal to whites; women remain unequal to men. This inequality reflects the historical legacy and continuing impact of discrimination. Yet inequality has declined over time. In considering these issues, the larger question is the degree to which people's location in the stratification structure is determined by birth or achievement. One of the paradoxes of modernity is that our very concern with gender and racial/ethnic stratification reflects a degree of movement (I would say progress) toward class-based stratification structures. When societies are stratified by class, unlike medieval estates, there is a greater (but far from total) emphasis on achievement. This historical transformation is one example of what I meant earlier in saying that people and, indeed, entire societies, now have greater choice in how they organize themselves.

The book is written primarily for students, but also for general readers who want to know more about how the distribution of valued resources occurs. I have tried to write simply and clearly. Although some jargon is unavoidable, I have kept it to a minimum. When technical terms are necessary, they are introduced, defined, and illustrated. Even so, most textbooks are boring. Having taught social stratification for over 25 years, I have found that the use of metaphors, vignettes, and even nursery rhymes can be useful pedagogical devices. So I sometimes invent people, families, and situations in order to introduce or describe sociological findings. Occasionally, these episodes are (I hope) mildly humorous. Underlying such efforts at relieving the tedium, however, is a serious issue: The great world trend has been movement in the direction of more democracy and less inequality (the two are connected). The United States is thus part of a transformative historical process. I am convinced that sociology can and should inform public debate about this trend as we move toward a new millennium.

L.B.

Acknowledgments

No author works alone. I would like to take this opportunity to thank those individuals who helped to make this book better. My most enduring debt is to Marion Willetts of Illinois State University. She read the entire manuscript and made valuable suggestions throughout. Various chapters were read by Chet Ballard of Valdosta State College, Bam dev Sharda of the University of Utah, Janis Weber of the University of Wisconsin at Stevens Point, Max Wilson of Flagler College, and Barbara Zsembik of the University of Florida. Their criticisms were extremely useful, often at crucial times. In addition, the following persons read the manuscript for Allyn & Bacon: James E. Gallagher, University of Maine; Myron Orleans, California State University–Fullerton; Allan Schnaiberg, Northwestern University; and George Wilson, University of Miami. Their comments were unusually helpful as I went about revising the manuscript. Finally, I would like to thank the staff in the federal documents section of the University of Florida Library. Paige Harper, especially, often went out of his way to help me find sometimes obscure government publications. I am most grateful.

Chapter *1*

Sociology and Stratification

Theoretical Perspectives on Stratification
  Karl Marx
  Max Weber
  Kingsley Davis and Wilbert Moore
  Ralf Dahrendorf
  Gerhard Lenski

A Strategy for the Study of Stratification
  Historical and International Dimensions of Stratification
  Levels of Analysis and Stratification
  Power and Stratification

All societies display stratification. The term conveys an image of geological strata, of layers stacked one upon the other. Like geological strata, societies are also composed of interconnected layers that display a hierarchical (or ranked) structure. The **structure of social stratification** can be defined as the distribution of valued resources in society. Such resources can be income, occupational prestige, power, and education, among many others. Possession of valued resources affects people's **life chances,** their ability to share in the available goods and services. The structure of stratification has three interrelated systems of ranking.

The first is by class. People in the same **class** tend to be relatively equal to one another in terms of valued resources. For example, those with similar levels of occupational prestige usually have (roughly) similar income and education. People in different classes tend to be unequal in these same terms. Such variations affect people's life chances. For example, housing location and size, alcohol consumption, health, even mate selection, all differ by class.

The second system of ranking is by gender. Although some decline in gender inequality has occurred in recent years, women and men continue to be unequal to one another in terms of income, occupational prestige, and other factors. Historically, traditional gender norms (buttressed by violence and its threat) meant that women have not only had less access to resources than men but also less autonomy in shaping their lives. Their life chances differed, and differ today as well.

The third system of ranking is by race and ethnicity. Members of racial and ethnic groups are often unequal to one another. For example, although differences between whites and African Americans in income and occupational prestige have declined in recent years, they remain significant. This fact means that African Americans (along with Hispanics, Asian Americans, and other minority groups) are less likely to be middle class than whites (non-Hispanics). This difference reflects the long-term impact of prejudice and discrimination. But even within the middle class, members of minority groups are often unequal to whites. This is partly because many are first-generation middle class—hence, their lifestyles are more precarious—and partly because they still endure prejudice and discrimination. As with gender inequality, racial and ethnic inequality affects people's life chances.

Although the geological strata seen on the side of a cliff appear to be static and unchanging, this is misleading. In reality, dynamic processes shape the formation of the earth. So examining the geological record requires looking at both stability and change. This is also necessary when studying the stratification structure. Because the distribution of scarce resources is unequal, people struggle to keep their share of goods and services and to obtain more. This struggle makes the relationship among the three ranking systems dynamic.

One way to understand the forces shaping the stratification structure is to think about the degree of emphasis on ascription versus achievement as "pure types" (to use a phrase of Max Weber's). **Ascription** refers to the use of non-performance-related criteria (such as class of origin, race/ethnicity, or gender) in evaluating a person. This is a complicated way of saying that people obtain positions based on birth. The extent to which certain types of people—say, white males—have advantages in seeking to become physicians indicates an emphasis on ascription. **Achievement** refers to the use of performance-related criteria that are equally applied to all persons (such as grade point averages, college degrees, skill requirements) when they are evaluated. This is a complicated way of saying that people obtain positions based on hard work and ability. The extent to which anyone—regardless of class of origin, race/ethnicity, or gender— can become a physician based on grades and other skills indicates an emphasis on achievement. Now imagine two societies, one based totally on ascription and the other on achievement. Although neither could actually exist, seeing them as end points on a continuum provides a way of classifying real societies: In some, ascription is more important than achievement, and in others, achievement is more important than ascription.

Although many people like to believe that we emphasize achievement in the United States, this is only partially true. Ascription remains fundamental. Family background in the form of class of origin, race/ethnicity, and gender strongly affect access to resources and, hence, one's life chances, regardless of how much ability people have or how hard they work. It makes a big difference if one is born rich or poor, white or brown, male or female. Nonetheless, achievement has become increasingly important over time in determining life chances, both in the United States and in Western societies generally. The story of the last century or two has been one of increasing choice in human affairs, both for individuals and societies. Choice leads to an emphasis on achievement. The rise of class as a system of stratification indicates this fact. It is not accidental that members of racial and ethnic minorities have sought greater income, prestige, and education based on their abilities, not inherited traits. So the tension between ascription and achievement shapes the stratification structure. This tension is expressed politically in the struggle for power.

This chapter introduces the sociological study of the structure of stratification. Because the basis of all science is theory, I begin by briefly summarizing the ideas of some of the most important theorists of stratification. With that background, I then outline a strategy for understanding the process by which access to valued resources is distributed.

Theoretical Perspectives on Stratification

The social sciences are relatively young disciplines. The first generation of sociologists did not appear until the latter part of the nineteenth century—people such as Karl Marx, Max Weber, Emile Durkheim, among others. More recently, such figures as Kingsley Davis, Wilbert Moore, Talcott Parsons, Robert K. Merton, Ralf Dahrendorf, Gerhard Lenski, and Jonathan H. Turner have increased theoretical understanding of the structure of stratification. By **theory,** I mean abstract knowledge about how and why empirical events occur. Although I shall be mildly critical of some of these scholars, you should bear in mind that they are pioneers who confronted many of the key problems faced by any nascent science: developing a model of the object of study, learning to ask testable questions, obtaining objective empirical information, and working out some tentative abstract hypotheses. I begin with Karl Marx.[1]

Karl Marx

The historical background for Marx's ideas lies in the enormous increase in productivity that resulted from scientific advances, the rise of capitalism, and the industrial revolution. According to Marx, the impact of these epic changes led to a paradox in the middle of the nineteenth century. Although increases in productivity meant that it had become possible for everyone to share in the available goods and services, including amenities (objects that increase comfort and pleasure), only a few people actually benefited: the very rich who owned capital (income-producing assets). The capitalists

---

[1]The following sketches are necessarily brief, and I have avoided citing the secondary sources. For more extended commentary and sources on Marx and Weber, see Turner, Beeghley, and Powers, *The Emergence of Sociological Theory* (1998). On the modern theorists, see Turner, *The Structure of Sociological Theory* (1998).

exploited the masses, who lived in great misery and depravity. In this context, Marx was both a revolutionary and a sociologist. As a revolutionary, he sought to overthrow the existing order and substitute collective control of society by the people so that, acting cooperatively, everyone's needs could be met and they could be free to develop their full potential as human beings. As a sociologist, Marx developed a theory that appeared to show such collective control is historically inevitable. The result, Marx and Engels wrote in the *Communist Manifesto,* would be a communist society in which "the free development of each is the condition for the free development of all" (1848, p. 112). In this context, Marx believed, the structure of social stratification would no longer involve the exploitation of the many by the few.

In developing his theory, Marx began with the simple proposition that in all societies people produce goods to satisfy their material needs. He called this proposition "the materialist conception of history." He meant that people's social relationships and values are inherently connected to the type of productive activity that exists. For example, family life is likely to be different in a hunting and gathering society from what it is in an industrial one, as is the form of government, education, religious beliefs, law, cultural values, and so on. These differences reflect the diverse ways people obtain food, clothing, and shelter, as well as the availability of amenities. This insight about the importance of producing goods to satisfy needs has endured. Modern political strategists say it differently—"It's the economy, Stupid"—but mean the same thing.

Marx continued by arguing that a relatively rigid stratification structure emerges in all societies based on private ownership of capital. As a result, he believed, an upper class of owners dominates the state and controls access to resources. While Marx's assertion is too strong today, those who own capital do have a great deal of power. It follows that they have a stake in maintaining the status quo. When he looked at social arrangements, Marx always asked a simple question, one that modern sociologists also ask: Who benefits? For example, in his greatest work, *Capital,* he showed how the capitalists' attempts at lengthening the working day and raising productivity in order to secure greater profit for themselves also increased workers' exploitation (1867). In every arena, at home, at work, in court, at church, and in the doctor's office, it is useful to ascertain who benefits from current social arrangements. The answer usually suggests which classes are the most powerful in a society.

It also suggests which classes are relatively powerless; that is, its members usually cannot overcome the disadvantages with which they are born. Because they do not own capital, most people must sell their ability to work in order to survive. This necessity means they continually recreate their own exploitation. Because autoworkers, for example, need cars to get to work each day, they return their wages to the company and its stockholders (most of whom are rich and powerful). And this is a generalized process: As they go about obtaining goods and services, working people return nearly all their income to the capitalists. They, in turn, reinvest their profits to make still more money. As Marx put it in *Capital,* "the circle in which simple reproduction moves alters its form and . . . changes into a spiral" (1867, p. 581). He meant that the exploitation of working people by capitalists is part of a self-perpetuating social structure.

Strangely, however, even though their interest lies in changing this social structure, most workers (nearly all of the population) accept the status quo. This is because they are taught by the schools, the media, government, and even religion to believe that their own exploitation is right and proper. One of Marx's goals was to explain to working people their true interests. For example, he argued that "religion is the sigh of the oppressed creature—the opium of the masses" (1843). He meant that religion diverts people's attention from their alienation and exploitation in this world by promising an illusion: happiness in the next world. Thus, he argued, the hidden impact of religious teaching is to make the masses blind to their interest in changing the status quo, thereby benefiting those who desire to maintain it: the capitalists. In this context, Marx said, **alienation** is widespread. That is, people see themselves as powerless, unable to control their own lives; most importantly, they do not understand that they are being exploited or how it is accomplished. The pervasiveness of alienation is a dominant theme in Marx's work. It constitutes the standard by which he judged societies. In a nonalienated world, people would use work not only to obtain goods and services but also to express their human potential. In a nonalienated world, the means of production (capital) would be used for the common good. In a nonalienated world, the stratification structure would be relatively fluid and people could move up based on achievement. But these possibilities, Marx believed, were impossible when the stratification structure is organized so that the few who own capital exploit the many, who must sell their labor to survive.

Marx divided the stratification structure into two parts: the bourgeoisie (capitalists) and proletarians (working class). While he recognized that this model was too simple, his purpose was to highlight what he saw as the increasingly rigid division within nineteenth-century capitalist societies between owners and nonowners of capital. This two-class division proved helpful to Marx because he emphasized that class conflict pervades all societies and constitutes the mechanism for historical change—the vehicle that will lead to a communist society. Thus, he believed, the transition from capitalism to communism was inevitable because capitalists created both the technology necessary for a communist society and the people capable of making a revolution: proletarians. He predicted that their number would increase over time and that they would become steadily poorer and more alienated. In the context of ever-worsening economic crises, Marx claimed, proletarians would become class conscious—which is to say they would not only understand how they were being exploited but also be willing to act to change the situation. With help from the Communist Party, the proletarians would start a revolution.

The proletarians, Marx said in the *Manifesto,* would begin by seizing control of the state, taking all capital from its owners, and centralizing the means of production. Although Marx's goal was human freedom, these measures lead inevitably to totalitarianism. Marx, in fact, forecast a temporary "dictatorship of the proletariat" (1875). Nonetheless, Marx was an optimist. The *Manifesto* ends with some of the most famous lines ever written (Marx & Engels, 1848, p. 134): "Let the ruling classes tremble at a Communist revolution. The Proletarians have nothing to lose but their chains. They have a world to win. WORKING MEN OF ALL COUNTRIES, UNITE!"

Although Marx was wrong in many respects, his writings contain important insights. I want to mention several themes running through his works that remain relevant to sociological inquiry.

The first is the emphasis on social structure. Marx was a structuralist, although he did not use that word. For example, his analysis in the *Manifesto* of the conditions under which proletarians transform themselves into a class-conscious revolutionary group does not deal with the decision-making processes or cost-benefit calculations of individuals. Rather, it shows that urbanity, education, political sophistication, and other factors influence large numbers of oppressed people to recognize their common condition and to overthrow capitalism. As an aside, mass movements of oppressed persons in capitalist societies, such as women and minorities, have typically sought to get into the class system rather than overthrow it; that is, they have sought an increasing emphasis on achievement rather than ascription. Nonetheless, implicit here is a modern structural approach; that is, a focus on identifying the parts of the stratification structure and showing how location in the society influences rates of behavior.

The second theme is the degree of fluidity in the stratification structure. Marx believed that it was becoming more rigid, that ascription was becoming more important as a determinant of the distribution of valued resources. But he had it exactly wrong: The stratification structure in modern societies is less rigid (more fluid) than in the past. As it turns out, class frees people. Considerable mobility based on achievement occurs in class-based societies. This movement, both upward and (less often) downward, indicates that ability and hard work are becoming more important in determining people's life chances. As mentioned earlier, however, more important does not mean decisive; Marx was partly right. Birth (ascription) continues to influence life chances. Research shows that two semipermeable barriers to mobility exist: between those who own capital and those who do not, and between the middle class and working class (see Chapter 3). Thus, even given a relatively high rate of mobility, the class structure reproduces itself from one generation to another. For example, those born of middle-class parents tend to become middle class themselves. Similarly, those born male or female, black or white, continue to have different life chances.

The third theme is the importance of class conflict. Marx believed that class conflict would be the historical mechanism by which a new, more humane society would emerge. Although his grandiose view of history was shortsighted, he was correct to emphasize that classes have different and often opposing interests. He was also correct in noting that these differences are often hidden by an ideology (a set of values) that seems reasonable. A key question is thus how values lead to and sometimes veil exploitation. This is another way of recognizing that social facts are not always what they seem to be—an essential sociological orientation. This insight can be applied to the other dimensions of stratification as well: One might wonder, for example, how traditional gender norms hide (or justify) the exploitation of women by men.

The fourth theme is the emphasis on power. For Marx, power was redemptive; that is, when the people held power, they would use it for the common good, to liberate human beings from exploitation. But the people can never rule—at least directly. In every society, a small group, an oligarchy, exercises power. In those societies that subsequently became communist, the necessity for representation meant total rule by the party, which justified its position by invoking the common good. This invocation was an ideological veil, however, as the party functioned much like a feudal aristocracy (Djilas, 1965; Voslenski, 1985). Despite revolutionary rhetoric, the practical issue is not whether the ends justify the means. It is, rather, can the means produce the ends desired; that is, can power unfettered by accountability produce individual freedom? The answer is no. History shows that capitalist, not communist, societies display less exploitation and alienation. Nonetheless, Marx's emphasis on where power lies in capitalist society constitutes one of his most enduring legacies. Those who own income-producing assets have more choices and more effective choices than those who do not.

The final theme is the importance of alienation and exploitation. As will become clear, even though social conditions have improved since Marx's time, it is still possible to identify powerless people who are taken advantage of unfairly. In general, Marx emphasized, knowing the context in which people make choices is as important as knowing the choices themselves. Yet alienation and exploitation are often hidden behind an ideological veil. Marx was correct in arguing that those with power generally use it to further their own interests. Observers who ask Who benefits? can sometimes pierce the veil.

Implicit in this discussion is a strategy for understanding Marx's work and, indeed, that of all the scholars considered here. That is, one should avoid hagiography, being too worshipful. The trick is to figure out a scholar's enduring contributions and move on. With regard to Marx (and the others), I have tried to identify some useful aspects of his intellectual legacy.

Max Weber

During the early part of this century, Max Weber rejected Marx's interpretation of history. Weber argued, correctly as it turns out, that a communist revolution was not inevitable. He agreed, however, with the dead revolutionary that people's class location produces different life chances. For example, the working class displays different levels of income, styles of consumption and leisure, and rates of unemployment than does the middle class. In addition, Weber agreed with Marx that the rich have great political power in modern societies due to their ownership of capital. In *Economy and Society,* Weber added to these insights in three ways (1920).

First, Weber stressed that people behave in terms of both their economic interests and their values. Unlike Marx, Weber saw that value-based behavior does not necessarily reflect alienation. For example, individuals occasionally refuse a job promotion with its higher salary if it requires moving to another state and leaving a community where they share religious and friendship bonds. Similarly, to the extent they can, parents often choose to pay (big bucks!) for their children's college education; in effect, they sacrifice investment opportunities. These examples show that people's actions cannot be understood solely in terms of their economic interests. Rather, interests and values constitute complementary bases for action.

The terminology Weber employed in making this point is confusing. He used the concept "class" rather narrowly to refer to people's economic situation as indicated by their source and amount of income. Weber believed that social life is becoming increasingly rationalized. The historical process of **rationalization** meant, he asserted, that social life is more and more dominated by methodical calculation based on scientific (which is to say objective) knowledge, with an emphasis on efficiency and control. Although he understood that such an emphasis freed people from the bonds of birth (ascription) and produced greater mobility based on achievement, Weber was a pessimist. He feared that as more areas of life became subject to measurement and control, people would be encased in an "iron cage" (rationalization run amok). This fear may be well grounded. Weber's analysis of rationalization applies to stratification because what he called class-oriented action involves economic calculations. It is, as he put it, "instrumentally rational" in the sense that means and ends are objectively identified based on knowledge.

In contrast, Weber used the concept "status" to refer to the values people hold and the evaluations they make of others' **lifestyle.** The term refers to people's way of living, as indicated by their consumption habits, use of leisure time, and fundamental choices and values. Some elements of lifestyle reflect moral stances while others constitute aesthetic judgments. For example, one's house and its furnishing as well as one's selection of wine or entertainment (the ballet versus professional wrestling) express lifestyle. It is also expressed by the educational goals held for children: public school versus prep school, the state university versus Ivy League college. Finally, lifestyle is expressed by such basic choices as gender roles in marriage and attitudes toward abortion. Such cases constitute what Weber called "status-oriented action." It is "value rational" in the sense that it reflects people's standards of honorable behavior.

"Class" and "status" are interrelated, of course, since lifestyle makes income possible and income makes lifestyle possible. Thus, Weber used the terms "class" and "status" to identify the different bases for action displayed by people at each layer of the stratification structure, who protect their economic interests and values by joining together in political parties or interest groups. But Weber's terminology has not been adopted. Rather, sociologists today use the concept *class* more broadly to refer to both economic and noneconomic similarities displayed by people in each stratum. The difference in terminology is illustrated in Figure 1-1. The area to the left of the vertical bar portrays Weber's distinction between "class" and "status," while that to the right suggests that modern sociologists include Weber's distinction in the single concept "class."

Weber's emphasis on the way status influences lifestyle is important because it sensitizes observers to the fact that people understand their location in the stratification hierarchy and actively maintain it. They do so by means of a simple mechanism: **discrimination,** the unequal treatment of individuals and groups based on their personal characteristics. In practice, discrimination results from the fact that lifestyle is rooted in family experience. Before individuals reach maturity, they participate in their family's claim to social prestige, its occupational subculture, and its educational level. They experience its religiosity, suffer its unemployment, and enjoy its leisure pursuits. Thus, even in the absence of formal organization, families in the same class share a style of life, attitudes, and many other characteristics. As a result—and this point is very important so pay attention—people from similar backgrounds need not communicate in order to identify those who are like themselves or to discriminate against others who are different. They act in concert without being organized to do so. This fact has significant implications: Status concerns lead to a consideration of the noneconomic

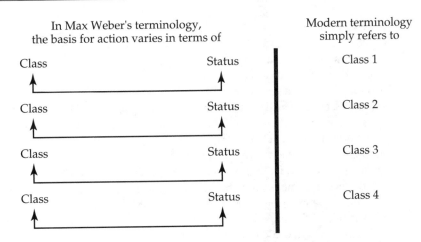

In Max Weber's terminology, the basis for action varies in terms of

Modern terminology simply refers to

Class   Status   Class 1

Class   Status   Class 2

Class   Status   Class 3

Class   Status   Class 4

Weber:

- Class-oriented action is concerned with economic interests, mainly the source and amount of income. It is instrumentally rational.

- Status-oriented action is concerned with values, as indicated by housing, friends, marriage partners, leisure-time activities, moral choices, and other elements of lifestyle. It is value rational.

Modern Sociologists:

- The term *class* is used to refer to both economic interests and values among people who resemble one another in terms of occupation, income, source of income, education, political power, and other characteristics.

FIGURE 1-1   Differences between Max Weber's and Modern Terminology

dimensions of stratification (about which more in a moment). They also indicate why ascription remains important.[2]

Even though they are not organized into groups, the members of each class act to maintain their distinctive lifestyle—they discriminate, in other words—in several specific ways (Weber, 1920, pp. 306, 935): (1) People extend hospitality only to social equals. Thus, they tend to invite into their homes, become friends with, eat with, and socialize with others who are like themselves. (2) People restrict potential marriage partners to social equals. Thus, they tend to live in neighborhoods and send their children to school with youngsters of others who are like themselves, with the result that their offspring generally marry someone with a similar lifestyle. (3) People practice unique social conventions and activities. Thus, they tend to join organizations, such as churches and clubs, and spend their leisure time with others who share similar beliefs

---

[2]There has been controversy over whether classes need to be organized in order to discriminate (Grusky & Sørensen, 1998). Some of the wording in this paragraph paraphrases lines from Reinhard Bendix, "Inequality and Social Structure: A Comparison of Marx and Weber" (1974).

and ways of living. And (4) people try to monopolize "privileged modes of acquisition," such as their occupational skills or capital.

These tactics are important because they lead to the inheritance of prestige, income, and wealth; they lead, in short, to the reproduction of the class structure from one generation to another as people obtain access to resources based on ascription. Like Marx, Weber emphasized the importance of power in social life, since those in the same class often act politically to close off opportunities to outsiders in order to protect their positions in society. By the term **power,** Weber meant the ability to achieve goals even if opposed by others. For example, because particular skills (say, in medicine or carpentry) acquired over time necessarily limit the possibility for obtaining other skills, rivals "become interested in curbing competition." So they join together and, in spite of continued competition among themselves, use whatever power they possess to close off opportunities for outsiders. Put simply, they make it difficult to enter a field. This process is why those children with the best chance of becoming, say, a physician or a carpenter, are born to parents who work in those fields. Such attempts at occupational closure occur continuously at all class levels, Weber said, and they are "the source of property in land [or capital] as well as of all guild [or union] monopolies" (1920, p. 342). Power, based on class and status considerations, insures that "privileged modes of acquisition" are preserved, people's lifestyles are protected, and the structure of stratification is maintained.

Weber added to Marx's insights in a second way by outlining a model of the class structure in more detail. Like Marx, Weber began with the recognition that the most fundamental division is between those who own capital and those who do not. He continued, however, by identifying additional classes within these two rubrics.

Among owners of capital, Weber sketched two classes, which he called rentiers and entrepreneurs. "Rentiers" comprise those who live off their investments and pursue a relatively nonacquisitive lifestyle, ranging from public service to indolence. "Entrepreneurs," in contrast, comprise those who own and operate businesses or pursue economic gain in other ways. It is essential to understand, however, that both groups are very rich and comprise a small proportion of the population. Thus, regardless of whether they work as an avocation or vocation, the possession of capital allows such persons to consume expensive amenities, influence public policy, affect the opportunity of others to acquire property, and monopolize status privileges (such as access to legislators—see Chapter 6). So despite their differences, wealthy, propertied classes have enormous power and access to valued resources.

Those who do not own capital also possess economically and politically important resources, mainly the worth of their services and skills. Weber divided these people, the great mass of the population, into two classes. The middle class comprises those whose services and skills do not involve manual labor: public officials, managers of businesses, technicians, white-collar employees, and members of the professions. Since their services and skills are in demand in industrial societies, such persons usually have higher incomes and more political power than those who work with their hands. Like the rich, middle-class people use their resources to enhance their life chances, influence public policy, and affect others' opportunities—albeit at their level. For example, they try to insure that their children attend "good" schools and end up with credentials that allow them to enter the professions (such as medicine). In so doing, the class structure remains stable. Without explanation, Weber divided people who do manual labor into three groups: skilled, semiskilled, and unskilled workers. It is unclear whether he saw these groups as separate classes or subdivisions within a single working class. In any case, like the rich and middle class, working-class people use their resources to establish a lifestyle and pass it on to their children. For example, they train their children in a trade, such as carpentry. Once again, the class structure is reproduced. As will be seen in Chapters 2 and 3, the class structure in the United States resembles the model originally sketched by Max Weber many years ago.

In this context, however, Weber emphasized that status concerns lead to discrimination—which suggests how class combines with the noneconomic dimensions of stratification. He argued that discrimination based on differences in lifestyle can evolve into **castes.** The term refers to an emphasis on ascription that is so extreme that mobility is prevented by legal and religious restrictions. Like Marx, Weber's underlying concern was with the degree of fluidity of the stratification structure.

Weber added to Marx's contributions in a third way as well: He laid the groundwork for objective social scientific research into the structure of stratification and other topics by arguing that sociology's goal ought to be to tell observers "what is" not "what ought to be." In this respect, the existence of sociology reflects the historical process of rationalization. In order to identify "what is," Weber argued that research should strive to be "value free" in the sense that data should be categorized in terms of clear concepts, proper rules of evidence must be followed, and conclusions should be based on logical inferences (1904). On that basis, sociologists can discover the facts, explain why they occur, discuss the available options, and (sometimes) suggest the implications of selecting one option over another. Sociologists should not, however, tell people what to do. Weber believed that social scientific knowledge can help people make informed choices based on their values, economic interests, or some other criterion. With luck, such choices will be wiser.

Now, producing objective knowledge is difficult; it is a goal pursued very imperfectly. One reason for this difficulty is that human beings possess will and volition. People often go their own way, with the result that findings are imprecise. Another reason is that sociologists are embedded in their subject matter. Those studying, say, gender stratification, bring to the topic their past experiences and values. Bias can follow. In order to reduce bias as much as possible, sociologists emphasize the **norms** characteristic of all sciences: skepticism and replication. The term refers to shared rules for behavior in specific situations. Sociology is characterized by a debunking motif, an emphasis on seeing beyond common sense. The norm of skepticism simply applies this orientation to research reports (or textbooks): Do not believe everything you read. The norm of replication calls on researchers to do more than criticize; they must repeat the research to see if the finding remains stable. These norms mean that at its best and over the long term, science is self-correcting. When findings seem accurate and stable, they are called **empirical generalizations.**

Alas, because people change, the social sciences carry a special burden in that even empirical generalizations are subject to revision (Lieberson, 1992). Such instability rarely happens in the natural sciences, which is why technology works. In the social sciences, however, findings vary over time and across societies. This is because human beings rebel, subvert the established order, enact new laws, and in other ways make history. (As I will describe later, they change the social structure.) Hence, observers can never be sure that what they find today will be true tomorrow. But this special burden carries with it an unexpected benefit: The social sciences are granted eternal youth (Weber, 1904, p. 104). Thus, the study of the structure of stratification and other topics always merits a new look.[3]

Kingsley Davis and Wilbert Moore

In the mid-1940s, Kingsley Davis and Wilbert Moore wrote an essay, titled "Some Principles of Stratification," that asked a simple question: What is the function of stratification for the society? Their answer was that its hidden impact is to "insure that the most important positions are conscientiously filled by the most qualified persons" (1945, p. 244). Put differently, stratification functions to insure each society's survival.

In all societies, Davis and Moore said, a division of labor exists in which positions are clustered in four functionally necessary areas: economic, political, technological, and religious. Tasks in these areas, they asserted, constitute functional necessities for the survival of a society. Thus, in each sphere, people must be motivated to fill positions and enact roles; some, for example, must become carpenters and others, physicians. Davis and Moore claimed that a few positions in each area are more important for societal survival than others and that they are also more difficult to fill because they require scarce talent, extensive training, or both. Hence, such positions must be more highly rewarded. Their example is modern medicine. Medical training is so long, costly, and burdensome, they argued, that few persons would become physicians if the position did not carry with it high rewards. Thus, they concluded, societies use unequal rewards (such valued resources as income and occupational prestige) to motivate people to obtain functionally important and difficult to fill positions in each of the four areas.

Sociologists are often skeptical of others' ideas, and, hence, the Davis-Moore analysis generated much debate. The conclusion of that debate is that the argument constitutes an illegitimate teleology and is usually untestable. A teleological statement imputes inherent purpose to a phenomenon. Thus, the purpose of an automobile is to provide transportation; it is designed and built with that goal in mind. The application of this notion to human societies, however, is dubious. While societies often set goals for themselves, such as landing a person on the moon, they are not designed for that purpose. Davis and Moore took an empirical generalization, the existence of stratification, and transformed it into a functional necessity. They thus avoided the key issues in the study of inequality: the struggle of people and groups (such as physicians) for power and other valued resources. Such a strategy cannot work. The thesis is nearly always untestable because the functionally necessary tasks and most important positions can-

---

[3]One impact of postmodernist thought has been to question whether objectivity is possible. It is argued that such a goal is somehow outdated because a text (of writing, of research) has no inherent meaning. With all due respect, I disagree. No science is possible without accurate knowledge of empirical phenomena.

not be identified without invoking values. As a result, Davis and Moore's analysis has been rejected by sociologists.[4]

This same judgment applies to functionalism as a theoretical tradition. Davis and Moore were students of Talcott Parsons, the best-known functionalist in sociology, whose work reveals both of the flaws outlined above (1951; 1954). Hence, functionalism is now passé, mainly for theoretical reasons but also for political ones. Indeed, it is easy to see how Davis and Moore's argument could be used to support the status quo in any society: Those obtaining the most resources would simply argue that their class position is necessary for the survival of society. Physicians have made this argument very successfully in the United States. Nonetheless, although functionalism has been rejected, the Davis-Moore essay and the theoretical tradition it illustrates contain two useful themes that remain relevant to the study of stratification.

One involves the simple act of looking for the functions of a social phenomenon. Although the term "function" is too vague for detailed empirical analyses (Goode, 1973), attempting to uncover the functions of poverty, unemployment, and other social facts is sometimes a good way of getting at their hidden consequences, a task that can be done without the problems afflicting Davis and Moore's analysis. They tried to identify the nonobvious effects of stratification, which is good sociology, only to go wrong by imputing generic needs to society. In contrast, Robert K. Merton, another student of Parsons, distinguished between the manifest and latent functions of social arrangements (1968). Like Marx, his point was that social facts are not always what they seem to be, that underlying interests and forces also exist, and that both aspects of reality must be understood. In this way, Merton argued, it is possible to see familiar issues in a new light, which can lead to discoveries about the nature of stratification.

In addition, functionalism provides a useful way of identifying the parts of the social structure, a problem Marx also struggled with. Although Davis and Moore asserted that the tasks they identified—economic, political, technological, and religious—constituted functional necessities for survival, one need not make this assumption. A more useful approach is to see them as empirical generalizations, subject to revision. Today, the parts are often termed **social institutions,** tasks with which every society must cope. Thus, in studying the stratification structure, observers typically look at how classes differ in terms similar to the items identified by Davis and Moore, Parsons, and others.

1. People's occupation, amount of income, and source of income are identified, since they indicate people's economic and political interests.
2. The rate and type of political participation and power are examined, since they influence economic, educational, and other opportunities.
3. The rate and type of crime is ascertained, since these are affected by class location.
4. The rate and type of religiosity is recognized, since they influence (and are influenced by) class location and values.

---

[4]International variations in mobility rates provide one context in which a quasi-functionalist hypothesis has been tested and refuted (see Chapter 3). See also the attempt at explaining occupational prestige hierarchies in functionalist terms in Chapter 2. For a recent critique of Davis and Moore, see Wallace (1997).

5. The level of educational attainment is investigated, since it is related to class location, political interests, and values.
6. Kinship characteristics are sketched, since they affect class location, economic and political interests, and values.

It is not hard to see that these characteristics, most of which are dealt with in subsequent chapters, are interconnected. For example, macroeconomic policies have an impact on street crime (the kind of crime that some poor and working-class persons commit) by altering people's employment situation. In any science, it is essential to develop a model that identifies the structure of the phenomenon under investigation (for example, the parts of the body or the atom) and shows how they are interrelated. As noted earlier, Weber sketched a model of the class structure, one of the vertical dimensions of the stratification structure. The functionalists added to this analysis by identifying the social institutions that appear characteristic of each society—the horizontal dimension of the stratification structure.

Ralf Dahrendorf

Functionalism constituted the dominant theoretical orientation in the United States from World War II until Ralf Dahrendorf's *Class and Class Conflict in Industrial Society* appeared in 1959. He argued that sociologists in the United States failed to realize the significance of class conflict in social life. Responding to Marx, Dahrendorf tried to reorient sociology so that it could be more realistic. Sociology, he observed, must become "an exact social science with precisely formulated postulates, theoretical models, and testable laws" (1959, p. ix). Unfortunately, Dahrendorf's execution of this strategy was flawed.

Dahrendorf began by developing a series of assumptions about the nature of society (1959, p. 162). They contradicted those of Davis and Moore, Parsons, and other functionalists:

1. "Every society is at every point subject to change; social change is ubiquitous."
2. "Every society displays at every point dissensus and conflict; social conflict is ubiquitous."
3. "Every element in a society renders a contribution to its disintegration and change."
4. "Every society is based on the coercion of some of its members by others."

Despite Dahrendorf's intention, these assumptions are unrealistic. After all, if society is continually subject to change (item 1), then organized social life would be impossible. More importantly, no science can assume relationships among the phenomena it is attempting to study. Although social scientists have a more difficult task than natural scientists because they are part of what is being analyzed (recall Weber), the fact remains that the scientific task is to test hypotheses.

In the next step, Dahrendorf transformed these assumptions into a causal model that sketches how people move into and out of relationships of authority. Not a Marxist,

Dahrendorf argued that possession of authority identifies people's access to valued resources and their interest in keeping what they have and adding to it. The result is class conflict. Although this idea has merit, its correctness is unknown because Dahrendorf asserted its truth by assumption. While there exist other flaws in his causal model, this problem is the most serious.

Finally, Dahrendorf developed a testable theory, which, he insisted, is derived from the model. This theory focuses on the conditions under which classes organize, the forms of class struggle, and the process of change (1959, pp. 236–40). While the theory comprises a large number of statements, I provide only one example here: In discussing the forms of class conflict, Dahrendorf proposed that "there is a close positive correlation between the degree of superimposition of conflicts and their intensity." In plainer language:

The more several conflicts overlap with one another, the greater their intensity.

In contrast to the assumptions outlined earlier, this hypothesis is useful. Because it is abstract (independent of time and space), it can be applied to many different empirical topics, not just class conflict. Nonetheless, it does not emerge from his model. Actually, Dahrendorf's theory constitutes an extrapolation of work by Marx, Georg Simmel (1908), Lewis Coser (1956), and others. This fact makes his theory less original than he asserts and calls his strategy for theory construction into question.

Although Dahrendorf's work is flawed, he contributed to the study of stratification in two essential ways. First, more than anyone else, he alerted sociologists in the United States to the fact that power and class conflict are built into the structure of stratification. Unlike the situation in Europe, U.S. sociology lacks a vibrant Marxist tradition, and, as a result, scholars were relatively insensitive to these issues. Thus, Dahrendorf observed that one need not be a Marxist to deal with the topics Marx raised. This point is important because, as indicated earlier, it is easy to show the continued relevance of his ideas. Second, in stating his propositions formally, Dahrendorf took theoretical analyses to a new level of sophistication. Theories could no longer be buried in discursive prose, a format that promotes vagueness and makes testing difficult. Dahrendorf is easy to criticize, mainly because he made his assumptions explicit, clearly identified his variables, defined them, and stated how they covary. Thus, while his work has been widely attacked, he fundamentally redirected sociological research so as to make it more realistic. Not many scholars can make such a claim.

Gerhard Lenski

Gerhard Lenski's 1966 book, *Power and Privilege,* constituted a decisive break with the past. Although marred by an attempt at synthesizing assumptions attributed to the functionalist and conflict approaches as well as an evolutionary framework (Nisbet, 1969), Lenski produced the first truly theoretical analysis of the stratification structure using international and historical data. His theory has two parts. First, he explained the basis for stratification and, second, he explained why it varies from one society to another. In so doing, he demonstrated "who gets what and why" in all societies over the course of history, a fairly impressive contribution.

In explaining the basis of stratification, Lenski focused on the distribution of power and privilege within societies. Like Marx, he emphasized the importance of producing goods and services. He distinguished between societies in which people produce only the minimum necessary for subsistence and those in which a surplus exists and must be distributed. In the former, Lenski hypothesized, people "will share the product of their labor to the extent required to insure the survival and continued productivity of those others whose actions are necessary or beneficial to themselves" (1966, p. 44). In plainer language, the first hypothesis is:

> *The more dependent people are on each other for survival, the more they will share the products of their labor with one another.*

Lenski reasoned that individuals usually act out of self-interest. While familiar with Weber's writings, Lenski asserted that values are not primary determinants of the stratification structure, especially prior to industrialization. Thus, human groups capable of producing few goods are necessarily small, communal, hunting and gathering societies, in which each individual is dependent on everyone else. For this reason, people share what they produce.

Whenever a surplus exists, however, the situation differs a great deal. "Power will determine the distribution of nearly all of the surplus possessed by a society," Lenski proposed (1966, p. 44). In covariance form, the second hypothesis is:

> *The greater the surplus of goods and services in a society, the more power determines their distribution.*

In short, as Marx, Weber, and Dahrendorf all emphasized, albeit in quite different ways, Lenski argued that power is highly correlated with access to valued resources, such as income, education, and occupational prestige.

In order to explain why the stratification structure varies from one society to another, Lenski focused on two main factors: the level of technology and the nature of the state. The former has its greatest significance prior to industrialization. As Lenski phrased the hypothesis: "Variations in technology will be the most important single factor determining variations in distributive [or stratification] systems" (1966, p. 90). In covariance form, the third hypothesis is:

> *The greater the level of technology prior to industrialization, the greater the productivity and inequality.*

The term **technology** refers to verified knowledge about the environment. Improvements in technology, Lenski argued, are applied to the practical task of producing goods and services for people to enjoy. The result, following from the second hypothesis (and as Marx suggested), is that those with the greatest power acquire nearly all the surplus. Put differently, they have access to most of the valued resources that are available. This process means that inequality is great and the stratification structure is rigid, so not much mobility occurs. As indicated, this situation exists in all preindustrial societies.

With **industrialization** (and capitalism, accompanied by scientific advance), however, human history changed forever. The term refers to the transformation of the economy as new forms of energy were substituted for muscle power, leading to a massive increase in productivity. Lenski asserted that two changes resulted. First, expanded production means that a small upper class cannot monopolize wealth and other resources and that mobility based on achievement becomes more widespread. Second, a "new democratic ideology" emerges, which not only emphasizes greater equality as a dominant value but also allows the many to combine against the few. (Note that after rejecting the importance of values, Lenski recognizes here that a belief in democracy fundamentally influences the stratification structure in modern societies.) The result of these two factors, he proposed, is that "advanced industrial societies will move even further from the traditional elitist ideal in which a tiny minority monopolizes both power and privilege. [But] this trend will stop substantially short of the egalitarian ideal in which power and privilege are shared equally" (1966, p. 327). Lenski's fourth hypothesis follows:

> *The greater the level of technology and the more democratic the state, the less inequality.*

Lenski emphasized, however, that this statement only means that the rich possess a lower proportion of the total wealth. They remain, according to the second hypothesis, the most powerful class, and they continue to control a disproportionate share of the wealth. Nonetheless, an important implication of Lenski's work is that achievement becomes more important in determining people's access to resources.

In testing the theory, Lenski used archeological, anthropological, and historical information on all the world's known societies. He used evidence skillfully and demonstrated the accuracy of each element of the theory—except perhaps the last. Whether inequality must decline with technological advance and the rise of democracies remains unclear (see Chapter 7).

Gerhard Lenski's work refined and tested ideas about the structure of stratification that scholars as different as Marx and Weber considered many years ago. In addition, because the elements making up the theory are stated explicitly, others can test them. Hence, even if part of Lenski's work is subsequently proven wrong, he decisively advanced knowledge of stratification.

Although their writings are flawed in various ways, the theorists reviewed here merit study, partly because they show how sociology has advanced and partly because they contain enduring lessons. Stripped of its radical millenarianism (a belief in the coming of an ideal, communal society), Marx's work illustrates the usefulness of a structural approach focusing on how class location affects the choices people have. In addition, his emphasis on the significance of class conflict directs modern sociologists to look for the different levels of power, economic interests, and values displayed by various classes. Further, Marx's stress on exploitation and alienation suggests the importance of ascertaining who benefits from public policies; sometimes the answer is not obvious. From Weber, modern sociologists take a recognition of the importance of class, an understanding that people's lifestyles and values often influence behavior, a model of the class structure (the vertical dimension of the stratification structure), an emphasis on power as a determining factor in social life, and a directive to do research that is as objective as possible. Davis and Moore, and functionalists generally, show that social arrangements frequently contain nonobvious dimensions, what Merton called *latent functions*. In addition, the functionalists offer an analytical model of the division of labor, the horizontal dimension of the stratification structure that remains useful. Dahrendorf reminds sociologists that issues related to class and class conflict can be analyzed outside a Marxist framework and that theories need to be stated formally. Finally, Lenski illustrates how a sound theoretical analysis can be developed and tested empirically. In so doing, he emphasized again the overriding importance of power in social life.

A Strategy for the Study of Stratification

The works above provide a preface for the study of stratification by introducing many of the issues that must be confronted in an analysis of this topic. There are at least two ways of taking advantage of such a review. One involves using previous writings as the basis for developing an abstract, more all-encompassing theory of stratification, as in Jonathan H. Turner's, *Societal Stratification* (1984). Turner translated the ideas of Marx, Weber, Davis and Moore, Dahrendorf, and Lenski into formal, quasi-mathematical theoretical statements and, on that basis, elaborates a general theory of stratification. He sees such a theory as one step toward a larger goal, the identification of the generic theoretical principles underlying all human behavior. Another approach, pursued in this book, involves using previous works as the basis for a middle range analysis of the stratification structure in the United States (Merton, 1968). Thus, I intend to build on the ideas of the theorists described above to tie together the research findings. Such a goal requires a method, by which I mean a strategy for explanation rather than a statistical technique. The strategy used here is to (1) assess the historical and international dimensions of stratification, (2) distinguish levels of analysis (individual and structural) for understanding stratification, and (3) examine how power affects the stratification process. These themes provide a vehicle for understanding how access to valued resources is distributed in the United States; they are also fundamental to sociological analysis of all aspects of social life.

Historical and International Dimensions of Stratification

Sociology at its best looks at the data along two dimensions: historical and international (Kohn, 1987). Historical data reveal how much change has occurred over time within one society, such as the United States. For example, in examining changes in racial and gender inequality, poverty, mobility, and other topics, I will extend the analysis back 100 to 200 years, or as far as plausible data are available. This is a particularly useful period to examine, since it marks the transition to modernity. International data indicate the extent to which inequality in its various forms occurs at similar rates in several nations. Such information provides a way to place the American experience in perspective. I will usually restrict international comparisons to Western industrial societies. Since these nations share a common cultural heritage and display advanced economies, their similarities and differences regarding the issues dealt with in this book can be especially revealing.[5]

Max Weber pioneered use of such data in his studies of the relationship between religion and the origin of capitalism (1905, 1913, 1917, 1920). Weber wanted to understand why capitalism as an economic system arose in Western Europe and ushered in modern life. Thus, he performed a "logical experiment" by systematically comparing various Western nations in the seventeenth and eighteenth centuries with India and China at the same time. He found that what distinguished Europe (and the United States) from these other nations was not the level of technology, a free labor force, or other factors. Rather, the West became unique due to the rise of the culture of capitalism as an unintended consequence of the Protestant Reformation (see Turner, Beeghley, & Powers, 1998). The term *culture of capitalism* refers to a set of values that support and justify making money. What happened was that behaviors undertaken for purely religious reasons, such as hard work aimed at acquiring wealth, were transformed over time into secular cultural values. These ethical standards, in turn, helped to usher in a new kind of society, one never before seen in history, a society based on class with a stratification structure that emphasizes achievement.

Weber's research strategy is significant because it can be used with any topic, not only stratification. As an aside, note that Weber's "logical experiment" alters the approach usually presented in methodology courses. There, students are taught to form a hypothesis and gather data with which to test it. In contrast, Weber's tactic is to begin by gathering data, which are then explained. This explanation is often multivariate in form, but the variables are related logically rather than mathematically. As I have tried to show elsewhere, this strategy is often useful in dealing with structural issues (Beeghley, 1999).

The use of historical and international data can lead to productive questions. For example, if the rate of poverty in the United States was high in the past (and it was), but is much lower now, one asks what has changed. Individual motives? Perhaps. But if the rate of poverty in this country is much higher than in Western Europe, one immediately wonders if structural barriers to opportunity exist that keep large numbers of people impoverished. The strategy, once again, is to look for explanatory factors that differ historically and internationally, and appear logically related to poverty. Science, it seems to me, is simply the art of asking questions. The idea is that there are no secrets. The facts of nature, social life, even people's unconscious motives can be discovered if one asks the right questions. In sociology, historical and international data provide an empirical basis for such queries. They lead to greater understanding. They also lead to a distinction between levels of analysis.

---

[5]Chapter 11 is an exception to this restriction. The concern there will be to place stratification in the United States in a global context.

Levels of Analysis and Stratification

In order to illustrate the importance of distinguishing levels of analysis, imagine you are enrolled in an art history course and must try to understand a painting by the Dutch impressionist, Vincent van Gogh. Let us assume it is *The Café Terrace at Night* (finished in 1888). In looking at the painting, one sees a humble establishment where people eat, drink, and (probably most importantly) talk. Like much great art, *The Café Terrace at Night* can be understood on several levels, and—this is important—each level displays different properties. At one level, you might use a spectroscope to inspect the paint's chemical composition. Such an examination is useful because of the bright colors typical of van Gogh's works. At another level, you might use a magnifying glass to study his technique with the brush. This analysis would be useful because van Gogh's strokes were often very heavy and slashing. At still another level, you might look closely at the painting from a short distance to see how the images fit together. At a final level, you might move several feet away to get an overall view. These last two levels are useful because distance alters what viewers see. What you should remember with this example is that each level of analysis not only provides different data, but also different explanatory variables. Yet explanation at each level is valid. And combining them leads to greater insight about the painting. So it is with the study of the stratification structure.

The initial task is to understand why individuals act. Only individuals vote or look for jobs. Only individuals justify their actions morally and live with the result. Only individuals give their lives meaning. The basis on which individuals make decisions is their personal experiences (which are not always conscious). Sociologists use the term **socialization** to describe these experiences. It refers to the lifelong process by which individuals learn norms and values, internalize motivations and (unconscious) needs, develop intellectual and social skills, and enact roles as they participate in the society (Brim, 1966). In plainer language, socialization refers to the process of growing up, with the addendum that it continues throughout life. In effect, each individual's personal experiences form a sort of prism through which she or he channels behavior. The dimensions of this prism can be formally stated:

1. Childhood interactions are usually more influential on individuals than later experiences.
2. Interaction in primary groups (such as family and religion) is usually more influential on individuals than interaction in secondary groups.
3. Interaction with people who are emotionally significant (such as parents, teachers, and friends) is usually more influential on individuals than interaction with ordinary persons.
4. Long-term interaction is usually more influential on individuals than short-term interaction.[6]

Knowledge of these experiences helps observers understand how individuals' backgrounds lead them to act as they do. A person's biography is composed of family,

---

[6]These principles are rarely stated formally. I first did so in "The Religious Switcher and Alcohol Use: An Application of Reference Group and Socialization Theory" (Beeghley et al., 1990).

friends, and enemies. It also comprises the schools attended, books read, television programs watched, religious faith adhered to, Scout troop joined, and orgies participated in. Eventually it will include the gang joined, the occupational group entered, the political party identified with, and all other experiences. With this background, then, a person learns what is expected (norms and values), develops personality characteristics (motivations and needs), and understands how to act (knowledge and skills). These are the elements of the socialization process defined above. Note the active verbs: Individuals attend, join, enter, and the like. Even when they are young, people choose. Socialization is an active—not a passive—process. It varies by class, race, and gender.

I mentioned that socialization continues throughout people's lives. In terms of the metaphor used previously, the prism through which individuals channel their behavior is not cut once, in childhood, say, and left that way forever. Rather, people periodically recut their own prism—that is, they change their behavior—in light of new experiences. As individuals move through life, they adopt a variety of **reference groups** along the way (Hyman, 1942; Merton & Rossi, 1968). The phrase refers to collectivities of people whose characteristics (values, norms, tastes, and patterns of action) are significant in the development of one's own attitudes and behavior.

Taken together, knowing how individuals are socialized and their choice of reference groups leads to understanding of their behavior. For example, poor people sometimes find that they have little control over what happens to them or their children. A person's job disappears. A child witnesses a murder on the street. Savings stored under a mattress (because no banks are available) are stolen. As such experiences cumulate, people become alienated. They lose hope and perhaps act out with drugs. Or they become angry and perhaps act out sexually or violently. These reactions do not happen as often as you might think, but they do happen. Although understanding does not excuse such behaviors, it does explain them.

While the connection may surprise you, you can see alienation as a dominant theme in the *Star Wars* movies. Darth Vader represents an alienated man, acting out in extreme ways. Luke Skywalker represents the redeeming social values Darth has rejected. In the penultimate scene, they are fighting to the death and, frankly, Darth is winning. Luke appeals to the goodness hidden inside Darth. Can he reject the seduction of the Emperor, who represents evil (or the devil, depending on your theology)? Ultimately, Darth overcomes his alienation, hurls the Emperor to his death, and, at the end of the movie, is reincarnated as Luke's father and reunited with Obi Wan Kenobi and Yoda. (The triune image was deliberate, I suspect.) The empire is defeated. One reason people feel so good after the movie is that it celebrates the triumph of individuals over great odds. Individuals, people believe, possess all the will and ability necessary. Like Darth and Luke, they need only use it. This belief may be why public policies in the United States often demand heroic action by people who are alienated and exploited. Such requirements are shortsighted, as the following chapters show. Not many people possess either Darth's or Luke's fictional courage.

Understanding why individuals act, however, provides only one kind of information. Just as a painting can be understood at different levels, so can social life. The structure of stratification must be considered.

The social structure influences rates of events. This basic idea reflects the fact that the rates of diverse events are characteristic of a society, not individuals. It can be applied to many phenomena, such as suicide (Durkheim, 1895), intermarriage (Blau et al., 1982), premarital sex and divorce (Beeghley, 1996), and drug use and homicide (Beeghley, 1999). In studying the structure of stratification, the following chapters reveal that it can be applied to such issues as rates of occupational mobility, poverty, job perquisites, voting, gender stratification, and racial and ethnic stratification. In each case, I will show that the variables affecting the rates of mobility, voting, and other phenomena differ from those influencing individuals to perform or endure those acts. This fact means that it is not possible to understand social stratification in the United States without focusing on structural variables.

Yet this orientation seems backward to many people, primarily because the ethic of individual responsibility is so pervasive in the United States. The origins of this value lie in the transformative effect of Puritanism, with its emphasis on each individual's personal relationship with God (Weber, 1905), along with the frontier experience (as myth and reality), with its requirement that individuals be self-reliant in order to survive (F. J. Turner, 1920). The long-term impact of these factors has produced in many persons a preference for focusing on individuals when thinking about social issues. For example, if the rate of occupational mobility is high (and it is), then most people argue (incorrectly) that it reflects each individual's hard work. Similarly, if the rate of voting is low (and it is), then most people believe (again, incorrectly) that nonvoters must be satisfied with the status quo. The underlying assumption in both examples is that the whole, the rate of mobility or voting, is no more than the sum of its parts—the individual actions making up the rate. This assumption, however, is incorrect. Just as water is qualitatively different—in touch, taste, and many other characteristics—than its component parts (hydrogen and oxygen), so the rate of social events is qualitatively different than its component parts (individual behaviors). From this point of view, it makes sense to suggest, by analogy, that the rate of mobility, voting, and other social phenomena reflect the social structure.

The theoretical basis for this orientation lies in Emile Durkheim's insight that it is "in the nature of the society itself that we must seek the explanation of social life" (1895, p. 128). He meant that structural phenomena exist externally to individuals, guiding their behavior in predictable ways. But guidance is not force and not all individuals react in the same way. His example had to do with suicide. Although this is a very solitary act, he showed that even in social contexts where the ties binding individuals to the society are strong—as among employed married people with children who regularly attend church—some suicides would occur. This fact is irrelevant to Durkheim's point, however, which was that the suicide rate would be lower in such contexts than in others, where the bonds tying individuals to the society are less (1895). Thus, if he was correct, then it should be possible to show how the social structure produces varying rates of events other than suicide, such as the level of mobility or poverty, independently of individual motives or behavior.

The reason why social structure affects rates of events is that it determines the choices available to people (Merton, 1968). Thus, people's location in the stratification structure (high to low) systematically influences their choices and their consequences. This argument can be formally stated as the *Class Structure Hypothesis:*

The lower the social class, the fewer choices people have and the less effective they are in solving personal problems.

But the impact of social class is interrelated with the other dimensions of stratification. For example, the *Gender Hypothesis* is as follows:

Women at every class level have fewer and less effective choices than do men.

Similarly, the *Minority Group Hypothesis* is stated as follows:

Minority groups at every class level have fewer and less effective choices than do whites (non-Hispanic).

Much of this book consists in demonstrating the usefulness of these hypotheses.

The rationale underlying these hypotheses is the same as Durkheim's: The structure of stratification is external to individuals, influencing both people's choices and their effectiveness. Paradoxically, then, while the total number (or rate) of a phenomenon—such as the proportion of people in each class who vote—reflects the sum of individual actions, that information does not explain its level. For example, as I shall describe in Chapter 6, an understanding of the motives for voting does not explain why working-class people go to the polls at a lower rate than middle-class and rich persons. Only knowledge of how the social context influences the choices available to individuals in each class can explain the magnitude of this phenomenon. For this reason, Durkheim said "social facts are things"; they have a reality independent of individuals.

I want to focus for a few moments on the Class Structure Hypothesis. Although I have cited Durkheim and Merton as the primary sources underlying it, each of the theorists reviewed previously also influenced its formulation. Thus, I interpreted (some would say misinterpreted) Marx in terms consonant with it. Virtually every theme in his writings can be considered in light of this hypothesis, without recourse to his revolutionary millenarianism. Similarly, Weber's emphasis on the influence of values on behavior and his depiction of the class structure focuses attention on how rates of events are affected. The functionalists contributed by identifying key elements of the social structure that influence the level of poverty, voting, and many other phenomena. Although his work is flawed, Dahrendorf pointed out how authority relations are built into the social structure. Finally, Lenski's emphasis on the significance of power in the distribution of valued resources in society is obviously consonant with the theory presented here.

The Class Structure Hypothesis has many practical implications. For example, one can pick any behavior by individuals—finding a spouse, obtaining an education, getting a job, purchasing a car, recovering from mental stress, any behavior at all—and, if the hypothesis is correct, poor persons will usually have fewer choices and be less able to resolve their personal problems than the members of other social classes, and this fact will be reflected in different rates of behavior by class. Moreover—and this is a key point—these differences will exist no matter how hard poor individuals work or how much ability they have. Such insight helps observers to understand why impoverished people sometimes make decisions that appear unwise from a middle-class vantage point.

The Class Structure Hypothesis reflects a more general argument that I want to repeat: The social structure influences rates of behavior. Yet, as also emphasized earlier: Individuals choose. In sociological jargon, they have agency. The relationship between individuals and social structure has been a (in my view, needlessly) controversial topic in sociology. The issues are the degree to which individuals can act independently (do they have choices?) and whether the social structure can be changed. The answers are as follows: First, individuals have a great deal of independence, but in practical terms their choices are not unlimited. You can, for example, choose to use a typewriter rather than a word processor. You can also choose to have many spouses. Since the first is inefficient and the second illegal, only a few persons make such choices. In this sense, then, the social structure exists externally to individuals and sets boundaries (which are sometimes wide and sometimes narrow) on behavior. Second, people can and do change social structures. How this process might occur and the difficulty involved can be suggested by using college football as an example.

There is a sort of class and race structure to college football, and people make choices within that context. In a game, for example, players operate within a set of rules that affects their behavior: Only ends and backs can catch forward passes, for example. In addition, players, many of whom are African American, often improvise during a play. But the structural question is who organizes the game and to whose benefit, and how do these issues affect the players? Let us begin with the coaches. They are nearly always white and are relatively well paid (indeed, they make serious money at major universities). Coaches, of course, decide who gets to play and at what positions. They also have a lot of influence over rules adopted by the National Collegiate Athletic Association (NCAA), since its governing body is made up of coaches. So they have power. For example, at their behest, the NCAA decided that when Coach Charisma induces an 18-year-old football player to sign a contract to play at State University, he is bound to the school even if Mr. Charisma moves on to a (better paying) position at another institution. So the players are bound by contract, but the coaches (usually) are not. In addition, along with coaches, athletic directors, university presidents, and NCAA administrators determine the rules under which games will be played and the eligibility requirements for players, among other things. Like coaches, these people are nearly always white males, and they make lots of money. Now if you happen to be an 18-year-old male with some football skill, your choices involve whether to take the right courses to become eligible, whether to play or not, and for whom to play. You cannot, however, negotiate about pay. You cannot even ask to be paid the minimum wage for all the hours put in practicing, attending meetings, lifting weights (often all summer), and playing in the games. In effect, you sign a contract to work long hours for room, board, and tuition. The result (sometimes) brings glory to the university and helps others make money. At the University of Florida, where I teach, the head football coach makes (via salary and other income-producing perquisites) nearly a million dollars per year. But others make money as well: announcers, television executives, stockholders of firms that advertise on football telecasts, to name only a few. Yet most participants think this situation is right and proper. This is so even though many (if not most) players at major universities fail to graduate. So they do not even get an education for their labors. One might say that college football is the sigh of the oppressed creature—the opium of the players.

Perhaps my sarcasm is unfair. But think about who has the wider range of choices and how effective they are. The players can choose to play or not. They can choose to attend (real) classes or not. Unless they organize themselves to strike before a big game or unless (until?) someone hires a lawyer to sue the NCAA, however, they will remain bound by contract even if a coach leaves. They will not be paid for their labors. So changing the structure of college football will be difficult for them. Coaches and administrators, on the other hand, make the rules. They can more easily change the structure of college football. But it would not be in their interests to do so, which means that paying the players (even minimum wage) is unlikely. My point: People at the top have greater ability to change the social structure than those at the bottom.

The structure of stratification is similar. I mentioned at the beginning of the chapter that the story of the past century or so has been one of increasing choice in human affairs. This fundamental change has a practical implication: The level of inequality—by class, gender, and race—is not accidental; it is chosen. As emphasized by every theorist, people with power use it to gain access to valued resources. And they use power to retain those resources.

Power and Stratification

Max Weber's definition of power as the ability of an individual or group to get things done, to achieve goals, even if opposition occurs, has become standard. It follows that people have power when they can choose to spend or withhold money, prestige, or other resources from others. They have power when, faced with a divorce, lawsuit, or mental stress, they can find the right lawyer or therapist to help them deal with the problem. They have power when companies and governments pay attention to their needs and desires. But power is not confined to individuals. Because the ability to achieve goals is highly correlated with class, people with similar interests often act in concert and discriminate against others, even though they are not formally organized into groups. Hence, it is not possible to understand the structure of stratification without focusing on the class basis of power. In addition, however, as with college football, white males occupy most positions of power in this country. Hence, power is also gender and race based.

As you should recall, a class consists of those persons with similar occupational prestige, education, income, and other characteristics. In every society, power is class based, and correlated with race and gender. This fact means that the very rich, both individually and as an aggregate, have more influence over access to valued resources than do middle-class people; that the middle class, in turn, has more influence over access to valued resources than do working-class people; and that the working class has more influence over access to valued resources than do poor people. This argument has many practical implications. It implies, for example, that rich people usually have a greater variety of choices and they are more effective in solving personal problems.

Similarly, as subsequent chapters will show, it suggests how to understand the distribution of wealth and poverty, the nature and level of benefits from income transfers, the level and kind of supervision on the job, the characteristics of housing occupied by different classes, the structure of political participation, and certain aspects of racial, ethnic, and gender inequality. In addition, this approach follows from theoretical analyses of stratification. This argument can be stated formally as the *Political Power Hypothesis:*

> *The higher the social class, the greater the influence over access to valued resources in the society.*

Here is an example of the political power of the rich. One problem such persons face is retaining as much income as possible after taxes. As I will show in Chapters 6 and 7, over the past few years the rich have persuaded Congress to transfer much of the tax burden from them to the rest of the population. As a result, despite what Lenski thought, income and wealth inequality have increased and are now at their highest point in U.S. history. Most of the time, tax breaks for the rich are justified by their benefits to "the economy" and to the majority of people through the so-called "trickle down effect." Such arguments are veils, of course, designed to hide the way in which the tax system channels income up rather than down. In reality, rich persons avoid paying taxes and retain most of their income because of their enormous political power. Put differently, the resources rich people have expand the range and effectiveness of their choices. Thus, instead of merely reacting to government policies, the rich decisively affect their formation. This fact provides them with enormous advantages over the members of other classes.

These advantages mean they can often affect how valued resources are distributed in society. Although it is true that every society displays stratification, the result of this dynamic process varies considerably. And this result affects people's life chances. Ken Griffey, Jr., apparently earns several million dollars each year to hit baseballs. Is he worth it? The owners of his team, the Seattle Mariners, think so. They charge huge amounts of money for tickets and television rights because people want to see Mr. Griffey display his peculiar skill. Chung-soon Kwon works at the fast food store where I buy my newspaper each day and earns about $15,000 per year. Is she worth it? Or, put differently, should she be paid a higher (more livable) wage? The company thinks she is worth that amount and no more. It could easily replace her if she had the temerity to ask for a raise. In the United States, the structure of stratification is more unequal than in other nations.

Summary

Social stratification can be defined as the process by which access to valued resources is distributed in society. Possession of valued resources, such as income, education, and occupational prestige, affects people's life chances. The structure of stratification has three dimensions: class, gender, and race/ethnicity. People in the same class tend to be relatively equal to one another in terms of occupational category, income, source of income, education, and other characteristics. People in different classes tend to be unequal in these same terms. The impact of traditional gender roles (buttressed by violence and its threat) means that women are often unequal to men. Because of prejudice and discrimination, members of different racial and ethnic groups are often unequal to one another. Although these differences have declined in recent years, they remain important.

In order to begin the analysis of stratification, the first section reviewed the works of previous theorists. Karl Marx proposed that in all societies people produce goods and that a structure of stratification emerges based on private ownership of the means of production. Capitalist societies display two classes, Marx said, the bourgeoisie and the proletarians. Class conflict is inevitable and will ultimately lead to a communist revolution. Although Marx was wrong, a number of sociological insights permeate his work: the emphasis on social structure, the degree of fluidity in the class structure, the importance of class conflict in shaping stratification, the emphasis on power, and the importance of exploitation and alienation.

Max Weber added to Marx's sociological insights by emphasizing that people act in terms of both economic considerations (which he termed *class*) and lifestyle or value considerations (which he termed *status*). By discriminating against others who are different, the members of each class (conceived broadly, see Figure 1-1) use their power to maintain their positions. In addition, Weber filled out Marx's model of the stratification structure by recognizing that the rich constitute two different groups, rentiers and entrepreneurs, and that those without capital can also be divided into at least two groups: the middle and working classes. Finally, Weber emphasized the importance of striving for objectivity. The goal of social science, he believed, should be to identify "what is" not "what ought to be."

Kingsley Davis and Wilbert Moore argued that stratification is the means society uses to motivate people to fill difficult and functionally important positions. Their analysis, however, is an illegitimate teleology and untestable. Nonetheless, functionalism contributed to the study of stratification by emphasizing the importance of looking at nonobvious (or latent) aspects of social life and identifying the key elements of the division of labor.

Ralf Dahrendorf argued that sociology should develop a set of assumptions about the nature of society, a model in which variables are linked by assumption, and a set of testable hypotheses. This orientation is very flawed. Nonetheless, Dahrendorf's work remains useful because he taught U.S. sociologists that problems of class and class conflict can be dealt with in a non-Marxist framework and illustrated the importance of formally stating hypotheses.

Gerhard Lenski developed a theory that explains why the distribution of power and privilege varies within and among societies, and tested his idea using historical and comparative data. He found that the more people are dependent on each other for survival, the more they will share the products of their labor. At the same time, however, the greater the surplus of goods and services, the more power determines their distribution. Among preindustrial societies, Lenski found that the greater the level of technology, the greater the productivity and the greater the inequality. Finally, Lenski proposed that the greater the industrialization and the more democratic the state, the less inequality. Empirically, the status of this last hypothesis remains unclear.

The second half of the chapter sketched a strategy for the study of stratification. The initial step is to assess the historical and international dimensions of stratification. Historical data reveal how much change has occurred over time within one society, such as the United States. International data show the extent to which inequality in its various forms occurs at similar rates in other nations. This research strategy, which parallels Max Weber's, constitutes a "logical experiment" that facilitates identifying the structural variables affecting rates of behavior.

The second step is to distinguish levels of analysis. This procedure is important because the psychological variables explaining why individuals act differ from the structural variables explaining why rates of behavior vary.

People act in terms of their personal experiences, which can be described by the socialization process. The term refers to the lifelong process by which individuals learn norms and values, internalize motivations and (unconscious) needs, develop intellectual and social skills, and enact roles as they participate in society. Socialization is an active process. As people move through life, they adopt a variety of reference groups—collectivities whose characteristics are significant to the development of their own attitudes and behavior. Taken together, knowing how individuals are socialized and their choice of reference groups leads to understanding their behavior.

The social structure affects rates of events—such as poverty, occupational mobility and the like—because it determines the choices available to people. The Class Structure Hypothesis follows: *The lower the social class, the fewer choices people have and the less effective they are in solving personal problems.* This hypothesis, along with the gender and minority group hypotheses, has practical implications. It means that regardless of the problem, poor persons will usually have fewer choices than members of other social classes, and this fact will be reflected in differences in behavior by class.

The third step is to look at how power affects access to valued resources. Power, the ability to achieve goals even if opposition occurs, is not confined to individuals; it is class based and correlated with race and gender. Again, this argument has practical implications. It implies that *the higher the social class, the greater the influence over access to valued resources in the society.*

Chapter 2

Social Class and Stratification

Occupational Prestige and Class Identification

"What do you do for a living?" It is a simple question, usually asked shortly after strangers are introduced. Except for the rich (an important exception), occupations provide the focus for people's lives, both psychologically and materially. The answer, then, is like a calling card—a shorthand summary of a person's claim to be someone with standing in the community. "I'm a lawyer." This answer tells you that the respondent has high prestige, possibly high income, and possibly some degree of power and influence. "I work at the hospital." This answer tells you that the respondent is not a physician, but has some lower prestige job. "I am unemployed at the moment." This answer tells you that the respondent not only does not earn an income but also, at least for now, has little social standing. Losing one's job is a major assault on a person's self-identity.

Students ask similar questions, and for the same reason: "Where do you go to school?" "What is your major?" The answers locate the respondent in the collegiate class structure. The need to obtain such information early in a relationship reveals an underlying characteristic of modern societies: People's self-identity and income stem from their most important and time-consuming activity, their jobs (Glick, 1995). This fact means that what people do each day and how it is evaluated constitute central issues in the study of stratification. One need not be a world-class (or even a good) lawyer or auto mechanic. The issue is how these tasks are evaluated.

The question "What do you do for a living?" carries another implication as well, since people often identify with a class based on their jobs. That is, they see themselves as, say, middle class, and this subjective sense of their location in the class structure guides interaction with others. Lawyers, for example, want to live in neighborhoods with others like themselves, who are also middle class. They share interests, ranging from who gets elected to whom their children marry. And, as both Weber and Marx observed, they act on these interests. This chapter focuses on people's sense of occupational prestige and class identification as indicators of class location.

Occupational Prestige

Occupational Prestige in the United States

The study of **occupational prestige** assesses the social standing of the jobs people have. It is measured by giving a set of cards to a random sample of people and asking them to rate the occupations listed therein according to their standing in the society. For example, among the jobs listed would be electrician. Respondents are asked to place this card on a ladder with nine boxes on it, signifying a range from the highest to lowest standing. The ratings for each job by each member of the sample are averaged to obtain a prestige score and all the occupations in the study are then placed in rank order. In the case of electricians, the score is 51, which is about in the middle of the hierarchy. Listed below are a few of the hundreds of occupations that are ranked, along with their scores (Nakao & Treas, 1994).

Physician	86
Lawyer	75
Registered Nurse	66
Public Grade School Teacher	64
Police Officer	61
Business Person	59
Electrician	51
Secretary	46
Automobile Mechanic	39
Real Estate Manager	38
Cosmetologist	36
Assembly Line Worker	35

Garbage Collector	28
Sales Clerk	28
Bartender	25
Janitor	22

As this short list shows, physicians and lawyers are among the highest-rated people in the United States; that is, they carry the most social standing. Most (but not all) of the high-prestige occupations are white collar; that is, the jobs do not involve manual labor. On the other hand, garbage collectors and janitors are among the lowest-rated jobs in the United States; that is, they carry the least social standing. Most (but not all) of the low-prestige occupations are blue collar; that is, the jobs usually require manual labor. Note, however, that the dividing line between white- and blue-collar workers is not precise: Some blue-collar jobs, such as electrician, outrank some white-collar jobs, such as real estate manager.

The Meaning of Occupational Prestige

The meaning of occupational prestige is significant because, along with ownership or control of capital, jobs are the major roles through which people obtain access to valued resources in modern societies. In *Occupational Prestige in Comparative Perspective,* Donald Treiman proposed one explanation (1977, pp. 1–25). As it turns out, I disagree with him; but this fact is useful because it provides a way of showing how sociologists question and evaluate one another's work.

Treiman argued that occupational prestige hierarchies result from the functional necessities faced by each society. Thus, he began by outlining a set of functional necessities that must be met if societies are to survive. Like all such lists, however, Treiman's is arbitrary and slightly different from that of previous scholars, such as Davis and Moore (1945) and Parsons (1951). His argument is that the functional necessity to obtain food and other commodities, exchange goods, develop shared values, and coordinate activities produces a division of labor. The task specialization inherent to any division of labor leads, in turn, to differences in power and privilege. These differences cause, finally, variations in prestige as people use the resources available to them. Unfortunately, this analysis reveals the flaws characteristic of all functionalist analyses. That is, it poses an illegitimate teleology (that every society has needs) and its presupposition (that the needs of society produce a division of labor) cannot be tested.

In contrast to Treiman, my preference is to explain the meaning of occupational prestige in terms of a simple hypothesis that can be tested: *The greater the skills required, the higher the prestige of an occupation.* Education provides a good (although not the only) indicator of the amount of skill required for a job (MacKinnon & Langford, 1994). As the ranked list of occupations implies, nearly all the jobs with higher prestige also require either a high level of formal education or considerable training (Nakao & Treas, 1994).

If I am correct, this argument suggests a different way of interpreting prestige rankings. That is, people symbolically reward those whose jobs indicate their skill, ability, and hard work by giving them respect. As a result, the hierarchy of occupational prestige carries important practical implications. People defer to their superiors, as indicated by their different occupations. They accept as equals those with roughly similar jobs. This fact affects people's lifestyle (and life chances), since those considered equals comprise the population with whom one typically entertains, marries, shares meals, and engages in other forms of intimate social interaction. Finally, people derogate their inferiors by making them acknowledge in some way their own inferiority and by avoiding intimate social relationships with them. For example, the use of titles such as "sir" and "Doctor" during interaction is often a tacit way for one person to recognize the prestige (and income) of another. Thus, prestige rankings embody society-wide patterns of domination and subordination, of power.

In everyday life, people do not think about prestige scores. They represent quantitative summaries of people's subjective judgments of others' standing in the society. Consider for a moment some of the differences between white- and blue-collar work. The image, white collar, suggests people who wear suits and ties on the job, and it is a fairly accurate symbol. As mentioned, white-collar jobs involve nonmanual labor. A college degree or professional training is often required of those in top-level jobs. People employed in these occupations usually sit behind desks, stay physically clean while working, and often have high income. They are usually paid at a fixed yearly salary rather than by the hour. In addition, a relatively high proportion of white-collar jobs entail supervisory responsibility and many involve the risks of entrepreneurial (or business) activity. White-collar people usually direct blue-collar people and often run or manage businesses. This combination of characteristics, not all of which occurs in every job, means that white-collar workers typically have more political power and higher occupational prestige than do blue-collar employees. These characteristics, along with income differences, indicate why white-collar people usually have more and better options available when confronted with personal crises, such as a divorce or a drug problem.

In contrast, the image, blue collar, suggests people who wear work clothes on the job and, as before, it is a fairly accurate symbol. As mentioned, blue-collar jobs often involve manual labor of some sort. People employed in these occupations frequently work with their hands, often become physically dirty while doing their jobs, and usually have less income and education than do white-collar workers. Most of the time, their occupations do not involve either supervising others or the risks of entrepreneurship. They are usually paid by the hour rather than at a fixed salary. This combination of characteristics means blue-collar workers generally have lower occupational prestige and less political power than do white-collar employees. They also have fewer choices when faced with personal crises.

Although these characteristics mean that blue-collar jobs often have lower prestige, they involve a wide range of skill. Service occupations—such as police officer (prestige score 61), cosmetologist (36), and bartender (25)—provide a good example. In a way, they are a special case of blue-collar work because these workers often stay clean. Moreover, some jobs require college education and carry great responsibility. Superior police officers, for example, must be both psychologists and crime fighters, a tough combination. The amount and difficulty of physical effort varies a lot in blue-collar occupations: In some automated industries, such as oil and chemical, the jobs are interesting but not physically arduous; in other industries, such as auto and steel, automation means boring and strenuous work. These variations mean that social scientific systems of classification are often imprecise.

Nonetheless, people make discriminatory judgments in everyday life (without hesitation) based on the answer to the question "What do you do?" Sometimes these appraisals are straightforward: "She and her husband are teachers and, hence, like us." Often, however, they are subtle. An auto mechanic (prestige score 39) I know, William Meadows, is a good example. Although he becomes rather dirty on the job, he charges me $40 per hour to repair my car. Moreover, he owns the business, so he is also a business person (score 59) with all the risks that entails. Mr. Meadows usually has two or three employees who also work on cars. He pays them (much) less than $40 per hour (with no benefits) and pockets the rest for himself. The business does well, and Mr. Meadows makes a good living; his home is on a lake in an exclusive development. He happens to be African American and so are most of his employees.

Racial/Ethnic and Gender Differences in Occupational Prestige

As implied, prestige rankings affect interaction between members of different racial and ethnic groups, and between men and women as well. "What do you do?" On average, African Americans and Hispanic Americans will state a lower-prestige job than people from other groups. For example, average prestige scores in one study were 51 for Asian Americans (the scale is 1–90), 49 for white Americans, 41 for Hispanic Americans, and 41 for African Americans (Xu & Leffler, 1992). These scores have practical implications. When I drop off or pick up my car, Mr. Meadows' employees sometimes greet me with "sir" (he never does). The tacit recognition of differences (and similarity) in prestige and power also occurs between men and women. This is so even though average prestige scores by gender are rather similar: Men's average is about 49 and women's 47 (Xu & Leffler, 1992). But this similarity is misleading. First, significant differences exist among women in various racial and ethnic groups. Second, many women are not in the labor force and, hence, do not obtain the social standing (and potential for economic independence) that follows from earning a living. "I am just a housewife." Third, as shown in Chapter 5, the occupational distribution of employed women and men differs; women work at lower-ranking jobs (for example, men as physicians and women as nurses). Thus, people's judgments of others' standing also reflect nonclass patterns of domination and subordination.

The Stability of Occupational Prestige over Time

The literature on occupational prestige is very long and has resulted in an empirical generalization: *Hierarchies of occupational prestige are similar over time within the same society.* Thus, the correlation in prestige rankings from one study to another are well above .90 in the United States (Nakao & Treas, 1994). This finding means that the rankings of, for example, physicians and nurses, have been essentially identical over time. This same result occurs in other nations as well. For example, in the Netherlands the correlation between 1953 and 1982 was .97 (Sixma & Ultee, 1984). In Japan the correlation between 1952 and 1964 was .96 (Treiman, 1977). When correlations approach 1.0, as these do, it means almost perfect agreement exists.

This same finding also occurs in less economically developed nations, such as Brazil, India, Nigeria, and the Philippines (Treiman, 1977). For example, in Poland the ratings correlated .93 from 1957 to 1975, and .94 from 1975 to 1987 (Sawinski & Domanski, 1991). There are problems with the samples for many of these studies, however. The data tend to come from urban areas, and respondents are often college students. Hence, they do not represent the entire population but, rather, its most Westernized segments. This problem becomes more significant with the next finding.

The Stability of Occupational Prestige across Societies?

Another empirical generalization is that *hierarchies of occupational prestige are similar across societies.* I have placed a question mark after this heading to indicate that even though this finding is stable, it may not be correct.

Donald Treiman assessed the hypothesis with data for 52 countries from all regions of the world (1977, p. 96). He reported that "all the available evidence points to the same conclusion: There is high agreement throughout the world regarding the relative prestige of occupations." He found a correlation of about .80 among all these studies. Although lower than the temporal correlation previously reported, this figure still means that substantial agreement exists from one society to another about which jobs carry the most and least standing. According to Treiman, whose book *Occupational Prestige in Comparative Perspective* remains the best analysis of this topic, this finding holds even when problems of terminology, weaknesses in the samples used, and disparities in type of society are resolved. But his conclusion is probably too strong. Findings are labeled empirical generalizations because, as in this case, a large number of studies have been done and the results are uniform. Nonetheless, it turns out that criticisms of this finding are serious enough to call it into question.

The first problem is with the samples. Treiman argued that it makes no difference whether the samples are composed of rural or urban people, college students or nonstudents, that the judgments of occupational prestige in Ghana, Mexico, Turkey, and other societies are essentially the same as in the Netherlands or the United States. Haller and Bills, however, recalculated (i.e., tried to repeat) Treiman's findings and showed that rural and urban people in various societies disagree regarding the evaluation of occupations (1979). This issue is important because many studies in less industrialized nations use samples of the population that are most influenced by Western values—college students and urban people, for example. Treiman argued that use of such samples does not matter. He may be wrong.

The second problem is the comparability of job titles across societies. Treiman went to extraordinary lengths to resolve this issue, but probably did not succeed. Many studies, especially of less developed societies, use very few occupational titles (only ten in some cases) that are comparable to those in the United States and other industrialized nations. Haller and Bills argued that this situation means the occupational structure itself is not comparable, since the vast majority of the jobs people do are so different. Their point is persuasive.

Surprisingly, then, despite the number of studies that have been done, the only way to resolve the issues mentioned here is with more data. Subsequent attempts at replication should be designed so as to address these two problems. Until that time, a less sweeping empirical generalization is more appropriate: *Hierarchies of occupational prestige are similar across all Western industrialized nations.* As a caveat, it is possible, as Haller and Bills suggested, that what Treiman found reflects a worldwide process of convergence: Less developed nations are becoming more industrialized and are increasingly influenced by Western values. If true, then similar occupational prestige hierarchies may emerge in these societies over time.

One last note before considering class identification. It is important for you to recognize that Treiman's book constitutes brilliant and enormously difficult work, one representing years of thought. It is an excellent example of high-quality social science. As Max Weber once suggested (1918), over the long run, all good scientific research is superseded as subsequent scholars address the same issues and bring more knowledge to bear on them.

Class Identification

Occupational prestige scores are assessments respondents make of others' social standing, based on their jobs. **Class identification** is an assessment respondents make of their own social class and the implications this evaluation has for their lifestyles. Sociological concern with this topic stems from Karl Marx's work. He was interested in understanding the conditions under which exploited groups would become class conscious and rebel against their oppressors. This concern, however, has proven to be less relevant in Western industrial nations because classes (at all levels) may act cohesively without revolutionary intent. For this reason, studies of class identification simply analyze people's ability to place themselves into a set of ranked classes and assess the meaning this placement has for their lifestyles and life chances.

Patterns of Class Identification

Class identification was first measured by Richard Centers in his seminal book, *The Psychology of Social Classes* (1949, p. 233). He asked this question: "If you were to use one of these four names for your social class, which would you say you belonged in: the middle class, lower class, working class, or upper class?" Subsequent research still uses essentially the same question, with results as shown in Table 2-1. The data show that most people have little difficulty placing themselves into a class and that most see themselves as either working or middle class. In 1945, just as World War II ended, Centers found that 51 percent of men identified themselves as working class and 43 percent as middle class. Since then, the percentages have become more even, with about

45 to 46 percent of both genders identifying with each class. Only about 4 to 8 percent identify with the lower class, probably because people perceive the term as invidious and do not wish to see themselves in this way. Even fewer people identify with the upper class, in part because research samples typically do not include rich persons (who are most likely to view themselves at the top) and in part because many of those who are well-off do not see themselves as such (Jackman & Jackman, 1983).

Patterns of class identification are highly correlated with occupation, such that blue- and white-collar men usually identify with different classes (Vanneman & Pampel, 1977). White male workers in blue-collar occupations with the lowest prestige scores nearly all see themselves as working class. White male workers in white-collar occupations with the highest prestige scores nearly all see themselves as middle class. White male workers in the middle section of the prestige hierarchy divide themselves based on their occupations; thus, given similar prestige scores, those in blue-collar jobs usually see themselves as working class and those in white-collar jobs usually see themselves as middle class. These findings remain after controlling for education and income. I will discuss the issue of employed women's class identification later on.

Patterns of class identification vary by race and ethnicity, as shown in Table 2-2. A plurality of whites (non-Hispanic) see themselves as middle class, 48 percent, compared to 43 percent identifying themselves as working class. The order is reversed, however, among African Americans and Hispanics, with a majority saying they are working class. As will be seen in Chapter 3, this pattern correlates with the occupational distribution of these two groups. Note that although Asian Americans identify in ways roughly similar to that of whites and this order conforms to their occupational distri-

TABLE 2-1   Class Identification among Men and Women, 1945, 1972, 1996

Class Identification	1945	1972	1996
		Men	
Lower Class	1%	4%	4%
Working Class	51	45	46
Middle Class	43	47	45
Upper Class	3	3	5
	98%	100%	100%
		Women	
Lower Class		5%	7%
Working Class		45	44
Middle Class		48	45
Upper Class		2	4
		100%	100%

Sources: Centers (1949); GSS (1996).

Note: 2% of the men in the sample did not answer the question in 1945.

bution, the sample size in Table 2-2 is so low that the results are not statistically meaningful.

These data imply the existence of discrete and identifiable classes in the United States, not just as statistical constructs but as subjectively relevant categories in people's minds. It appears that working-class and middle-class labels reflect a class division between those who do manual and those who do nonmanual labor; they are not merely prestige judgments (Vanneman & Pampel, 1977, p. 435). Thus, people see their jobs as an indicator of their location in the class structure: Those with similar occupational characteristics generally see themselves as belonging to the same class. This argument is consonant with studies of social mobility presented in Chapter 3, in which the division between blue- and white-collar work will be shown to constitute a semipermeable barrier to upward and downward mobility.

The Meaning of Class Identification

In his analysis of the stratification structure, Max Weber argued that people who share common lifestyles and values tend to discriminate against others who are different. He said that this process occurs naturally, without classes being formally organized, as people enjoy each other's hospitality and friendship, marry, select houses and neighborhoods in which to live, and practice social conventions with others who are like themselves. These social conventions are often revealed in subtle ways. For example, my impression is that the location of the television set and the amount of time spent watching it are class related. If true, in working-class houses, the television is often the center of attention in the living room, and it is nearly always turned on (TBA, 1991). In middle-class houses, however, the television is often in a room other than the living room and is not turned on so much. Assuming for a moment that I am correct, the issue is not whether this rather innocuous social convention is better or worse, good or bad. Rather, the issue is that such differences, which are correlated with class, express people's lifestyles and values.

TABLE 2-2   Class Identification by Racial and Ethnic Group, 1996

	White	African	Hispanic	Asian
Lower Class	5%	9%	12%	12%
Working Class	43	56	53	40
Middle Class	48	33	34	48
Upper Class	4	2	1	0
	100%	100%	100%	100%

Source: GSS (1996).

Note: The sample size for Asian Americans is only 40, so the results are not statistically meaningful.

Weber, in short, was right. When people identify with a class, they are saying something, in a symbolic way, about their experiences and their lifestyle preferences: They are identifying those with whom they prefer to interact in intimate ways, and they are commenting upon their taste in entertainment and other leisure time activities. This fact is clearly shown in the best analysis since that by Centers, Jackman and Jackman's *Class Awareness in the United States* (1983, pp. 21, 195). In this study, nearly 80 percent of the respondents reported they feel strongly about their class identification, which confirms it is important to them.

Just how important can be seen when the notion of class identification is linked to other arenas of life. The Jackmans found that people expressed "a marked tendency toward preference for [social] contact with one's own class," especially with regard to friendship choice, neighborhood preference, and marriage partners. For example, more than half of those people who identify themselves as working class say they prefer living in working-class neighborhoods and a similar proportion of those who identify as middle class assert a desire to live in middle-class neighborhoods. As it turns out, these preferences are realized in practice, since class, racial, and ethnic segregation characterizes most U.S. cities (Harrison & Weinberg, 1992). Such segregation means that informal interaction, friendship ties, and other forms of relatively intimate social relationships are usually class based. I will return to the topic of social class and housing, and to the consequences of racially and ethnically similar friendship ties in subsequent chapters. With regard to marriage, Jackman and Jackman reported that people who identify themselves as poor or working class usually prefer that their children "marry up." That is, they want their children to marry someone from a higher class. This preference reflects the fact that marriage can be a vehicle for upward mobility in terms of standing in the community. In contrast, people who see themselves as middle and upper class generally want their children to marry someone from the same class. It turns out, however, the spouses in most marriages come from similar class backgrounds. Hence, this most intimate form of interaction is typically class based. In sum, the evidence suggests that patterns of class identification reflect a fundamental division in U.S. society. People from different classes have different lifestyles, and these variations affect life chances.

A Note on Employed Married Women

I observed earlier that all good scientific research is superseded as subsequent scholars address an issue. The problem of class identification among employed married women illustrates this process. Women who are housewives generally assume the class of their husbands. This process is called "status borrowing." It makes sense in a context in which a woman has no other source of standing in the community. The situation is not as clear-cut in the case of employed married women, since they have an independent source of prestige and income in the society. Past research supports two different hypotheses.

The first is the *Status-Borrowing Hypothesis:*

> *Employed married women ignore their own jobs and education, and consider only their husband's characteristics in deciding with which class to identify.*

This argument implies, for example, that a secretary or an elementary school teacher married to an electrician would see herself as working class, since her husband's job involves manual labor. The logic behind the hypothesis lies in traditional gender norms (see Chapter 5). From this point of view, women's primary adult roles should revolve around the household: bearing children, rearing children, and caring for their husbands. Hence, their major interest should be in the home—even if they are employed. By extrapolation, then, such women should see their position in the community as resulting from their husband's job. Solid, technically sound research supports this hypothesis (Felson & Knoke, 1974; Jackman & Jackman, 1983).

The second argument is called the *Status-Sharing Hypothesis:*

> *Employed married women take both their own and their husband's characteristics into account in deciding with which class to identify.*

This argument implies rather different patterns of class identification among employed married women. For example, on the one hand, a secretary married to an electrician might see herself as working class because, even though she has a white-collar job and has many of the fringe benefits connected to white-collar occupations, she nonetheless performs the lowest prestige white-collar work. On the other hand, the same person might emphasize the fact that her job is white collar regardless of her relatively low income, assess her husband's job as a highly skilled and relatively prestigious occupation, and identify herself as middle class. (Recall that the occupational prestige score for electricians is higher than that of many white-collar jobs.) In each case, respondents evaluate both spouses' positions in the community when determining their overall social standing. Hence, status sharing occurs. The logic behind the status-sharing hypothesis lies in egalitarian gender norms. From this point of view, women and men should be equal; that is, equally obligated to support the family, rear children, and care for one another. By extrapolation, then, employed married women should see their position in the community as resulting from a combination of their own and their husband's characteristics. Again, technically sound evidence supports this hypothesis (Ritter & Hargens, 1975; Van Velsor & Beeghley, 1979).

Obviously, both the hypotheses and the empirical findings cited above flatly contradict each other. Both cannot be right. Or can they?

Beeghley and Cochran examined this issue and showed that the research just cited may be correct, even though the findings are contradictory (1988). Rather, the inability to confirm one or the other hypothesis may reflect changing gender norms. Thus, over the past few years, U.S. society has been moving, in fits and starts, from a belief in traditional gender norms to an acceptance of egalitarian gender norms. Such changes do not come easily or quickly because they involve drastic alterations in the way people view themselves, the world in which they live, and the way they organize their lives. Previous research may simply reveal this confusion: At one time respondents display a status-borrowing pattern and at another a status-sharing orientation.

Yet there must be some method of sorting these differences out, and Beeghley and Cochran suggested that married women's orientation to gender norms might provide a way. They argued that such normative orientations set the context in which married women adopt either a status-borrowing or a status-sharing stance. Hence, they tested the following hypotheses:

1. Employed married women who believe in traditional gender norms will consider only their husband's characteristics in deciding with which class to identify.
2. Employed married women who believe in egalitarian gender norms will take both their own and their husband's characteristics into account in deciding with which class to identify.

In testing these hypotheses, Beeghley and Cochran used married women's support for the Equal Rights Amendment (ERA) and their attitudes toward married women working outside the home as indicators of gender norms. They found that those supporting the ERA and favoring women's employment use a status-sharing approach in identifying with a class. In contrast, those opposing the ERA and opposing married women's employment, even though they have a job themselves, use a status-borrowing approach in identifying with a class. Beeghley and Cochran concluded by predicting that, as an increasing proportion of women work outside the home and more people of both genders accept egalitarian gender norms, the status-sharing hypothesis will be supported by an increasing proportion of employed married women.

One last observation: It is important for you to recognize that neither the findings reported by Beeghley and Cochran nor their prediction ends the matter; nor do recent data showing that employed wives use a status-sharing approach (Davis & Robinson, 1998). Gender norms remain in flux, and further research on this and related topics will show the direction in which they move. It is in this sense that Max Weber described the social sciences as blessed with eternal youth.

"What do you do for a living?" It is a question that has become meaningful only recently. In William Shakespeare's play, *Romeo and Juliet,* for example, set in the sixteenth century, one's job was less important than one's name. Being a Capulet or a Montague, or associated with one of these families, clearly indicated high status in Verona. Such persons were due respect. With industrialization and the rise of capital-ism, however, the criterion by which people evaluate each other has changed. One's name remains important, of course, but what people do and the class with which they identify provide an initial guide to their place in the community and the respect they should be given.

Summary

This chapter describes the implications people's jobs have for their class location and suggests the meaning such views have for their lifestyle. Studies of occupational prestige assess the social standing of occupations. The basis for prestige assignments appears to be the level required in various jobs. Prestige hierarchies indicate patterns of domination and subordination characteristic of the class structure. These hierarchies vary by race/ethnicity and by gender. There are two main empirical generalizations: The hierarchy of occupational prestige is stable over time within and across societies. The second generalization—stability across societies—however, probably needs to be modified. It is more likely that hierarchies of occupational prestige are similar across all Western industrial nations.

Class identification assesses the extent to which people see themselves as belonging to different classes and the implications this has for their lifestyles. In the United States, people find it easy to identify with a class, mainly the working and middle classes (see Table 2-1). Class identification is highly correlated with occupation and says a great deal about people's lifestyle: for example, who they live near, their friends, and potential marriage partners. Patterns of class identification among employed married women are unclear, mainly because of changing gender norms. When this factor is controlled for, however, the finding becomes intelligible. It appears that employed married women who accept egalitarian gender norms use a status-sharing orientation, while those who accept traditional gender norms use a status-borrowing orientation in selecting a class with which to identify.

Chapter 3

Social Class and Stratification
Mobility and Status Attainment

William H. Gates was a prominent lawyer in Seattle in the 1950s. On October 28, 1955, his son, William H. Gates III, was born. As he grew up, young Bill developed an abiding, indeed compulsive, interest in computer programming. Eventually, he founded the Microsoft Corporation, bought DOS, and in 1981 persuaded IBM to use a revised version of it as the operating system for its line of personal computers. When Microsoft became a publicly traded stock corporation in 1986, its chief executive officer, Bill Gates, became an instant multimillionaire (Wallace, 1993). It is said that he is now worth billions. Mr. Gates's experience implies important questions. Can you and I become billionaires? More prosaically, how much opportunity is there—really? What factors determine people's occupational location (and, hence, their income, prestige, and ultimately their life chances)? In a relatively rigid society, people usually obtain jobs based on their birth—the jargon term is *ascription*. By contrast, in a relatively fluid society, people are more likely to get positions based on their ability and hard work—achievement. As described in Chapter 1, all societies can be classified by their degree of emphasis on ascription or achievement. In general, class-based societies display greater emphasis on achievement.

Sociologists answer these sorts of questions by measuring (based on observation) mobility and status attainment. **Mobility** refers to changes in people's occupation, either intra- or intergenerationally. Intragenerational mobility occurs during people's own lives. Intergenerational mobility occurs from parents' occupations to children's. In both cases, the question being asked is this: How many people move and how far? The answer, of course, is in terms of rates of movement and the explanation is structural. In presenting the data in the next section, I shall focus on intergenerational mobility when looking at the United States and intragenerational mobility when comparing this country with others. As you will see, the findings are parallel. **Status attainment** is the study of how individuals enter specific occupations. The question here is this: What combination of ascribed and achieved factors leads individuals into one occupation rather than another and why? The answer, of course, is social psychological—either directly or indirectly. As an aside, precisely because mobility and status attainment are assessed only in terms of people's occupations, such analyses say nothing about how ownership of capital (such as stock in the Microsoft Corporation) leads to opportunity, success, and power. I will return to this issue.

Social Mobility

Social Mobility in the United States

In order to describe long-term rates of intergenerational mobility, the flow of people out of and into occupations must be shown. This task requires an understanding of how the occupational structure changed over time. In the past, there was not much variability in the occupational structure; most people were farmers. In 1800, for example, 74 percent of the labor force was engaged in farming occupations, a figure that was probably an all-time low at that time (USBC, 1975, p. 139). It fell steadily over the century, to 55 percent in 1850 and 38 percent in 1900. People left farming jobs, moved to cities, and took new jobs. By 1900, as Table 3-1 shows, a sizeable working class had developed, defined as people doing nonfarm blue-collar work: about 45 percent of the population. Most of these jobs involved very hard, physically arduous tasks. Little mechanization existed, at least by today's standards. In addition, a small middle class had formed, about 18 percent of the population (at most). These people worked inside, and most of them did not do manual labor.

As displayed in Table 3-1, the occupational structure has continued changing over the past century. Today, only 3 percent of the population works on farms, and about 39 percent in blue-collar jobs. Although such work remains arduous and, often, physically dirty, mechanization has transformed it. Tractors (sometimes with air conditioning) substitute for horse-drawn plows. Powered equipment makes blue-collar jobs easier and increases productivity—which is to say people get more done in less time. Nonetheless, most of these people are working class in prestige and class identification. Finally, the table shows that the majority of employed persons, 58 percent, now work in white-collar jobs. Most are middle class in prestige and class identification.

Table 3-1 illustrates the long-term pattern: People have moved off the farm and into working- and middle-class jobs, often in historically new occupations. It is probable that Emily Perrin produced the first quantitative study of mobility in 1904. She compared the occupations of fathers and sons in order "to determine how far ancestral bent and how far environmental conditions influence a man in his choice of occupation in life" (1904, p. 967). Put differently, she wanted to understand how family back-

TABLE 3-1   Occupational Distribution, 1900, 1950, and 1997

	1900	1950		1997
White Collar			*White Collar*	
Professionals	4%	9%	Professional Specialty	14%
Managers	6	9	Executives and Managers	15
			Technicians	3
Sales	5	7	Sales	12
Clerical	3	12	Administrative Support	14
Total White Collar	18%	37%	Total White Collar	58%
Blue Collar			*Blue Collar*	
Crafts	11%	14%	Precision Production	11%
Operators	13	20	Operators	10
Laborers	12	7	Handlers & laborers	4
Service	9	10	Service	14
Total Blue Collar	45%	51%	Total Blue Collar	39%
Farmers	38%	12%	Farmers, Foresters, Fishers	3%
Total	101%	100%	Total	100%

Sources: USBC (1975, p. 139), USDL (1998, p. 174).

Note: Percentages do not add to 100 because of rounding. As implied by the name changes, the occupational categories are not exactly comparable between 1950 and 1997.

ground and achievement affect a person's occupation. As mentioned earlier, subsequent scholars divided Perrin's questions in two: the study of mobility rates and status attainment by individuals.

The best early analysis of mobility was Pitirim Sorokin's, *Social Mobility*, originally published in 1927. Sorokin, like all subsequent observers, recognized that a job is most people's main source of income and prestige in modern societies. Thus, he focused on how fathers' occupations were linked with their sons' occupations and thereby charted the rate of mobility across generations. The emphasis on the nexus between fathers and sons made sense at the time because few women were employed and most people believed they should remain at home (see Chapter 4). Sorokin analyzed the data then available, including Perrin's, and concluded as follows (1927, pp. 435–39): First, much intergenerational occupational inheritance occurs. For example, he noted that "the hereditary transmission of occupation still exists. . . . The fathers' occupation is still entered by the children in a greater proportion than any other." Second, a lot of intergenerational mobility takes place such that a significant proportion of children move into different (usually higher prestige) occupations than their fathers. Third, intergenerational mobility is usually short distance. In his words, "the closer the affinity between occupations, the more intensive among them is mutual interchange of their members." Although Sorokin's data were not very good, his findings anticipate later research.

Such research has developed reasonably accurate data for the late nineteenth century and for the 1960s, 1970s, and 1980s. The result is three major findings about mobility rates among men.[1]

First, there is a great deal of occupational inheritance in the United States. The dominant intergenerational pattern is for fathers in white-collar occupations to have sons who also work in white-collar occupations, while fathers in blue-collar jobs generally have sons who also work in blue-collar jobs. The extent of occupational inheritance means that the class structure is reproduced from one generation to another as people with a certain level of access to resources pass them on to their children. Unlike Sorokin, by the term "inheritance" I do not mean that sons take the same job as their fathers or even enter the same occupational category. Rather, they end up in the same social class: as white-collar or blue-collar workers, respectively. Panel A of Table 3-2 illustrates this finding. It shows, for example, that even during the nineteenth century, most sons of professional workers ended up in the white-collar work force. Similarly, most sons of blue-collar workers and farmers followed in their fathers'

---

[1]The data on which these findings are based come from four studies. (1) Avery Guest et al. (1989) examined the link between fathers' and sons' occupations during 1880–1900. Their data are better than those Sorokin had. (2) In *The American Occupational Structure*, Peter Blau and O. D. Duncan (1967) analyzed a sample of 20,700 men, aged 20–65 in 1963. (3) In *Opportunity and Change*, David Featherman and Robert Hauser (1978) examined a sample of 10,500 men aged 21–65 in 1973. These samples represent the noninstitutionalized male population at the two points in time. Their size is important. Most random samples are considerably smaller, typically around 1,500 persons, and carry an error term of about plus-or-minus 3 percent. Large samples like these display a much lower error term, plus-or-minus 1 percent or less. (4) Michael Hout (1988) assembled data for the period 1982–1985. His sample, while more typical in size, includes both men and women.

TABLE 3-2   Occupational Mobility among Men, 1880–1900, 1963, 1973, and 1982–1985

Panel A: Illustrations of Intergenerational Occupational Inheritance among Men

Year	Percent	Result
1880–1900	56%	of the sons of professionals became white-collar workers
"	78%	of the sons of service/laborers became blue-collar workers
"	60%	of the sons of farmers became farmers
1963	68%	of the sons of salaried professionals became white-collar workers
"	72%	of the sons of laborers became blue-collar workers
1973	68%	of the sons of salaried professionals became white-collar workers
"	71%	of the sons of laborers became blue-collar workers
1982–1985	72%	of the sons of salaried professionals became white-collar workers
"	60%	of the sons of laborers became blue-collar workers

Panel B: Illustrations of Intergenerational Occupational Mobility among Men

Year	Percent	Result
1880–1900	26%	of the sons of crafts workers became white-collar workers
1963	41%	of the sons of crafts workers became white-collar workers
1973	45%	of the sons of crafts workers became white-collar workers
1982–1985	45%	of the sons of crafts workers became white-collar workers

Panel C: Illustrations of the Difficulties of Long-Distance Intergenerational Occupational Mobility among Men

Year	Percent	Result
1880–1900	3%	of the sons of farmers became professional workers
1963	<1%	of the sons of farmers became professional workers
1973	<1%	of the sons of farmers became professional workers
1982–1985	0%	of the sons of farmers became professional workers

Sources: Guest, Landale, and McCann (1989, p. 359); Blau and Duncan (1967, p. 28); Featherman and Hauser (1978, p. 535); Hout (1988, p. 1396).

Note: Occupational categories are not the same from one study to another.

footsteps. Thus, most sons (and daughters, see below) inherit the class of their parents, which suggests that ascription remains important. This was true in the nineteenth century, and it remains true today.

The sons of farmers, however, constitute an anomaly. Although they displayed high levels of occupational inheritance during the nineteenth century, the historical pattern has been for them to move into blue-collar occupations where farm-related skills could be used. This trend means that there are now two occupational classes in the United States: white-collar workers and blue-collar workers, with farm workers constituting a recessive class. The boundaries of these classes form semipermeable barriers to social mobility.

The usual interpretation of this finding is that the need for the prestige of being "white collar" together with the lack of saleable manual skills prevents a great deal of downward mobility among the sons of white-collar workers. Similarly, much upward mobility into white-collar jobs is prevented by lack of necessary skills and, often, lack of respect for those sorts of jobs. Many blue-collar people do not believe that "pencil pushers" really work. After all, they do not sweat or get dirty or become physically tired from their jobs. The result is the reproduction of the class structure.

Second, social mobility is widespread in the United States. This empirical generalization means that, despite the first finding reported above, the occupational structure is relatively fluid. Panel B of Table 3-2 provides illustrations. I am using craft occupations in the table because they comprise the highest prestige blue-collar jobs (see Table 3-1 and Chapter 2) and constitute a sort of jumping off place for upward mobility. Thus, about 26 percent of the sons of craft workers became white-collar workers during the years 1880–1900. This rate increased significantly during this century. By 1963, it had risen to about 41 percent and by 1973 to about 45 percent. Beginning in the 1890s (and probably earlier), each generation of men has been upwardly mobile compared to their fathers (Biblarz et al., 1996). All this movement suggests that there has been lots of opportunity in the United States over the last two centuries and that the importance of achievement has increased.[2]

Widespread mobility is one of the markers of capitalism. This process has a twin impact. On the one hand, it signifies the rise of class as a system of stratification, with its emphasis on achievement (rather than birth) as a basis of location. Most people interpret the historical process of intergenerational upward mobility as liberating. On the other hand, as the occupational structure has changed over time (Table 3-1), the historical pattern has been for some occupations to be destroyed (especially those requiring manual labor) and others to be created (especially those involving nonmanual labor). You should understand—and this is an important point, so pay attention—that the people in occupations that have been destroyed are usually not the same ones as those in occupations that have been created. Thus, some people lose: their jobs, livelihood, self-concept, houses, even their marriages and children (see Chapter 9). Capitalism is liberating, but it is also vicious.

In order to gain a preliminary quantitative appreciation of this process, please look back at Table 3-1, noting the rise in the number of people in sales and service jobs coupled with the decline of those in precision production and operative jobs between 1950 and 1997. Most of these changes occurred in the last 20 years, and they indicate

---

[2]The pattern of mobility portrayed by these two findings has been common over a much longer period than portrayed here. Although analyses are hampered by unsystematic data, it appears that intergenerational inheritance coupled with relatively high rates of upward mobility describe the occupational structure since the seventeenth century (Pessen, 1971; Williamson & Lindert, 1980). I will comment on this issue again when describing the historical trend in the distribution of wealth in Chapter 7.

fundamental dislocations in the labor market (DiPrete & Nonnemaker, 1997). High-skilled and (relatively) high-paying blue-collar jobs in industry have declined; they have been replaced by lower-skilled and (significantly) lower-paying jobs, mostly in sales and service sectors. Moreover, this change does not reflect purely economic forces; it also indicates political decisions. Governments today can, if they wish, affect the rate of change and the degree of job protection ordinary working people have. Two results are greater inequality (see Chapters 7 and 11) and an increase in the number of working poor (see Chapter 10).

Third, short distance movements exceed long distance ones. In their now classic work, *The American Occupational Structure,* Peter Blau and O. D. Duncan mimicked Sorokin's words: "The closer two occupations are to one another in the status hierarchy, the greater is the flow of manpower between them" (1967, p. 36). Panel C of Table 3-2 illustrates the pattern by showing how few people move long distances. Thus, in 1880–1900 only 3 percent of the sons of farmers moved to the top of the prestige ladder by becoming professional workers. More recently, such mobility has occurred less than 1 percent of the time. Do not be mislead by the 0 percent for 1982–1985; it reflects the small sample size. A little (very little) long-distance mobility takes place.

Recent data on women's intergenerational mobility show patterns similar to those of men (Hout, 1988, p. 1395). First, a great deal of occupational inheritance takes place. For example, 95 percent of the daughters of salaried professional fathers become white-collar workers, usually above the level of clerks. Second, much mobility occurs. For example, 74 percent of the daughters of craft worker fathers became white-collar workers. This figure falls to 37 percent, however, if administrative support workers are excluded. When women work for pay, they are often guided into "support jobs," such as clerks; that is, they take jobs that involve assisting men. Finally, most movement is short distance. For example, fewer than 1 percent of daughters of farmers become professional workers. These data, however, understate the differences between men and women. Biblarz and others, for example, found little change in women's rates of occupational mobility since the 1880s (1996). They suggested that "gender-based occupational discrimination" (another way of talking about the importance of ascription) has always inhibited daughters' occupational mobility and continues to do so.

Mobility data on minority groups are limited to African Americans, and their historical pattern is much different than that for whites. As recently as 1962, only 5 percent of African American men had professional or managerial jobs (Featherman & Hauser, 1978, p. 326). Unlike whites, however, little occupational inheritance occurred for men in these categories. Rather, the sons of African American professionals usually displayed downward mobility: 63 percent of them had service, operative, and laborer jobs. More generally, the vast majority of African American men—68 percent—were employed in these three occupational categories in 1962. And nearly all of them displayed great occupational inheritance from one generation to another. Thus, unlike whites, who have often advanced intergenerationally, the debilitating effects of discrimination kept most African American men confined to menial jobs regardless of their parents' status. The year in which these data were collected is significant, as it was just prior to passage of the Civil Rights Act of 1963 and other measures. This fact suggests that between the end of the Civil War and the mid-1960s, little opportunity existed for African Americans, regardless of their family resources, ability, or hard work. I will argue in Chapter 5 that the Civil War freed African Americans in name but not in fact.

Since the 1960s, however, the situation has changed considerably. The class structure among African Americans elongated, as it also has, presumably, among Hispanics and other minorities. Table 3-3 suggests how much change has occurred. Nearly half of all African Americans (men and women) are white collar, and 20 percent are in professional and managerial jobs (11 percent plus 9 percent in the table). Moreover, although this conclusion is tentative, it appears that the pattern of mobility is beginning to resemble that of whites: occupational inheritance (in particular, a greater rate of inheritance at the upper-occupational levels) and an increasingly high rate of upward mobility compared to the past (Featherman & Hauser, 1978; Davis, 1995; Fosu, 1997). Thinking back to Chapter 2, it will be interesting to see if African Americans' class identification changes as well (Table 2-2). As already mentioned, these changes reflect the impact of the Civil Rights movement. When people became free, they began displaying upward mobility. Table 3-3 also shows the occupational distribution of Hispanics, revealing that a smaller proportion, 38 percent, are white collar compared to both African Americans and whites (non-Hispanics). My guess is that the figures in the top half of the distribution are all-time highs for Hispanics. Assuming you believe that greater equality among racial and ethnic groups is better, then these data suggest that progress has occurred over the last 30 to 40 years. Remember, however, that Table 3-3 shows that a much higher proportion of whites work in the higher-prestige and higher-paying jobs. Moreover, the children of African Americans still display significantly higher rates of downward mobility than do whites (Davis, 1995). So a great deal of

TABLE 3-3   Occupational Distribution among Whites, African Americans, and Hispanics, 1997

	Whites	African Americans	Hispanics
Professional Specialty	16%	11%	7%
Executives & Managers	16	9	8
Technicians	3	3	2
Sales	13	9	9
Administrative Support	14	17	12
Total White Collar	62%	49%	38%
Precision Production	12%	8%	13%
Operators	9	14	16
Handlers & Laborers	3	6	6
Service	12	22	21
Total Blue Collar	36%	50%	56%
Farmers, Foresters, Fishers	2%	1%	6%
Total	100%	100%	100%

Source: USDL (1998, p. 174).

inequality remains. This double finding—progress (and freedom) along with continued inequality (and discrimination)—will be the theme in Chapter 5.

For now, however, it is important to examine international mobility data. After all, you should wonder if this country is unique. For example, if the rate of mobility in the United States is higher (or lower) than in other nations, then it is useful to ask why this difference exists.

Social Mobility in Other Nations

Presenting mobility data internationally, however, can be tricky because studies in the United States, England, France, and other European nations do not use the same occupational categories. This problem has been dealt with in *The Constant Flux: A Study of Class Mobility in Industrial Societies* by Robert Erikson and John H. Goldthorpe (1993, p. 331). They found that mobility rates in the United States are neither much higher nor lower than in similar nations. This fact is illustrated by intragenerational mobility. You should recall that the issue here is how many people are mobile over the course of their careers. Presented below are the chances of men who begin their careers as skilled blue-collar workers (roughly equivalent to precision production workers in Table 3-1) ending up as professionals, managers, and technicians:

Sweden	22%
United States	20%
England	16%
France	15%
Ireland	8%

These data lead to two conclusions. First, with regard to the United States, the intragenerational finding presented here parallels the intergenerational finding presented earlier: Most people are occupationally stable, while a significant (although smaller) proportion are mobile. Second, although U.S. mobility rates are not unique, there is considerable international variation. Thus, in the United States and Sweden, the odds of a man who begins his career as an electrician ending up as an engineer are about one in five. In England and France, however, they are about one in six, and in Ireland one in ten. So these three nations display less mobility than does the United States.

Social structures display three tendencies, all of which are illustrated by the study of mobility. First, they are stable over time. This is why so much occupational inheritance occurs. Comprising networks of relationships and values that tie people together, social structures set the range of opportunities and limitations that are available. So people grow up within a context that provides specific skills and experiences: schools, role models, and the like. Hence, the class structure is reproduced as the children of farmers learn to appreciate the land, children of blue-collar families learn how to work with their hands, and children of white-collar families learn how to succeed in school. I am being stereotypical, of course, simply to point out that there is a great deal of intergenerational occupational inheritance. Second, social structures change over time.

The rapidity of change, however, is a new phenomenon in history. This is why so much mobility occurs. For example, productivity increased when people invented machines to take advantage of fossil fuels. Not only was more food produced, but also problems of coordination arose and more white-collar jobs were created. The plausible range of opportunities expanded. Hence, mobility became widespread as people took advantage of new choices. Third, social structures vary internationally. This is why differences in mobility occur from one nation to another. In the next section, I offer an explanation for each of these tendencies.

Social Structure and Mobility

The Reproduction of the Class Structure

Recall that the first finding reported in this chapter is that most of the sons of blue-collar workers end up as blue-collar workers. And when their daughters are employed, most of them end up either in white-collar support jobs or as blue-collar workers. The result is that they are always economically insecure, regardless of how hard they work (see Chapter 9). Similarly, most of the sons of white-collar workers end up as white-collar workers. And when their daughters are employed, they too end up as white-collar workers, typically in jobs above the level of administrative support. What I am interested in, then, is the reproduction of the class structure over time, in other words, the continuing impact of ascription.

A Vignette

In order to suggest how this process occurs, I have constructed a vignette about a game of Monopoly as it might appear if it were organized to reflect reality. The purpose of this little fantasy is to provide you with a subjective sense of what the data mean.[3]

The game of Monopoly embodies fundamental values characteristic of the United States, especially beliefs about equality of opportunity and the virtue inherent in competitive striving for success. In the game as it is actually played, each participant starts with an equal amount of money, $1,500. By combining luck (symbolized by the roll of the dice) and shrewdness (symbolized by purchase and auction decisions), competitors seek economic success. The point to remember about the game is that everyone begins with the same chance of winning. After all, a game is only fair under such conditions, and no one wants to participate in a contest in which some of the players have an unfair advantage at the beginning. Although many people believe that life is like a game of Monopoly and that their class position represents their reward for hard work, this attitude is self-deceptive; for the real world is rather different in that some people are born with more advantages than others and the results of their hard work vary accordingly.

---

[3]The name of the game, Monopoly, is the trademark of Parker Brothers for its Real Estate Trading Game (Beverly, MA: Parker Brothers Division of General Mills Fun Group, Inc., 1935, 1946, 1961). An earlier version of this vignette appeared in my *Living Poorly in America* (Beeghley, 1983).

Here is a fictional version of Monopoly, one that is more analogous to the real world than the actual game. Begin by imagining that four groups of people are participating and that they compete both as individuals against all other individuals and, in certain situations, as members of their respective groups. Also, imagine that the game board is much larger than usual because there are so many contestants.

Group One is very small; in fact, its members are statistically insignificant. They are almost never included in sample surveys. But they are relatively advantaged at the start of the game, for they begin owning some property and possessing lots of Monopoly money, say, $5,000 each. In addition, the members of this group take care of the bank and, because of their enormous responsibility, get two rolls of the dice each turn. Thus, while these people are not statistically significant, they are of great substantive importance.

Group Two is very large but its members have considerably fewer advantages with which to begin. They have no property and about $2,000 each. Nonetheless, they believe as an act of faith that they and everyone else playing the game can be like Bill Gates and move into Group One if they work hard enough.

Group Three is also very large but its members are even more disadvantaged at the beginning of the game. They have no property and only about $1,000 each.

Group Four is smaller but still significant in size. Its members, however, are the most disadvantaged of all. They not only own no property and have very little money, about $500 each, but also they do not know all the rules of the game. Perhaps as a result, they often (more or less randomly) lose a turn and frequently pay more than list price for properties and fines.

One final point about this game. No one can stop competing; no one can quit striving for success. Any players who run out of money or go to jail are required to beg for more cash, pay their penalties, and continue playing—indefinitely.

In this context, then, the competition begins. Now Monopoly is a game played by individuals, and it would be easy to measure the process by which each participant acquired income and property and thereby found a place in the game. This would be the Monopoly equivalent of status attainment, of course. While such an analysis would be useful in order to understand precisely how individuals in the various groups behave, it would be misleading to extrapolate an explanation of the game as a whole based only on the analysis of the experiences of individuals. This is because the players were divided into groups with unequal advantages when the game began. An interpretation that does not recognize this fact, which does not ascertain the structure of the game, has to be misleading.

If, however, one takes a more holistic (or structural) view, it becomes possible to sketch the results of the game in a plausible way. The members of Group One, the rich, will generally remain well off unless they are very unlucky or unwise (in fact, downright stupid). This is because they began competing with many built-in advantages and share some of them; for example, they pool their "get out of jail free" cards. Furthermore, given their responsibility for taking care of the bank, a few of them illegally "borrow" money occasionally while other players are not looking. When caught, of course, they are (sometimes) forced to pay back what they stole.

Similarly, the members of Group Two will, with some variation, maintain their positions. Although upward mobility into Group One and downward mobility into Group Three will occasionally occur, most movement will be within Group Two itself and of relatively short distance. These people generally ignore the fact that few of them actually move into Group One and take satisfaction in being better off than less-advantaged persons. They attribute this fact to their hard work and ability rather than the advantages with which they began.

The members of Groups Three and Four are obviously in the most precarious positions. While some upward mobility into Group Two does take place, most move-ment will be short distance, usually within or between the lower-level groups. Security is always uncertain for these participants in the game, mainly because the resources available to them are so minimal that it is difficult, on their own, to make much headway. Nonetheless, nearly everyone in these two groups works hard and accepts their position in the game.

Some members of Groups Three and Four, however, become **alienated**; that is, they believe they are powerless to influence their own lives. Alienated people find that dominant norms and values are hopelessly remote, even meaningless. Thus, some readjust their goals and only play by going through the motions. Others, however, just sit at the game board passively while their tokens are moved for them. Still others (surprisingly few) pull out guns and use them to alter their economic situation. But given spatial arrangements separating the various groups, their victims are usually other members of Groups Three and Four. When caught, these people are sent to jail for long periods.

With apologies to the many dedicated scholars working in the field, this fictional vignette reflects the major findings in the study of social mobility: While a great deal of mobility occurs, most of it short distance, the class structure is reproduced over time because occupational inheritance predominates.

The Inheritance of Social Class

The vignette is useful because it highlights the fact that the rewards of hard work go mostly to those who start life with some advantages. This result is why the mode is occupational inheritance—from blue collar to blue collar and from white collar to white collar. It is also why, as explained later, ascribed factors systematically influence status attainment at every stage. Thus, even though people can no longer directly inherit class position and even though they must get and keep jobs based on achievement, ascription remains fundamental to understanding the stratification structure. People's family background is significant not only because it allows them to obtain educational creden-tials that qualify them for better jobs, but also because it provides them with knowl-edge, interpersonal skills, social contacts, values, psychological traits, and other less obvious benefits that enable them to obtain and keep better jobs. I shall return to this issue in a few moments.

In addition, the vignette is useful because it suggests how the rate of mobility is affected by the social structure. As the fictional Monopoly game is constructed, no amount of individual effort will change the fact that most people will not cross class boundaries and those who do will go only a short way. To repeat: The social structure sets the range of opportunities available to individuals. This is why the research reported previously shows that reality mirrors the vignette.

Finally, the vignette is useful because it highlights a fundamental omission in both the mobility and status attainment literatures: The findings do not reflect the existence of an upper class, the rich. Despite the use of "random samples," survey research cannot account for either the characteristics or the impact this small class has on the structure of stratification. This is because the rich make themselves inaccessible to survey researchers. One does not simply walk up to the doors of rich persons and hand them questionnaires. Yet, despite their statistical insignificance, the substantive importance of this small aggregate is enormous—for they possess capital and wield enormous political power as a result. These factors, the importance of which Marx and Weber emphasized, make the occupations of rich people relatively unimportant as determinants of class. In effect, researchers have examined mobility and status attainment only for the vast majority of people, for whom occupation determines their class, and ignored the group for which it is not important. The omission of the property-owning class leads to an emphasis on individual achievement as the mechanism for mobility. It also leads to an image of the United States as being without classes and class conflict. In this sense, mobility research is a throwback to a pre-1950s orientation, prior to the time Ralf Dahrendorf alerted U.S. sociologists to the importance of class conflict. Yet there remains the reality of mobility.

The Long-Term Pattern of Mobility

Even though most people are occupationally stable, the data show that the United States has displayed a relatively high rate of upward mobility over time. Common sense suggests that individuals are upwardly mobile because they work hard and have ability. And this is true. But, as is so often the case, a focus on individuals does not explain why the rate of mobility has been so high over the last century. In reality, the explanation for this fact has little to do with individuals' skill or motivation. Rather, the social structure changed over time such that a great deal of upward mobility became possible for certain kinds of people. The factors causing the high rate of mobility can be stated formally, as in the following hypothesis:

> The rate of mobility in the United States reflects the impact of (1) industrialization, (2) class differences in fertility rates, (3) immigration rates, and (4) affirmative action for white males.

Industrialization

The new forms of energy that became available beginning in the nineteenth century—such as steam, fossil fuels, and (later on) nuclear energy—allowed the substitution of machines for human and animal muscle power and led to a radical increase in productivity. Such changes mean that machines now perform many tasks that animals and people used to do. As a result, the number of farming and blue-collar jobs declined and the number of white-collar jobs expanded. More specifically, the three occupational categories that expanded most over the last 150 years were professionals, executives and managers, and administrative support while the two that declined the most were farmers and farm laborers, and laborers in manufacturing (Blau & Duncan, 1967). These changes exerted an enormous impact on everyone's lives. Put simply, without the tremendous increase in white-collar jobs over the last century, most people would still be farmers today and the rate of social mobility would have been very low. Hard work would not have produced mobility, no matter how much ability people possessed. In sum, "changes in the occupational structure are the only source of systematic variation in rates of intergenerational occupational mobility" (Hauser, 1975, p. 585).

What happened is that as the economy was transformed vacant job slots were created in the top sectors, which served as a "pull" factor stimulating upward mobility. Thus, while no individual was forced to be upwardly mobile, these jobs existed; they were attractive in terms of pay, perquisites (privileges), and other characteristics (such as the ability to remain physically clean and avoid manual labor); the result was that many individuals strove to attain them. It is important to understand, however, that the motives or abilities or any personal characteristic of those who filled them cannot explain the existence of these jobs. They reflect changes "in the nature of the society itself" that produced a high rate of mobility over time (Durkheim, 1895, p. 128). People's options expanded.

Class Differences in Fertility Rates

The term **fertility rate** refers to the average number of children each woman has. With the exception of the post-World War II "baby boom," the long-term trend in fertility rates has been downward. The average woman born in the early 1800s had about eight children, while the average woman born since 1935 has had about two (Cherlin, 1992). But the fertility of women from different classes has probably always varied such that lower-class women had more and upper-class women had fewer than average. Scattered data from throughout the nineteenth century show this tendency clearly (Whelpton, 1928; Jaffe, 1940). Data from 1910, when the process of industrialization was in full swing, also display this pattern: Rural and farm women had around five children on average, urban women married to blue-collar workers had around four children, and urban women married to white-collar workers had about three children (Graybill et al., 1958). These differences are significant, since large families in farming and lower-level blue-collar occupations provided most of the people to fill the increasing number of jobs that opened above them in the stratification hierarchy. In effect, class differences in fertility constituted a historical "push" factor, stimulating upward mobility in the United States.

Immigration Rates

The United States is a nation of immigrants, and the years from 1870 to 1920 saw the highest level of immigration in U.S. history. In the decade from 1900 to 1910, for example, the immigration rate was 10 persons per 1,000 U.S. citizens, an all-time high (USBC, 1997b, p. 10). These new residents typically entered the society at the lowest rungs. Nonetheless, immigration laws during this period required that new arrivals come equipped with skills (Lieberson, 1980). The sheer force of numbers combined with education, literacy, and other vocational abilities constituted another "push" factor, stimulating upward mobility (Sibley, 1942). Thus, "the pressure of displaced manpower at the bottom and the vacuum created by new opportunities at the top [started] a chain reaction of short distance movements throughout the occupational structure. This push of supply at the bottom and pull of demand at the top [created] opportunities for upward mobility from most origins, as the vacancies left by sons moving up [were] filled by sons from lower strata" (Blau & Duncan, 1967, p. 66).

The significance of class differences in fertility rates and immigration rates has declined in recent years. Since about 1920, for example, the level of immigration into the United States has been kept at one or two persons per 1,000 citizens. Similarly, although class differences in fertility continue to exist, they have declined over the years.

Affirmative Action for White Males

The term **affirmative action** refers to public policies giving advantages to members of one group over others. Historically, such benefits have gone to white males. They could achieve. Women and members of minority groups have been held back by ascribed barriers.

Unequal treatment has been built into the social structure in the form of **traditional gender norms.** These are rules of behavior emphasizing that men and women ought to have separate spheres: Women should bear and raise children, and take care of their husbands. Men should provide for the family economically and dominate public life. In the past, such norms were implemented by denying women the right to vote, despite the fact that they were productive citizens. Such norms were also used to justify driving women out or keeping them out of high-prestige and high-paying jobs in medicine, education, business, and the like. Although these norms are changing, as indicated by the fact that many forms of unequal treatment have become illegal in recent years, they continue to influence behavior. This can be seen in the informal, hard-to-identify mechanisms that favor men's economic and political success (see Chapter 4). In addition, the conflict over abortion and other aspects of sexual behavior indicates the continuing salience of traditional gender norms. Thus, if women's reproductive roles ought to be the center of their lives, then birth control and abortion should be illegal (or at least very hard to get). This result would inhibit women's occupational success, as it did in the past. But if women's and men's nonreproductive roles ought to be balanced with their reproductive roles, then birth control and abortions should be readily available. This result would facilitate women's occupational success. I discuss these issues in Chapter 4. For now, it is worth noting that the impact of traditional gender norms is reflected by the decision of all researchers, beginning with Emily Perrin and continuing until recently, not to analyze mobility among women. Sociologists, who are sometimes not very prescient, simply assumed that women belonged at home—thereby legitimating gender discrimination. The norms underlying such behavior enhanced mobility by white males.

Affirmative action has also benefited white males at the expense of African Americans and other racial and ethnic groups. In Chapter 5, I argue that three factors inhibited mobility by nonwhites. First, variations in the conditions of settlement—free versus slave and citizen versus debt peonage—placed people of color at a disadvantage.

Second, patterns of prejudice and discrimination (especially institutionalized discrimination) inhibited occupational success. And third, affirmative action aimed at whites, mainly males, promoted their occupational success. The impact of such policies can be seen in the nineteenth century land acts and the development of land grant colleges, which provided conduits of mobility that were unavailable to African Americans. Although discrimination has become illegal today, I will describe in Chapter 5 some mechanisms by which it continues. The result has been greater upward mobility by white males.

These elements of social structure—industrialization, class differences in fertility rates, immigration, and affirmative action for white males—existed independently of individuals and influenced them, affecting their range of choices. People's behavior was directed in certain ways rather than others by factors over which they had little control. Thus, the structure of stratification developed a large number of open channels for achievement by some white males but considerably fewer and shorter channels for those individuals with the greatest inherited disadvantages. This is why women, African Americans, Hispanics, and others display lower rates of mobility: They were born to the wrong parents, worked in the wrong industry, or lived in the wrong region of the country. It is a grim fact that people with disadvantaged parents can be paragons of hard work and morality but most will remain poor or live on the edge of poverty.

International Variations in Mobility

Attempts at showing the relationship between social structure and international variations in mobility rates have a long history. One hypothesis has dominated the literature:

In every society, the greater the industrialization, the more equality of opportunity, upward mobility, and similarity in mobility rates.

Initial analyses seemed to confirm the argument. Lipset and Zetterberg found, for example, that "the overall pattern of social mobility appears to be much the same" in every Western industrial society (1959, p. 13). But, alas, subsequent researchers could not replicate their findings, even using the same data (Miller, 1960). More recently, the hypothesis was modified to state that cross-societal similarity in mobility rates occurs after controlling statistically for cultural, demographic, and political differences among these nations (Featherman et al., 1975). But even this version has been refuted. Nonetheless, the argument will not go away. In the most recent analysis, Erikson and Goldthorpe showed that the occupational structure did not change at the same time, at the same rate, or to the same degree in various Western nations. They concluded that there is "no evidence" of similarity in patterns of mobility in Western industrial societies (1993, p. 102). This fact was illustrated earlier with data on intragenerational mobility, which varies greatly from one nation to another. Internationally, then, the interplay between inheritance and achievement is best described as trendless or, to use their phrase, a "constant flux." So the hypothesis is false. Nations, as Lenski observed, can now choose; they can regulate the degree of mobility (and inequality) (1966).

If there is no trend, then interest focuses on the decisions various nations make. In this context, please recall my earlier discussion of how highly skilled and (relatively) high-paying blue-collar jobs in industry have declined—replaced by lower-skilled and (significantly) lower-paying jobs, mostly in sales and service. This mobility occurred in response to economic and technological developments, as they were mediated by political decisions. Public policies, for example, can affect worker's job security when industries are contracting, their ability to obtain support (welfare) when jobs are lost, the ease with which people can move from an industry that is contracting to (new, perhaps different jobs in) an industry that is expanding, and the ease with which persons in, say, their 50s or 60s can exit from the labor force altogether. DiPrete and his colleagues found tentative support for the following hypothesis:

> *When jobs decline in an industry, the less job security, the fewer the labor market boundaries, then the greater the emphasis on individual resources in determining occupational mobility (1997).*

They looked at four nations and found that the United States protects worker job security less and places the fewest barriers between jobs in different industries. These decisions lead to more emphasis on individual resources. It follows, as mentioned earlier, that there has been a lot of mobility into sales and service occupations in recent years. This statement, however, does not do justice to the impact such changes have on people's lives (see Chapter 9). Sweden was next, displaying somewhat greater job security and labor market boundaries. The Netherlands and Germany were rather similar and better yet at protecting individuals from the impact of economic and technological change. A lot of controversy exists about the wisdom of these policies. In this country, the dominant view (held by those with the power to make decisions) is that "the market" ought to determine where the jobs are. Whether this opinion serves as a veil for protecting economic and political interests of the rich and powerful is something you need to decide. In any case, remember that "the market" operates in a political context; jobs are created and destroyed in light of political as well as economic decisions. In every Western nation, those with power can influence how much mobility occurs.

But who has power? I will consider this issue in Chapters 6 and 7. For now, I want to shift the level of analysis from mobility rates to status attainment by individuals.

Status Attainment

Individuals make decisions in the context in which they find themselves. They enter an occupation based on the way their parents' status produces advantages and disadvantages, their own efforts and abilities, and a large degree of luck. (Most people do not want to recognize this last element.) In *The American Occupational Structure,* Peter Blau and O. D. Duncan showed that this process can be studied as a causal sequence that identifies not only the factors in individuals' lives that influence attainment but also how much each factor affects subsequent ones (1967, p. 163):

> *We think of the individual's life-cycle as a sequence in time that can be described, however partially and crudely, by a set of classificatory or quantitative measurements taken at successive stages. . . . Given this scheme, the questions we are continually raising in one form or another are: How and to what degree do the circumstances of birth condition subsequent status? And how does status attained (whether by ascription or achievement) at one stage of the life-cycle affect the prospects for a subsequent stage?*

All subsequent research on status attainment reflects the impact of Blau and Duncan's path-breaking work.

Status Attainment in the United States

The major variables in the status attainment process are shown in Figure 3-1, which depicts a sequence of ascribed and achieved factors. A person's background (as indicated by parent's social class) influences one's occupational status attainment, both indirectly because of its strong relationship to educational accomplishments, but also directly. Thus, while the importance of ascribed factors is greatest when a child is young, family influences affect a child's accomplishments throughout life. At the same time, however, achievement at each stage of life decisively affects prospects at subsequent stages. This fact means that issues over which individuals have more control assume greater importance with age. The boxes in the figure are numbered to correspond with the order of the findings reported next.[4]

1. *Father's education, father's occupation, mother's education, and family income are all highly correlated, and each influences status attainment at all stages of a child's life.* The social class of a child's family, including the mother's characteristics, directly affects each stage of status attainment: the development of ability, academic performance, the evaluations of significant others (such as parents, teachers, and friends), the child's educational and occupational aspirations, the child's educational attainment, and the child's eventual occupational attainment. Because the variables in box 6 are grouped together in order to simplify the presentation, the effect of family background on a child's first job and eventual occupation is not shown. Remember, as noted already, that a direct but lessened relationship exists between them. The impact of a person's family on that person's occupational success fits with most people's intuitive observation. This is a case where research shows that "common sense" is correct.

2. *Ability influences every subsequent stage of the status attainment process.* People of high ability usually do better than those with less. "Ability" is usually measured by either an achievement or intelligence test and, hence, refers to academic aptitude rather than to other kinds of skills. Thus, ability most strongly affects academic performance (for example, grade point average) and educational attainment. But ability also influ-

---

[4]The figure summarizes many studies. See Blau and Duncan (1967), Sewell et al. (1970), Featherman and Hauser (1978), Hout and Morgan (1975), Alexander et al. (1975), Jencks et al. (1979), Krymkowski (1991), England (1992), and Duncan et al. (1998).

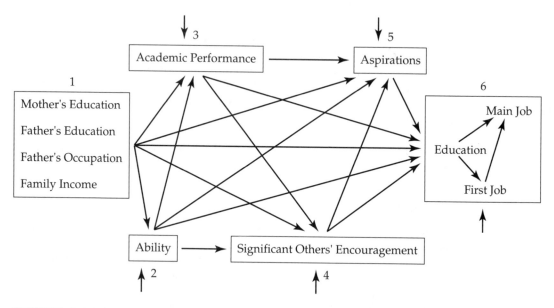

FIGURE 3-1   The Process of Status Attainment in the United States

ences some intervening variables: a child's educational and occupational aspirations and the encouragement a child receives from various significant others. Finally, in addition to education, ability also affects first job and main job. As an aside, you should remember that while ability has a biological basis, its development is socially determined (Duncan et al., 1998). Thus, middle-class children often possess advantages over others who have the same ability, with the result that they enter school better prepared and, hence, display better performance. The long-term impact increases the odds of success for middle-class children.

   3. *Academic performance directly influences subsequent status attainment: the level and kind of encouragement received from others, aspirations, and eventual educational and occupational attainment.* The dual impact of the schools becomes apparent early in people's lives. On the one hand, the schools facilitate achievement. Ambitious parents encourage and prepare their children, who enter the schools ready to use their abilities. As a result, they receive encouragement from teachers, develop aspirations, and get tracked into a college preparatory curriculum. They become less likely to drop out of schools and more likely to attend college (Haveman & Wolfe, 1995). And a college degree is often what separates those in the middle class from those in the working class. On the other hand, school personnel often use ascriptive (nonperformance) criteria in evaluating and placing children. Teachers expect, and get, better performance from middle-class students (Rosenthal & Jacobson, 1968). Just as important, however, track placement typically reflects class background (Oakes, 1985). Tracking is how the public schools prepare some students for college and others with vocational skills (Jencks et al., 1972). My guess is that this practice constitutes a reaction to large class size: Heterogeneous groups of 25 (or more) are much harder to teach than 15 or so.

Tracking makes teaching large groups easier. Class size is a function of funding, of course, much of which is dictated by middle-class voters (see Chapter 6). In this context, then, the schools provide some children with a vehicle for upward mobility. For most, however, they lock people in place.

4. *Significant others' encouragement affects aspirations and educational and occupational attainment.* The term **significant other** was coined by the psychiatrist Harry Stack Sullivan (1940), who used it to refer to people who are emotionally important to individuals and, hence, especially influential on them. Sullivan emphasized that the impact is strongest when individuals are young. Thus, parents, teachers, and peers constitute significant others who affect children's aspirations and their ultimate educational and occupational attainment (Sewell & Shah, 1968a; 1968b). This influence occurs in combination with the effect of academic performance and other previously mentioned variables. Thus, children develop aspirations according to the evaluations they receive from others and their own self-assessment based on their academic performance, familial obligations, and the like. Further, children's peers are also significant others who influence the development of aspirations and educational and occupational attainment.

5. *Educational and occupational aspirations influence educational and occupational attainment.* **Educational aspirations** refer to children's plans and expectations about their ultimate level of schooling, such as going to college. **Occupational aspirations** refer to the kinds of jobs children expect or would like when they become adults. Aspirations are the filter through which significant others influence children. Thus, parents who have college degrees provide role models and encouragement for their children to attend college. In addition, when people's friends comprise children of parents with college degrees, a collective expectation about college attendance develops. The result is higher educational attainment. In contrast, children raised in different contexts often develop lower aspirations, which result in lower educational attainment.

6. *Educational attainment strongly influences occupational attainment, both first job and main job.* College attendance is crucial to getting many white-collar jobs. The best predictor of college attendance remains family background, with all the other variables shown in Figure 3-1 serving as filters for this factor. It has been known for a long time that middle-class children are much more likely to attend college than working-class or poor children, even if the latter have high ability (Coleman et al., 1966; McPherson & Shapiro, 1998). What happens, of course, is that parents at the top of the class structure are more likely to encourage higher education and more capable of making it happen. This is so even if their children do not have as much ability as others, at least when measured by standardized tests. At the same time, however, a smaller but significant proportion of working-class parents whose children display high ability also get their children into college. Interestingly, class of origin does not predict either performance once a person enters college or graduation from college. And graduation is important. Those with a college degree have a significant occupational advantage over those without one. This fact means that in the race for prestige (and income), it is not attendance but the credential that counts. In this regard, the dual impact of education becomes clear once again. On the one hand, an educational credential constitutes a vehicle for preserving class boundaries. Middle-class parents ensure that their children reap the rewards of prestige and income associated with white-collar jobs. On the other hand, a significant minority of working-class children get into and complete college, and their achievement translates into white-collar prestige and income. To repeat: The status attainment process constitutes an interrelated chain of ascribed and achieved factors. This is also true for African Americans (and probably other minority groups) and women.

The status attainment process shown in Figure 3-1 describes African Americans' experiences as well as whites' (Winship, 1992). Yet this fact masks significant change that has occurred. Blau and Duncan's data showed that during the 1960s African Americans were less able than whites to pass on whatever status advantages they achieved. With the passage of time, however, more intergenerational continuity is occurring among African Americans, and racial differences in educational and occupational attainment have declined (Jaynes & Williams, 1989). Nonetheless, it remains true that, on average, African Americans and whites begin at different status levels and end up at different status levels. This is, of course, also true for other minority groups. Put bluntly, while everyone benefits from increased schooling, white males still benefit more. This variation reflects discrimination. Alas, models of the status attainment process, such as Figure 3-1, do not include this factor as a variable, which means that they do not get at the key issue.

The situation is similar with regard to gender differences (England, 1992). The status attainment process is similar for women and men. But significant variations exist: Mothers' characteristics affect daughters' status attainment more than fathers' do. Women's first job tends to be higher in prestige then men's, but men's main job increases their prestige more. This difference occurs because women get locked into jobs (as clerks, for example) without a promotion ladder. Ultimately, however, while the status attainment model shown in Figure 3-1 describes both women's and men's experiences, it reveals little about their differences. It reveals little, in short, about discrimination.

Status Attainment in Other Nations

As it turns out, the process of status attainment appears to be similar in all Western industrial nations. You should understand, however, that problems of data comparability exist, the models used include fewer variables than shown in Figure 3-1, and the studies only deal with males. Given these caveats, the findings can be summarized as follows (Treiman & Ganzeboom, 1990; Krymkowski, 1991):

> *1. Family background exerts a weak but significant and direct impact on children's occupation.*
>
> *2. Children's education exerts a strong and direct impact on their occupation.*

Note that I have phrased the finding in gender neutral terms, under the hypothesis that the process is similar for men and women.

While the pattern is similar across Western societies, however, significant variation exists. Treiman and Yip examined five nations: the United States, West Germany, Great Britain, Netherlands, and Sweden (1989). They found that the relationship between father's occupation and son's job is much lower in Sweden than in the United States and other nations, while that between son's education and his job is much higher. This finding suggests that ascription is less important than achievement in Swedish society. The Netherlands, by contrast, displayed the highest relationship between father's and son's jobs, and the lowest relationship between son's education and job. This finding suggests that ascription has a greater impact in the Netherlands, compared to the United States and other nations.

The process of status attainment illustrates how ascription and achievement combine in modern societies to affect where people end up in the class structure. Children participate in their family's social network, developing contacts and connections as a result; they enjoy their family's economic benefits; and in the family they develop skills, knowledge, and other abilities. So people's class of origin indicates the opportunities with which they begin seeking a place in society. At the same time, what individuals accomplish makes a difference.

The Individual and Status Attainment

Social class matters. Recall for a moment the Class Structure Hypothesis:

The lower the social class, the fewer choices people have and the less effective they are in solving personal problems.

The number of choices people have and their effectiveness is important because status attainment occurs within a specific class context, one in which some people (and families) have fewer advantages than others.

This section illustrates how the status attainment process occurs by sketching a vignette about two fictional families: the Smiths, a working-class family on the edge of poverty, and the Joneses, a middle-class family. Be warned: The differences between the two families are portrayed in ways that emphasize the disadvantages of growing up near poverty and the advantages of growing up middle class. Hence, this sketch does not do justice to the full range of familial experiences children in different classes have. There is some danger of caricature, of assuming that the family background of poor and working-class children is always inferior to that of middle-class children. Nothing could be further from the truth. Nonetheless, the types of events depicted here are class related. Poor and working-class families are more likely to display characteristics like the Smiths while middle-class families are more likely to resemble the Joneses. This difference is reflected in the socialization process and, as a result, in status attainment. As a last point, problems of prejudice and discrimination are not considered here, either by race/ethnicity or gender, as they will be discussed in subsequent chapters.

A Vignette

Jane and Edward Smith are married and live in Cedar Key, Florida, a town of about 1,000 people on the Gulf Coast. Jane's mother and father both have high school degrees. Her mother works as a waitress and her father earns an uncertain living fishing in the Gulf. Edward's mother graduated from high school and works as a retail clerk. Although his father did not finish high school, he works steadily as a self-employed electrician.

They married when they were both 17 years old. Jane was pregnant at the time with her first child, named Mary. At age 19, they had a second child, Emma, and at 20 a third, Sam. Initially, they tried to establish their own household, but moved back into Jane's parents' home on two occasions. Living conditions were crowded, which added stress (Beeghley & Donnelly, 1989). For several years, they had spells of unemployment and part-time employment. They received public assistance twice, totaling about a year and a half. They are now 30, and work full-time in, respectively, a textile mill and food-processing plant. Jane operates a machine and earns about $16,000 yearly. Edward is a nonunion electrician, earning about $25,000 yearly.

The initial financial hardships the Smiths experienced meant that the children spent the early years of their lives in an environment of economic want without satisfaction. In this context, they learned that their parents cannot control what happens to the family: how much there is to eat, what kind of house they live in, and other fundamental aspects of life. Although Jane and Edward stayed together and eventually achieved a stable living standard, their lifestyle remains precarious. Children internalize this knowledge; it becomes part of their interior vision of the world and their place within it; and it affects their behavior throughout life. They may learn, for example, to live for the moment, since waiting around for future rewards is likely to bring disappointment. What such orientations mean in terms of the socialization process is that children learn to believe they are vulnerable and not in control of what happens to them. This lesson affects future behavior in school, making it more difficult to succeed occupationally later on.

In addition to the financial limitations, the Smiths married and started a family while still young themselves. Hence, the children were raised by parents who were still, in years and experience, children themselves. Because Jane and Edward passed from girl and boy to wife and husband to mother and father so swiftly, they had little time to integrate and assimilate the psychological orientations and behaviors necessary for their new roles. So, at least initially, they lacked both marriage and parenting skills. As before, this fact means that their children's early years were spent in an environment in which want without satisfaction was everywhere, only in this case the thing wanted was psychological security. To be raised by people who are unsure of their own adulthood can mean that children are responded to in very inconsistent ways. In this case, Edward and Jane have always been loving parents. There were, nonetheless, periods of neglect in which their own needs (they were young adults, remember, 18 to 22 years of age) took precedence over their children's needs. Moreover, they struggled economically and lived in a crowded environment. Inevitably, they fought sometimes. There were some occasions when Edward and Jane took out their frustrations on the children: They hit them. The long-term effects of such lack of predictability are straightforward: Children become angry and frustrated and, as a result, display inconsistent and inappropriate behavior. For example, they may be aggressive in the wrong way or passive at the wrong time. Such characteristics have important negative implications for success in school and for occupational attainment later on.

Finally, the Smith children grew up with some other limitations. Neither Jane nor Edward were read to when they were little, and, hence, did not recognize the importance of reading to their own children. Moreover, other forms of stimuli—piano lessons, trips to museums, computer camps, and the like—were unavailable either because of the cost or the Smith's rural location. Such experiences help prepare children for school and expose them to the dominant culture. These activities are important when children enter school and throughout the school years. Teachers can identify which children are going to have difficulty in the early grades. Those who have not learned certain skills—naming colors, counting, the alphabet, among others—enter the school at a disadvantage. The Smiths' oldest child, Mary, is a good example. Mary was enrolled in Cedar Key Elementary School at age five and was a low achiever from the beginning. Jane Smith met with the teachers and tried to respond to their suggestions, but was not forceful in dealing with them. By the beginning of third grade, Mary was placed in a special education class even though she tested at normal intelligence. Mary is now in middle school, reading at an elementary school level. Last summer, as every summer, Mary and her siblings stayed with their grandmother and spent much of the day watching television. One suspects that her educational and occupational future is dim.

Yet children have different experiences. Recall that schools have a dual impact, facilitating high achievement that is independent of family background for some. The Smiths' minister, as luck would have it, was an undergraduate music major and saw that Emma (the middle child) had unusual musical ability for a little girl. He encouraged the child, even buying her a violin. With the Smiths' support, he taught Emma for several years, and she did well. He also paid for her to attend a music camp each summer. As a result of this attention, teachers have now taken an interest in her, both academically and musically. Although prediction is difficult, Emma's long-term educational future seems brighter, as does her occupational future.

In the jargon sociologists use, the Smiths lack financial capital (money), human capital (employment-related skills), and social capital (maturity, interpersonal skills, and knowledge of the larger culture). But the terminology does not get at the many practical problems they faced. My hope, of course, is that the vignette is at least suggestive of these problems. I also hope that it suggests their underlying courage. Against the odds, they have grown up, stayed together, worked hard, and raised their children in as stable an environment as possible. (As an aside, you may have noted that I did not mention the Smiths' youngest child, Sam. If you want to know what happens to him, look ahead to Chapter 10. The Smiths' lives take a turn for the worse when Edward loses his job because the company moves the fish plant to Mexico where labor is cheaper.)

Harriet and Peter Jones live in Evanston, Illinois, an upper-middle-class suburb of Chicago. Harriet's parents both have advanced degrees. Her father is an engineer, and her mother a computer programmer. Peter's parents also have advanced degrees. His father is an accountant, and his mother an elementary school teacher. Thus, as with the Smiths, both Harriet and Peter come from similar class backgrounds. Unlike the Smiths, however, Harriet and Peter remained in school and started their careers before thinking about marriage. They met at age 26 and married at 28. Their child, Everett, was born two years later. Harriet works as a reporter, and Peter is a college professor. Their combined income is around $100,000 per year. Not only is their income high, but also Harriet's parents gave them the money for the down payment on their house in an exclusive area with good schools.

Being raised in a relatively affluent environment produces many advantages. It has never occurred to Everett to wonder about food. Moreover, their home is large and, hence, it has been easier to separate when people become frustrated with one another. So compared to the Smiths' children, Everett experienced a more stable and predictable lifestyle from a very young age. He learned that life is not precarious and that delaying immediate gratification will often bring greater rewards in the future. Thus, his interior vision of himself included a sense of personal efficacy (the ability to solve problems and overcome obstacles) and a belief that he has some control over what happens to him. Such experiences fundamentally affect behavior in school, making it easier to succeed subsequently as an adult.

In addition, the Jones' child was "affluent" in a second way as well. Harriet and Peter were mature when Everett was born. Secure in their adulthood, they responded to him as consistently as possible and tried to create a family environment in which he could thrive. One result is a high level of verbal and interpersonal skill. Such characteristics produce more success in school and increase the level of achievement as an adult.

Finally, Harriet and Peter were able to provide their child with many experiences—preschool, lessons, camps, computers at home, and the like—that increased his cognitive skills. So Everett entered school knowing his colors, able to count, and capable of using the computer to find sites his parents did not want him to see. Nonetheless, it became apparent in the first grade that Everett was a low achiever. Harriet and Peter attacked the situation directly: They consulted with the teacher and principal, volunteered to work in the classroom, had the child tested, worked with him daily at home, had him tutored over the summer, requested (and got) a more structured second grade teacher. Everett was working at grade level by the end of second grade. He is now in middle school, performing well, and is a good athlete. Last summer he attended a baseball camp, a basketball camp, a music camp, and a computer camp. One suspects his eventual educational and occupational prospects are bright.

To use jargon again, Harriet and Peter Jones have financial, human, and social capital. Some of these advantages came from their parents. The house down payment is a tangible example; less tangible, but no less real, were the development of aspirations that led them to attend college and delay marriage. Other advantages reflect their own hard work. The long-term result is the probability of relatively high educational and occupational achievement for their child.

A caveat: As indicated earlier, I intend these examples to portray how the status attainment process occurs and the relative advantages middle-class people enjoy. You should understand, however, that some middle-class people have children but dodge parenting; they are unable to put their children's needs before their own. Some are absent due to their occupational ambitions. Some abuse their children. Some use their children as weapons during divorce. At the same time, many working-class and poor families are stable and nurturing. So you should take the Smith and Jones examples as illustrative of the impact of social class on status attainment, not definitive.

Socialization and Status Attainment

Socialization, you should recall, is the lifelong process of learning norms and values, internalizing motivations and (unconscious) needs, developing intellectual and social skills, and enacting roles. Although this process continues throughout life, its importance is greatest when one is young. As summarized in Chapter 1, childhood interaction, primary group interaction, interaction with significant others, and long-term interaction are usually very influential on individuals. In the language of status attainment research, which is one way of restating socialization theory: Parent's occupation and income affect children's abilities, school performance, teachers' encouragement, aspirations, education, and occupation. Of course, children have increasing say in this process as they get older. The vignette comparing the Smith and Jones families is designed to suggest some aspects of this process, as revealed by research. A key finding is that *the higher the family income (especially in early childhood), the greater the achievement of children* (Duncan et al., 1998). The reason for this relationship is that family income affects the quality of the home environment: nature of parent-child interaction, opportunities for learning, and the physical condition of the home among other factors.

Think about the differences in parent-child interaction portrayed in the vignette. The Smiths are good people who struggled mightily, indeed heroically, to establish a stable family life—and they succeeded. Nonetheless, much of their interaction, between themselves and with their children, was harsher than occurred within the Jones family. The finding is this: *The lower the family income, the greater the economic pressures and the greater the stress between parents—which leads to harsher parent-child interaction* (Conger et al., 1997). It follows that *the harsher the parent-child interaction, the lower children's self-confidence and the lower their achievement* (Conger et al., 1997). These findings are why I speculated that Mary Smith's future looks bleaker than that of Everett Jones. But such results are not inevitable. Recall that significant others besides parents affect status attainment. This is why I had a minister recognize Emma Smith's musical talent, altering the odds of her finishing high school and, perhaps, attending college. The future is not given; it is impossible to know what will happen to Mary, Emma, or Everett. But there is no question that the quality of the home environment—in this case parent-child interaction (along with that of others who are emotionally significant)—affects their future.

Opportunities for learning, defined broadly to include all aspects of life, not just schooling, also affect people's future. Consider, as just one example, the different way Mary and Emma Smith spend their summer compared to Everett Jones. But formal schooling is vital. The status attainment literature shows that *the higher the parents' social class, the higher the children's educational attainment.* And, of course, *the higher the educational attainment, the higher the occupational attainment.*

One reason for these findings is that middle-class people dominate the public schools. They are most capable of attending a school board meeting, a parents' night, a teacher conference, or a disciplinary meeting with the principal. People whose work makes them less physically tired at the end of the day, who possess private transportation, who have access to child care, and who enjoy paid leave time built into their jobs will attend such meetings at higher rates. As a result, their children's educational needs are better served: Teachers take a more personal interest, are more tolerant, and are quicker to spot (and resolve) potential problems. Consider the different experiences of Mary Smith and Everett Jones, which I (loosely) extrapolated from Annette Lareau's *Home Advantage: Social Class and Parental Education in Elementary Education* (1989). She explored the way in which and the effectiveness with which middle- and working-class parents interact with teachers. A hypothesis follows: *The less knowledge and self-confidence parents have, the less likely they are to see themselves as the status equal of teachers.* If the hypothesis is correct, working-class parents who see themselves as unequal to teachers are likely to be less forceful and less effective than middle-class parents. This is why the vignette portrayed different outcomes for Mary and Everett—with long-term consequences. Social class matters: The domination of the public schools by middle-class people means that their children have a better chance to succeed.

Another reason for these findings is that the educational resources available to children vary by class. For example, it has been estimated that youngsters whose parents are in the top fifth of the income distribution benefit from twice the educational resources, in simple dollar terms, as do children whose parents are in the bottom fifth (Jencks, 1972). There is no reason to believe this estimate has changed. Such variation means that poor and working-class children have fewer opportunities to learn than do middle- and upper-class children. For example, my impression is that the availability of computers in the classroom is directly related to the socioeconomic status of the students served. In addition, exposure to computers outside the school—at computer camps, at private after-school workshops, or at home—is undoubtedly class related. As you will see in Chapters 9 and 10, the budgets of poor and working-class families rarely allow for the purchase of home computers. Yet computer knowledge will be an essential skill in the next few years. This example could be extended to class size, laboratory equipment, library materials, and the like. Again, these differences in educational resources mean that middle-class and rich children have a better chance to succeed.

A final reason for these findings is that school success does not depend solely on ability; it also reflects preparation for school along with such personality traits as self-discipline, being able to take direction, intellectual (as opposed to emotional) behavior orientations, and hard work independent of intrinsic task orientation. Fewer poor and working-class children are likely to have these characteristics (especially when they are the children of young parents), and there is considerable evidence that the educational system does little to build such traits (Bowles & Gintis, 1976). Rather, those students who lack self-discipline, who are less able to follow direction, who too often react emotionally, and who are unable to work without immediate rewards are frequently stigmatized. Such students are often behind academically when they arrive in kindergarten or first grade, have negatively charged personality traits, and end up staying behind academically—regardless of their abilities. More generally, as noted earlier, students from all classes are usually placed in ability groups—tracked—with others like themselves (Oakes, 1985). Such tracks are correlated with social class. So children and their peers belonging to the same track function as role models for one another and reward each other's behavior, whether it is appropriate or not. This is fine for middle-class youngsters, less fine for people from other backgrounds, for it means there exist built-in differences in the chance to succeed. These experiences constitute an essential aspect of the socialization process.

As a final comment, many individual teachers try hard to help children who appear less able or less well-adjusted. They usually fail over the long run. Yet the impact of the minister (it could have been a teacher) on Emma's life suggests that we ought to notice that some succeed. What these facts mean is that poor and working-class children more often enter school behind others and when this occurs they usually do not catch up. This failure means, in turn, that the educational system reproduces the stratification structure.

This description of the social psychological basis for status attainment provides a rather different view of the structure of stratification than that held by many researchers (e.g., Blau & Duncan, 1967). They emphasize, rightly, the high rate of mobility, and show how education and other achievement variables contribute to that process. I emphasize, rightly, the stability of the class structure and show how family background and education facilitate that process. Both of us are correct. Can you and I become billionaires? We are more likely to win one of those state-run lotteries.

Summary

The study of mobility focuses on changes in people's occupation, either intra- or intergenerationally. The study of status attainment focuses on how individuals enter specific occupations. Together, these topics indicate the relative emphasis on ascription and achievement in the stratification structure. Describing trends in mobility and status attainment requires an understanding of how the occupational structure changed over time (Table 3-1). The long-term pattern has been for people to move off the farm and into working- and middle-class jobs.

The major findings in the study of mobility are as follows (Table 3-2): (1) The dominant tendency is for inter- and intragenerational stability, (2) nonetheless, mobility is widespread, and (3) most movement is short distance. The paradoxical combination of stability and mobility has characterized the United States since the seventeenth century. Recent data indicate that women and men show similar patterns of mobility. Historical trends in mobility for African Americans have differed significantly from that for whites, with less occupational inheritance and more downward mobility. Since the 1960s, however, racial differences in patterns of mobility have begun declining.

Although it has been hypothesized that industrialization would produce similar patterns of mobility in all societies going through this transformation, the argument has been rejected. Mobility rates in other nations similar to the United States display a "constant flux." It has been shown, however, that U.S. rates are not uniquely high or low compared to other nations.

The class structure is stable across generations because people in each class pass their resources (wealth, education, interpersonal contacts, and the like) on to their children. When U.S. society is examined in a historical context, it becomes clear that the most important factors affecting mobility rates are structural: industrialization, class differences in fertility rates, immigration, and affirmative action for white males. Thus, the rewards of hard work go mainly to those who start out with some advantages. Note that the literature on mobility focuses on occupations and does not recognize the significance of a capital-owning class whose members' prestige and power in the society is not dependent on their jobs.

Blau and Duncan first identified the mechanisms of the status attainment process. They showed that it reflects an interrelated chain of ascribed and achieved variables. Their model was elaborated on by the inclusion of a set of explicitly social psychological factors (Figure 3-1): family background, ability, academic performance, significant others' encouragement, aspirations, educational attainment, first job, and main occupation. Subsequent work shows that the basic status attainment model also describes the experiences of African Americans and women, with the caveat that it does not take the impact of discrimination into account. The status attainment process in other Western industrial nations resembles that in the United States.

Underlying the status attainment process is socialization, which varies by social class. Because children from different classes often (not always) have different experiences at home and at school, their status attainment varies accordingly.

Chapter *4*

Gender and Stratification

Historically, men were supposed to focus their lives on producing an income and participating in public life. This emphasis meant that the value placed on achievement, fairness, equality of opportunity, and hard work to get ahead has been applied mainly to white males. Thus, it is no accident that a woman would be asked, "What does your husband do?" at social gatherings. Men's status in the community depended on what they did for a living—on their productive activity outside the home. It indicated their place in the stratification hierarchy, their share in the distribution of valued resources. Historically, men were breadwinners. Women, by contrast, were supposed to reproduce, raise children, and care for the home. This emphasis meant that educational and occupational opportunity was restricted, no matter how much ability women had or how hard they worked. Rather, women's position in society was ascribed (set by birth); as wives, they were attached to men, accompanied men, and helped men succeed. They did not, at least publicly, lead or dominate men. It would have been odd to ask a man, "What does your wife do?" Women were breadservers. This rather rigid gender-based ranking system has meant that women have had less access to valued resources. Hence, at every class level they have had less autonomy, less freedom to make life choices, and more restricted life chances. The name for these different expectations for men and women is **traditional gender norms** (Beeghley, 1996).[1]

Until recently, these different expectations based on birth were accepted as right and proper. When I was growing up in the 1950s, a popular television series, *Father Knows Best,* epitomized these values. In the series, the main character was Jim Anderson. He left each day in the family's only car to sell insurance. His wife, Margaret, stayed home—isolated and dependent. She watched the children, cleaned house, ordered groceries, prepared dinner, and provided any other support services Jim needed. Minor problems occurred in each episode that Jim would resolve, since, of course, "Father knows best." Looking back, the popularity of this series suggests, at least to me, women's enormous ability to take a (bad) joke. After all, it was pretty clear that one sex was supposed to be the domestic servant of the other.

Despite traditional gender norms, some women have always worked for pay, especially those who were poor, members of minority groups, or immigrants. But so-called protective laws and discrimination forced most women into dead-end jobs. Such practices enjoyed overwhelming support. A 1945 Gallup poll asked the following question: "Do you approve or disapprove of a married woman earning money in business or industry if she has a husband capable of supporting her?" Only 20 percent of women and 16 percent of men approved. Most people thought women should remain at home, like Margaret Anderson, regardless of talent or hard work (Niemi, 1989, p. 225).

That so few people approved of women as achievers is reflected in *The Social Meaning of Money* (1994) by Viviana Zelizer. She showed that as the middle class expanded between 1870 and 1930 or so (see Chapter 8), husbands usually controlled the family's money and wives did not know how much their husbands earned. Household funds were either given to wives on an as-needed basis or by allowance. But many men opposed allowances, according to Zelizer, because they gave wives more indepen-

[1]The next three paragraphs use phrasing from my *What Does Your Wife Do? Gender and the Transformation of Family Life* (Beeghley, 1996, p. 125).

dence. Thus, middle-class women developed various strategies to acquire more money. They went through their husband's pockets for change, had shopkeepers put fake items on bills and took cash instead, kept money from goods and services produced at home (for example, by renting rooms and sewing), and saved money from housekeeping expenses. Because working-class families had lower and more unstable incomes (see Chapter 9), their situation differed. Zelizer said that these husbands often held back some money for their own use and gave the remainder to their wives. These wives were also generally ignorant of their husbands' earnings. For both middle- and working-class women, this ignorance reflected a legal fact: Family income belonged to husbands. They earned it; they had the right to spend it. Thus, although men like Jim Anderson often had many fine traits, they kept their wives economically dependent.

Today, gender norms are changing. They are becoming more egalitarian. Women have entered the labor force, and it has become more common for husbands to be asked, "What does your wife do?" As this query implies, norms about earning money have changed. A random sample of people was recently asked the question about married women working for pay: Now 83 percent of women and 84 percent of men approve a wife's employment (GSS, 1996). These high percentages, however, are a little misleading: What people say and what they do often differs. Hence, most analyses of gender inequality find that although much has changed, much remains the same. This duality—the decline of gender stratification coexisting with its continuation—constitutes the theme of this chapter.[2]

Dimensions of Gender Stratification

Although traditional gender norms appear to be giving way, albeit slowly, to egalitarian gender norms, this process is not inevitable (nothing in history is) and is fraught with uncertainty (change always is). By **egalitarian gender norms,** I mean expectations that both women and men should balance their reproductive and productive tasks, and that when women engage in productive tasks they should be evaluated in terms of performance-related criteria that are equally applied to all.

Gender Stratification in the United States

Labor Force Participation

When women are not employed, they may have access to resources (such as husband's income) but rarely control over them, which makes them unequal to men and makes their life chances inferior to those of men. For this reason, the single most important change in women's roles over the past century is the steadily increasing proportion who

---

[2]A note on terminology: **Gender** refers to the social roles women and men play. Variations in roles reflect norms and values existing externally to individuals, who are taught them at very young ages. In contrast, the term "sex" refers to biological differences between men and women. The distinction between gender and sex (or sexual) makes it easier to understand that the inequality existing between men and women in the United States is socially constructed (Howard & Hollander, 1997, p. 11).

participate in the paid labor force. Not only is employment the key to improving life chances, paid work outside the home is a rejection of traditional gender norms. This is so even among those women who state (sometimes passionately) that they are not feminists; employment carries the potential for economic independence. In 1890, about 80 percent of all men were in the labor force, a figure that has remained relatively stable throughout this century. In comparison, in 1890, only 17 percent of all women were employed. This latter percentage rose steadily over the century to 59 percent in 1997 (Hayghe, 1997, p. 42). Thus, about three-fifths of all women now work outside the home. These data, however, include unmarried women who usually must support themselves. Hence, traditional gender norms apply with less vigor.

The labor force participation rate of married women, especially those with children, is of greater significance in light of traditional gender norms. These data are presented in Figure 4-1. It shows that in 1890 only 5 percent of all married women participated in the labor force. These persons were mainly poor, members of minority groups, and immigrant women who could not, because they were impoverished and

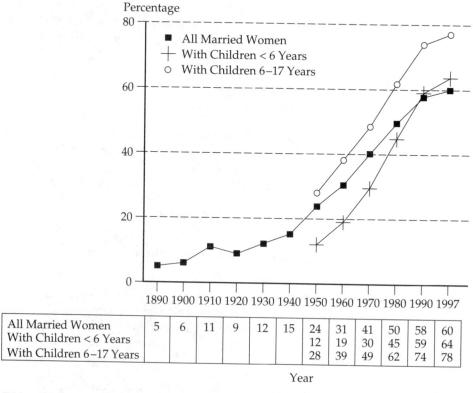

	1890	1900	1910	1920	1930	1940	1950	1960	1970	1980	1990	1997
All Married Women	5	6	11	9	12	15	24	31	41	50	58	60
With Children < 6 Years							12	19	30	45	59	64
With Children 6–17 Years							28	39	49	62	74	78

Year

FIGURE 4-1 Labor Force Participation of Married Women with and without Children, 1890–1997

Sources: USBC (1975, p. 133; 1996a, p. 400); Hayghe (1997).

discriminated against, live according to traditional gender norms. If a woman ever worked for pay during these years (and most did not), they did so only prior to marriage. But this pattern has changed. The percentage of married women participating in the labor force has increased steadily until, in 1997, 60 percent worked outside the home. Although the data do not go back so far in time, the figure also reveals that married women with children increased their employment rate over the years. While only 12 percent of those with preschool-aged children worked for pay in 1950, this proportion climbed to 64 percent in 1997. Similarly, among married women with school-age children, the labor force participation rate rose from 28 percent in 1950 to 78 percent in 1997. Thus, most women in the prime earning years are now employed.

The fundamental change in people's life chances that results from employment can be illustrated by juxtaposing it with the changing divorce rate. Please look again at Figure 4-1, noting the overall pattern of increasing labor force participation. Now imagine a line depicting the divorce rate that rises in a way roughly parallel to the lines in the figure. The divorce rate rose steadily over the last century until about 1970 when it leveled off at around 50 percent (Beeghley, 1996). In covariance form, the finding is as follows:

> *The higher the rate of women's labor force participation, the higher the rate of divorce.*

In considering this finding, recall Marx's point that the context in which people make decisions is fundamental to understanding rates of behavior. In a social context in which few women are employed, as existed at the turn of the century, a relatively small proportion of them sought a divorce, simply because they could not be economically independent (since they had no job skills or their skills had eroded during their years as mothers and homemakers) and they did not have much opportunity to meet other adults. Similarly, only a small proportion of men sought a divorce because they were obligated to continue supporting, more or less indefinitely, both their former family and any new family they formed. Furthermore, legal and religious sanctions along with the fact that most people lived in rural areas created additional barriers to divorce. In this situation, most people had to maintain their marriages even if they had broken down.

The social context, however, has changed in several ways. Because of industrialization, advances in medical technology, and other factors to be explained later, women have entered the labor force. This historical process means that a higher proportion of women will end their marriages, simply because they enjoy a modicum of economic independence and take advantage of opportunity. Similarly, a higher proportion of men will seek a divorce, simply because they have fewer economic obligations to their wives. The recent leveling off of the divorce rate suggests that it may have reached its natural limit—at least under current conditions.

Paradoxically, however, the changes described here do not indicate gender equality. (Recall: Much has changed; much remains the same.) One reason is that half of all married women are still homemakers and the other half still earns, on the average, far less than do men. Another reason is that women have difficulty obtaining equitable divorce settlements (Weitzman, 1985; Weitzman & MacLean, 1992). Hence, differences in earnings mean they usually endure a loss of living standards, with many ending up poor (see Chapter 10). Finally, child custody is nearly always given to women, who must often manage without help from their former spouses. While child support laws exist in every state, they are not well enforced. Men becoming independent more easily, while wives and children are worse off does not reflect gender equality.

Occupational Segregation and Prestige

Although change has occurred, women and men still work at different jobs. Table 4-1 illustrates this fact by displaying both the current level of occupational segregation by gender as well as changes that occurred between 1970 and 1997.

Let us look first at the current level of occupational segregation. The table depicts the percentage of women in the major occupational categories established by the Census Bureau as well as selected detailed occupations. Column (3) shows that women are bunched in specific major occupational categories. For example, 79 percent of all administrative support workers are female, compared to only 44 percent of all executives and administrators. Similarly, 59 percent of all service workers are female, compared to only 9 percent of all precision production employees.

This same pattern occurs when the detailed occupations are examined, as in column (5). For instance, only 26 percent of all physicians are women, compared to 94 percent of all nurses. Similarly, 76 percent of all teachers are women, compared to only 10 percent of all engineers. This pattern of occupational segregation also holds with regard to specialization within fields. For example, women physicians mainly specialize in fields such as pediatrics, psychiatry, and obstetrics, rather than, say, neurosurgery. The last is a much higher-paying specialty. A similar situation occurs among teachers (data not shown in Table 4-1). For example, 84 percent of all elementary school teachers are women, compared to 58 percent of all secondary school teachers and only 43 percent of all college professors (USDL, 1998, p. 174).

Column (5) also shows that occupational segregation occurs in nonprofessional jobs as well. For example, 66 percent of all retail sales clerks are women, compared to 44 percent of all sales representatives. Similarly, 18 percent of all protective service workers, who are primarily police officers and firefighters, are women, compared to 95 percent of all private household workers, who are primarily maids. These data mean that occupational segregation by gender is pervasive in the United States. Much remains the same.

Nonetheless, much occupational segregation has declined. Thus, columns (4) and (5) show that the proportion of female physicians rose from 10 percent to 26 percent, computer programmers climbed from 24 percent to 30 percent, sales representatives increased from 17 percent to 44 percent, and bartenders expanded from 21 percent to 57 percent. Although these data only refer to selected occupations and the format of presentation does not control for outside influences, virtually all studies show that while the extent of occupational segregation by gender remained stable for most of this century, it decreased substantially beginning in the 1970s (Jacobs, 1990; Goldin, 1990).

One of the major changes in occupational segregation by gender (not shown in the table) has occurred among African American women. In 1940, three-quarters of

TABLE 4-1 **Women as a Percentage of all Workers in Major Occupational Categories and Selected Detailed Occupations, 1970 and 1997**

(1)	Major Occupational Category, %		Detailed Occupational Category, %	
	(2)	(3)	(4)	(5)
Occupational Category	1970	1997	1970	1997
White Collar				
Executive, Administrative and Managerial	19	44		
Marketing Manager			8	35
Financial Manager			19	49
Professional Specialty	44	53		
Architect			4	18
Engineer			2	10
Teacher			71	76
Registered Nurse			97	94
Physician			10	26
Technician	34	52		
Engineering Technologist			9	19
Computer Programmer			24	30
Sales	41	50		
Sales Representative—Finance & Business			17	44
Retail Sales			62	66
Administrative Support	73	79		
Supervisor			56	60
Secretary			98	98
Bank Teller			87	90
Blue Collar				
Precision Production	7	9		
Mechanic			3	4
Extractive			2	1
Construction			2	2
Machine Operator	40	25		
Textile Machine			79	72
Truck Drivers			2	6
Handler & Laborer	17	20		
Stock and Freight Handlers			13	25
Service	69	59		
Bartender			21	57
Private Household			96	95
Protective Service			7	18
Farming, Forestry, Fishing	9	19		
Farm Operator & Manager			5	23

Sources: Rytina & Bianchi (1984); USDL (1998b, p. 174).

African American women were doing private household and farming work. Today, although still overrepresented in private household jobs, their occupational distribution resembles that of white women; that is, it resembles that shown in column (5) of Table 4-1 (King, 1992). One suspects that occupational segregation has declined among Hispanic and Asian women as well, since it is doubtful that the changes described here apply only to one group (see Chapter 5).

Even though much change has occurred in recent years, these data understate the level of occupational segregation still existing in the United States (Reskin & Padavic, 1994). For example, women and men in the same job category often work for different companies, with significant economic consequences. Thus, high-priced restaurants employ waiters (men) whose income is relatively high, while low-priced restaurants employ waitresses (women) whose income is relatively low. Moreover, men and women in the same job category work in different industries, again with significant economic consequences. Thus, women are often employed in the textile industry where the pay is low, while men work in the petroleum industry where the pay is high. Finally, even when men and women appear to have similar jobs within a company, the former often has more and the latter less income and authority. Just because a woman has the title "Manager" does not necessarily mean she controls resources or makes fundamental decisions.

In general, job segregation means lower prestige. Nurses have a lower level of occupational prestige than physicians. Elementary school teachers enjoy less honor in the community than do college professors. Administrative support workers constitute the lowest prestige white-collar category. Similarly, service workers usually enjoy less prestige than do precision production workers. Textile workers have less prestige than truck drivers. And private household workers endure lower standing than protective service workers. This pattern can be expressed as an empirical generalization:

> *The higher the proportion of women in an occupation, the lower its occupational prestige.*

But more than prestige inequality is involved in the different jobs women and men perform. Table 4-1 also reveals that employed women tend to be clustered in jobs that resemble traditional roles: assisting men, caring for children, and picking up after others. Nurses, after all, appear to assist doctors. Elementary school teachers not only impart knowledge, but also (and just as importantly) they socialize the very young, a task traditionally assigned to women who remain at home. Finally, private household workers pick up and clean other people's houses, while police officers and firefighters protect them. This last example provides an excellent image of how traditional gender norms have been transmuted to the workplace.

There are other consequences of occupational segregation. For instance, it means that women's chances for self-fulfillment are lower because many of the jobs they hold are more boring and require less intellectual effort than those of men. More important, however, occupational segregation means that women earn less money and are less able to be economically independent. This fact, of course, affects life chances.

Income Differences

In the past, many people accepted the idea that women should earn less then men. Today, however, everyone agrees—99 percent in a recent Gallup Poll—that women working at the same jobs as men should receive equal pay (GP, 1994, p. 187). This support means that achievement values are currently viewed as applicable to women, at least with regard to income on the job. Unfortunately, however, this ideal is not realized in practice.

In *Understanding the Gender Gap: An Economic History of American Women,* Claudia Goldin showed that women's income was about 54 percent of men's in 1890 (1990, p. 60). Panel A of Table 4-2 shows that women still earned only 54 percent of men's income in 1950. Since then, the earnings of women employed full-time increased slowly and fitfully. As of 1997, women's median income was 74 percent of men's. Equality is still a long way off.

Just how far off can be seen by examining gender differences in income by skill level, as displayed in Panel B of Table 4-2. Educational attainment is the indicator of skill. Panel B shows that at each higher level of education, women earn more; at the same time, however, at each level of education, women earn only 60 to 69 percent as much as do men. In addition, Panel B provides one of my favorite examples of gender inequality: The earnings of high school educated women are identical to those of

TABLE 4-2   Women's and Men's Income

Panel A: Women's Median Income as a Percentage of Men's, 1950–1997 (Year-round, full-time workers, 18 years of age and older)

Year	Women's Income as % of Men's
1950	54%
1960	61
1970	59
1980	60
1990	70
1997	74

Panel B: Mean Income by Gender and Education, 1997 (Year-round, full-time workers, 18 years of age and older)

Education	Men's Mean Income	Women's Mean Income	Women's Income as % of Men's
Elementary (< 9 years)	$22,700	$15,000	66%
High School Degree	32,600	22,700	69
College Degree (or more)	66,400	41,600	63

Source: USBC (1998d, p. 30).

elementary school educated men. These data can be summarized in the form of two empirical generalizations. *For both genders, the greater the skill level, the higher the income.* This fact means that achievement pays off. However: *At every skill level, men earn significantly more than women.* This fact means that ascription remains a powerful force.

But less inequality exists among young men and women. The following data are median incomes of two age ranges of women and men employed full-time in 1997 (USBC, 1998f, p. 31).

Age	Women	Men	Women's Percentage
25–34	$25,100	$31,100	81%
45–54	$29,400	$42,400	69%

These ages identify people starting their work lives and in their peak earning years. As shown, older women earn only a little more than younger women on average; this is because the former have often left the labor force for extended periods of time and suffered more from discrimination (issues discussed later). Younger women, however, have incomes closer to those of younger men, which may mean they suffer less discrimination. As before, racial and ethnic variations exist.

Gender Stratification in Other Nations

Women are also stratified along these same dimensions—labor force participation, occupational segregation, and income—in other Western industrial nations. Shown below are international comparisons of women's labor force participation in 1994 (USBC, 1997b, p. 846).

Netherlands	57%
France	60
Germany	62
United Kingdom	66
Canada	68
United States	71
Sweden	74

Thus, the United States has a relatively high level of employment compared to that of other nations. But these data hide significant variation. Employed German women, for example, are more likely to work part-time (Blossfeld & Rohwer, 1997). In all these nations, women display a high level of occupational segregation, with Canada and the United States having the lowest (Anker, 1998, p. 176). Finally, income inequality by gender is significant in each country, with Sweden displaying the least and the United States the most (UN, 1989, p. 13). In certain respects, then, American women are better off, while in other respects they are worse off. This conclusion assumes, of course, that you believe egalitarian norms are better—a position justified by values, not science.

The information presented in this section suggests the duality mentioned earlier: (1) Gender inequality has declined significantly in recent years, and (2) a great deal still exists. The continuity of gender inequality is shown by the many women who remain out of the labor force and the high level of occupational segregation and income inequality. The reduction in gender inequality is revealed by rising female labor force participation along with declining occupational and income inequality. I will offer hypotheses to account for these patterns later in the chapter. Now, however, it is important to recognize that the difficulty most women have becoming economically independent, regardless of skill, indicates not only the continued salience of traditional gender norms but also how few women exercise authority and how many are victimized.

Some Consequences of Gender Stratification

Authority and Gender

The term **authority** refers to the legitimate exercise of power. As Max Weber observed, those with authority assert a right to make decisions affecting others, who believe they have a duty to obey (1920). This shared definition of right and obligation usually means that force does not have to be used. Thus, from the point of view of traditional gender norms, men have the right to exercise authority in the United States. Women's acceptance of male authority is reflected in traditional marriage vows: They pledge to love, honor, and obey. Although this prerogative has been challenged in recent years (marriage vows are changing), men dominate public life.

In economic matters, men, not women, set policy. Internationally, U.S. companies apparently have the highest proportion of women in management jobs in the world (ILO, 1997). That is, however, not saying much. Of the top five best-paid corporate officers in each Fortune 500 company, fewer than 3 percent (exactly 61) are women (Catalyst, 1997). Moreover, in these large companies, only 10 percent of all corporate officers at any level are women. Thus, men decide the height of assembly lines, which affects women's ability to work in better paying blue-collar jobs (recall the distribution in Table 4-1). Men decide how occupations are to be evaluated, which may be part of the reason engineering is seen as more important than teaching. Pay levels follow.

This same pattern occurs in government. Men, not women, make laws and dictate how they will be enforced. Only 8 percent of all senators and 11 percent of all members of the House of Representatives are women. It is not accidental that until just a few years ago women were denied many basic civil rights. These included the ability to own property, obtain credit, and sue in court. Men made these laws. They still do. When bills about day care, or Head Start, or domestic violence (wife or child abuse) come before Congress, women have little impact.

Religion is no different. Men, not women, talk to God. Only 14 percent of all members of the clergy are women (USDL, 1998b, p. 175). Those religious groups excluding women from leadership roles do so for varying reasons. Most, however, appear to assert that although men and women are equal in the eyes of God, however known, scripture says men ought to be in positions of formal leadership. It should be no surprise, then, that God is defined as masculine and those interpreting His intentions have always justified men striking and chastising women and children (Greven, 1991). It should no surprise that, in His name, they chose to defend developing embryos over the needs of women. It should be no surprise that some Protestant faiths still assert that every woman should "submit herself graciously" to her husband's leadership (Neibuhr, 1998).

The situation is similar in court. Men dominate; they decide how laws are interpreted and enforced. It is not accidental that child support payments in the United States are set very low and are poorly enforced (USBC, 1995b).

When people seek medical treatment, men dominate. They decide who should enter the field and its priorities. So men define who is sick and how they will be treated. In fact, organized medicine drove women from the field during the nineteenth century (Starr, 1982). It is not accidental that this process began just when abortion became a safe medical procedure and increasing numbers of women sought to regulate their fertility (Luker, 1996).

Finally, men dominate higher education. Walk down the hallway where administrators and faculty are housed; nearly all are men. The secretaries, of course, are women. This pattern also includes sociology (Beeghley & Van Ausdale, 1990). It is not accidental that just 30 years ago, women's studies courses and departments were unheard of. It was assumed that analyses of women's experiences would yield little new insight. This assumption was, of course, buttressed by sociological theory (Acker, 1973).

Although much change has occurred, women in authority remain rare—and deviant. Imagine women in jobs of real authority: as the chief executive officer of General Motors, as the majority leader of the United States Senate, as the parish priest. Think about how women in positions of dominance are described: "lady policemen" and "lady doctors." The diminutive term, "lady," relegates those performing such roles to unequal status. It implies they should not be there. This situation also occurs on campus, where the expression "lady" designates many women's athletic programs—as in "Lady Gators" and "Lady Bruins." Women's sports are, of course, always unequal compared to men's. Thus, the term *lady* still implies to many, as it always has, that women belong in the home, where men can protect them. Unfortunately, the paradoxical result of traditional gender norms is that women are not protected—either at home or at work.

Victimization and Gender

Although often unrecognized, traditional gender norms and the inequality that follows lead to female victimization. Sexual harassment, rape, wife abuse, and child sexual abuse all involve the assertion of power by men over women. **Power** refers to people's ability to achieve their goals, whether legitimate or not, even if opposition occurs. Power often requires force or coercion. I mentioned earlier that authority relies on a shared acceptance of the right to dominate. In this case, traditional gender norms imply agreement that men belong on the job and women at home, dependent. Nonetheless, anyone approached by an armed police officer knows that the threat of force always underlies authority. Relations between men and women are similar. The combination of differences in physical size and men's dominance of public life means that the threat of force always exists and sometimes occurs. Women become victims. They are the only exploited people I know of who have been idealized into powerlessness.

Sexual harassment occurs under one of two conditions. First, a person pressures another for sexual cooperation as a condition of employment (such as hiring or promotion). Second, an intimidating or hostile environment is created in the workplace. The courts have held that these criteria also apply to educational institutions, specifically to professors and students. Nearly all sexual harassment is directed by men toward women (Schneider, 1991). In addition to extorting sexual cooperation, harassment occurs via repeated phone calls or letters, repeated pressure for dates, repeated physical touching, and repeated sexual remarks. More "subtle" mechanisms for creating a hostile working environment include plastic displays of sexual body parts or nude pin-ups used as dartboards. The only limit to making women know they are unwelcome at work is men's imagination. Millions of women experience insults and assaults merely by choosing to work for pay rather than remain at home.

Sexual harassment is widespread. Various studies show that a significant proportion of employed women are sexually harassed (Wagner, 1992). For example, 37 to 48 percent of female physicians report they have been harassed—in medical school, during their internship, and in medical practice (Frank, 1998). Yet many, if not most, women find that sexual harassment is a crime without a remedy. In *Measure for Measure*, written around 1603, Shakespeare shows why. In Act II, scene iv, Isabella tells Angelo:

> *With an outstretch'd throat I'll tell the world aloud*
> *What man thou art.*

Angelo responds:

> *Who will believe thee, Isabel?*
> *My unsoil'd name, the austereness of my life,*
> *My vouch against you, and my place i' the state,*
> *Will so your accusation overweigh,*
> *That you shall stifle in your own report*
> *And smell of calumny.*

Like Angelo, harassers often try to make the victim the victimizer by accusing her of making untrue assertions harming his reputation (calumny). Like Angelo, they then move on with their careers, becoming chairs of academic departments (including sociology), administrators in Fortune 500 corporations, and judges and politicians (Engelberg & Sontag, 1994).

The consequences of sexual harassment are adverse (Wagner, 1992). Victims sometimes lose their jobs, either by being fired or quitting (Coles, 1986). Sometimes their lives are transformed: They lose self-confidence, become anxious, and suffer from headaches, ulcers, and other physical ailments. Some become clinically depressed; this term does not mean they merely feel bad. Everyone feels bad sometimes. Rather, **depression** occurs when people become psychologically incapacitated; they lose interest in daily activities for an extended period; they have little energy, feel worthless, and find it difficult to concentrate; they sometimes contemplate suicide; they often use and abuse drugs. As should be clear, harassers use sex as a means to power. As women enter traditional male occupations, men often become insecure; they believe women are invading their territory. In order to regain control of their situation, they try to put women "in their place" in the only way they know how: sexually. The resulting trauma inhibits occupational and economic success for many women.

So does rape. It is estimated that almost 700,000 rapes of adult women occur each year (NVC, 1992). Since about 60 percent of all rape victims are children under 18, this estimate probably covers less than half of all such assaults. By extrapolation, about twelve million women have been raped at some point in their lives. Rape keeps women unequal in two ways. First, fear of rape leads many women to alter their behavior (Koss, 1993). At an early age, women learn to avoid placing themselves in situations where they may be vulnerable, such as working at night. Yet many high-prestige and well-paying jobs require such extra hours. Thus, women who have not been raped are victims to the extent they change their behavior, act cautiously, do not take a particular job, or avoid an opportunity out of fear. But 75 percent of rape victims know the assailant, who is a father, husband, boyfriend, or friend (NVC, 1992). Second, actual victims display many problems (NVC, 1992). About 30 percent become clinically depressed at some point in their lives, while another 31 percent develop **post-traumatic stress disorder.** The term refers to reactions to trauma: intense anxiety, inability to concentrate, becoming easily startled, nightmares, flashbacks, and insomnia. Physical symptoms are common: stomach aches, ulcers, and bulimia, among others (Dansky, 1997). In addition, rape victims are more likely to use and abuse drugs of all sorts. Finally, about 33 percent of rape victims contemplate suicide and 13 percent eventually try it. So the impact of rape is long-lasting. Like sexual harassment, rape is an assertion of power by men, a means of controlling women and keeping them in their place—at home and out of the labor force (Searles & Berger, 1995).

So is **wife abuse:** threatening or harming one's wife or companion. Men initiate most violence in families, which is why I use this term rather than the more common "spouse abuse" (Kurz, 1993). In 1996, official data reveal (and probably understate) more than 960,000 women were victims of violence by intimates, nearly all by men (USDJ, 1998, p. 3). Over all, about 14 percent of women say they have been physically abused by their husbands, partners, or boyfriends (GP, 1997b). In addition to physical injuries, abused women suffer in other ways as well. Although numbers are hard to obtain, battered women are at greater risk for post-traumatic stress syndrome, depression, and suicide (Herman, 1989). Once again, the issue is power: keeping women dependent. Abused women have less occupational or economic success over time (Lloyd, 1998).

Child sexual abuse has the same impact. This is the molestation or sexual penetration of children by adults. Statistics show that about 20 percent of all girls and 9 percent of all boys are sexually abused as children, usually by adult males, with nearly 400,000 incidents every year (NRCCSA, 1992). As with the other behaviors described here, child sexual abuse is about power rather than sex (Herman, 1981). Thus, male adults engage in sexual behavior with young persons in order to feel powerful and in control. The victims frequently react by feeling powerless (Jacobs, 1994). Men who are victimized tend to have inconsistent responses, some become depressed and others aggressive (often toward women). Women who are victimized also tend to become depressed and to see themselves as dependent on men. Such women often become sexually active at younger ages and endure early pregnancy (and abortion or birth), early marriage, and early divorce (Boyer & Fine, 1992; Stock, 1997). Victims of both sexes frequently use and abuse drugs, and think about suicide. These results limit their employment and income as adults.

This discussion suggests that women need to be protected from men rather than by them. If a few men assert power via sex, all men benefit to the extent that women stay home, stay dependent, and provide domestic service. Thus, while it may never occur to men like Jim Anderson to threaten women like Margaret, their family life is buttressed by the victimization of women. In *Trauma and Recovery,* Judith Lewis Herman emphasized that the most common location of trauma for women is the family and workplace (1992). Such locations continue to be regulated by traditional gender norms. Because these norms dictate that men ought to dominate women, they lead to silence when trauma occurs. In fact, Herman argued that it is the silence that haunts women even more than the crimes themselves: bystanders' denial that crimes have been committed. She said that the study of trauma endured by women depends on a political movement for equality: **feminism,** which refers to both an ideology and a social movement emphasizing that women and men should be equal. Feminism seeks the generation of egalitarian norms for women and men. It argues that the roles women play as adults cannot be like those of men until women are no longer victimized, until sex is no longer a means of power by men over women.

The Individual and Gender Stratification

Think about certain events in the life of Carol Hanson. She enrolls at Keene State College with excellent test scores and good grades. Nearly any major is available to her. She initially considers engineering and takes a couple of courses. Ultimately, she selects education.

Carol graduates at age 23 and begins teaching in an elementary school. She marries Bertram ("Bertie") Robinson, who is still working on his engineering degree, so Carol supports them for two years. After Bertie graduates, they leave the hills of New Hampshire and settle in Mayberry (well, why not?). She teaches fourth grade for five years and also does nearly all the housework. Then Bertie is offered a job in (can you believe this!) Metropolis. Carol opposes the move; they argue, and at one point Bertie throws the phone at Carol, giving her a black eye. They move. After relocating to a big new house, they decide to start a family (a common pattern). After the birth, Carol, now 30, quits her job and focuses on childrearing, housework, and taking care of Bertie. After three years, she begins teaching again but starts near the bottom of the salary scale because her previous tenure only partially transfers. Thus, Carol's income is less than both Bertie's and that of others who obtained their teaching certificate at the same time but remained in the labor force. Carol continues, of course, to be responsible for child care and housekeeping. After two years, Bertie gets another job offer. Carol again opposes the move, but to no avail. They move to (it had to be) Gotham City. A second child is born, and Carol quits working. She returns to teaching after two years. Once again she starts near the bottom of the salary scale. Five years pass. Bertie is now making serious money but hating his rat race. He begins seeing his (much younger) secretary, Ms. Bimbo. After the divorce, he takes his engineering degree (remember, Carol supported him), his pension (Carol provided support services while this was building), Ms. Bimbo, and the dog Toto back to Kansas. Because Carol has a good job, she receives no income support. What she gets is child custody and child support. After a short time, however, the latter stops. So Carol takes care of her children on her teacher's salary of $30,000 per year.[3]

Though stereotypical, the vignette reflects the experiences of many women. Carol decided on a teaching career instead of, for example, building highways. Women often select occupations that require helping others (Bridges, 1989). One reason for this choice lies in her socialization at home (more on this in the next section). Another reason is that she became serious about Bertie and married him at a relatively young age. Such women often lower their aspirations (Murrell, 1991). She quit her job twice and did not go back to school for an advanced degree in order to relocate with her husband. Such decisions are very common (Presser, 1994). Finally, she went through a divorce and found child support to be unreliable. Again, this is common: About half of women who obtain support receive the full amount; about one-fourth collect half and one-fourth get nothing (USBC, 1995b, p. 7). Note that, except for the breakup of her marriage and its consequences, each of these choices was Carol's. Women often make such decisions. Why?

Women's Choices

When people enter the labor force, they make decisions about what skills to acquire and the relative priority their job will have compared to leisure time, child care, housework, and the like. Economists postulate an "efficient" job market in which these choices affect income variations (by gender, race/ethnicity, or any other ascribed characteristic). From this point of view, Carol earns less than Bertie because she is less productive. Productivity is assessed by people's **human capital:** their skills (education, work experience, and tenure on current job) and employment priorities (labor force continuity, choosing part-time employment, absenteeism due to a child's illness, and leaving a job due to a spouse's mobility). This argument can be phrased as the *Human Capital Hypothesis:*

> *The fewer skills people acquire and the lower the priority employment has versus other activities, the lower their income.*

Education and work experience reveal the job skills individuals like Carol and Bertie have chosen to develop, their employment priorities, and, hence, income. So Carol's

---

[3]I used a similar vignette in my *What Does Your Wife Do? Gender and the Transformation of Family Life* (Beeghley, 1996, p. 145).

selection of education over engineering produced skills (presumably) worth less than Bertie's. In addition, she chose to stop working (for pay) on two occasions, which also made her "less productive." This argument is generalizable beyond the vignette. Many women make similar decisions, which—although laudable—make them less productive. This angle of vision suggests, then, that such women deserve lower incomes because they are less skilled and less devoted to (paid) work. They value (economists would say they have a "taste for") housework, child care, and following their husbands. Earnings inequality follows.

Well, okay. But three observations suggest there is more going on here than gender-related differences in "taste." First, if I understand the logic of the Human Capital Hypothesis correctly, it implies that women emphasizing family obligations would pick jobs that fit with these activities. Many of the occupations in which women cluster (shown in Table 4-1), however, do not fit with caring for children and husbands. For example, hours are usually less flexible. Secretaries and private household help must typically keep rather rigid schedules. Nurses must often work nights and weekends. In fact, men's jobs often have more flexible hours, more unsupervised leave time, and more sick leave and vacation, which means that their jobs are more compatible with family responsibilities. Second, the hypothesis implies that single women (whose family responsibilities are less) would cluster in higher-prestige, higher-paying occupations. This does not occur; such women's jobs are no different from those of married women (Reskin & Padavic, 1994). These observations imply that "productivity" is not the only source of gender-related differences in income, that the job market is not "efficient." Third, tests of the hypothesis suggest just how inefficient. Only about 40 percent of the variation in men's and women's income results from so-called human capital factors (England, 1992a, p. 27). This finding means that the Human Capital Hypothesis can only partly explain why women like Carol make less money than men. More is going on here.

Discrimination against Women

The "more" that is going on is **discrimination.** The term, you may recall from Chapter 1, refers to the unequal treatment of people or groups because of their personal characteristics. Today, such behavior is often illegal. Not at home, however, and I would like to argue that the unequal treatment of women and men begins there. First, the various forms of victimizing women constitute discrimination. When Carol objected to moving to Metropolis, Bertie threw the telephone at her. From that moment on, Carol was aware that force might be directed either at her or the children. More generally, the threat of wife abuse, rape, and child sexual abuse makes all women careful. Second, discrimination occurs during divorce when the tangible assets (a house) and the intangible assets (a pension) are divided (Beeghley, 1996). Although Carol's relationship with Bertie was intimate, in callous economic terms they were business partners for many years: She provided support services while he obtained a degree and made a career. She followed him from place to place, always providing services in the expectation that she would gain economic security in return. Then he walked away with Ms. Bimbo. It is a common tale, but true, and wives are treated unequally, especially when they have their own (less remunerative) careers and pensions. Third, discrimination at home goes beyond these acts of power to the more subtle issue of teaching women and men to accept traditional gender norms (Valian, 1998). Even when children are infants, parents project their gender expectations onto children. As children grow up, data show that girls and boys perform different chores: Girls cook and clean, boys remove garbage and mow the grass. Moreover, as Virginia Valian showed, in play children learn "appropriate" adult roles (1998, p. 36). Playing with dolls and doll houses constitutes practice for adult responsibilities; girls learn to enjoy and to want to do what they will have to do as adults. Why do you suppose Carol, who was career oriented, so readily accepted her responsibilities at home? Boys' play, by contrast, turns into men's play. Few boys become cops or robbers, or major league baseball stars; many men practice target shooting and play softball and watch sports on television. These behaviors do not teach them to enjoy caring for others. Children actively try to make sense of their environment. They see their parents' division of household labor and learn expectations for their own behavior. Now there are many who would disagree with this third point, mainly, it seems to me, because they do not want to face the implications of their values. I will return to this issue when dealing with social structure and gender stratification.

Discrimination starts at home, but continues at work. The Equal Pay Act of 1963 and the Civil Rights Act of 1964 prohibit discrimination against women in earnings and occupation. Other federal legislation forbids discrimination in education, housing, and credit. Despite these laws, a great deal of covert discrimination occurs in the workplace. The methods used to prevent individual women from obtaining a job are straightforward: recruitment and screening practices.

When employers decide to hire people, they must recruit candidates (Beeghley, 1996). One relatively efficient way of doing this is by word-of-mouth. Simply posting a notice or notifying employees often generates applicants. Current employees direct men and women to "gender-appropriate" jobs in line with an an employer's preferences (even if unstated). Another approach is to use an employment agency. Because such agencies only get paid if they produce satisfactory candidates, they have an incentive to violate the law and refer the types of applicants an employer desires: for example, women in secretarial and men in managerial jobs. What happens, of course, is that employers and agencies develop informal understandings about the kinds of persons to be referred for particular jobs. A third approach is to place advertisements in the media. This tactic sometimes allows overt but hard to discover discrimination. For example, a "gender-inappropriate" respondent (say, a male asking about a secretarial job or a female inquiring about a telephone repairer's job) is informed that the person responsible for hiring is not available that day. A few minutes later, however, a "gender-appropriate" caller claiming similar credentials would be told to come for an interview. This tactic is only one of many used by employers. A final approach is to fit a job for an "inside" candidate. My suspicion is that this happens more in government and academia—where advertising of job openings is required by law—than in private industry where such pretenses are not necessary.

After recruiting job candidates, they must be screened, eliminating those who are ineligible or inappropriate. In so doing, it is legal to use subjective evaluations of job candidates. Thus, an interviewer's judgments about an applicant's "appearance," "self-confidence," "emotional makeup," and many other characteristics constitute appropriate criteria for hiring or not hiring someone. In this context, an employer's gender role stereotypes about women can easily enter the decision-making process. For example, the difference between a man who has "self-confidence" and a woman who is "too pushy" is very subtle, but the result can be very discriminating. Another screening device is the selective waiver of educational and experience requirements, a tactic that occurs most often in white-collar jobs. For example, let us say that a job is advertised requiring a master's degree and five years of experience. Let us say further that the two best applicants are a woman with a bachelor's degree and ten years of experience and a man with a master's degree and one year of experience. Which person is hired depends on the employer's evaluation of the trade-off between experience and education, and the kind of person an employer is most comfortable with on the job. Now consider the way minority persons fit into this process. Imagine comparing Hispanic or African American women and men to white men when the mix of education and experience must be weighed. The result can be very discriminatory, especially over the long run as employers consistently juggle criteria in favor of white males.

In sum, when the choices women make and the possibility of discrimination are combined, then the reason why many individuals achieve less than their skills suggest they should becomes clear. Yet this form of analysis remains incomplete. As I argued in previous chapters, it cannot reveal why the overall rate of female accomplishment is so low. It remains unclear why women make the choices they do. After all, if it is not economically smart to become a housewife, why have so many normally intelligent women chosen this lifestyle over the years? In order to answer this question, it is necessary to look at the way the social structure influences people's options.

Social Structure and Gender Stratification

In George Bernard Shaw's play *Pygmalion,* originally produced in 1914, the main character, Henry Higgins, wonders why women cannot be more like men (1957). Well, they can. The data presented earlier show that much change is occurring in precisely that direction: Women have entered the labor force and obtained—on their own— valued resources: prestige, education, income, and power. Women are more equal to (or like) men today than they were in the past. Even the data on female victimization reflect this fact because such events are now controversial. Yet much remains the same: The data continue to show that—in every area—women remain unequal to men. It is useful to pause and think about this problem more abstractly.[4]

In Chapter 1, I noted that the forces shaping the stratification structure, with its three systems of ranking (class, gender, and race/ethnicity), can be conceptualized by the degree of emphasis on achievement versus ascription. To the extent that performance-related criteria equally applied to all are used to evaluate people and to the extent these evaluations affect the distribution of valued resources, a society empha-

[4]*Pygmalion* later became a Broadway musical and then a movie under the title *My Fair Lady.*

sizes achievement. The data suggest that the United States is moving in this direction and, in this sense, women and men are becoming more alike. Conversely, to the extent that non-performance-related criteria based on birth are used to evaluate people and to the extent such evaluations affect the distribution of valued resources, a society emphasizes ascription. The importance of gender as a system of ranking indicates an emphasis on ascription, as suggested by the *Gender Hypothesis:*

> *Women at every class level have fewer and less effective choices than do men.*

Although this is not the place to test this hypothesis, the data presented earlier are consonant with it: At every class level, women's life chances, their ability to share in the available goods and services, still reflect their dependence on men rather than their own achievement.

As this duality reveals, societies are not monolithic entities. Historical change usually means that contradictory tendencies coexist. The decline of gender stratification coupled with its continuation illustrates this phenomenon. The next two sections provide a structural explanation for each.

The Decline of Gender Stratification

The ideal of equality of opportunity for both men and women has become more widespread. As indicated, this is another way of talking about the applicability of achievement-oriented values to both genders. My hypothesis that accounts for this change is as follows:

> *The decline of gender inequality reflects: (1) Industrialization, (2) female labor force participation, (3) advances in medical technology, (4) legal changes, and (5) the rise of feminism.*

Industrialization

In the past, most people lived on farms, scratching a living from the soil. Husbands and wives did this together, using a simple division of labor to produce what they needed to survive. There was little surplus.[5] In this context, women were indeed like men: They worked at backbreaking productive tasks. Since modern labor-saving devices did not exist, the work required of women—baking, making soap, brewing beer, harvesting garden crops, managing barn animals, and much more—was very difficult. It is absurd to think that women were incapable of heavy work (Easton, 1976). In addition, bearing children was a constant burden. The average woman became pregnant many times and bore six to eight children (Cherlin, 1992). In this context, childbirth was a productive act because in a few years children produced more than they cost.

The situation remained similar in the cities when capitalism emerged. In his *Autobiography,* published in 1795, Benjamin Franklin described how his wife,

---

[5]Recall Lenski's finding that mutually dependent people share what they produce when there is no surplus (Chapter 1).

Deborah, assisted "cheerfully in my [printing] business, folding and stitching pamphlets, tending shop, purchasing old linen rags for the papermakers, etc." (1961, p. 92). Note that Franklin specified that it is "my business." In the nascent cash economy in which men were formally in charge, women's work constituted unpaid labor. Typically, the goods produced at home by unpaid female workers were partly consumed and partly sold or traded (Goldin, 1990). But no matter how such products were used, my point is the same as already stated: Productive activity occurred at home, where both women and men worked.

Industrialization changed this situation. As noted previously, the term refers to the transformation of the economy when new forms of energy substituted for muscle power, leading to advances in productivity. The application of technology based on fossil, steam, and other forms of energy requires a more complex division of labor than that found at home. It also requires workers to gather at one site in order to minimize the cost of energy, raw materials, transportation, and distribution. So production shifted away from home. In a context in which controlling pregnancy and birth remained difficult, most women remained at home. Men left; they worked to earn an income and support their families.

Industrialization did more, however, than separate home and work: It lead to a decline in gender inequality by creating opportunities for women as well as for men, mainly because the organization and type of work changed. As productivity increased, it became necessary to emphasize administration, coordination, and record keeping. Put simply, more white-collar workers were required. As shown in Table 3-1 (in the mobility chapter), the percentage of white-collar workers rose from 18 percent in 1900 to 58 percent in 1997. Brain power supplanted muscle power, which meant that women could compete on equal terms with men. The result was that women entered the paid labor force in increasing proportions over time.

Female Labor Force Participation

In her autobiography, written around 1905, Dorothy Richardson described her life as a working woman in the late nineteenth century (O'Neill, 1972). She left home at age 18 and moved to New York City. There she worked for a variety of companies in entry level positions. She titled her book *The Long Day* in order to emphasize the length of the working day, the hard labor, and the low wages. During the latter part of the nineteenth century, the average employed person worked ten hours per day, six days per week. Despite such requirements, Richardson eventually enrolled in night school, acquiring education and some commercial skills. She then became a stenographer and, to use her word, "prosperous"; that is, she achieved economic independence (O'Neill, 1972, p. 267). The ability of people like Richardson to earn an income has become more typical as this century has progressed.

Women's increased labor force participation lead to a decline in gender inequality because an income, even a low one, means they need not be economically dependent on men. It changes women's options and changes family life. Some, like Dorothy Richardson, could be like men: They could support themselves. Such women sometimes never married, especially those with college degrees (Rothman, 1984). They simply remained employed (Goldin, 1990). Most women, of course, married. During the early years of this century, marriage usually meant that women quit their jobs. As time passed, however, this pattern changed as married women increasingly entered the labor force. They did so mainly in response to expanding economic opportunities, such as those produced by industrialization, rather than to declining opportunities for their husbands (Chinhui & Murphy, 1997). This fact, however, has important implications—on the divorce rate, for example. People with jobs do not have to endure a marriage filled with sorrow. Thus, female employment has an insidious implication: A rejection of traditional gender norms. The demand for equality follows, as day the night, from economic independence. This is why I said earlier that all employed women are feminists, in fact if not ideology, since their jobs give them both a source of prestige and the potential to live on their own.

Although industrialization provides opportunity and labor force participation an income, these two factors will not lead to gender equality unless women can control fertility. This ability required advances in medical technology.

Advances in Medical Technology

Advanced technology usually creates new choices. It allows behaviors that were impossible or immoral just a few years ago, and thereby creates social problems (Beeghley, 1999). The invention of the rubber condom, the intrauterine device, and the birth control pill contributed to rising rates of premarital sexual intercourse (Beeghley, 1996). Similarly, the development of tools and techniques for performing safe abortions raised moral issues that continue to divide the nation (Luker, 1984). The nonobvious issue underlying both these problems, however, is women's roles. Specifically, should women's reproductive roles take precedence over their productive roles?

The answer to this question is now clear. Advances in medical technology lead to a decline in gender inequality by providing women the opportunity to regulate whether and when to give birth. Although significant limits on the ability to control fertility still exist, women can increasingly balance their various roles. Without this opportunity, they cannot take advantage of the transformation of the economy. Without this opportunity, employed women will be shunted into dead-end jobs they can easily enter and leave. When pregnancy and birth can occur without warning, without planning, women must be dependent on men for economic security. This fact can be suggested by a simple mental experiment. Imagine that industrialization is occurring and neither birth control nor abortions are available. In such a context, a bright woman wants to go into civil engineering. But is it wise for an engineering school to admit her? One can argue that, like most women, she will marry and become pregnant many times (eight to twelve in the nineteenth century). In such a situation, one can argue that most women will not be able to use their training. Moreover, even if she obtains a degree, who would (or should) hire her? After companies invested time and money in her, she would have to quit. Now there were exceptional women who succeeded under these circumstances. But they were few. For most of history, sexual differences between men and women meant that the latter had to bear children whenever pregnancy occurred.

Yet the opportunity created by advances in medical technology was not immediately available because the law restricted women's ability to take advantage of applied medical knowledge. They enjoyed neither civil nor reproductive rights. This fact had to change in order to increase women's (and men's) choices.

Legal Changes

In democratic societies, laws not only regulate behavior, they also serve as codified norms. They represent people's collective judgment about right and wrong behavior. They identify, preserve, and protect ways of thinking and acting that citizens believe are important. As such, people with different characteristics are often treated differently under the law. Children, for example, have both special rights and special restrictions. Their unique treatment is justified because children are viewed as relatively powerless against adults. Until recently, women have been treated differently as well. I shall describe women's unequal treatment under the law along two dimensions: civil rights and fertility rights.

The denial of civil rights to women was justified as "protective legislation." One category of laws imposed maximum working hours for women. For example, no state had enforceable laws limiting women's hours of work prior to the 1880s. By 1919, however, 40 states had enacted such statutes (Goldin, 1990, p. 190). Another category allowed discrimination against women in hiring and job retention. Thus, married women could not be hired as teachers in 61 percent of all school districts in 1928; they could not be retained after marriage in 52 percent of all school districts (Goldin, 1990, p. 161). These laws constitute one reason women quit their jobs at marriage: They were forced to. Still another category of laws made occupational segregation legal. As a result, women were typically tracked into jobs without promotion ladders while men were tracked into jobs with promotion ladders. Thus, in 1940, a sample of 260 companies with more than 19 employees revealed that 74 percent explicitly restricted some jobs to women and 70 percent restricted some jobs to men (Goldin, 1990, p. 112). This discrimination was not only legal, companies were proud of such policies. In addition to restrictions on hours of work, hiring and retention, and job type, many other limits on women's rights existed—again, by law. These constraints meant that women were unable to act as fully endowed citizens, as adults. They were denied the right to choose the kind of work they did, to strive for economic success, and to obtain power and prestige apart from men. They were denied the right to achieve—simply because they were women.

Two contradictory interpretations of protective legislation exist (Goldin, 1990, p. 192). One is that young, single, employed women were prone to exploitation, so they had to be protected, like children. Moreover, it is argued, such laws ultimately benefited all workers, male and female. Hours of work per week, for example, dropped from about 60 in the nineteenth century to about 40 by 1930. Another interpretation, however, is that these laws were designed to restrict opportunities available to women. Many protective statutes were passed during the period 1880–1930, when the economy changed and women entered the labor force. It can be argued that they were not designed to protect women at all. They were, rather, reactions by men and their representatives (male legislators) to increased competition and an attempt at retaining their power and privilege—within both the family and society. Conveniently, such statutes were justified in terms of traditional gender norms. My impression is that while many of those seeking to protect women were well-intentioned, their efforts were short-sighted.

The drive to protect women did not occur without conflict. Some feminists proposed equality. For example, shortly after women obtained the right to vote in 1919, the National Woman's Party was organized and, under the leadership of Alice Paul, introduced the Equal Rights Amendment. Although equality is a morally powerful stance, such efforts were relatively ineffective for many years. From about 1890 until 1960, the law emphasized women's "protection." This constituted a collective normative judgment about right and wrong behavior. It expressed a simple value: Women should not be equal to men; they should remain dependent, like children; their access to valued resources should be determined by ascription.

This collective judgment changed, like so much else, during the 1960s, when women gained full civil rights. The legislative history of the Civil Rights Act of 1964 is interesting, however, because the inclusion of women occurred by accident. The Act did not mention equal rights for women until the day before its passage when a southern congressman introduced an amendment to include sex along with race. Reportedly, some male members of Congress laughed, seeing it as a joke (Bird, 1968). The southern strategy, it appears, was to load the bill with a variety of "absurd" amendments in order to defeat it. They miscalculated. As a result, women are now supposed to be treated equally in seeking and keeping jobs. Coupled with the Equal Pay Act of 1963, which requires that men and women be paid equally for equal work, Title IX of the Educational Amendments Act of 1972, and other statutes, the legal basis for gender discrimination ended. Thus, the trend in law was transformed. Norms, codified into law, dictate that women and men should now be evaluated by performance-related criteria applied equally to all.

This is a clear instance of the change from ascription to achievement orientations. As I will emphasize in Chapter 5, when Thomas Jefferson wrote that "all men are created equal" the concept of equality was initially applied very narrowly: to white men who owned property. Historically, however, the trend toward greater inclusiveness has proven to be inexorable: Immigrants, religious minorities, racial and ethnic groups, and women have sought to be treated as full citizens. The logic is that human beings should not be treated unequally based on their personal characteristics.[6] Women, however, find themselves in a peculiar situation because only they can bear children. It is hard to imagine gender equality without the ability to regulate pregnancy and birth.

The second dimension of unequal treatment under the law was the denial of fertility rights, including both preventing and terminating pregnancy. Such rights have been restricted by law until recently. Thus, beginning about 1870 and continuing in various states until the 1960s, the distribution of contraceptive information and devices was illegal under obscenity statutes (Reed, 1978). Similarly, every state made abortion illegal between 1860 and 1890 (Luker, 1984). Now there are two ways of interpreting restrictions on birth control and abortions. One is that they were statements of moral

---

[6]It is not much of an extension to include sexual orientation. By what logic should homosexual men and women be treated unequally under the law?

principles: Sex outside of marriage is wrong, and abortion is murder. But as mentioned earlier, the underlying issue is the roles women can play, both in the family and in the larger society. These laws made women's reproductive ability the center of their lives. Barring celibacy, women's ability to obtain an education, have a career, enter politics, and participate equally in all spheres of life could be undermined at any time by pregnancy and birth. Hence, these laws kept women at home, like children, unequal to men. It is not accidental that they were passed during the same period as so-called "protective" legislation. As opportunities increased with industrialization, men (and some women) sought to keep women at home. It did not work.

As with civil rights, the denial of reproductive rights began to end during the 1960s. In a series of decisions, the Supreme Court declared that women and men had a right to obtain birth control regardless of their age or marital status. Legislative enactments facilitated this right. Various states, led by California in 1967, began changing their abortion laws. Ultimately, however, the Court's 1973 decision in *Roe* vs. *Wade* invalidated all state laws proscribing abortions. Hence, the collective judgment of society is now different. The law guarantees women's ability to work for pay and, indeed, to participate fully in every area of society. Underlying these legal changes was the rise of feminism.

The Rise of Feminism

The drive for equality by oppressed people usually requires an ideology and a social movement. Feminism provides both. Ideologically, it emphasizes that men and women should be equal. Most feminists support the development of egalitarian gender norms. Without this orientation, the traumas experienced by women—the arbitrary denial of a job, rape, abuse—remain personal tragedies. As such, Judith Lewis Herman remarked, the process of bearing witness becomes meaningless (1992). Traumatic acts are not acknowledged; they are forgotten. But placed in the context of a movement for equality, these same acts are understood as examples of oppression, of tyranny. They allow victims to find a transcendent meaning in their experiences. They galvanize others and translate a personal tragedy into a social problem.

Feminism leads women to see themselves as individuals capable of doing more than bearing children. According to Carl Degler, the Protestant Reformation, the Enlightenment, the abolitionist movement, the development of capitalism, and the French Revolution, among other factors, all contributed to a recognition by some women that they could fill productive roles in society (1980). A feminist movement followed.

The history of the feminist movement is usually described in two waves (Cott, 1987). The first wave took place between the years 1848 and 1920 or so. Beginning with the Seneca Falls Convention of 1848, women began pressing for the removal of barriers to education and political participation. The mobilizing issue was the right to vote. This goal served as a symbol of women's status as full-fledged citizens: Women voters are adults, like men. Apart from this issue, not all feminists of the period shared the same goals. Some argued for equality while others emphasized the uniqueness of women. Many of the latter supported "protective" legislation of the sort described earlier. After passage of the Nineteenth Amendment to the Constitution, which secured the right to vote, the movement became quiescent. Protection seemed like enough, with the result that the many traumas women experienced went unnoticed, at least publicly. The second wave emerged during the 1960s and continues to the present. Responding to a new-found ability to prevent pregnancy, to ideological manifestos (for example, Betty Friedan's *The Feminine Mystique* [1963]), the Civil Rights movement, and other factors, women began organizing again. The National Organization for Women was founded in 1967 to press for full equality. As before, however, the feminist movement has various branches, each of which pushes a somewhat different agenda (Ferree & Hess, 1985). In all of them, however, the mobilizing issues have been birth control, the right to an abortion, and ending violence against women. These goals serve as symbols of women's ability to control their lives. Without this ability, equality remains an illusion.

Notice how a variety of historical events has coalesced. Feminism arose just as capitalism combined with industrialization to transform the economy. The ideology of equality buttressed expanded opportunity. In this context, women joined the labor force in steadily increasing numbers. Advances in medical technology, the fruits of scientific progress that originated several centuries ago, made it possible for women to regulate and control pregnancy and birth. Even though legal changes were delayed and continue to be contentious, they finally allowed women to regulate fertility. These changes, of course, were stimulated not only by the existence of technology but also by the overarching value of equality. One of the dominant trends in Western history has been the freeing of individuals from dependence on others, another way of placing emphasis on achievement. Increasingly, when men and women join together, they do so out of desire, not need; and they remain together as a (truly) free choice rather than out of dependence. The historical trend is clear: increasing equality between men and women.

The Continuation of Gender Stratification

Despite the changes described above, gender inequality continues. Why is this so? The answer must be structural. My hypothesis is the following:

The continuation of gender inequality reflects (1) traditional gender norms and (2) institutionalized discrimination.

Traditional Gender Norms

As noted earlier, traditional gender norms direct women and men into different spheres. According to this convention, then, the choices men and women make ought to be different. Even though they may be smart or creative, or both, and even though they may desire to become artists or scientists, women should focus their energy on family obligations. Most followed this dictum until recently. They became housewives, dependent on their husbands. Those who were employed worked at menial jobs, for low pay, or both, enduring discrimination. In a historical context where their choices were highly restricted, these ordinary women found whatever satisfaction they could. In certain respects, this situation has not changed. I have selected four indicators of the continuing salience of traditional gender norms:

   1. A significant minority of women do not work for pay. Thus, Figure 4-1 reveals that 60 percent of all married women are in the labor force, an all-time high. This datum means, of course, that the remaining 40 percent of all women do not have an income. Excluding the aged and disabled, they are housewives, dependent on their husbands for economic support. Whether they like it (or admit it) or not, they adhere to traditional gender norms.
   2. Voluntary part-time employment is common among women: About 27 percent of employed women have part-time jobs, most by choice (USDL, 1998b, p. 27). In comparison, only 11 percent of men work part-time. Women choose part-time employment to reduce the role conflict arising from job and family obligations. This priority is another way of adhering to traditional gender norms, of remaining dependent on their husbands.
   3. Most employed wives have lower incomes than their husbands. Even though spouses usually have similar levels of education, wives earn only 69 percent as much as husbands (Winkler, 1998). So wives are more dependent on husbands than husbands on wives. This economic relationship usually occurs by choice, as indicated by family decisions to relocate for husbands' jobs—even when wives are opposed, even when wives' incomes suffer as a result (Bielby & Bielby, 1992). Income differences are important because they translate into power within a marriage: When a man earns the most, he can impose his desires on his wife. Moreover, wife abuse is more common and harder to stop when women are more economically dependent on men (Herman, 1992). The fact that many women remain dependent reflects and reinforces traditional gender norms.
   4. Finally, the division of labor in most homes remains unequal. For example, employed women spend 33 hours per week on household tasks, compared to 14 for men (Blair & Lichter, 1991). Women spend nine hours per week preparing meals, compared to two for men. Women spend almost eight hours cleaning house, compared to less than two for men. And men are blissfully ignorant of what this means: "I just never knew, until my wife made me look, that dust gathered under a bed" (Horsfield, 1998). The only areas in which men spend more time are outdoor tasks and auto maintenance. Even when household jobs are shared, women usually organize and supervise them. Thus, men "help" women do "their" work. This orientation means that women labor for much longer hours than their husbands. It means that employed wives have two jobs: one at home and one at work. Interestingly, they usually view this situation as fair (Valian, 1998). I always thought the comic's assertion that "a man around the house is an inanimate object" was too extreme, but it describes many marriages and reflects traditional gender norms.

   These four indicators reveal the degree to which many people believe that women ought to focus on breadserving and men on breadwinning, and that everyone will be happier as a result. Such beliefs perpetuate gender inequality.

Institutionalized Discrimination

The inequality of women and men is also buttressed by **institutionalized discrimination:** the unequal treatment of individuals or groups based on their personal characteristics that is embedded in the social structure. I have selected two indicators of institutionalized discrimination against women.

1. Rosabeth Moss Kanter proposed that a skewed gender ratio in competitive contexts affects women's ability to succeed (1978). This insight can be expressed by the *Isolated Woman Hypothesis:*

> *The lower the proportion of women in a work group, the greater the discrimination.*

Please look back at Table 4-1. It shows that women remain rare in many competitive jobs, like engineering and medicine. Such work settings usually display a skewed gender ratio: a large proportion of men and a small proportion of women. Most of the latter occupy entry-level positions. Discrimination occurs as one result.[7]

Because there are so few of them, women are highly visible to peers and supervisors, which creates performance pressures: One's mistakes cannot be hidden. Furthermore, women are expected to avoid making men look bad, even in a competitive situation. As might be expected, women in high-visibility jobs sometimes respond inconsistently, which makes their behavior unpredictable and social relations difficult. A self-fulfilling prophecy can occur in that women are expected to fail and do, often with a little help from male colleagues and supervisors. Women in such contexts have few choices. They can try to overachieve, a difficult tactic. Alternatively, they can seek success more covertly and thereby limit their visibility. Rosabeth Moss Kanter speculated, plausibly, that the so-called "fear of success" among women really constitutes an attempt at keeping a low profile in a threatening context, thus preventing retaliation (1978).

Women also have difficulty succeeding because a skewed gender ratio produces polarization. Boundaries are established that isolate the "female intruder." Thus, men meet informally, become friends, enjoy lunch, and have drinks after work with those who are like themselves. They exclude female colleagues from socialization into the company: sources of information, knowledge of short cuts, and other factors vital to advancement. Sometimes these processes occur without (much) malice; rather, the female intruder is simply different, threatening, and left out as a result. Polarization allows opportunity for discrimination via sexual harassment and other means. For example, one (seemingly innocuous) strategy is to interrupt the flow of group events in some fashion—for example, by asking if it is okay to swear or apologizing for doing so.

---

[7]Underlying this argument is an insight associated with Georg Simmel: Variations in group size constitute structural facts that decisively influence rates of behavior (Simmel, 1908). For example, a small group will always have a higher rate of intermarriage with a large group (Blau et al., 1982). Thus, if two African Americans marry two whites in a population of 10 African Americans and 100 whites, then 20 percent of the African Americans and 2 percent of the whites married out.

The question emphasizes to a woman that she is different, that she disrupts normal behavior merely by her presence, that she is an intruder. Such forms of harassment inhibit success in a context where work behavior is already visible. Faced with exclusion, women have several strategies, none of which is satisfactory. One is to accept isolation, which means living without important information and making unnecessary mistakes. Another is to try becoming an insider by proving loyalty to the group. This tactic often means turning against other women. Kanter suggested, again plausibly, that a skewed gender ratio is the structural source of the so-called "queen bee syndrome," women discriminating against other women. Still another strategy is to be loyal to the work group without discriminating against other women; for example, not participating in prejudicial conversations or discriminatory actions. This tactic is difficult because male colleagues must acquiesce. Men can force a woman to choose sides.

Finally, women find it difficult to succeed in a skewed gender ratio context because they are assimilated into the work group on men's terms, which precludes advancement due to roles forced on women. For example, a woman may be expected to be nurturing toward her male colleagues, behavior more appropriate within the family than on the job. She may be treated as a seductress (regardless of her actions). She may be regarded as the group's pet. An independent stance on her part can result in being labeled an "iron maiden," the tough woman, with all the unflattering connotations that phrase conveys. This last reaction sometimes occurs when a talented woman succeeds despite male opposition. As Kanter observed, it is a reaction by men toward a woman who demands "treatment as an equal in a setting in which no person of her kind has previously been an equal" (1978, p. 984).

2. Occupational segregation provides a second example of unequal treatment built into the social structure. As shown previously, men decide how jobs are evaluated and paid, and women and men usually work at different jobs. As new occupations developed over the last century (male) employers "gendered" them; they set wages and organized tasks with either men or women in mind. This process still occurs (Acker, 1990). As a result, women usually have lower paid jobs involving helping and nurturing others, while men usually have higher paid jobs with authority. Thus, the skills involved in building highways and bridges are deemed to be worth more than those involved in building children. I use the phrase "building children" to stress that, like the structures (male) engineers design, children are constructed; someone must teach them to be adults. In his book, *Childhood,* Melvin Konner concluded that "children are living messages we send into the future, a future we will not see. . . . In effect we are building the house of tomorrow day by day, not out of bricks or steel, but out of the stuff of children's bodies, hearts, and minds" (1991, p. 428). Yet engineers are paid very high wages compared to teachers and childcare workers because men have determined that constructing highways is more difficult and more significant than children. This decision is, of course, political not economic. In my view, it would be more correct to see men and women with different skills (England, 1992a, p. 18). In any case, institutionalized occupational discrimination has two parts. Employers first segregate men and women, then pay the latter lower wages, even if their jobs are of comparable worth. Once this fact is recognized, the data presented earlier make sense.

Taken together, traditional gender norms and institutionalized discrimination constitute inertial forces, preserving inequality between men and women. Much remains the same.

But think back: In October 1781, George Washington defeated Lord Cornwallis at the Battle of Yorktown. This win over the British forces, I would suggest, did not end the American Revolution. Nor did the signing of the Treaty of Paris two years later. Nor did the Constitution's adoption in 1789. Despite their importance, these events only marked the end of part one of the struggle for freedom. They secured for white men certain fundamental rights: to vote, to be represented, and to obtain an education and a job based on hard work and ability. They reflected a long-term process by which white men are increasingly evaluated based on their achievements.

Women had none of these rights. They were still evaluated based on ascriptive criteria. Part two of the American Revolution began in a chapel in Seneca Falls, New York, in July 1848, where 240 people gathered and issued a declaration of the rights of women against men's oppression. It asserted that "we hold these truths to be self-evident: that all men and women are created equal; that they are endowed by their Creator with certain inalienable rights; that among these are life, liberty, and the pursuit of happiness." It went on to outline most of the elements necessary for the freedom and equality of women: the right to vote, to obtain an education, and to secure a job and income, among others. The Seneca Falls Declaration had little impact at the time. As the existence of this chapter indicates, gender still constitutes a system of ranking separate from class. But the moral force of ideas is strong. The Declaration began a fundamental transformation not only in the way men and women relate to one another but in stratification processes generally. Much has changed. Perhaps in the future, class will supercede gender as a basis for stratification.[8]

Summary

Married women's labor force participation rate rose steadily through this century. In addition, married women with children also increased their rate of employment (Figure 4-1). One implication of these changes is a higher divorce rate, which does not necessarily benefit women. While some changes have occurred in recent years, men and women are still occupationally segregated (Table 4-1). This fact means they are unequal in both prestige and income. Among full-time employed workers, women earn about 74 percent as much as men (Table 4-2). There appears to be less difference, however, among recent entrants to the labor force.

Nonetheless, men still exercise authority in the United States, and women are still victimized, as indicated by sexual harassment, rape, spouse abuse, and child sexual abuse. Underlying all these differences are traditional gender norms. Quantitative research shows that women's own choices, their skills and labor force attachment, only

---

[8]The "Seneca Falls Declaration" is worth reading; it can be found on the internet at *http://civnet.org*. See also Ellen C. Dubois, *Feminism and Suffrage* (1978).

account for about 40 percent of the income difference between the genders. Thus, another cause of the inequality experienced by individual women must be discrimination.

The history of this century reveals a duality: the simultaneous decline of and perpetuation of gender stratification. It is hypothesized that five variables have led to a decline in gender stratification: industrialization, female labor force participation, advances in medical technology, legal changes, and the rise of feminism. In contrast, two variables are hypothesized to continue gender stratification: traditional gender norms and institutionalized discrimination. The former is indicated by the high proportion of women not working for pay, voluntary part-time employment by women, the economic dependence of women on men, and men's opposition to housework. The latter is indicated by the gender ratio common in competitive groups and occupational segregation.

Race/Ethnicity and Stratification

This chapter tells the story of Jefferson's Dilemma (Shipler, 1993). In the *Declaration of Independence,* written in 1776, Thomas Jefferson declared: "We hold these truths to be self-evident, that all men are created equal. They are endowed by their creator with certain unalienable rights, such as life, liberty, and the pursuit of happiness." A revolution was fought and a new nation established based on this value (Lipset, 1963). The simple phrase "all men are created equal" implied that African American and white men have the same rights and should be allowed to succeed in light of their talents, skills, and willingness to work. It implied, in short, that achievement-oriented criteria should be applied to all. The Declaration established a new moral standard for people to live up to.

But Jefferson did not live up to this standard. He was a slave owner. His only book, *Notes on the State of Virginia,* written in 1785, shows that he believed in the inferiority of those enslaved. So he and the other founders of the new nation excluded African slaves from the promise of the new nation. He thus created a dilemma: a choice between freedom and equality for all versus freedom for some and slavery for others. There is evidence that Jefferson recognized the difficulty this choice represented. The original draft of the Declaration contained an indictment of slavery that the Continental Congress deleted. In *Notes,* he forecast the long-term harm to the nation created by a division into free and unfree. Yet he freed only two slaves during his lifetime and only five in his will. He may (or may not, depending on whom you believe) have fathered children by one of his slaves, Sally Hemings. Jefferson never resolved his dilemma.[1]

Nor have we. Two definitions are necessary in order to consider this issue: The term **race** refers to groups identifiable in light of their physical traits, such as skin color. Thus, African Americans, whites, and the various Asian minorities are typically defined as races. The term **ethnic group** refers to aggregates with distinctive social and psychological characteristics, as indicated by their nationality, religious heritage, and other unique elements of their background. Thus, the Irish and Italians are typically defined as ethnic groups. So are persons who came from or whose ancestors came from various Hispanic and Asian nations. The current U.S. population is about 265 million people. Of this number, about 72 percent are white, 13 percent African American, 11 percent Hispanic American, 4 percent Asian American, and less than 1 percent Native American (USBC, 1997b, p. 18). Although useful, these racial and ethnic categories are completely arbitrary. They are metaphors for the divisions tormenting this nation.[2]

These divisions have existed since the beginning. In 1790, just after the Constitution was adopted, 60–80 percent of the white population was of English origin (USBC,

---

[1] In *An American Sphinx: The Character of Thomas Jefferson,* Joseph Ellis argued that the evidence is inconclusive (1997). In *Thomas Jefferson and Sally Hemings: An American Controversy,* Annette Gordon-Reed made the strongest case I have seen in favor of Jefferson's paternity (1997).

[2] As a convention, when I refer to "whites" the reference excludes Hispanics, who can be of any race. You should understand that "race" is meaningless genetically; skin pigmentation merely reflects adaptations to climate (Cavalli-Sforza et al., 1995). Racial distinctions are only meaningful because we attach meaning to them. Moreover, few "Hispanic" or "Asian" people see themselves as sharing a common culture (de la Garza, 1992; Takaki, 1989). Rather, they identify with their ethnic group—for example, as Chinese Americans or Mexican Americans. Thus, the names serve as a way to present data.

1975, p. 1168). Hence, all other groups have not only been forced to adapt to English norms and values but also to endure their prejudice and discrimination. **Prejudice** refers to people's hostile attitudes toward others in a different group or toward other groups as a whole (Allport, 1954). **Discrimination** refers to the unequal treatment of individuals and groups due to their personal characteristics, such as race or ethnicity.[3]

Although prejudice and discrimination have been widespread throughout U.S. history—one need only mention 200 years of slavery and 100 years of segregation—the situation has changed in recent years. Attitudinal surveys show that most people now embrace the value of equality, especially when phrased as equality of opportunity, and that the level of prejudice has declined (GP, 1997a). Despite this acceptance, however, many people oppose policies designed to provide equal opportunity for all. Thus, like Jefferson so long ago, many people find it hard to implement the value of equality. For example, although nearly all whites say that African American and white children should be able to attend the same schools, that support depends on the school's racial composition. Thus, 97 percent of whites claim to have no objection if their children's school has "a few" African American students. But if "more than half" the children are African American, the proportion of whites objecting rises to 59 percent (GP, 1997a, p. 17). Moreover, 66 percent of whites oppose busing children to achieve integration (GSS, 1996). Similar differences occur when whites are questioned about access to housing, jobs, and other basic issues. Thus, even though whites now accept equality, they remain like the founders of the new nation: not only willing to tolerate discrimination but also to actively discriminate. Underlying unequal treatment, of course, are feelings of hostility. Perhaps the best single indicator of prejudice lies in attitudes toward intermarriage. Jefferson (said he) opposed unions between whites and African slaves, and most whites opposed intermarriage until recently. In 1958, 96 percent of whites disapproved of marriage between the races. By 1997, however, only 41 percent of whites and 23 percent of African Americans disapproved (GP, 1997a, p. 19). These data suggest that while attitudes are changing, a gap continues to exist between what people say and what they do. As with gender, this chapter will show that while much has changed, much remains the same. Jefferson's Dilemma is our dilemma.

Dimensions of Racial and Ethnic Stratification

Over time, the United States has become one of the most heterogeneous nations on earth, filled with a cacophony of racial and ethnic groups. It is alluring to think we have become a melting pot where disparate people live together in relative harmony. But history suggests conflict and exploitation have been and are more common.

---

[3]Although the population was mostly English, they came from varying backgrounds. In *Albion's Seed: Four British Folkways in America,* David Hackett Fischer showed that English immigration occurred in four waves from different regions, and that people from each differed in speech, courtship and marriage customs, religious rituals, attitudes toward education and freedom, and other ways (1989). These differences appeared where they settled—New England, Virginia, the Delaware Valley, and the Colonial backcountry—and the legacy of the original immigrants can still be found in these areas.

Racial and Ethnic Stratification in the United States

In order to begin, it is useful to distinguish between absolute and relative change. "Absolute change" refers to a difference over time. For example, if the median income of African American families changed from about $1,900 per year in 1950 to about $28,100 per year in 1997 (and it did), then most are better off. This assertion remains true even after taking inflation into account. "Relative change" refers to a difference in relationship to some other group, such as whites. For example, if during the same period the median income among white families changed from about $3,400 per year to about $47,000 per year (and it did), then the relative relationship between the two groups has not altered very much. In both 1950 and 1997, African American families earned about 56 to 60 percent as much as white families (USBC, 1975, p. 297; 1998f, p. 13). Over the last century, most minority groups improved their situation absolutely. In relative terms, however, a considerable gap often exists. I illustrate these patterns by examining civil rights, infant mortality, residential segregation, and occupation and income.

Civil Rights

Civil rights refers to citizens' legally guaranteed opportunity to participate equally in the society. For example, those possessing civil rights can vote, eat where they choose, buy stock or a house if they have the money, educate their children, obtain a job, and marry whomever they wish. Civil rights guarantee individual freedom. Without civil rights, entire groups are evaluated based on nonperformance criteria—ascription. For those without civil rights, the law itself can be and has been used as a mechanism for exploitation (Aguirre & Turner, 1993).

When the Constitution was adopted in 1789, only property owners who paid taxes could vote, which meant only English men enjoyed civil rights. Over time, accompanied by much protest and violence, those who did not own land and various white ethnic groups (German, Scandinavian, Irish, Italian, and so forth) obtained a legal guarantee of equal participation.

Native Americans were less successful. Whites always agreed, by treaty, to treat Native American tribes fairly, as sovereign nations. But these groups were unfamiliar with Western notions of property (for example, land titles and transfers). So whites used the law to take their land and thereby removed the basis for political sovereignty from Native American nations (Churchill & Morris, 1992). Similarly, until recently the Bureau of Indian Affairs, run by whites in Washington, also used the law to limit Native American civil rights (Deloria, 1992).

Those of Asian ancestry were also less successful. The few Chinese and Japanese immigrants who came to the United States in the nineteenth century faced very high levels of prejudice and discrimination (Takaki, 1989). One example of unequal treatment was the passage of restrictive immigration laws to keep the population of Asian heritage people small. Another was the seizure of property and confinement of U.S. citizens of Japanese descent to internment camps located east of the Rocky Mountains during World War II (CWRIC, 1982). In comparison, citizens of German descent neither lost their land nor were jailed. Thus, while European immigrants had to overcome many obstacles, the barriers faced by Asian Americans were more significant.

Hispanic people fared no better. By origin, the Hispanic population is about 60 percent Mexican American, 12 percent Puerto Rican American, and 5 percent Cuban American, with the remainder coming from various Central and South American nations. Historically, the early settlers from Mexico displaced the Native Americans and regarded the Southwest as their homeland, until the Anglos (whites) invaded and made the Southwest part of the United States. Subsequently, Mexican Americans were treated as second-class citizens, segregated and deprived of civil rights. Similarly, in the North the small communities of Puerto Rican Americans were kept segregated and denied their rights, partly by custom and partly by law. More recent immigrants from Cuba and other nations have endured less discrimination, benefiting from legal changes that have occurred over the past 30 years or so.

Finally, the Civil War's promise of freedom was empty as African Americans went from slavery to serfdom in the form of sharecropping. After the war, the South began a campaign of terror against the former slaves that not only denied them civil rights but also placed them in a system of segregation and debt peonage lasting for another century (Kennedy, 1995; Oshinsky, 1996). The South lost militarily but won substantively during Reconstruction, and the North acquiesced. It has been said that 200 years of slavery and its 100-year aftermath were America's original sin.

In the 1950s and 1960s, however, the structure of discrimination broke down as court decisions and legislative enactments made most forms of unequal treatment illegal. For example, in *Brown* vs. *Board of Education,* the Supreme Court ruled in 1954 that segregated school systems violated the Constitution. This decision was but one, although a key one, in a series of acts by which the Court struck down the legal basis for discrimination. Furthermore, the struggle by minority groups for equal rights moved to the streets during this same period. Their unruliness was initially nonviolent, becoming violent later (Feagin & Hahn, 1973). In this context, Congress passed a series of civil rights acts designed to outlaw all forms of discrimination. As a result, denial of the right to vote became illegal, access to public accommodations was guaranteed, and the right to equal educational opportunity was declared, among many other changes.

Discrimination due to skin color is now illegal in the United States. In this area, then, African American, Hispanic, and Asian citizens improved their situation both absolutely and relatively. Civil rights, however, do not mean equality of opportunity. One indicator of continuing inequality is the differing ability of newborn babies to survive.

Infant Mortality

The **infant mortality rate** refers to the number of live babies who die within the first year of life. It serves as a useful example of inequality of living standards because it reflects people's level of nutrition, sanitation, housing, and medical treatment. Here are infant mortality rates in 1900 for various white groups and African Americans. The numbers refer to deaths per 1,000 live births (Lieberson, 1980, p. 46).

Native whites	142
English immigrants	149
German immigrants	159

Italian immigrants	189
African Americans	297

Thus, white immigrant groups displayed higher rates of infant mortality than did native whites at the turn of the century. This means immigrants endured lower living standards than natives. They were unequal. In comparison, however, the African American infant mortality rate was far higher than that of immigrants and more than double that of native whites. The magnitude of these differences suggests that even though the living standards of white immigrants were low, African Americans confronted far more discrimination.

This fact has not changed, even though infant mortality rates declined steadily over time. Here are data for 1996, in deaths per 1,000 live births (NCHSa, 1998, p. 4):

Asian Americans	5
Hispanic Americans	6
White Americans	6
Native Americans	10
African Americans	14

Not only is the mortality rate of African American babies still double that of whites, it is the same as that in Bulgaria and greater than that in the Philippines (USBC, 1997b, p. 833). Thus, although much has changed—everyone is healthier today—much remains the same. But whites, who live in different neighborhoods, rarely notice these differences in equality of opportunity.

Housing Segregation
The degree to which groups are isolated from one another because they reside in different neighborhoods affects the price of housing they can obtain. It affects the quality of education available. It affects employment opportunities. It affects the probability of criminal victimization. It affects access to community services, such as libraries and parks. It exposes children to neighborhood disorganization (for example, drugs). It affects every aspect of life (Massey & Denton, 1993). Isolated groups are nearly always worse off than the majority. For this reason, housing segregation provides a useful indicator of relative inequality by race and ethnicity.

Prior to World War I, African Americans were not especially isolated from whites (Lieberson, 1980, p. 259). In the North, the average African American person lived in a neighborhood in which only 7 to 10 percent of the residents were also African American; nearly all the rest were white. This situation was possible because the African American population in the North was small. But whites reacted to African Americans' migration to the North during the years 1920 to 1970 by increasing their isolation, by segregating them (Harrison & Weinberg, 1992). Although the Fair Housing Act of 1968 was designed to prevent such discrimination, it has no enforcement mechanism. So in 1990, the average African American lived in a neighborhood in which 63 percent of the residents were also African American. Segregation means inequality.

The level of residential isolation is less for other groups, with the exception of Native Americans—many of whom reside on reservations (Harrison & Weinberg, 1992). Thus, the average Hispanic person lives in a neighborhood in which 52 percent of the residents are also Hispanic. You should remember, however, that many Hispanics, such as those of Cuban ancestry, look white. So they endure much less segregation (Massey & Denton, 1993). Among Asian Americans, the average person lives in an area in which 28 percent of the residents are also of Asian heritage. This lower level of housing segregation suggests that these groups are seen as less threatening by whites, partly because they remain small populations. As a result, their relative social position is better. A similar pattern occurs with occupation and income.

Occupation and Income

Historically, the United States has been characterized by a rigid pattern of occupational segregation. Whites worked at higher-prestige and higher-paying jobs than Hispanics, African Americans, Asians, and Native Americans. But this situation has altered somewhat over the past 30 years, as shown in Table 5-1. The table reveals that only 6 percent of African Americans worked in white-collar jobs in 1940, compared to 49 percent in 1997. Similarly, only 19 percent of Hispanics worked in white-collar jobs in 1960, compared to 39 percent in 1997. Note, however, the lack of change in the percentage of white-collar Hispanics from 1990–1997. About 66 percent of Asian Americans now work in white-collar jobs. Finally, only 45 percent of Native Americans were in white-collar jobs in 1990. Although some of the data are more incomplete than I would like, it is clear that the gap between whites and other groups has become smaller over time. This relative change indicates less inequality.

Although the pattern of declining inequality can also be seen below when a few detailed occupations are considered, the change is not very great (USBC, 1974, p. 352; USDL, 1998b, p. 174). Begin by scanning across the rows for African Americans in 1970 and 1997: In each case, their percentages have increased, which suggests declining inequality. Temporal data for other groups are not available over this same time.

TABLE 5-1   Percentage of Racial and Ethnic Groups in White-Collar Jobs, Selected Years, 1940–1997

	1940	1950	1960	1970	1980	1990	1997
White Americans	35%		44%	48%	54%	60%	61%
African Americans	6		13	24	37	44	49
Hispanic Americans			19	22		39	39
Asian Americans						64	66
Native Americans						45	

Sources: USBC (1998a; 1998b; 1998c; 1998e).

Note: The system of occupational classification changed between 1970 and 1980. Blank cells indicate that data are not available.

	African Americans		Hispanic Americans
Job Category	1970	1997	1997
Architects	2%	3%	4%
Engineers	1	4	4
Physicians	2	4	5
Lawyers	1	3	4
Insurance agents	3	8	5
Electricians	3	6	9
Firefighters	2	12	5
Police	6	18	8

Despite these (minimal) changes, job segregation remains. Now look down the columns. Although African Americans are 13 percent of the population, in 1997 they comprised only 3 percent of architects and 3 percent of lawyers. Similarly, while they are about 11 percent of the population, Hispanics comprise only 4 percent of architects and 4 percent of engineers. These data show continuing absolute inequality.

Data on income reveal continuing relative inequality. As shown in the next list, the income of families varies by racial and ethnic group, and the rank order follows that displayed in Table 5-1 (USBC, 1998a; 1998b; 1998f).

	Year	Median Family Income
White American	1997	$47,000
Asian American	1996	46,400
African American	1997	28,600
Hispanic American	1997	28,100
Native American	1990	21,700

Asian and White Americans have the highest family incomes, with African and Hispanic Americans significantly lower. Native American families are much worse off than any other group.

As noted, the United States is a heterogeneous society, comprising a variety of racial and ethnic groups who are unequal to one another. The differences in access to valued resources (life, housing, jobs, and income) portrayed here are not unique. Other nations show a similar pattern.

Racial and Ethnic Stratification in Other Nations

In comparison to the United States, most European nations are relatively homogeneous by race and ethnicity. The United Kingdom is an exception, due mainly to its colonial legacy. Hence, I am going to present data on racial and ethnic inequality in the United Kingdom and compare it to the United States. I focus on a crucial issue: unemployment. This indicator of inequality is useful because, as will be shown in more detail in Chapter

9, those without jobs are economically deprived, display a lower self-concept, and are more likely to endure familial disruption, among other problems.

The United Kingdom has a population of about 54 million persons, of whom 1.5 percent are Black from various Caribbean and African nations, 1.5 percent are of Indian origin, and smaller percentages from Pakistan, Bangladesh, and other Asian nations. Thus, racial and ethnic minorities in the United Kingdom constitute about 5 percent of the total population (ONS, 1997, p. 31).

Table 5-2 displays unemployment rates in the United States and the United Kingdom by race and ethnicity. It reveals that whites in both nations are significantly less likely to be out of work than members of racial and ethnic minorities. Other indicators of inequality, such as those used earlier in this section, show that racial and ethnic minorities suffer discrimination similar to that in the United States (Field et al., 1981; Joshi, 1989).

The data presented in this section lead to three conclusions. First, inequality in the United States has declined in certain areas, such as civil rights and occupation. This is true in both absolute and relative terms. Second, a great deal of inequality in living standards continues to exist, as indicated by infant mortality rates and residential segregation. Finally, racial and ethnic inequality in the United States resembles that in the United Kingdom. These conclusions show that we have not become a melting pot. Rather, the social divisions established when the new nation was formed have endured.

TABLE 5-2 Unemployment by Racial and Ethnic Group, United Kingdom and United States

	Unemployment Rate
United States	*1997*
White Americans	4%
Asian Americans	5
Hispanic Americans	7
African American	9
United Kingdom	*1997*
White	6%
Indian	8
Pakistani	20
Black	21
Bangladeshi	23

Sources: USDL (1998, p. 153); USBC (1998a); Sly et al. (1998, p. 12).

Some Consequences of Racial and Ethnic Stratification

The passage of civil rights laws during the 1960s fundamentally changed the relationship between whites and minority groups, creating opportunities where few had existed before. Some have taken advantage of these opportunities. Others have been left behind. One unintended result has been the creation of an **underclass:** people who are persistently poor, residentially concentrated, and relatively isolated from the rest of the population. More graphically, the term connotes people confined to a ghetto (an area inhabited by only one group). Such persons are easy to overlook, which raises the odds that the problem will become worse. In the United States, the underclass comprises whites residing in parts of Appalachia, Native Americans on reservations, Hispanics in some communities, and African Americans. The last group comprises about 60 percent of the underclass, so they are the focus in this discussion (Ruggles, 1990, p. 112).

Over the course of this century, many African Americans left the rural South for cities in the North. They were looking for freedom from serfdom; they met a trap in the form of housing segregation. As described by Massey and Denton in *American Apartheid: Segregation and the Making of the Underclass,* African Americans endure high levels of housing segregation in every U.S. city (1993). Moreover, they showed that 16 large cities with a high proportion of African Americans exhibit hyper-segregation: Very few African Americans reside in integrated areas; most are confined (I use the term deliberately) to neighborhoods that are nearly all Black. Their level of isolation is far greater than that of other minority groups. The rising rate of poverty that developed in the 1980s (sketched in Chapter 10) worsened the problem.

Today, large areas of the nation's central cities are composed of the most disadvantaged segments of the African American population. Many lack work experience. Indeed, unemployment is the key problem (Wilson, 1996). Most manufacturing jobs used to be located in central cities, which meant that relatively uneducated people could find work. Over time, however, these jobs have moved to the suburbs, which are inaccessible to central city residents. Hence, many have learned to live without employment. All about them, they see others in similar circumstances.

An **anomic** setting exists, as people still learn—at home, at school, and in the media—that hard work leads to success, but find they cannot obtain it via employment (Merton, 1968). So the young mature without seeing stable families with parents leaving for work every day and children going to school. The reaction of people forced to live in such contexts is predictable. Many lose hope. Many become **alienated;** they believe they have little control over their lives and that attempts at improving their situation, getting out of the ghetto, are fruitless. The result is also predictable: high rates of crime, drug use, and sexual acting out (Crane, 1991).

Some alienated people become angry, and some angry people become violent. Crime becomes normal, an illegitimate means to "success." For example, 75 percent of the inmates in New York state prisons come from only seven neighborhoods in New York City, all of them African American and Hispanic (Clines, 1992). The carnage is very self-destructive. Murder is now the leading cause of death among African American men, aged 15 to 24 (NCHS, 1996, p. 31). In psychological terms, one suspects that when young African American men kill young African American men, they are shooting into a mirror. The impact is widespread. A high percentage of young African American men live in jail. Those not incarcerated feel unsafe. Children are traumatized, with many negative consequences (see Chapter 10).

Some alienated persons turn their anger inward. Their self-loathing sometimes leads to drugs. Like the psychotropic substances middle-class people obtain via prescription, alcohol, crack cocaine, and heroin lessen the pain. In this context, the roles of drug pusher and hustler have become more attractive and more widespread (Anderson, 1990, p. 76). Someone must distribute the product. But unlike the drugs obtained by middle-class people, the distribution of illegal substances is regulated by violence. So many neighborhoods look like war zones—filled with people preying on one another. Children are sometimes born addicted. Trauma is widespread.

Finally, some alienated people use sex as an outlet for anger. Men and boys make women and girls pregnant. Women and girls desire to become pregnant and give birth. After all, in an anomic setting, making babies is one of the few tasks at which people can be successful. It becomes a mark of one's existence in an environment that denies their significance. They fail to see the long-term negative consequences. The following percentages of babies born to unmarried women by race and ethnicity indicate how extreme segregation, race and ethnicity, and the creation of an underclass lead to conduct. The data are for 1996 (NCHS, 1998b, p. 46):

African American	70%
Puerto Rican American	61
Mexican American	38
Cuban American	25
White American	22

African Americans display the highest rate of unmarried births. Among Hispanics, the rate of unmarried births corresponds to the degree of housing segregation and the proportion whose members look white (Massey & Denton, 1993).

These reactions to being placed in an anomic situation are not race specific. Whenever groups of people live in an upside-down world, they respond similarly (Inniss & Feagin, 1992). Thus, Liverpool, England, resembles many U.S. cities except that its population is almost completely white. As in the United States, manufacturing jobs have left, and 25 percent of its citizens are unemployed. In fact, long-term unemployment has become normal for many persons, especially young adults. Poverty is rampant. Located outside the economic mainstream, poor people are concentrated together and isolated from the rest of the nation. They constitute a white underclass. And the same problems appear: high rates of violence, drug use, and sexual acting out.

Alas, the impact of an underclass, a result of three centuries of exploitation, cannot be easily fixed. Individuals with little hope cannot change their worldview overnight. The level of racial and ethnic inequality and its consequences lead to several questions that I want to consider: (1) In what context does discrimination against individuals occur, and what is its impact? The other questions are structural: (2) Why have members of some racial and ethnic groups succeeded at greater rates than others? (3) What factors maintain the level of racial and ethnic inequality shown previously?

The Individual and Racial and Ethnic Stratification

I have always liked nursery rhymes. "Humpty Dumpty sat on a wall. Humpty Dumpty had a great fall." Have you ever thought about why Humpty fell? He was just sitting there. Being an egg and, hence, oval, he probably took precautions to prevent falling. So it is unlikely that he fell accidentally. But maybe some of the other eggs were not used to seeing eggs like him on top of the wall. Maybe they thought eggs like him ought to remain at the bottom. Maybe they resented eggs like him being so high and mighty. So someone pushed Humpty. The reason: He was a brown egg. "All the king's horses and all the king's men could not put Humpty together again." Disliking Humpty, maybe they did not try very hard. In fact, maybe they were glad to see him fall. After all, a white egg would replace him. This interpretation may be flawed (!), but it does make sense of the story. And it suits my purpose: People of color have always been pushed off the wall of opportunity by prejudice and discrimination.

Moreover, the interpretation suggests some of the conditions under which prejudice and discrimination occur. The *Contact Hypothesis,* for example, emphasizes the importance of interaction and familiarity:

> *The less experience people from different groups have with one another, the more likely are members of the dominant group to display prejudice and discriminate.*

The reason for such hostility is that people usually see the world from the perspective of their own group and, without personal experience, develop negative stereotypes about those who appear different (Case et al., 1989; Fuchs & Case, 1994). Prejudice, after all, is simply a way of judging others without knowing anything about them (which is why I suggested the importance of being used to seeing someone who is different in an equal or superior position in the rhyme). Such judgments lead to discrimination (which is why I suggested that someone pushed Humpty). Two venues in which people become familiar with others in different groups are schools and neighborhoods. But they remain segregated.

Another situation in which prejudice and discrimination occur is when people from different groups seek the same jobs, land, or other valued resources (a spot on the wall). The *Resource Hypothesis* summarizes the argument:

> *The more people from different groups compete for scarce resources, the more likely are members of the dominant group to display prejudice and discriminate.*

What happens is that the members of the dominant group want to protect their material interests and develop rationalizations about those at the bottom to justify keeping them there (Aguirre & Turner, 1993). Such reasoning justifies practices that would otherwise be seen as unjust. (This is why I suggested that "all the king's horses" might stand by while Humpty lay broken.) More sociologically, limiting people's occupational success by not hiring others of a different race (or gender) functions in the same way.

The Civil Rights revolution of the 1960s was supposed to have ended such problems. Yet civil rights did not change whites' racial attitudes and their tendency to treat others unequally. The data presented earlier show this fact clearly. But numbers lack evocativeness. They do not reveal the daily slights and slaps that individuals who are not white must endure. They do not reveal how such events prevent individuals from achieving their full potential, and they do not suggest how people try to scale walls, only to be pushed off when success occurs. I am going to discuss two locations in which discrimination continues to exist: public places and organizations. Although the focus is on African Americans, the logic of this argument applies to all minority groups.

Public Place Discrimination

Most whites do not think about how the color of their skin affects their treatment by others. Most African Americans, however, confront their color and its implications every day. This is because when they are away from family and friends—in public places—they have little protection from discriminatory behavior. Discrimination can take several forms (Allport, 1954).

One strategy for discrimination is avoidance (Staples, 1994). Hailing a cab in a large city, for example, can be a difficult process for minority individuals. Many drivers avoid picking up minority persons—especially men. It is a chance to discriminate freely without being caught. Middle-class African Americans take this behavior as evidence of whites' true feelings. More subtly, whites may routinely cross the street to avoid them and stop talking in elevators when they enter. I have seen whites take their children away from play sites (a jungle gym, for example) when joined by dark-skinned children. So it becomes important to make whites feel safe. Some African American males apparently whistle classical music while walking down the street as a sign they are not dangerous (Bradley, 1997). Such actions make daily life more stressful for the victims.

Another strategy is rejection (Graham, 1995). Providing poor-quality service is one way. African Americans find that getting seated in restaurants often takes a long time. While waiting, they are sometimes handed coats to be checked. When they are seated, it is in the back by the kitchen door (even when other tables are available). Then the meal arrives cold. Plain old harassment while going to work is another example of rejection: being frisked on suburban commuter trains and mistaken for a delivery boy when entering the building where one works. Finally, rejection occurs in the office. Clients wonder "Why did I get the black lawyer?" (or accountant, doctor, and so forth); this concern is manifested in questions about qualifications ("Where did you get your degree?") that would not ordinarily be asked. Such experiences mean that ordinary interaction is often tinged with stress and anger.

A third strategy is verbal and nonverbal harassment. Racial epithets occur—when it is safe: from passing cars, from across the street. The targets are both adults and children. The "hate stare" attempts intimidation without overt violence. Such forms of psychological assault must usually be endured without reply. A response is often either impossible or dangerous. Then parents must explain hate to their children. Stress mounts.

The final strategy is violence in some form. Whites throw cans or bottles from moving cars. Occasionally, when middle-class African Americans find themselves in the wrong area, they are pulled from their cars or accosted on the street. Sometimes they are "merely" threatened. The police are of little help. In fact, the police are often perpetrators. In one study of police violence against citizens, 93 percent of the episodes involved white officers assaulting African Americans (Lersch, 1993). Events like this are constant possibilities, and they make each day more difficult.

Such experiences wear people down. They do not occur "once a week, once a month. Every day that you live as a black person, you're reminded how you're perceived in society." One individual describes the long-term implications (Feagin, 1991, p. 119):

> *If you think of the mind as having 100 ergs of energy, and the average man uses 50% of his energy dealing with the everyday problems of the world . . . then he has 50% more to do creative things that he wants to do. Now that's a white person. Now a black person also has 100 ergs; he uses 50% the same way a white man does . . . , so he has 50% left. But he uses 25% fighting being black and what that means. Which means he really only has 25% to do what the white man has 50% to do, and he's expected to do just as much as the white man with that 25%. . . . You just don't have as much energy left to do as much as you know you really could if you were free, [if] your mind were free.*

In my classes, white students sometimes say that minorities are too sensitive. A small slight should be ignored, whites say. And it usually is. But imagine the effect of being repeatedly pushed off a wall, broken, and having no one help. The cumulative impact can lead to rage. It can explode unpredictably. Interaction becomes difficult. Success becomes harder.

Discrimination by Organizations

Civil rights laws mean that discrimination by people in organizations is now illegal and those wishing to act on their prejudice must be covert. As before, I am going to point out some of the strategies used by whites against racial and ethnic minorities.

One area in which unequal treatment occurs is in housing. Historically, the white public, real estate agents, and government acted overtly: As African Americans migrated to the North during the years after World War I, they were trapped in ghettos far more systematically than previous waves of European immigrants or Asian or Hispanic Americans (Massey & Denton, 1993). The strategies used to create and maintain African American ghettos were direct: (1) Whites used violence (riots, bombings, physical harassment, and threatening letters) to intimidate African American families purchasing a home in white areas. (2) Whites formed "neighborhood improvement associations" and placed restrictive covenants in deeds—thereby making the sale of a home to African Americans illegal. (3) White realtors guided African Americans to ghetto areas to increase demand; thereby increasing prices and profits. They controlled the size of the ghetto by "blockbusting." They would sell an African American family a home just outside the ghetto. They would then incite whites to flee and purchase the other houses on the block at low prices. They then sold those homes at high prices to African Americans. (4) After World War II, whites in the Federal Housing Administration and Veterans Administration established housing guidelines that promoted low-cost mortgages for whites living in suburbs—leading to the largest increase in home ownership in U.S. history—by whites. African Americans were left out.

Most whites supported these cruel actions. In 1942, 84 percent of all whites agreed that "there should be separate sections in towns and cities for Negroes to live in" (Massey & Denton, 1993, p. 49). Similarly, in 1962, 61 percent of whites agreed that "white people have a right to keep blacks out of their neighborhoods if they want to and blacks should respect that." In 1984, 28 percent agreed with this same assertion; in 1996 12 percent agreed (GSS, 1996). Yet, as I suggested at the beginning of the chapter, a gap often exists between attitudes and actions. Most cities remain segregated. Although whites seem accepting of open housing, they actually discriminate against African American neighbors, especially if there is more than one.

Banks and real estate companies are aware of this gap and continue to (covertly) discriminate today. There is an old Eddie Murphy sketch (probably from *Saturday Night Live*) that suggests the cruelty involved: A perfectly dressed Murphy is applying for a home loan. The lenders greet him with a smile, give him the application, and assure him it will be carefully considered. After Murphy leaves, the lenders dissolve in laughter and throw the application away. When a white person enters and asks for an application, the lenders open the vault and tell him to take what he needs. The skit is chilling in its accuracy. Regardless of income, African Americans are more likely to be denied loans than whites (Massey & Denton, 1993, p. 108).

Realtors also smile and then deny African Americans and Hispanics the ability to rent or buy homes in white neighborhoods. In Worcester, Massachusetts, one outfit placed the word "Archie" next to houses not to be shown to African Americans or Hispanics. In Orange County, California, a realtor simply told minority applicants—falsely—that no apartments were available (Herbert, 1998). These specific examples are generalizable. When housing audits are done, African American, Hispanic, and white applicants with matched characteristics approach realtors seeking housing, either to rent or buy. The data below suggest that discrimination against minorities occurs nationwide: They are shown fewer units in white areas, steered to minority neighborhoods, and given fewer facts about units they are shown (Fix & Struyk, 1993, p. 20).

	Denied Opportunity to see Houses	*Denied Information about Houses*
Black Renter	46%	15%
Black Buyer	50	8
Hispanic Renter	43	12
Hispanic Buyer	46	8

When neighborhoods remain segregated over time, it is reasonable to hypothesize that discrimination is occurring. Remember: The issue here is not that white areas are intrinsically better; it is that resources accompanying housing lead to unequal opportunity.

Another area in which organizations discriminate is when employees must be hired. Since perfect job candidates rarely apply, imperfect candidates must be evaluated. Consider: The Aardvark Company advertises a job requiring a Master's degree and five years of experience. Imagine that the two best applicants are (1) a Hispanic male with a Bachelor's degree and ten years' experience and (2) a white male with a Master's degree and one year's experience. Aardvark hires the white male due to his educational qualifications. Now imagine that Aardvark has another opening and the two best applicants have reverse qualifications (the Hispanic with more education and less experience). This time Aardvark hires the white male due to his greater experience. After this process occurs many times, a work force will remain white and male—but no discrimination has occurred because the "best" applicant was always selected.

Again, the example is generalizable. Hiring audits show that when a young Hispanic with an accent applies for a job advertised in the newspaper, about 31 percent of the time he or she will be denied an application, refused an interview, or not hired (Fix & Struyk, 1993, p. 22). A similar outcome takes place about 20 percent of the time when a young African American applies. When an organization's work force remains segregated, a reasonable hypothesis is that discrimination is occurring. Opportunity remains unequal as a result. Yet, as argued in Chapter 1, emphasizing individual experiences leaves the analysis incomplete.

Social Structure and Racial and Ethnic Stratification

As a result of civil rights laws, the obvious manifestations of prejudice are gone now, like a bad dream. Members of minority groups seem to be everywhere, sometimes in positions of high prestige and income. In this context, it seems to me, many whites no longer want to think about the race problem in this country. They want to see the United States as color blind, as they say it should be. Yet whites accept discrimination, partly because many harbor prejudice. This section focuses on the link between social structure and racial and ethnic stratification. I offer answers to the remaining questions posed earlier.

Historical Variations in Racial and Ethnic Group Mobility

People often wonder why more African Americans have not succeeded. The numbers are revealing. As recently as 1940, only 6 percent of all African Americans were white-collar workers. Although the gap has closed over time (see Table 5-1), African Americans, Hispanics, and Native Americans lag behind whites. Because this result seems odd, it sometimes leads to thoughtless conclusions. After all, many people can point to their own relatives (Germans, Irish, Italians, and others) who struggled and eventually succeeded in a new society. More recently, various Asian minorities have done relatively well, suggesting that the United States remains a land of opportunity. African

Americans have done less well. At the risk of unduly simplifying a very complex historical process, I offer the following hypothesis:

> *African Americans' relative lack of economic success in comparison to other immigrant groups reflects historical differences in (1) conditions of settlement, (2) prejudice and discrimination, and (3) affirmative action.*

Conditions of Settlement

This factor refers to the situation in a group's homeland and the United States at the time of immigration (Smith, 1987).

The first condition was the circumstances under which immigration occurred. That is, some groups came to these shores voluntarily while others arrived involuntarily and remained as slaves. Voluntary immigrants responded to changing conditions in their homeland. For example, the German and Irish people who settled in the Midwest from 1820 to 1840 had been driven off land they had occupied for generations. This was a fairly typical experience. Other immigrants, already urban, had skills or trades in demand in the United States. In fact, U.S. companies actively recruited immigrants. In all cases, the motive for leaving was the promise of a better life. With the passage of generations, many of these people became successful. In contrast, African people were taken from their homes to this continent involuntarily as forced (often skilled) labor. Slavery produced profit—for others. Plantation owners, of course, gained directly. But northern ship owners, bankers, and others, also benefited from slavery. Forced labor was essential to the early development of capitalism. Generations passed during which enslaved people could not take advantage of the opportunities available to others.[4]

The second condition of settlement was the opportunity presented by the geographical size of the North American land mass. Europeans saw themselves as inheriting an open continent. (The existence of Native American people was never seen as more than inconvenient.) As a result, it seemed possible to accommodate many white groups as the frontier moved westward. Slaves could not take advantage of this situation.

The third condition of settlement was the opportunity presented by **industrialization.** Recall that the term refers to the transformation of the economy by the substitution of new forms of energy for muscle power. Early in the nineteenth century, people with basic skills were needed: stone masons, bricklayers, loggers, carpenters, and the like. Later on, the ability to operate (or learn to operate) machines became important. Moreover, throughout this period, opportunities for merchants and traders grew expo-

---

[4]Many African slaves were imported precisely because they possessed needed skills. They were multilingual, experienced in agricultural production, or possessed craft skills. For example, in *African Americans at Mars Bluff, South Carolina,* Amelia Wallace Vernon showed that English-born planters knew nothing about growing rice; hence, Africans with this knowledge were brought in to perform this task (1993). In *Slave Counterpoint: Black Culture in the Eighteenth Century Chesapeake and Lowcountry,* Philip D. Morgan described how the character of slavery and race relations developed over time, and how Africans struggled to preserve both a degree of personal independence and the survival of African cultures (1998). Vernon showed that they were surprisingly successful in that some of these cultural traditions endure today, despite centuries of oppression.

nentially. In short, the economy was expanding, the occupational structure was being transformed, and millions of new arrivals benefited. Slaves did not.

In the years after the Civil War, immigrants from Russia, Scandinavia, Italy, and other places came here. The frontier was wide open and many immigrants built farms on the prairie. Others settled in cities and found economic niches suitable for their skills. In the South, however, President Andrew Johnson pardoned ex-Confederate soldiers and allowed them to legally reclaim their land. They used the law to convert most of the former slaves into sharecroppers and trap them in a system of debt peonage (Smith, 1987). A few years later, white southerners imposed Jim Crow laws in order to institutionalize discrimination in the South, where most African Americans still lived (Woodward, 1966). This process effectively prevented freedom for another century.

Although this description is sketchy, it does suggest that the conditions of settlement encountered by various white ethnic groups were relatively advantageous. Over time, these differences led to assimilation and group success for whites. In comparison, African Americans were relatively disadvantaged.

Prejudice and Discrimination

People in every society tend to discriminate against those who are different. Furthermore, the more different, the greater the discrimination. Feelings of prejudice often underlie such unequal treatment. The nineteenth century United States, for example, was viciously anti-Catholic in outlook. There is little doubt that this prejudice led to discrimination. Yet a continuum of desirability clearly existed during this period (Lieberson, 1980). Native whites, the majority of the population, were of northern European ancestry and tended to rank immigrants from these nations as the most desirable. Next came central and southern Europeans, most of whom were Catholic. The Japanese and Chinese occupied a third rank. Deep-seated racial prejudice meant that the United States reacted against even small numbers of Asian immigrants. In 1924, after restrictions effectively cut off immigration, fewer than 150,000 persons of Japanese ancestry lived in this country. The Asian population of the United States remains very low even today. Finally, African Americans fell into the lowest rank, suffering more prejudice and discrimination than any other group (except Native Americans). The data on residential segregation and infant mortality described earlier merely suggest the difficulties faced by the former slaves and their descendants.

The southern and central Europeans were not so different from those already here, mainly the English. They shared a common culture and often were not physically identifiable. As a result, they could melt into the new society, changing their name, dress, accent, and the like. Moreover, their immigration constituted a response to economic opportunity. Some returned to their homeland when their lives in this country proved too harsh. Their home governments could (and sometimes did) pressure the United States not to discriminate. These governments also encouraged immigration to the United States and provided assistance to migrants after their arrival. Despite anti-Catholic sentiment, such factors reduced prejudice and discrimination directed at southern and central European immigrants.

In contrast, newly "freed" African Americans remained concentrated in the South, especially in rural areas. They were visible due to skin color and came from cultures that were devalued. Their "freedom" was not a response to economic opportunity, and, given colonization of the African continent, no home government existed to protect them. While their freedom might have meant economic opportunity in the North, this possibility went unrealized (NACCD, 1968, pp. 143–44).

> *Had it not been for racial discrimination, the North might well have recruited southern Negroes after the Civil War to provide labor for building the burgeoning urban-industrial economy. Instead, northern employers looked to Europe for their sources of unskilled labor.... European immigrants, too, suffered from discrimination, but never was it so pervasive. The prejudice against color in America has formed a bar to advancement unlike any other.*

Finally, hostility toward and unequal treatment of African Americans also influenced the nature and quality of education made available to them.

In making this comparison between European immigrants and African Americans, I do not mean to imply that the former's assimilation was easy; it is never easy to start over in a new society. I do mean to suggest, however, that assimilation of southern and central European immigrants was easier because they endured less prejudice and discrimination. Until very recently, African Americans had to cope with pervasive hostility and unequal treatment that was built into both U.S. custom and law. These factors prevented freedom. It is very difficult for people to be occupationally successful when they are denied civil rights. Although manifestations of prejudice and discrimination tend to be covert today, they continue to inhibit mobility. Historically, the problems of prejudice and discrimination have been made worse by government policy.

Affirmative Action

As noted in Chapter 3, **affirmative action** refers to public policies giving advantages to members of one group over others. Such policies have become controversial in recent years, mainly because many whites believe it is unfair to do more than guarantee civil rights to the entire population. Policies designed to ensure opportunity by requiring integrated education or the hiring of minority persons (and women) seem discriminatory. They are. It would be nice to have a color blind society, but we do not. Although this problem can be seen in terms of fairness or morality, the underlying political issue is, as always, power. Racial and ethnic relations always involve obtaining *A Piece of the Pie,* as Stanley Lieberson titled his study of this topic (1980). When society is seen as a pie to be consumed, the referent is a metaphor for the distribution of valued goods in the society: jobs, land, education, wealth, prestige, power, and the like. People are willing to fight, to discriminate, to use the law in order to obtain (or retain) their "fair" share. "Fair," of course, depends on the observer. Most groups do not diet; they desire a bigger rather than smaller piece of the pie. So the question becomes who is going to divide it up. In this section, I briefly describe how government has responded to racial and ethnic groups over time. In so doing, I hope to place the problem of affirmative action into perspective.[5]

---

[5]The metaphor is also, of course, a way of restating Gerhard Lenski's finding that in every society power determines the distribution of surplus goods and services (see Chapter 1).

One piece of the pie is land. I mentioned earlier that German immigrants settled in the Midwest. This location was not accidental. The Land Act of 1820 provided them some pieces of the pie. Immigrants could obtain 80 acres of land on credit, with payoffs at $1.25 to $2.00 per acre. Such prices made the land essentially free. After the Civil War, the federal government wished to open up the area west of the Mississippi River. Accordingly, it subsidized railroad expansion and passed the Homestead Act of 1862, among other policies. Scandinavian immigrants, like many others, settled throughout the Plains States under terms that allowed anyone who farmed 160 acres for five years to purchase them for $10. Again, such prices meant that the land was given away. Coupled with access to eastern markets via the railroads, the Scandinavians worked hard for a piece of the pie. This is another way of describing affirmative action, of course—the provision of opportunity for white immigrants.

In comparison, newly freed African Americans were promised 40 acres and a mule in the aftermath of the Civil War. In fact, under an executive order by General William Tecumseh Sherman, nearly a half-million acres were divided into 40-acre plots and, along with mules, horses, and food, were turned over to former slaves. In 1869, however, President Andrew Johnson rescinded the order and pardoned former Confederate officers. Reconstruction meant that freedom was short-lived. But if this commitment of land and the means to farm it had been kept, as J. Owens Smith suggested in *The Politics of Racial Inequality,* millions of second- and third-generation freed African Americans would have been upwardly mobile (1987). Like the Germans and Scandinavians, they would have worked hard to possess part of the pie. Instead, former Confederates reclaimed their lands and kept "freed" slaves in their place. Denied opportunity, African Americans found success difficult.

Another piece of the pie is access to education. In 1862, Congress passed the Morrill Act, which funded land grant colleges in every state. According to Smith, the federal government spent more than $250 million (in the nineteenth century!) under the principle that "every citizen is entitled to receive educational aid from the government" (1987, p. 115). The idea was that the children of farmers should be able to go to college. Yet this massive outlay of money did not go to "every citizen." In fact, it was directed at whites, especially in the South. The University of Florida, where I teach, did not admit a single African American student until 1969. Instead, a few African American colleges were established, largely due to the efforts of private philanthropic organizations. Donated by whites, receipt of the little money available depended on accepting a philosophy of "racial adjustment." (This was a euphemism for knowing one's place.) In 1890, the second Morrill Act led to the creation of separate land grant institutions in the South, such as Florida A & M. Poorly funded, these institutions kept southern states eligible for federal support while providing poor quality education to very small numbers of African American youth.

This last statement summarizes the educational opportunities available to African Americans in the South from the time of the Civil War until recently. Lieberson reviewed the situation and offered the following hypothesis (1980, p. 149):

The greater the proportion of African American citizens in an area, the less educational opportunity available to them.

By less educational opportunity, he meant inequality in virtually every aspect of the public schools: funding, teacher training, supplies, length of the school year, and so forth. Just to give one example, there were simply few schools African Americans could attend. In 1911, only 64 high schools were available to African American students in the 18 southern states. There were none in Atlanta and other major cities. The situation was only a little better in the North. Thus, with regard to educational opportunity, the United States has a history of affirmative action—directed toward whites. Lieberson showed conclusively that in every context where African Americans have had a chance at education, they began catching up to whites.

A third piece of the pie is access to a job. Even without access to land or education, it is plausible to argue that the absence of job discrimination would have made upward mobility easier for African Americans. Discrimination was rampant, however. I noted previously that prejudice led northern employers to recruit European immigrants for factory work after the Civil War. These industrialists soon found African Americans to be useful as strikebreakers (Grossman, 1989). Although European immigrants also served as strikebreakers, in due time they joined the union movement. African Americans were excluded.

Partly as a result, when Congress passed a series of bills in the 1930s designed to allow workers to organize, African Americans were again excluded. The most important of these bills was the National Labor Relations Act (NLRA) of 1935. This initiative placed wages, hiring policies, layoffs, and other issues under the rule of law rather than the "goodwill" of an employer. In addition, worker organization under the NLRA facilitated other benefits: good credit rating, group insurance, group discounts, easier qualification for home loans, and the like. Working people were thus issued pieces of the pie. Although African American leaders lobbied for an antidiscrimination clause to be included in the NLRA, the New Deal coalition of President Franklin Roosevelt depended on the support of southern legislators. In addition, northern members of Congress did not care about discrimination. After all, few African Americans were allowed to vote. As a result, the NLRA left unions free to discriminate, which they did. Over the years, Smith argued, jobs were parceled out by whites to kin, friends, and others like themselves (1987). Here is an example: The National Apprenticeship Act of 1937 established government training programs under union control for skilled workers. This program covered not only blue-collar jobs but also training as occupational and physical therapists, librarians, medical technicians, and many others. In 1964, the same year the Civil Rights Act was passed, the federal government paid $4 million in job subsidies. Over nearly 30 years, virtually all the participants in this program were white. Once again, the historical pattern reveals affirmative action for whites. African Americans were left at the starting gate, as they had been a century before.

In sum, the answer to the question with which this section began is that more African Americans have not succeeded because structural impediments of U.S. society stacked the odds against them. Whites placed these limitations there. The few African Americans who succeeded overcame great obstacles in order to do so.

In describing affirmative action, Stanley Lieberson's metaphor of a piece of the pie has been used to illustrate how power affects which groups get a bigger share of the distribution of valued resources. Over time, whites have used public policy to provide opportunity for whites at the expense of African Americans. During the 1960s, however, and continuing for the last 30 years or so, the federal government developed policies designed (very imperfectly) to provide some opportunity for minority groups to increase their share of the pie, especially in terms of access to jobs and education. Such policies have been mildly effective; one example is the increase in the proportion of African, Hispanic, and Asian Americans in white-collar jobs. During the past few years, however, many whites have begun protesting that such policies are unfair, and this assertion is true. The protest reflects an underlying (albeit inchoate) goal: Whites want to retain their share of the pie.

Racial and Ethnic Stratification Today

In Chapter 1, I observed that racial and ethnic stratification constitutes one of three interrelated systems of ranking. In that context, however, I gave class a certain priority, arguing that *minority groups at every class level have fewer and less effective choices than do whites.* Although this argument cannot be tested here, it provides a way to understand racial and ethnic stratification today:

> *Racial and ethnic stratification reflects (1) the reproduction of the class structure and (2) institutionalized discrimination.*

Reproduction of the Class Structure

A great deal of racial and ethnic inequality occurs as the unwitting result of individuals acting normally to raise a family and seek success. As they do these things, people from each class use their resources in order to protect their lifestyle and pass it on to their children. This process can occur without anyone discriminating. The result, however, is the reproduction of the class structure—that is, its stability over time. Although much mobility occurs in this country, Chapter 3 showed that the mode is for occupational continuity across generations. Hence, parents employed in blue-collar jobs tend to have children who work in blue-collar jobs, while parents employed in white-collar jobs tend to have children who work in white-collar jobs. This continuity reflects class-related differences in opportunity. The Monopoly vignette in Chapter 3 illustrated this process. Think about the data presented here in terms of the vignette. At every class level, different levels of infant mortality mean not only that fewer minority children survive, but also that those that do have fewer opportunities. At every class level, housing segregation means not only that minority children are isolated from whites, but also that they have fewer opportunities. Occupational and income differences have a similar impact. Precisely because they have less opportunity to succeed, the odds of occupational mobility are stacked against many minority children—simply by their class of origin.

Now perform a mental experiment, assuming for a moment that discrimination no longer exists. In such a context, the success of people—African American, Hispanic, Asian, Native American, or white—would simply reflect some combination of the class location from which they start along with their ability and skills (their achievement, in other words). But the legacy of past discrimination means that many minority group persons come from working-class and poor backgrounds. Hence, the tendency of the class structure to reproduce itself insures that race and ethnicity will continue to be a basis for stratification for many years to come. Although the assumption underlying this "experiment" is incorrect (since discrimination still exists), it provides a means for explaining how the class structure affects the current pattern of racial and ethnic inequality. Its impact is magnified by unequal treatment.

Institutionalized Discrimination

A great deal of inequality results from **institutionalized discrimination**—the unequal treatment of people with different physical or social characteristics—that is embedded in the social structure. In many cases, such unequal treatment occurs without awareness or intention; no one is trying to discriminate. My example involves the process of finding a job. Most people learn about jobs informally, by word of mouth (Corcoran et al., 1980). They rely on relatives and friends in their social networks as the primary source of information (Grieco, 1987; Morris, 1992). This pattern is most characteristic of blue-collar work openings, which tend to require fewer educational credentials as a condition of employment.

This manner of learning about jobs has enormous implications, mainly because whites, African Americans, Hispanics, Asians, and Native Americans usually partici-pate in different social networks. For example, whites tend to work at different jobs than do Hispanics and African Americans. Their children go to different schools. They live in different neighborhoods. They also attend different churches (Beeghley et al., 1981; GP, 1997a, p. 13). These variations identify the boundaries of the social networks in which members of each group participate. The presence of such boundaries indicates how the social structure affects interaction patterns: contact, friendship formation, and the like. The members of each group lead separate lives. As a result, individual whites, African Americans, Hispanics, Asians, and Native Americans tell their relatives and friends about different job opportunities. Hence, even in the absence of prejudice, this process produces a high level of occupational segregation—and, hence, inequality.

Here is a hypothesis that follows from the fact that most people hear about jobs through word of mouth:

> *At each skill level, the more members of a minority group currently employed in an organization, the greater the number of their job applicants and the greater the rate at which they will be hired.*

Assuming for a moment this hypothesis is correct (it should be tested), part of the reason lies in whom one knows. As indicated, people helping a relative or a friend obtain a job are not trying to discriminate. An additional reason why the hypothesis may be accurate is that other factors also influence whether people obtain jobs. For example, having heard about a job, people must then actually apply for it, undergo some type of screening by a potential employer, and get hired. These procedures allow ample opportunity for prejudice to lead to discrimination. They suggest why the work force in many organizations remains segregated.

Sometimes structural factors and individual motives combine to produce discrimination. My example is the racial/ethnic ratio on the job. The term refers to the proportion of African Americans, Hispanics, Asians, or Native Americans in relationship to whites. For example, in a social context where about equal proportions of minority group members and whites work in an organization, it is difficult to discriminate in hiring or promotion. This is partly because potential victims have allies. In addition, the social context is likely to display egalitarian norms buttressed by policies prohibiting discrimination. These structural characteristics influence individuals, making them less able to act on their prejudices (Blanchard et al., 1991). Conversely, it becomes easier to discriminate in hiring and promotion in an organizational context where the racial/ethnic ratio is skewed and whites hold the vast majority of jobs. This is partly because victims do not have allies. In addition, the social context is unlikely to display egalitarian norms or antidiscrimination policies. In such situations, even persons of good will tend not to take affirmative action seriously and those with prejudicial motives can act. As a result, the hiring and advancement of minority group persons becomes difficult.

The way in which a skewed racial/ethnic ratio on the job influences success can be illustrated by applying Rosabeth Moss Kanter's ideas to this topic (1978). As described in Chapter 4, she focused on how differences in the gender ratio affect the ability of women to advance in a corporate hierarchy. She argued that when only a few women work in a competitive environment dominated by men, occupational success is more difficult because the women's job performance is highly visible, boundaries separating the two genders coalesce, and assimilation into the work group is often on men's terms. It seems to me that the situation for Hispanics, African Americans, Asians, and Native Americans is analogous and that the hypothesis can also be applied to their experiences in similar contexts. Thus previously presented data show that the entry of minority group members into white-collar occupations is relatively recent and that few minority group members work in the professions. While no information about the number of Asians, African Americans, Hispanics, and Native Americans in management and executive positions was displayed, they often occupy entry-level positions. Hence, these persons tend to be treated as tokens, in Kanter's sense of the word; that is, they are seen as representatives of their category, all African Americans, all Hispanics, and the like. They become symbols rather than individuals. They often have trouble advancing, I would suggest, precisely because the structure of the work environment—the racial/ethnic ratio—stacks the odds against them. It provides a context in which discrimination can occur, and this is probably true regardless of how much ability people have or how hard they work. I should emphasize, however, that this hypothesis needs to be tested with data.

In any case, the continuation of racial and ethnic inequality in the United States today is not accidental. It reveals the impact of the reproduction of the class structure and institutionalized discrimination. These factors, in turn, reflect the conditions of settlement of various groups, the degree of prejudice and discrimination these groups endured over time, and the history of affirmative action directed toward white ethnic groups.

Alan Wolfe argued recently that the struggle for civil rights during the 1960s is really the story of how the United States became a modern—which is to say, class-based—nation. He pointed out that Dr. Martin Luther King, Jr. "had to overcome the determined resistance of terrorists without conscience, politicians without backbone, rivals without foresight, and an F.B.I. Director so malicious that he would stop at nothing to destroy a man who believed in justice" (1998, p. 12). Put more sociologically (but less evocatively), Dr. King and others strove to replace ascription with achievement as the basis for people's position in society. The task is far from complete. We still live with Jefferson's Dilemma.

Summary

The United States has always confronted a dilemma: freedom and equality for all versus freedom for some and slavery or discrimination for others. The historical dimensions of racial and ethnic inequality must be assessed in both absolute and relative terms. African Americans, Hispanics, Asians, and Native Americans were systematically denied civil rights throughout U.S. history until passage of civil rights laws in the 1960s. In other arenas, however, change has not been so great. Although significant absolute improvement has occurred, infant mortality rates of African Americans have always been about double those of whites. African American housing segregation has increased over the course of this century. Although data for Hispanics and Asians does not go back very far, they are much less segregated. Although occupational segregation has been the norm in the United States historically, increasing proportions of African Americans, Hispanics, Asians, and Native Americans are employed in white-collar jobs (Table 5-1). In the highest prestige positions, however, far less change has occurred.

Most western industrial nations are relatively homogeneous compared to the United States. The United Kingdom, however, displays a significant minority population. Comparing unemployment rates in the two nations shows that minority groups fare less well in both (Table 5-2).

The major consequence of racial and ethnic inequality discussed in this chapter was the creation of an underclass comprised of a large proportion of African Americans. This was an unintended result of passage of civil rights laws in the 1960s. Members of the underclass typically live in anomic settings and display a high level of alienation. Crime, drug abuse, and sexual acting out are common results. This is so regardless of race.

It was hypothesized that most discrimination against individuals occurs when people lack familiarity with others who are different and when members of different groups compete for scarce resources. Some whites who have not had much contact with members of minority groups tend to avoid them in public places, reject them in subtle but significant ways, harass and intimidate them, and subject them to violence in some form. Although discrimination in and by organizations is illegal, it is also easy. Some examples involved housing and hiring.

In order to understand why more African Americans have not succeeded, it is useful to examine historical variations in racial and ethnic group mobility. The key issues involve the conditions of settlement, patterns of prejudice and discrimination, and affirmative action. The conditions of settlement refer to voluntary versus involuntary migration, and the opportunities presented by the geographical size of the United States and industrialization. Prejudice and discrimination have always affected African Americans, Hispanics, Asians, and Native Americans more than whites. Affirmative action has always benefited whites more than any other group. At the structural level, the most important factors producing racial and ethnic inequality today are the reproduction of the class structure and institutionalized discrimination. The latter is not always intended, as illustrated by the process of learning about available jobs. Sometimes, however, structural factors, such as the race/ethnic ratio on the job, combine with covert individual discrimination.

Political Participation
and Power

Traditional democratic ideals assert that all citizens should participate equally and have equal influence on the political process. The term **pluralism** summarizes this ideal state of affairs. Pluralism embodies two overarching values. First, the competitors should act within the rules to influence public policy. Because such procedures are followed—as when citizens vote, representatives decide, and judges interpret—decisions about societal goals, priorities among goals, and the distribution of valued resources are accepted as legitimate by the people, even those whose interests are harmed. Make no mistake: All political decisions involve winners and losers. Second, access to the political arena should be open so that any person or group can compete for power. This injunction is the reason for the term *pluralist*. The idea is that everyone can vote, support candidates and causes, and lobby representatives. So the political process ought to display many competing individuals and groups. Such competition holds public officials accountable for their decisions. In this context, one in which today's losers may be tomorrow's winners, people accept political outcomes. Further, because everyone has multiple ties, as indicated by their religion, gender, race, ethnicity, occupation, community, and other affiliations, a balance of power exists among competitors. Thus, in a pluralist society no one group dominates because new coalitions are always forming (Dahl, 1967). When this "ideal" resembles reality, decisions are made and conflicts resolved without violence. The result is a stable society, a democracy. The key to such stability is widespread **political participation,** which refers to people's attempt at influencing either who gets elected or the appointments, policies, and laws passed by government (Conway, 1991, p. 3).[1]

Yet there is an inherent dilemma built into pluralism that, in practice, moves real societies—even democracies—rather far from the "ideal." **Power,** remember, is the ability to achieve goals, even if opposition occurs (Weber, 1920). Politics, like capitalism, is a competitive process; the point is to limit other participants' ability to achieve their goals. So it makes sense to suppose that those with the most resources would have the most power, as stated in the *Political Power Hypothesis* in Chapter 1:

> *The higher the social class, the greater the influence over access to valued resources in the society.*

But power is difficult to observe, especially with the methods normally used in the social sciences. One can only see its manifestations indirectly in terms of who decides what issues are important, who holds the key positions, and who has a say-so in the big decisions. These people usually comprise a relatively small aggregate.

In *Political Parties,* first published in 1911, Robert Michels recognized this fact by posing the "iron law of oligarchy." That is, in every society a small group of people, perhaps several thousand, dominate the political process and influence not only who benefits, but also the overall political agenda and the range of choices available to

---

[1]This portrayal of a pluralist society is an "ideal type," to use a phrase of Max Weber's (1920, p. 6). The strategy consists of setting up an example that is logically perfect and then assessing empirically (by observation) how actual occurrences differ from the "pure" construct. For further information, see Turner, Beeghley, and Powers, *The Emergence of Sociological Theory* (1998).

people. They have power. The basis for membership in the oligarchy is usually wealth, but other factors contribute as well: such as family background, group membership, institutional location. An elite always exists, simply because ordinary people cannot participate in governing decisions on a day-to-day basis.

So the issue in a democratic context is not the existence of elites with power; it is, rather, the degree to which decision makers are accountable to the public as a whole. Several observers have argued in recent years that U.S. democracy is threatened because accountability is low. For example, in *Who Will Tell the People,* William Greider asserted that we now have a "mock democracy" in which ordinary citizens are cut out of the decision-making process at the national level (1992). Voters, mainly the middle class, are provided just enough to keep them happy. In the meantime, partisans with money set the agenda for the nation behind the scenes and, hence, behind the backs of ordinary people. The result is a high level of inequality and the ever-present potential for unruliness. Whether this analysis is correct is something for you to decide.

Types of Political Participation

Voting

Democracy is usually taken to mean rule by the people, either directly or through their elected representatives. Outside of small groups (such as juries), direct democracy is impractical; so in most contexts democracy refers to representative government. Elections function simultaneously as a method for citizens to express their desires and to hold decision makers accountable. If a political system is to resemble the pluralist ideal, however, electoral procedures ought to maximize participation. One way to achieve this goal is to make voting as easy as possible. The United States, however, makes voting difficult because, unlike other nations, it requires individuals to register first. Once registered, people can vote on Election Day. But, as I will show in a few moments, satisfying this two-step requirement is more difficult for poor and working-class people, who vote at a much lower rate.

Although elections provide an important mechanism for holding decision makers accountable, they do not end the political process; they begin it. After all, people pursue their interests (they exercise power) as public issues are defined, policies considered, and laws implemented. Will decision makers listen to voters or to someone else?

Partisanship

The "someone else" refers to partisans, people who identify with, work for, and try to influence a party, candidate, or issue. During elections, the range of involvement can vary from casual to intense: wearing a button, doing volunteer work, and—most importantly—contributing money. Between elections, the main form of partisanship consists of **lobbying,** the attempt at influencing legislators or other decision makers in favor of (or against) a specific cause. Average voters sometimes lobby. They might, for example, telephone a member of the school board or write a note to their congressional representative. These contacts are taken very seriously by decision makers; they know that people who contact them in this way are especially likely to have voted and to vote again. Also, those who contact officeholders can then be solicited for campaign contributions at the next election. Contributions provide the lubricant for successful lobbying. Individuals and PACs (Political Action Committees) are effective to the extent they can either funnel money to a person's campaign fund or provide income that appears legitimate. This is true for both self-styled liberals and conservatives. Thus, understanding the twin issues of accountability and power in a democracy requires recognizing the role of money in elections.

Both voting and partisanship involve "working within the system" or, perhaps, "working the system." No matter which interpretation you prefer, participation in these ways means that people follow the rules. They win and lose, and go on to fight other battles—without disruption, without violence. Yet a tension exists between these types of participation: voting versus money. Everyone can vote—if they are registered. Only a few can contribute money to campaigns. The question in a democracy is this: To what degree are decision makers accountable to voters or contributors? Some people, however, are left out altogether, and I want to pause to say a few words about them.

Unruliness

Voting and partisanship are important because they lead to benefits: better city services, tax breaks, jobs, and so forth. Voting and partisanship also lead to a sense of power. Voters and campaign contributors do not take to the streets when they become dissatisfied. They elect a new mayor, senator, or president to represent their interests. Those who neither vote nor contribute are left out. They often feel powerless (the jargon term is **alienated**), and this feeling is realistic. When they become angry, as periodically happens, they become unruly—sometimes in violent and destructive ways. During the 1960s, poor people and racial and ethnic minorities took to the streets repeatedly (Gamson, 1975; Piven & Cloward, 1977). Similar events have occurred more recently in Los Angeles, Miami, and other cities (SA, 1994). The obvious interpretation is to see such episodes as riots. From this point of view, the perpetrators are criminals, who should be prosecuted for vandalism, mugging, even murder. While there is merit to this angle of vision, a less obvious interpretation also exists: One can see anger in the streets as rebellions on the part of oppressed people. They are political acts by individuals for whom few options exist. From this rather different angle of vision, violence and other forms of unruliness are not merely protests, they constitute claims to be considered (Coser, 1967, p. 84). But collective violence only occurs under conditions of extreme frustration; it is a form of political participation, a signal to those with power (who are generally insensitive) from those left out of the system. Unruliness, then, constitutes the political underbelly of a democratic system. It is ignored with peril.

The Rate of Voting

Voting is the primal democratic act; it is the first and most important indicator of a democratic society. All other modes of participation are adjuncts to this act. After all, partisans may contribute money to influence electoral campaigns and gain access to the winners. Furthermore, based on their access, they may lobby for the creation of laws beneficial to themselves (and against those that would harm them). But even if partisans are successful, elected representatives must ultimately appeal to ordinary citizens. Voters, then, can hold decision makers accountable—at least in principle. Alas, the data show that many citizens do not vote.

Voting in the United States

Historically, the number and characteristics of citizens eligible to vote has steadily expanded. As explained in Chapters 4 and 5, voting was restricted to white male property owners over age 21 when the Constitution was adopted. Over the years, however, all adults have gained the ability to participate, regardless of property owner-ship, immigrant status, race, or gender. This process occurred mainly because those left out of the democratic process fought to be included (Gamson, 1975; Williams, 1977). There is a lesson here: The extension of the franchise resulted from unruly (and often illegal) activities—riots, demonstrations, and other forms of protest—by those ex-cluded from a presumably pluralist system. Such persons had no other option. The outcome has been, at least in principle, a more truly democratic society.

But that principle is not fully realized today. While all adults are eligible to vote, relatively few do. This fact is revealed by Figure 6-1, which displays the rate of voting in presidential elections from 1876–1996. In the 1996 election (see the far right of the figure), only 49 percent of the adult population voted. Yet the figure shows that turnout has not always been this low. In fact, among those eligible, there was a time when most people voted; almost 80 percent of all eligible citizens took part in presidential elec-tions during the last quarter of the nineteenth century. Moreover, in the nonsouthern and most densely populated states, turnouts during the years 1874–1896 were much higher than the rates displayed in the figure. For example, average turnouts were 93 percent in Indiana, 92 percent in New Jersey and Ohio, 89 percent in New York, 83 percent in Pennsylvania (Burnham, 1980). In nonpresidential election years during this period, these same states had average turnouts of 84 percent in Indiana, 77 percent in New Jersey and Ohio, 68 percent in New York, and 71 percent in Pennsylvania. It thus appears that nearly all eligible citizens voted in those states where most of the popula-tion lived.

This, then, is the first important point: The current low rate of voting is not inevitable. It cannot be explained away as due to the lack of motivation by poor and working-class persons. Some try; they argue that those who do not vote must be satisfied with public policy (for a review, see Conway, 1991, p. 2). This argument, a sort of "politics of happiness," implies that poor and working-class people must be the most satisfied of all citizens, since they vote at the lowest rates (Eulau, 1966). This interpretation is not only absurd, it masks a hidden reality: The middle class and rich dominate the political process in the United States and receive most of the benefits.

A qualifying note. During the late nineteenth century, women and young adults could not vote by law. Moreover, although African Americans gained the franchise after the Civil War, it was taken from them by whites' imposition of Jim Crow laws

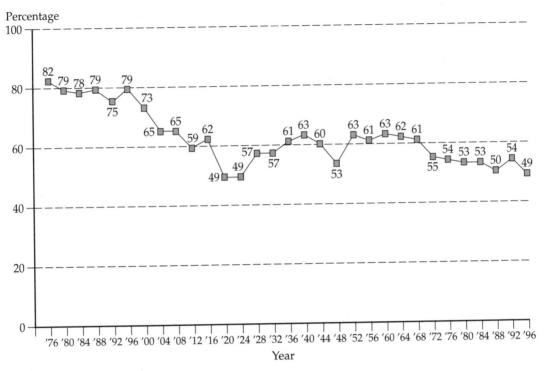

FIGURE 6-1   Rate of Voting in U.S. Presidential Elections, 1876–1996

Sources: USBC (1975, p. 1071; 1997b, p. 289).

during the 1880s (Woodward, 1966). So the argument that low rates of voting can be avoided should be interpreted with caution for now.

Figure 6-1 shows that turnout began dropping with the presidential election of 1900. As I will explain later, laws requiring registration were introduced in every state during this period. Participation rates stabilized at around 65 percent until the election of 1920, the first time women had the franchise. Voting returned to the 60 percent level in subsequent elections (with the exception of 1948) and stayed there until the election of 1972, when it declined once more to around 50 to 55 percent.

Since just under half of all adults in the United States now vote, the necessary majority to choose the president and other public officials elected at the same time is about one-quarter of the electorate (half of 50 percent). Turnout during off-year elections is even less; for example, only 39 percent of the population voted in House of Representative races in 1994 (USBC, 1997b, p. 289). Although part of the reason for low turnouts in off-years is the large number of relatively uncontested House seats, the more important reason (as I will show later) has to do with registration laws and other structural factors. These low voting rates in off-year elections mean that many decision makers—senators, representatives, governors, state legislators, and local officials—are selected by only 20 percent (or less) of all eligible citizens (half of 39 percent). Lower voting rates mean that a relatively small proportion of the population chooses elected public officials.

Because the United States makes voting contingent on registration, it is important to examine the relationship between them. Table 6-1 displays the proportion by income of all adults who reported they registered and voted. Please look down columns (2) and (3). Note that as people's family income increases, the percent reporting that they registered and voted increases as well. Now look down column (4). While the percentage of those registered who reported voting rises with income, the rate of increase is not nearly so great as in the other columns. If those with the very lowest family incomes are excluded (less than $9,999), these data reveal that 75–90 percent of those registered also vote at all income levels.

The fact that nearly all registered persons vote has been true for many years. For example, in the last eight presidential elections, the proportion of those registered who voted has ranged from 83 to 91 percent (USBC, 1998h, p. 1). These data, along with the table, lead to the second point you should remember: The turnout rate among those registered resembles that which existed in the nineteenth century. The level of voting among registered poor and working-class persons is similar to those with higher incomes. So, low rates of voting can be avoided.

Voting in Other Nations

The pattern of electoral participation is much different in other industrial societies. In Western Europe as a whole, turnout levels above 70 percent are common. This fact is

TABLE 6-1   Participation in the 1996 U.S. Presidential Election by Family Income

(1)	(2)	(3)	(4)
Family Income	Percent Registered	Percent Voted	Percent Registered Who Voted
All Incomes	**74%**	**64%**	**84%**
< $9,999	48%	33%	69%
$10,000–14,999	53	40	75
$15,000–24,999	58	46	79
$25,000–34,999	65	52	80
$35,000–49,999	71	59	83
$50,000–74,999	77	67	87
> $75,000	82	74	90
Percent Difference Lowest to Highest	**34%**	**41%**	**21%**

Source: USBC (1998f, p. 6).

illustrated by voting turnout in recent elections for the five nations shown here (UN, 1997, p. 195):[2]

Sweden	1994	87%
Germany	1998	82%
United Kingdom	1997	71%
Canada	1994	67%
United States	1996	49%

As turnout levels show, other Western democracies have far higher levels of electoral participation. Moreover, in most of these nations, the lower classes have voting levels nearly as high as the middle class and rich. For example, the following data display turnout in the 1994 Swedish parliamentary elections by family income in Swedish Crowns (SC, 1996, p. 395):

≤ 59,000	88%
60,000–109,000	88
110,000–159,000	91
160,000–209,000	96
≥ $210,000	95

They reveal that nearly everyone votes and that turnout hardly varies by class in Sweden, with only an 8 percent difference in turnout between the poor and rich. This variation is far less than occurs in the United States, which displays a 41 percent variation (see column (3) of Table 6-1). In fact, class differences in Swedish voting resemble those found in the United States among people who are registered (see column (4) of Table 6-1). Thus, the third point you should remember is that international data show turnouts resembling both the level of voting seen in this country in the late nineteenth century and the percent of registrants who vote. Neither low rates of participation nor vast differences by social class are inevitable.

It is wise to be cautious about these data, especially for the United States in the nineteenth century. Some scholars have argued that turnouts during this period may be artificially high because of vote fraud (Converse, 1972). In my judgment, however, the data are reasonably accurate, at least with regard to the total rate of participation (Burnham, 1980). The problem of fraud during elections of this period is a separate issue. All observers agree that most elections were controversial and competitive— usually decided by small margins. So high rates of participation make sense. Moreover, as shown above, the levels of voter turnout reported in Figure 6-1 for the late nineteenth century United States are consonant with the proportion of middle-class and rich people who vote today, the proportion of registered citizens who now vote, and European turnout rates. These similarities suggest that reported levels of participation in the last quarter of the nineteenth century are plausible.

[2]Turnout in the 1998 German elections is courtesy of the German consulate in Atlanta.

Most fraud during this period involved vote buying, voter intimidation, miscounting of votes, and the manipulation of small numbers of ballots in highly competitive elections (Argersinger, 1986; Allen & Allen, 1981). Thus, the nature of the ballot is extremely important. Prior to 1890, each party printed and distributed its own ballots, called "party strips" or "tickets," which listed all its candidates. These ballots were of varying size and color, which made it difficult to conceal one's preference as the ballot was dropped into the box. Voting during this period was raucous and public. Citizens selected one ticket, sometimes for a price, and turned it in—in full view of everyone gathered around the polling place. Adoption of the Australian ballot at the turn of the century changed this situation (Rusk, 1970). This type of ballot identifies all the nominees for office on one piece of paper and asks voters to mark their choices. It not only reduces the possibility of fraud but also makes it easier for people to vote a "split ticket"—that is, they can select candidates from both parties.

It should be mentioned that self-reports of registration and voting tend to be higher than the actual numbers recorded, which accounts for the variation in turnout reported in Figure 6-1 and Table 6-1 (Piven & Cloward, 1988). Despite this difference, the logic of the analysis remains accurate, and the interpretation offered here makes sense of the data.

But why do people vote? Well, partly as an act of patriotism. More importantly, however, they support candidates and causes that will protect their interests. In so doing, they want to hold decision makers accountable for the policies they enact. Since the data show that middle-class people dominate voting, it should not be surprising that public policy often caters to the interests of this group. Yet, as indicated earlier, money talks. And it affects public policy.

The Role of Money in Elections

To the ordinary voter, politics seems straightforward. Candidates present themselves in a campaign via television commercials, sound bites on the nightly news, public forums, and other venues. Based on their stands on the issues, people select the winners on election day. This pluralist-like view is accurate but incomplete. The real (but not always obvious) business of campaigns is conducted over the telephone, at cocktail parties, and at private meetings with wealthy contributors. The real business of politics is money. Politics and money are like a person and a shadow, inherently connected. Those with money have a source of power (the ability to achieve their goals) not available to ordinary voters. This fact means that those with money constitute another set of people to whom decision makers must be accountable. In order to see why money provides power, consider the cost of winning.

The Cost of Winning

Winning an election often depends as much on the quality of commercials as the quality of a candidate. This fact means that it costs so much money to be elected to public office that one must be wealthy or well-connected or both to conduct an effective campaign.

Listed below are the average amounts spent by the winner and loser, respectively, in congressional campaigns during the 1996 election (CRP, 1998):

	Winner	*Loser*
Senate	$4,700,000	$2,800,000
House of Representatives	$ 700,000	$ 300,000

These averages hide sharp variations in expenditures (CRP, 1998). Representative Newt Gingrich of Georgia, who spent $5,600,000 to retain his seat, ran the most expensive House campaign in 1996. Campaign expenses are usually much higher in Senate races because they are statewide. Senator Jesse Helms, who spent $14,600,000 to retain his seat, ran the most expensive Senate campaign in 1996. The principle that running for office costs a lot of money applies to campaigns at all levels. Whether one is trying to become a governor, state legislator, or city commissioner, the point is the same: It is necessary to pay for television and radio spots, staff salaries, transportation, and the myriad tasks that must be performed in a modern campaign. Money is essential to winning.

Money, Winning, and Reelection

Here is an empirical generalization:

The more money spent on a political campaign, the greater the odds of winning.

In order to illustrate this fact, please look at the gap between the amount spent by winners and losers in elections for the House of Representatives displayed above. In 1996, winners outspent losers by an average $400,000, or 67 percent. Most House races, in fact, are financial mismatches: The winner outspends the loser by more than ten-to-one (Makinson & Goldstein, 1994). This principle—that winners nearly always outspend losers—applies to elections at any level. And most winners are incumbents being reelected. In 1996, 94 percent of the members of the House of Representatives who ran for reelection won. The average percentage of incumbent reelection since 1960 is 93 percent. Similarly, 91 percent of senators running for reelection won. The average reelection rate in the Senate since 1960 is lower, 81 percent. Again, this principle—that incumbents usually win reelection—is true at other levels: city, county, and state. This finding is partly because incumbents have many natural advantages. Their name recognition is high; they provide services to their district or state; they receive regular news coverage; and they enjoy the congressional franking privilege, which allows them to mail "newsletters" and other items to constituents without paying postage. The most important reason for their reelection, however, is that incumbents have an established network of contributors, both individuals and Political Action Committees (PACs). Thus, except when challengers are already wealthy or have personal ties with people who can generate huge funds, they face a difficult race. Most lose.

Where Does the Money Come From?

Challengers lose because interested individuals and PACs support incumbents with money—lots of it. Here is a political axiom: Money is attracted to power like a moth to light. Although business-oriented PACs are usually most comfortable ideologically with Republicans, they made it a point to spread their largesse more or less equally to Republicans and Democrats when the latter controlled the Congress (CRP, 1998). Prior to the 1994 elections, for example, Democrats received 51 percent of all business PAC money. Then everything changed: The Republicans gained a majority in both the Senate and House in that election. Since that time, most business PAC money has gone to Republicans. The data below are campaign contributions during the 1996 election (CRP, 1998):

		% Democrat	% Republican
Business	$454,674,000	34%	66%
Labor	49,258,000	92	8
Ideological/Single Issue	29,346,000	49	51

Business contributions come from every industry imaginable: agriculture, communications, utilities, defense, finance, medical treatment, law, transportation, and many others. Labor contributions come from some of the same industries, at least where unions exist. Ideological contributions come from liberal and conservative groups, abortion groups (both sides), human rights groups, organizations interested in reducing or enhancing gun availability, and the like. The data reveal that business contributors overwhelm labor and ideology. At least 85 percent of PAC contributions to Congressional campaigns come from business interests.

I say "at least" because the data listed do not include other sources of money, most of which also comes from business interests. Under the law, candidates for federal office can spend as much as they can raise. (The Presidency is an exception.) Citizens can contribute $1,000 to a candidate per election (or $2,000 for, say, a primary and general election) along with $20,000 to a national political party and $5,000 to a Political Action Committee per calendar year. But these limits are easily evaded. Wealthy individuals wishing to give large amounts do so in the names of their spouse, children, and every relative and friend they have. Corporations direct higher echelon employees to do the same thing. In addition, unlimited contributions go to political parties, which use them for candidates' campaigns; this is called "soft money" or "sewer money," depending on whom you talk to. Finally, PACs can spend money directly in support of candidates but independently of their campaign organizations. Of course, informal coordination occurs. So, on top of the amounts already mentioned, millions more go to support candidates. All citizens are presumably equal in this process. Campaign contributions are a fundamental form of political "speech" and, hence, protected acts. Anyone can contribute. But who can afford to? The average poor family, with an income of less than $16,000 obviously cannot. The average working-class family, with an income of, say, $45,000 will sometimes contribute $100 to $200 to a union's political action committee. This is one way in which working-class people obtain some (but not much) clout in Washington. Even among the middle class, families with incomes of $80,000 per year, trying to establish long-term financial security, do not have a lot of money to give away. They generally do so through their professional organizations. Accountants, physicians, clinical psychologists, and even sociologists are organized and maintain lobbying operations in order to influence legislation. They do so via campaign contributions. In the end, however, only members of the "donor class" have the funds to give thousands of dollars to political campaigns. They are rich, white, and over age 45. More than half of large campaign contributors (defined here as giving more than $200) in 1996 had talked with their Congressional Representative since the election (Wilcox, 1998). This percentage is understated, of course; those who give big bucks can pick up the phone to talk to their Senators or Representatives, even the Congressional leadership. When was the last time you (or your parents) called Senator So-and-So on the telephone?

Two Examples

Two of the most powerful individuals in the United States are Dennis Hastert, a Republican, who is Speaker of the House, and Richard Gephardt, a Democrat, who is the Minority Leader. They provide convenient examples of the role of money in elections. Both men raised vast sums in order to be reelected in 1998: Gephardt, $5,000,000, and Hastert, $1,000,000 (CRP, 1998). Both vastly outspent their opponents—Gephardt by 16 to 1, Hastert by 39 to 1. Listed below are the top five sources of campaign contributions, with the amounts given:

Gephardt		*Hastert*	
Lawyers	$590,000	Finance	$182,000
Finance	490,000	Health	135,000
Misc. Business	373,000	Misc. Business	103,000
Labor	360,000	Communications	88,000
Health	293,000	Energy	81,000

Thus, like elected officials at every level, the leaders of the House of Representatives in both parties depend on large contributions to maintain themselves in office. The aggregation of these contributions by category (finance, etc.) leads to an important insight: PACs and individuals run in packs, like wolves on the hunt. And such animals want to be fed. Less polemically, people do not spend such large sums of money on a whim. Campaign contributions are investments and those making them expect results. They expect their interests to be protected. Where does that leave ordinary citizens? What about the public's interest?

Social Structure and Political Participation

The pluralist ideal is that people act within the rules to influence public policy and that everyone has access to the political arena. Data presented in this chapter, however, show that people in different classes participate at different rates and in different ways.

In effect, elected decision makers are held accountable by two constituencies: middle-class people with votes and rich people with cash. In this section, I present structural hypotheses about each.

The Structure of Voting

In a society that comes close to the pluralist ideal, in which everyone has access to the political arena and voters hold decision makers accountable for their decisions, money would have less impact. This is because parties and candidates would have to appeal to the interests of and mobilize all citizens in a context in which everyone votes. This process seems to occur in Western Europe. It does not occur in the United States. These differences reflect the structure of voting. Voting procedures are designed so that the poor are least able, while the middle class and rich are most able to participate. My hypothesis is:

> *The rate of voting in the United States reflects the impact of (1) Election Day, (2) registration requirements, (3) voting procedures, and (4) separation and frequency of elections.*[3]

Election Day

The day on which elections are held influences participation rates. In many Western European nations, as in Sweden and Germany, elections occur either on Sunday or a national holiday, which means leisure time is available to vote. This fact helps to explain why electoral participation rates are very high in these nations, usually between 80 percent and 90 percent, and class differences are minimal. In contrast, Election Day is a working day in England, Canada, and the United States; one result is that participation rates are significantly lower in these nations and class differences are greater. Voting on a working day is a structural barrier to participation. Those who overcome this obstacle in the greatest numbers have longer lunch hours, leave time built into their jobs, more physical energy at the end of the day, child care available, and a belief in their own efficacy. These traits, however, are class related, which is one reason why voting is also class related in the United States.

Registration Requirements

In Western European nations, the state automatically registers all citizens to vote, a fact that partly accounts for their high voting rates. Only in the United States are citizens responsible for their own registration. This requirement makes voting a two-stage process, each stage of which differs in place, kind, and time (Timpone, 1998).

In order to vote, people must go to two different places: a registration office well before Election Day and polling booth on Election Day. In the past, registration was often very difficult because it usually involved a trip to city hall or the county seat

---

[3]This section draws on material from my "Social Class and Political Participation: A Review and an Explanation" (Beeghley, 1986) and "Social Structure and Voting in the United States: A Historical and Comparative Analysis" (1992).

during working hours. Passage of the National Voter Registration Act (NVRA, or "motor voter" law) in 1992 partially changed that situation. Under the law, states are supposed to offer citizens the opportunity to register when they appear at driver's license and motor vehicle offices, welfare departments, military recruiting stations, and public libraries. Although citizens must still appear at these places during the day, the idea is to make registration easier. Prior to the 1996 election, however, only 16 states (including the District of Columbia) had actively implemented the law, and most of them already had some form of "motor voter" laws in place prior to passage of NVRA. Another 17 states passively implemented the law, which means that while people could register to vote at motor vehicle offices, they were not encouraged to do so. The additional 18 states simply refused to implement the law. Based on this array, an analysis of the initial impact of the NVRA indicates that the 16 states making registra- tion easiest also displayed significantly higher turnout in the 1996 election (Martinez & Hill, forthcoming). Note, however, that even though registration has become easier in some locales, it must still happen: Voting remains a two-step process. Registration still occurs in a place separate from the polling booth. This fact is important because even seemingly minor inconveniences, such as changing the distance to polling places, affects voter turnout (Timpone, 1998). Moreover, the motor voter law does nothing to increase citizen mobilization (about which more in a few moments).

Registration is also a different kind of act than casting a ballot. Voting is a political decision; and (especially if the ballot is simple) only requires that voters decide whose positions best reflects and protects their own interests. In contrast, registration is an administrative act, with which some people are uncomfortable. Those most likely to have these attitudes are working-class, poor persons, and those who are unfamiliar with professional settings.

Finally, a significant amount of time exists between registration deadlines and Election Day, which constitutes one of the strongest deterrents to registration (Teixeira, 1992). A century and a half ago, the French observer Alexis de Tocqueville noted the significance of this time difference: "As the election draws near, intrigues grow more active and agitation is more lively and wider spread" (1954, p. 135). He thought a presidential election is like a national crisis, which motivates people to get involved— by voting. But the average closing date for registration is three weeks prior to Election Day. This time span means that by the time motivating events occur, such as presiden- tial debates, the deadline for registration has already passed in many states. Indeed, when states with same-day or no registration are compared with other states, the former display about 10 percent higher levels of turnout (Highton, 1997).

The original rationale for imposing registration was to prevent electoral corruption. Yet there has been no fraud in Ohio or North Dakota, which have never required registration. Nor has it occurred in other Western nations. Finally, as noted earlier, it is likely that introducing the Australian ballot reduced corruption more than registration. If registration is unnecessary to prevent corruption, then such requirements must have a less obvious purpose. One guess is that registration assures middle-class dominance of this aspect of the political process.

The impact of Election Day and registration on voter turnout is displayed in Table 6-2, which shows that nations with the highest rates of voting maximize the opportunity

to vote by holding elections on a rest day and by not imposing registration requirements. Nations holding elections on working days have, in effect, imposed a barrier to
voting that some people cannot cross and, hence, they display lower levels of participation. The United States, which places the most restrictions on the opportunity to vote by
holding elections on a working day and requiring registration, reveals the lowest rate of
electoral participation. While these variables clearly influence voter turnout, I would
like to mention two additional factors that also seem plausible even though fewer data
are available.

Voting Procedures

Voting procedures probably influence participation rates. In the nineteenth century,
citizens simply dropped a preprinted ticket into the ballot box. While this practice made
voting easy, it prevented people from splitting their tickets; that is, choosing candidates
from various parties. As mentioned before, adoption of the Australian ballot made it
easier to vote a split ticket and reduced the possibility of fraud. Because citizens can
exercise more choice, this change seems inherently democratic, but it also requires
greater knowledge and reading skill. Even today, I would guess that the odds of citizens
voting a straight or split ticket varies by the nature of the ballot (which differs from state
to state). In addition, increasing the complexity of the ballot also increases the difficulty
of voting. More recently, another procedural change has been the introduction of voting
machines and computer punch cards. While these devices speed tabulating results, they
complicate electoral procedures still more. Although few data are available, they
probably inhibit electoral participation rates among those who are less sophisticated,
especially the poor.

Separation and Frequency of Elections

The separation of local, state, and federal elections, together with their frequency, also
probably influence participation rates. People in the United States go to the polls for
different purposes in different elections and, partly as a result, participation rates are
very low and class differences are great. State and federal elections are generally
separated: Only 14 states ever schedule gubernatorial contests in presidential election
years (Jewell & Olson, 1978, p. 50). Similarly, local elections are usually held apart

TABLE 6-2   Rate of Voting and the Electoral Structure in Five Countries

Country	Rate of Voting	Election on Work Day	Registration
Sweden, 1994	91%	No	No
Germany, 1998	82%	No	No
United Kingdom, 1997	71%	Yes	No
Canada, 1994	69%	Yes	No
United States, 1996	49%	Yes	Yes

Source: UN (1997, p. 195).

from other contests: Only 17 percent of all cities larger than 25 thousand people hold elections concurrently with either state or federal campaigns (Karnig & Walter, 1977). Finally, many areas hold bond and special district elections at still different times. With so much diverse election activity, some people find it difficult to obtain information about candidates and issues, and thereby maintain an interest in voting. Those who are most capable and, in fact, cast ballots at the greatest rate, have access to more intellectually demanding media, have friends and colleagues who are interested in these various contests, belong to groups with a stake in the outcomes, and have the time and energy to vote. Such persons are overwhelmingly middle class and rich.

The separation of electoral contests means that people in the United States go to the polls often. In one study of six states, citizens voted twice a year between 1972 and 1976 (Boyd, 1981). While this number may not seem like much, frequent trips to the polls are more difficult for the poor and working class than the middle class and rich, especially in view of all the obstacles cited earlier. Furthermore, 19 states purge their rolls of nonvoters every two years (Wolfinger & Rosenstone, 1980), which means that citizens who focus on the "more important" federal elections will often have to reregister and, prior to so doing, will not have their interests represented at the state and local level. More of these persons are working class and poor than any other class.

In sum, while any individual can presumably go to the polls, the structure of voting means that middle-class and rich people dominate this form of participation. The poor and working class are least capable of voting on a working day, getting registered, coping with voting procedures, and overcoming the problem posed by separate and frequent elections. These facts exist externally to individuals, decisively influencing rates of participation. Thus, for those at the lower end of the stratification hierarchy, the political system may seem open but it is closed in fact.

The reason why it remains closed is depicted by Figure 6-2, which is a model of the impact of structural inhibitions on the ability to vote. As shown, such barriers reduce the rate of electoral participation by working-class and poor persons, producing a lower turnout. Over time, low rates of participation lead candidates to stress policies and support the interests of those who vote: middle-class and rich persons. In addition, and this fact is not displayed in the figure, these individuals engage in partisan activities at higher rates. In such a context, of course, lower levels of voting are reinforced. As a result, political parties and candidates lose interest in mobilizing the poor and working class; they neither contact nor spend much effort at involving those who tend to be nonvoters anyway. In this context, the figure shows that two interrelated consequences follow. First, since no one teaches working-class and poor people that their interests might be different from those of other classes and since working-class and poor persons do not become energized, they do not display unique orientations and attitudes, and they vote at lower rates. This fact leads candidates not to stress their interests or contact them. Second, low rates of voting combined with an unwillingness to mobilize the working class and poor (because there is no payoff in terms of votes) leads public officials, candidates, political parties, and middle-class voters to defend structural barriers to electoral participation. Fear of fraud, fear of "uninformed" voters, and an amorphous—perhaps unarticulated—sense of self-interest buttresses this position. The

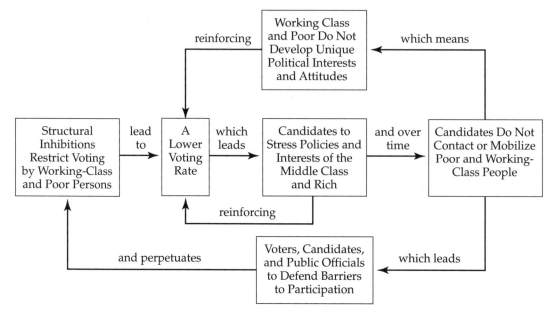

FIGURE 6-2   The Impact of Structural Factors on the Rate of Voting in the United States

Source: Beeghley (1992, p. 281).

long-term result, then, is that structural barriers to voting are maintained in a self-perpetuating process.[4]

This result has practical political implications. A low rate of voting, especially when concentrated among the working class and poor, means that decision makers do not have to appeal to the interests of nonparticipants. Instead, satisfying those who vote becomes the goal, which suggests one reason why middle-class people receive more benefits than do those with less prestige. But voting constitutes only one source of power. The rich have others.

The Structure of Partisanship

Anyone can be a partisan. The average person, however, votes (or does not vote) and lets it go at that. This is because most decisions made "inside the beltway," the freeway that surrounds Washington, D.C., seem remote to their lives. But the policies that result mean tens of millions of dollars to companies and large fortunes for individuals. It is a rarefied world, one where business and politics converge. The rich predominate in this world. They are active partisans, trying to influence legislation at every stage. The

[4]In *Why Americans Don't Vote,* Piven and Cloward described a similar model in prose form (1988, pp. 16–23).

structural basis for their partisanship is wealth; but other factors also exist that are correlated with wealth. My hypothesis is as follows:

The sources of partisanship are (1) money, (2) family background, and (3) institutional location.

In considering this hypothesis, recall the "iron law of oligarchy." Only a few people dominate the political process. How accountable are they when the structure of voting means that so few citizens exercise the franchise?

Money

The first and most important political resource in the United States is clearly money. You will not understand politics until you see it as a series of exchanges between candidates who need votes and those who have the money to pay for campaigns. It has become common for members of Congress to solicit a campaign contribution soon (sometimes immediately) after concluding a meeting with a lobbyist (Abramson, 1998). The overriding need for money means that elected officials pay attention to and respond to those with cash and to those who vote, in that order. Nonvoters are ignored, unless they become unruly. These priorities occur because of the correlation between level of campaign spending and winning elections.

Now campaign contributions are not necessarily bribes—nor are the vacations, payments for "speeches," or sky-box tickets to the Super Bowl and Kentucky Derby that members of Congress casually accept (Barlett & Steele, 1994, p. 213). One would have to be cynical to see them in this way. . . . Rather, what contributors and gift givers say they are "purchasing" with their monetary support is access, the ability to make their case, to be heard in the policy-making and rule development process. Thus, since rich people contribute disproportionately, they have more access to decision makers, more ability to have their interests get a hearing. This is how power works. The empirical generalization is:

The higher the social class and the greater the campaign contribution, the greater the access to public officials.

Access means influence. At every stage of the legislative, rule-making, and rule-enforcing process, the rich have more impact than any other class. A simple thought-experiment can illustrate why: Remember the costs of winning described earlier and imagine yourself as a member of Congress considering legislation to deny corporations the ability to deduct debt from their taxes. This issue is important, as will be described in Chapter 7, because it would inhibit companies from using debt to take over other companies; the result of such takeovers is often economically destructive and serves only to enrich the financiers engineering the deals. Suppose your secretary tells you that two telephone calls have come in at once; one is from an ordinary constituent and the other from a wealthy contributor. Which call would you take? And whose position would be most persuasive to you? This logic is why public policy generally favors the interests of those contributing to campaigns: the rich.

It should be noted that campaign contributions constitute only one way lobbyists (whether individuals or PAC representatives) influence legislators. Decision makers often rely on lobbyists for information, since in many cases they are experts in the field, capable of explaining complex and difficult subjects clearly. Lobbyists also court public officials with gifts, honoraria for "speeches," and personal favors (for example, tickets to special events). These gestures make legislators and lobbyists friends who are obligated to one another. Further, on specific issues, lobbyists can often generate "grass roots" support for their positions by having ordinary citizens write, telephone, and visit legislators (Mitchell, 1998). These contacts work because members of Congress (and decision makers at every level) want to please their constituents, especially those who are likely to vote. Finally, lobbyists often come from similar backgrounds and share personal associations and values with legislators. In fact, they are often former colleagues (Barlett & Steele, 1994). At least 128 former members of Congress are registered lobbyists, as are countless more former Congressional staffers (Mitchell,1998). Such similarities make them intellectually and psychologically compatible with one another, easing talk. For these reasons, then, the rich often have access to policy makers. Recall that many donors report talking to their Congressional representatives (Wilcox, 1998).

Family Background

A second source of partisanship is family background (Davidson, 1995). Thus, while dairy farmers and physicians form PACs and often influence legislation by means of campaign contributions and lobbying, their impact is rather specialized. In contrast, social ties stemming from family background give many wealthy people far-reaching political influence. These connections are reflected in the exclusive prep schools they attend, the exclusive fraternities and (to a lessor degree) sororities they belong to, and the private clubs they join (Domhoff, 1970, 1974; Ingham, 1978). These groups not only provide an informal context in which business deals are made, but also serve as forums for political discussions with decision makers. The poor, along with the working class and middle class, are systematically excluded from such groups. In general, the rich often come from a family background similar to that of decision makers and this fact, combined with their financial resources, allows them access.

Institutional Location

In addition to money and family background, a third source of partisanship is institutional location. In this context, the term "institutional location" refers to one's job, but not just any old job. Rich people have their interests represented simply because they occupy positions of power in the United States. For example, Dye identified about 7,300 elite positions in the United States (1983). Approximately 4,300 of this total are in the corporate sector, comprising the heads and boards of directors of large corporations; another 2,700 are in the "public interest" sector, comprising the owners and heads of mass media companies, philanthropic foundations, law firms, and civic organizations; and 300 are in the governmental sector, comprising the highest elected and appointed officials in the United States. Dye argued that the people occupying these elite roles are atypical of the U.S. population; that is, they are predominantly white, male, and rich or upper-middle class in origin—just like the donors described earlier. Ordinary people do not perform these roles. Those few who do enjoy access and influence.

In sum, money and status (in the form of family background and institutional location) count. Those who possess these traits have access to decision makers; and those with access can often make their case. The strategies used are very simple, the results perverse.

Money and Anomie

Here is a common scenario on Capitol Hill in Washington (or in your state capitol or city hall). A serious problem is identified. Various ways of dealing with the issue are debated. Instead of adopting the best alternative, however, the "solution" passed actually protects the interests of those contributing to Congressional campaigns. Lawmakers, of course, describe the act as a reform and stress that it is in the public interest. This is a veil. Politics is never about finding the "best" solution to a problem. Politics is about finding the answer that can be passed by a legislative body. In figuring out what can pass the House and Senate (or your legislature or city commission), one of the oldest sayings in politics should be kept in mind: "You gotta sleep with them who brung ya." In most cases, "them who brung ya" are those who supplied the cash for political campaigns.

For example, ordinary citizens become sick because of money contributed to political campaigns (PC, 1998). I know this statement is incendiary, but consider: Every year about 20,000 people eat contaminated food and are poisoned by E. Coli bacteria. Some die. Government regulatory efforts have been underfinanced and ineffective for years. It is probably not accidental that the food industry has given out more than $41,000,000 in campaign contributions over the last decade. This money was not given on a whim or as an act of altruism; it was an investment designed to yield greater profits. A similar process occurs with the cost of medical treatment, medicine, student loan interest rates (ever wonder why they are higher than mortgage rates?), phone rates, television cable costs, and many other issues. Campaign contributions affect ordinary citizens' daily lives and enrich those who give them.

Campaign contributions also affect the lifestyle of the rich. In *America: Who Really Pays the Taxes,* Barlett and Steele pose a dilemma: You want to avoid paying taxes—legally (1994, p. 213). What do you do? To whom do you turn? Well, if you have to ask, then you will likely have to pay your bill in full. On the other hand, if you are rich and knowledgeable in the ways of Washington, the strategy is very simple. First, you contribute large amounts of money to the campaign war-chest of your Representative and Senator for the next election. Better yet, contribute to many Representatives' and Senators' campaigns. Second, you hold testimonial dinners for them, soliciting contributions from others in the process. Third, you organize a symposium on a topic of interest and invite them to speak at it, for an honorarium of course. It would help, by the way, if this event occurred on a Caribbean island in the middle of February. (This is not a fanciful example.) Finally, and most important, you hire as lobbyists people who have experience writing tax laws and know current members of Congress. This would include former members, former congressional staffers, and former employees of the Treasury Department. As noted earlier, there is often a revolving door that goes back and forth between government work and lobbying, and government work and related private sector employment. With luck, this strategy will result in what Barlett and Steele called a "designer tax bill." Two examples follow.

1. Some designer tax bills go to corporations and their stockholders. Attempts at changing the so-called Tax Reform Act of 1976 illustrate this process. Under this statute, companies manufacturing products in Puerto Rico can take the resulting profits tax free. This tax expenditure was designed to create jobs on the island.[5] It turned out, however, to be "inefficient." In 1985, for example, the average job created by these companies paid wages of about $14,000 while the average corporate tax break per job was $22,000. In fact, 14 corporations received more than $100,000 per job created. According to Barlett and Steele, this section of the tax code cost the government (that is, taxpayers) $3.2 billion between 1985 and 1990 (1994, p. 242). Even this figure understates the total taxpayers lost because companies wrote off the cost of product development against U.S. tax returns, then produced the product in Puerto Rico, claiming the profits tax free. Although Congress considered repealing this tax expenditure in both 1986 and 1993, it declined after an avalanche of lobbyists persuaded members that the "common good" required it. (The veil again.) This lobbying was accompanied, of course, by campaign contributions and the other strategies mentioned above. The result provides a good example of how power works. Although the fight over this issue was probably reported in the media, it is relatively arcane to ordinary people, which meant that little opposition existed. The result also provides a good example of who benefits. While this tax break goes to corporations, stock ownership is very concentrated; the richest 10 percent of the population owns 85 percent of all corporate stock (see Chapter 7). So the rich are the prime beneficiaries of such public policies.

2. Other designer tax bills go directly to (rich) individuals. Barlett and Steele provided several examples, among them is the following section of the Miscellaneous Revenue act of 1988 (1994, p. 221): "(7) Special Rule.—In the case of the rehabilitation of the Willard Hotel in Washington, DC, section 205(c)(1)(B)(ii) of the Tax Equity and Fiscal Responsibility Act of 1982 shall be applied by substituting '1987' for '1986.'" Such "special rules" are inserted into bills promising "tax reform" or "fiscal responsibility" by individual members of Congress, with the acquiescence of their colleagues. What happened in this case is that renovation work on the Willard Hotel, a Washington, D.C., landmark, fell behind schedule and rich investors were going to lose special deductions originally lobbied for and promised in a "special rule" inserted into the "Tax Equity and Fiscal Responsibility Act of 1982." So the beneficiaries talked to a member of Congress, probably on the House Ways and Means or the Senate Finance Committee, and asked for an extension of benefits, which they received. Once again, this is how

---

[5]As I will explain in Chapter 8, "tax expenditures" are provisions of the tax code that provide special or selective reductions in taxes for certain groups of citizens or corporations.

power works. (Neither poor nor working-class people can talk to their Congressional representative and say: "My unemployment benefits are running out, so please extend them for another year.") There was no opposition to this section of the statute, mainly because the public did not know about it. Whenever tax bills are passed, members of Congress develop sound bites for the nightly news, making statements like "This is a major effort to simplify the tax law and make it more equitable" (Barlett & Steele, 1994, p. 252). Such sonorous platitudes have little relationship to reality. Rather, as William Grieder suggested, they are exercises in mock democracy, in deceiving those who are cut out of the decision-making process (1992).

In a pluralist society, at least in its ideal form, everyone acts within the rules to influence public policy and access to the political arena is open so that any person or group can compete for power. One way to obtain power, of course, is to enact rules that subvert pluralism, that prevent some citizens from participating. Indeed, that is just what has happened as the impact of poor and working-class voters has declined over the years (recall Figure 6-2). The result, I would like to suggest, is perverse: the development of an **anomic** social structure. That is, a disjunction exists between conventional values, such as deciding on public policies and resolving conflicts without violence, and the legitimate means to achieve them, by voting, for example. Voting is important because it leads to benefits: better city services, tax breaks, jobs, and so forth. It is also important because it reduces the room decision makers have to maneuver when dealing with elites. If everyone (or nearly everyone) voted, elected officials would be forced to pay more attention to everyone's needs, and this country would move closer to the pluralist ideal.

But since so many people do not vote, candidates for office find themselves in a peculiar situation. To be successful they must campaign as though they care about improving the lives of ordinary citizens. In governing, however, politicians as decision makers must satisfy the interests of those who voted and those who provided the money to help them be elected. This is why inequality has increased in recent years. For example, top tax brackets were reduced from 70 percent to 50 percent in 1981, and then to 28 percent in 1986, before rising to 36 percent in 1993. As a result, the rich can now retain an enormous amount of income and become even wealthier than in the past. In addition, as will be shown in subsequent chapters, a "hollowing out" of the income and job structure occurred such that lower-middle-class, working-class, and poor people are increasingly left behind.

These changes raise an obvious question: Why has the middle class supported public policies that are mostly beneficial to the rich? In *The Culture of Contentment,* John Kenneth Galbraith offered an answer (1992, p. 27). He speculated that people who come near the top of the class hierarchy develop a sense of entitlement, a feeling that their positions and benefits reflect merit: their virtue, intelligence, and hard work. Economic doctrine, then, accommodates that view. In Galbraith's pithy description, supply-side economics argues that "if the horse is fed amply with oats, some will pass through to the road for the sparrows." Phrased this way, the crackpot nature of the scheme becomes clear. Nonetheless, it provided an intellectual veil for fundamental changes in public policy. Galbraith suggested that the enormous benefit to the rich was accepted by middle-class people as "the price the contented electoral majority pays for being able to retain what is less but what is still very good" (1992, p. 26). In effect, it appears that the middle class allowed the rich to be favored in return for some limited economic protection for itself.

In Chapter 1, I offered a simple hypothesis extrapolated from the writings of theorists on stratification:

> *The higher the social class, the greater the influence over access to valued resources in the society.*

Although not a test of the hypothesis, the logic of the argument presented here fits with it. In this context, it is worth speculating about some possible options for change that would move the United States toward the pluralist ideal described earlier. Two come to mind: First, while money will always play a role in elections, mandating full disclosure of contributors prior to elections would provide the public with a clear idea as to whom candidates would be accountable once in office. Second, eliminating registration and making voting day a holiday would expand the electoral base to which candidates must appeal. These changes, alas, are unlikely.

Summary

The political process in the United States can be compared to an "ideal type," called "pluralism." In a pluralist system, people act within the rules to influence public policy, and access to the political arena is open so that everyone can compete fairly. A dilemma results, however, because groups with power want to limit the ability of others to participate. Three types of participation were reviewed: voting, partisanship, and unruliness.

Although the proportion of adults eligible to vote expanded steadily over time, the actual rate of voting has declined since the turn of the century (Figure 6-1). Today, only about half of those eligible participate in presidential elections and voting is dominated by the middle class. But this fact is not inevitable. (1) About 70 to 80 percent of those eligible voted during the last quarter of the nineteenth century. (2) Today, about 80 percent of those registered actually vote (Table 6-1). (3) Similarly, about 70 to 80 percent of adults vote in other Western industrial societies.

In order to understand elections, it is important to understand the role of money. The cost of winning has risen steadily over time. Most officeholders are reelected, mainly because they spend the most money. Incumbents raise money from large contributors, both individuals and political action committees, or PACs. Contributions from people and organizations tied to business overwhelm those with labor and ideological affiliations. Decision makers are accountable, then, to those who supply the money necessary to win elections.

Voting rates are influenced mainly by the day on which elections are held and the registration requirement (Table 6-2). They are also probably affected by voting procedures and the separation and frequency of federal, state, and local elections. A model of the structure of elections shows the impact of a situation in which middle-class people dominate: Candidates lose interest in the working class and poor because they do not vote, the working class and poor fail to see their interests, and everyone defends barriers to participation (Figure 6-2).

Although anyone can be a partisan, the rich possess the resources to most effectively pursue their interests. Money, family background, and institutional location mean that the rich have more access to decision makers than do members of other social classes. They take advantage of access in order to receive benefits.

Chapter 7

The Rich

The rich are not like you and me. The poor are characterized by relatively low wages and periodic dependence on public aid as a source of income. Working- and middle-class people rely on their occupations for income and prestige. Indeed, because these three classes comprise nearly the entire population, the usual tendency is to focus on people's occupations as the key to understanding their lifestyles and life chances. This is the logic, for example, underlying the literature on social mobility and status attainment reviewed in Chapter 3. But the rich are different: They own capital.

    The ownership of capital, income-producing assets, directs attention not only to the distribution of income, but also to the distribution of wealth. A family's wealth comprises everything it owns minus its debts. The things owned range from stocks and bonds to automobiles, real estate, and all other items that can be converted into money. Debt includes mortgage and auto loans, credit card balances, and the like. Although information about both income and wealth provides significant information, I focus on the distribution of wealth in this chapter, postponing discussion of income distribution until Chapter 8. This emphasis is useful because wealth is more unequally distributed than income (Wolffe, 1995). And the major source of wealth is income-producing assets.

In considering this topic, you should remember that capital can be used in different ways. Thus, Max Weber distinguished between two types of property owners: "rentiers," who live off their capital, and "entrepreneurs," who work their capital to increase its value (1920). Although a complete understanding of the rich would use this distinction to show differences in lifestyle and political influence, I shall not pursue it here, mainly because information on the different types of wealthy people is sparse and not much social scientific research has been done.

This lack of research on the rich reflects their affluence. Living poorly in the United States is regarded as a social problem worthy of study, which means scholars can obtain grants from government agencies to investigate this issue and, given their situation, impoverished people are relatively defenseless when observers come to the door. In contrast, being wealthy is not regarded as a social problem, so there is little money available to investigate this issue. Moreover, not only can the rich protect themselves from social scientific voyeurs, they also usually seek to remain as obscure as possible. (There are exceptions, but such persons are looked down upon by their peers.) As a result, even the most rudimentary information about the social and economic characteristics of rich persons is hard to obtain. Nonetheless, it is possible to provide reasonable estimates of the number and economic characteristics of wealthy people in the United States.

The Characteristics of the Rich

Counting the Rich

The rich comprise a relatively small percentage of the population. In order to count them, it is necessary to focus on income tax and estate tax data, both of which provide information about individual wealth. Since income tax reports are filed each year and include descriptions of people's sources of income, this information is particularly useful in discussing the rich. The main weakness of income tax data, as I shall describe below, is that citizens have considerable latitude to understate their income. By law, an estate tax return must be filed when people die owning assets valued at more than $650,000. Thus, since mortality rates by age, gender, and class are known, a sample can be drawn which represents the population of living persons with assets worth more than $650,000—a fairly well-to-do group. The main weakness of estate tax data is that wealthy people often choose to reduce the size of their estate before dying by distributing their capital to family members or placing it in trust. In general, then, you should assume that the figures given in this chapter provide conservative estimates of the number of rich people, the level of their wealth, and the source of their wealth.

Information from income tax returns provides an initial way of counting the rich, as displayed in Table 7-1. Column (2) of the table reveals that about 3 percent of all tax returns (filed by individuals and couples) show an adjusted gross income of $200,000 or more in 1995. The way to understand Table 7-1 is to recognize that adjusted gross income is income for tax purposes, not total income received during a year. "Adjusted gross income" represents taxable income after a series of deductions are subtracted from families' and individuals' gross (or total) income. These deductions (called tax expenditures) are for such things as business expenses, depreciation of income-producing assets, individual retirement accounts, capital gains exclusions, and the like. They make it possible for people, mainly the upper-middle class and rich, to show an income for tax purposes that is much lower than their actual gross income. Regardless of the data source or cutting point used, it should be apparent that the rich constitute a relatively small segment of the U.S. population.

I would like to argue that, after all the imprecision is taken into account, about 3 percent of the U.S. population should be considered rich, roughly five million people. This small aggregate can be divided into two types. First, most of those with yearly incomes between, say, $200,000 and $1 million are job-rich—for example, physicians, athletes, and corporate executives. They live well, often in large homes in exclusive neighborhoods. In fact, their most valuable asset is typically their house, which they acquired with income from their jobs. Many of these people, especially at the lower end of the continuum, would define themselves as upper-middle class. So the dividing line between these two categories is not precise. Second, the owner-rich comprise a much smaller group; these are people who live off their ownership of capital: mainly stocks in large corporations, government and corporate bonds, business ventures, and commercial real estate. These people are truly wealthy.

TABLE 7-1   The Distribution of Tax Returns and Adjusted Gross Income from Wages and Salaries, 1995

(1) Adjusted Gross Income (AGI)	(2) Percent of Tax Returns	(3) Percent of AGI from Wages and Salaries
$0 – < 15,000	4.5%	49%
$15,000 – < 30,000	13.3	72
$30,000 – < 50,000	25.0	84
$50,000 – < 75,000	28.8	85
$75,000 – < 100,000	13.7	84
$100,000 – < 200,000	11.1	74
$200,000 – < 500,000	2.7	61
$500,000 – < 1,000,000	0.7	51
$1,000,000 plus	0.2	31
	100.0%	

Source: IRS (1998a, p. 29).

The Basis of Great Wealth

The basis for great wealth is ownership of income-producing assets, especially corporate stocks and bonds. The impact of such assets is shown in column (3) of Table 7-1. Those tax returns displaying adjusted gross incomes of less than $100,000 receive nearly all their income from wages and salaries. Thus for the vast majority of the population, their jobs constitute the center of their lives. But those returns showing adjusted gross incomes above that figure reveal a steadily increasing proportion of income resulting from asset ownership. Between $100,000 and $1 million, people still depend on their jobs but the benefits from owning capital increase steadily. Finally, among persons with an adjusted gross income above $1 million, only 31 percent of it derives from salaries; the remaining 69 percent comes from capital. The data shown in Table 7-1 reflect an empirical generalization:

> *The higher the income, the greater the reliance on capital as the source of income.*

This fact has important implications because those who obtain income based on capital have several advantages over those who live on wages and salaries. One advantage is economic security. People without capital who work for a living can be injured, laid off, or see their occupational skills erode if they pause to start a family. Their lifestyle is always precarious as a result. And lifestyle is another advantage. People who derive high income from assets can choose to be employed or not, and, since nearly all of them do work, they can select an occupation that suits their interests and develops their human potential most fully. Persons without capital do not enjoy this luxury. A final advantage, one discussed in Chapter 6, is political influence. Although they constitute only a small segment of the population, those who have a great deal of money also possess considerable political clout. These advantages are built into the structure of stratification in the United States, which is predicated on private ownership of capital.

Top Wealthholders

At the extreme end of the stratification structure, a few people are very rich. Table 7-2 depicts the distribution of top wealthholders in the United States, based on estate tax data. The term "top wealthholders" refers to persons with assets valued at $600,000 or more. The table shows that these people constitute a rather small segment of the population: about 4.1 million persons, or (roughly) 2 percent of all adults. The table also reveals that the distribution of wealth is skewed such that the very richest persons make up a steadily smaller proportion of the population. Thus, the bottom row shows that about 12,000 individuals have a net worth of more than (often far more than) $20 million. Their average is far higher than that figure. This group of top wealthholders constitutes the super-rich in the United States today, a rather small, elite aggregate of people who possess enormous assets and (when they wish) exercise considerable political influence.

Wealth is relatively concentrated in the United States. For example, as shown below, the top 1 percent of families is worth more than the bottom 90 percent, and this relationship has been stable for some years (Kennickell, 1997, p. 30).

Net Worth, 1995

Top 1%	$7.2 trillion
Next 9%	6.8 trillion
Bottom 90%	6.5 trillion
	$20.5 trillion

Put proportionally, these data show that the richest 1 percent of families owned a stunning 37 percent of the nation's wealth and the top 10 percent own 68 percent. That does not leave much for the remainder of the population. And these proportions have not changed very much over time.

Table 7-3 elaborates on this issue by displaying the assets owned by the rich and the rest of the population. The richest 1 percent own most of those assets that provide significant income. In 1995, they owned 56 percent of bonds, 72 percent of business assets, 45 percent of trust funds, and 35 percent of nonhome real estate. The single asset that goes up in value the most over time is stocks; the richest 1 percent of the population own 43 percent of all privately held stocks. Although many ordinary people invest in the stock market, the poorest 90 percent of the population own only 16 percent of all stocks. The ownership pattern is reversed for assets that bring in little income. The poorest 90 percent of the population own 66 percent of most residential housing, most of which is mortgaged (often heavily). This debt means that an average family that purchases a home for, say, $100,000, will pay three times that amount in interest to a lending agency—owned by the rich. As will be shown later, this interest is deductible from income tax, which placates middle-class people (see Chapter 8). Similarly, 81 percent of all installment debt is owed by the poorest 90 percent of the population. Someone lives rather well off the interest payments. The combination of assets and liabilities shows that wealth is concentrated in this country.

TABLE 7-2   The Distribution of Top Wealthholders, 1995

Size of Net Worth	Number of Top Wealthholders	Percent of Top Wealthholders
< $600,000	1,008,000	24.40%
$600,000–1 Million	1,647,000	39.80
$1–2.5 Million	1,138,000	27.50
$2.5–5 Million	230,000	5.60
$5–10 Million	74,000	1.80
$10–20 Million	27,000	0.65
> 20 Million	12,000	0.25
	4,137,000	100.00%

Source: Johnson (1998).

TABLE 7-3   Assets and Debts by Level of Wealth, 1995

	Level of Wealth			
	Top 1%	Next 9%	Bottom 90%	Total
Assets				
Owned Mainly by the Richest 10% of the Population				
Bonds	56%	35%	10%	101%
Business Assets	72	21	8	101
Trust Funds	45	43	13	101
Stocks	43	42	16	101
Non-Home Real Estate	35	46	20	101
Other Assets[*]	32	39	29	100
Owned Mainly by the Poorest 90% of the Population				
Checking Accounts	17%	26%	58%	101%
Money Market and Other Financial Accts.	27	35	38	100
Pension Accounts	16	41	43	100
Life Insurance	17	28	55	100
Home	8	26	66	100
Automobiles	5	18	78	101
Debts				
Held Mainly by the Richest 10% of the Population				
Non-Home Real Estate	34%	41%	25%	100%
Held Mainly by the Poorest 90% of the Population				
Installment and Credit Card	10%	10%	81%	101%
Home Mortgage	5	17	78	100

Source: Kennickell (1997).

Note: Some totals do not add to 100% because of rounding.

[*]Antiques, paintings, jewelry, oil leases, and all other economically valuable assets.

The data above focus on individual wealth. Using individuals as the unit of analysis makes sense as long as they serve as a proxy for a nuclear family. Most people today think of the family as comprising adults living together, often with their immediate children. Family members typically have much less contact with relatives in their extended family, such as aunts, uncles, and cousins. But such ties are vitally important to the owner-rich. This is so for two reasons (Allen, 1990). First, kinship indicates who can share in the family fortune. Thus the founders pass on wealth to children; they, in turn, marry and bear children, passing on wealth again. This continuing process involves an ever-widening range of people and, it would seem, diminishes the fortune. Yet great wealth usually remains intact. This fact leads to the second reason family ties are important to the rich: Family members combine their assets via trusts and holding companies so as to control many large corporations. It turns out, then, that families, not individuals, own most fortunes.

Here is a simple example taken from Michael Patrick Allen's *The Founding Fortunes: A New Anatomy of the Super-Rich Families in America* (1990, p. 11). Prior to his death in 1976, J. Paul Getty controlled a majority of stock in Getty Oil, receiving dividend income of about $29 million per year. This stock was worth about $2 billion at the time. But Getty was not really a billionaire. The reason is that while he controlled the stock, he did not own it. He served as the trustee of a trust established by his mother, voting the stock and receiving dividends from it. Both he and his sons were lifetime beneficiaries—entitled to the income but unable to touch the principal. The trust will not be dissolved until the death of the last surviving grandchild. At that time, a holding company will probably be formed in order to preserve the principal for subsequent generations. In effect, the assets of this fortune constituted the collective property of the entire family. According to Allen, this pattern is typical among the rich, and it carries important implications. In the data displayed above, the many individual members of the Getty family are included in the top 1 percent even though in reality they function as a unit. Allen presented data and a host of interesting stories about 160 families, each of which were worth at least $200 million in 1986. This is a rather small community of people who have tremendous economic and political resources.

The Historical Trend in the Distribution of Wealth

The historical trend in the distribution of wealth, especially the share possessed by the very rich, is a matter of considerable controversy. Many people, even today, agree with the French observer, Alexis de Tocqueville, that the United States is and always has been a relatively egalitarian society (Pessen, 1971). In *Democracy in America,* originally published in 1835, Tocqueville argued that in the United States an equality of "condition gives some resources to all members of the community [and] prevents any of them from having resources to any great extent" (1954, p. 250–58). Furthermore, Tocqueville asserted, "most rich men were formerly poor" and when wealth is amassed, it is not passed on to relatives but circulates with "inconceivable rapidity." In contrast to this argument, a few observers claim that wealth always has been highly concentrated in the United States. Gabriel Kolko, for example, argued that "a radically unequal distribution of income [and wealth] has been characteristic of the American social structure since at least 1910 and despite minor year-to-year fluctuations . . . no significant trend toward income equality has appeared" (1962, p. 13). The way to resolve this controversy, of course, is with data and a hypothesis that interprets them. I begin with the latter.

The Kuznets Hypothesis

Like Gerhard Lenski, the economist Simon Kuznets hypothesized that when less economically developed societies, such as Brazil and Nigeria, are compared to more economically developed societies, such as the United States and Sweden, the relationship between economic growth and inequality is curvilinear in the form of an upside down U (1955). Think of the curve as having the shape of a bowl turned upside down. The *Kuznets Hypothesis* is:

> *Inequality of wealth and income increases during the early phases of economic growth when the transition from preindustrial to industrial society is most rapid, stabilizes for awhile, then decreases in the later phases of industrialization.*

This pattern is not accidental, Kuznets said. Economic growth, especially in the early stages, cannot occur without large-scale capital formation. Those who are not rich spend all or nearly all their income. Only rich persons can invest their incomes in sufficient quantity to transform a society from preindustrial to industrial. The result, however, is greater inequality, as wealthy people reap a considerable return on their investments. But Kuznets argued that a variety of factors produce a stable and then a declining level of inequality as industrialization advances. One of them is what Kuznets called "legislative interference" with the free market, by means of inheritance taxes, government-induced inflation (which erodes the value of wealth), and other public policies. Such "interventions," Kuznets suggested, "reflect the view of society on the long term utility of wide income inequalities" (1955, p. 9). Another factor reducing inequality over time is demographic: The rich usually have a lower birth rate than the rest of the population, which means their share of total income and wealth declines. An additional factor reducing inequality is continued economic growth combined with freedom of opportunity. This process occurs because the rise of new industries means that old wealth declines in value and is superseded by new wealth while, at the same time, workers are upwardly mobile, shifting from agricultural and low-skill jobs to higher-paying blue- and white-collar occupations. Thus, the Kuznets hypothesis says that the impact of political, economic, and demographic factors first raises, then stabilizes, and, over time, reduces inequality as economic growth continues.

This hypothesis implies that a historical process occurs. Yet the data used to test it are nearly always cross-sectional: comparisons of less- and more-developed societies existing today. One reason for this strategy is that such information is readily available. In any case, the hypothesis implies a historical pattern that needs to be traced empirically. In the following paragraphs, I sketch the trend of wealth inequality in the United States from colonial times to the present. The result will show that the Kuznets hypothesis must be modified.[1]

The Colonial Era

The colonial era constituted a preindustrial period and the overall level of wealth inequality remained relatively low. It was greater, however, in colonial cities than in

---

[1]The Kuznets hypothesis is most useful for describing the relationship between economic growth in Western industrial societies. It can only provide a partial account for economic growth in developing nations today (see Chapter 11).

rural areas. Edward Pessen, for example, shows that as early as 1693, the richest 10 percent of the population owned about 24 percent of the wealth in Chester County, Pennsylvania, and that a century later, in 1793, the richest 10 percent owned approximately 38 percent of the wealth (1971, p. 1019). Although wealth was unstable during the colonial era, it appears to have been similarly concentrated in Salem, Boston, and New York (Williamson & Lindert, 1980). These cities, however, comprised a very small proportion of the total population, less than 10 percent. The vast majority of people lived in rural areas and on the frontier, where conditions were much more equal. Thus, the single most reasonable estimate I know of is by Williamson and Lindert in *American Inequality: A Macroeconomic History* (1980, p. 38). They surmised that in 1774, on the eve of the Revolution, the richest 1 percent of free households owned about 13 percent of the wealth.

The Nineteenth Century

The first half of the nineteenth century is often called the "age of equality" in America. Yet this is the period in which industrialization began in the United States and, in contrast to Tocqueville's description, it is also a period of sharply increasing inequality. Figures for New York City are typical. In 1829, the richest 4 percent of the city's population owned about 49 percent of the wealth. By 1845, they owned approximately 66 percent (Pessen, 1971, p. 1022). A similar trend occurred in the South, where the richest 10 percent of families held about 72 percent of the wealth in 1830 and 82 percent in 1860. Thus, the first really great fortunes were amassed in the early nineteenth century, as a few millionaires and multimillionaires appeared.

Not only did great wealth inequality exist in the United States during the first half of the nineteenth century, but, despite Tocqueville's claim, most wealth was acquired by inheritance and was very stable over time. Pessen observed that only a small proportion, between 2 percent and 6 percent, of the rich were born poor (1971, p. 1006). The dominant pattern was apparently for inherited wealth to be built up to higher levels with each generation. Essentially, Pessen concluded, "the extent of an individual's early wealth was the major factor determining whether he would be rich later." This pattern remains true today (Allen, 1990; Solon, 1992). I shall return to the problem of the origin and expansion of wealth later in this chapter.

During the second half of the nineteenth century, the economy continued its transformation, and the distribution of wealth stabilized at very high levels of inequality. For example, in 1860 the richest 20 percent of the population probably owned more than 90 percent of the wealth in Baltimore, New Orleans, and St. Louis (Gallman, 1969). Data for ten other cities show a similar pattern (Soltow, 1975). As was typical in the nineteenth century, urban areas displayed more inequality than rural or frontier regions. Thus, Williamson and Lindert reported that in 1870 the richest 1 percent owned 27 percent of the nation's wealth and the richest 10 percent owned 70 percent (1980, p. 46). They concluded that the best interpretation of the pattern to this point is that "wealth concentration rose over most of the period 1774–1860, with especially steep increases from the 1820s to the late 1840s. It should also be noted that these two or three decades coincide with early industrial acceleration." In other words, the

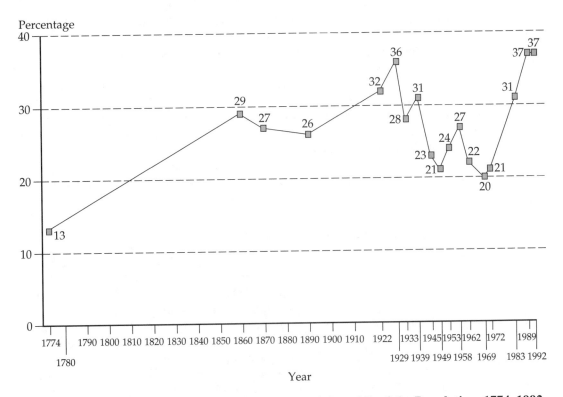

FIGURE 7-1 **Share of Personal Wealth Held by Richest 1% of the Population, 1774–1992**

Sources: Williamson and Lindert (1980, pp. 38–39); Schwartz (1985, p. 11); Kennickell and Woodburn (1992, pp. 38–40); Wolffe (1995, p. 67).

expansion of wealth inequality during this period corresponds to that predicted by the Kuznets hypothesis.

The Twentieth Century

The extraordinary concentration of wealth reached in the nineteenth century declined slightly during World War I, but rebounded so that, by 1929, the richest 1 percent of all adults owned about 36 percent of the wealth, an all-time high to that point in history. Beginning with the depression, however, wealth inequality declined. The extent of its decline is shown in Figure 7-1, which depicts estimates of the share of the wealth held by the richest 1 percent of the population for selected years over the past two centuries.[2]

In addition to scattered data for the period 1774 through the 1920s, the figure shows that the share of the wealth held by the richest 1 percent of all adults fell to about

[2]The population base for the estimates in Figure 7-1 varies: 1774, free households; 1860, free adult males; 1870, adult males; 1890, families; 1922 to present, all adults.

21 percent in 1949, rose slightly during the 1950s, and dropped again in the 1960s. Between 1962 and 1982, the richest 1 percent of American adults held approximately 20 to 23 percent of the total wealth. Thus this period constituted a time of rather stable and, in historical terms, a relatively low level of wealth inequality.

Hence, the long-term historical pattern through the 1970s suggests—tentatively— that the Kuznets hypothesis may be correct. Wealth inequality apparently increased with the onset of accelerated economic growth in the early part of the nineteenth century, remained very high between the Civil War and the Great Depression, then declined and stabilized at a relatively low level after 1930. On this basis, Williamson and Lindert concluded, "the American record thus documents a 'Kuznets inverted U' for wealth inequality" (1980, p. 63). Alas, sometimes conclusions do not last long in the social sciences. Figure 7-1 shows that the story does not end in the 1970s.

The Trend Since 1980

Thus the figure presents data for the 1980s and 1990s revealing sharply increasing wealth inequality. In fact, the richest 1 percent now owns about 37 percent of the wealth, an all-time high. (This result parallels data showing increasing income equality to be presented in Chapter 8.) So Kuznets is wrong, or at least partially wrong: Inequality does not necessarily decline with advanced economic development (Neilsen & Alderson, 1997). What does happen when the economy is transformed by industrialization is that greater choice becomes possible in human affairs.

Indeed, the story of the last two centuries or so is one of increasing choice. Based on advances in science (leading to industrialization), the development of capitalism, and increasing individual freedom, we now possess greater control over every dimension of life: social, biological, and environmental. As a result, behaviors that were impossible or immoral just a short time ago now seem both possible and moral. The development of values appropriate to this new situation constitutes one of the central dilemmas of our time (Beeghley, 1999).

With regard to the Kuznets hypothesis, then, the new information means that it must be modified in the following way:

> *Inequality of wealth and income increases during the early phases of economic growth when the transition from preindustrial to industrial society is most rapid, stabilizes for awhile, and then becomes subject to negotiation.*

It is known, of course, from Lenski's work, that power determines the distribution of surplus in most societies (1966). So the basis of this negotiation will be political: Which classes can influence public policy so as to garner as much wealth and income as possible, ideally without prompting the losers to revolt (Allen & Campbell, 1994). This is tricky business. I am arguing in this book that the rich and the middle class dominate the political process—the rich because they have the most money to spend and the middle class because they have the most votes. The data presented in Figure 7-1 suggest that the rich had enormous influence over public policy during the 1980s.

As noted in Chapter 6, during the 1980s so-called supply-side economic theory was used to justify reducing taxes on the rich on the grounds that the benefits of their investments would "trickle down" to the rest of the population via increased jobs and increased tax revenue. The logic behind the assertion that reducing taxes would increase tax revenues was never clear, at least to me (but see Galbraith, 1992). But the crackpot nature of the argument was ignored, with the results shown in Figure 7-1. Recall that I suggested how the political process produced such consequences in the last chapter. For now, it is time to look at the origin and expansion of great wealth.

The Origin and Expansion of Wealth

In the United States, most people believe that hard work and ability will produce occupational and, by extrapolation, economic success. From this point of view, which is basic to classical economic theory as well as popular belief, the way to great wealth is through a process of long-term, self-limiting behavior in which savings accumulate over time. Wealth, it is said, results from delaying gratification in the present in order to save, invest, and reap even greater rewards in the future. In the real world, however, great wealth, such as that depicted in Table 7-2, is nearly always inherited.

Here is a hypothesis that expresses the probable relationship between wealth and inheritance:

> *The greater the wealth, the more likely a person is to have inherited rather than created it.*

The statement is labeled a hypothesis because the evidence for it is mixed. My view, however, is that the reason more conclusive data are not available lies in the greater ability of wealthy persons—compared to members of other social classes—to conduct their affairs in private. Thus, with some notable exceptions, most of the really great fortunes existing today appear to be based upon inheritance (Allen, 1990).

But how is great wealth created in the first place? And how is it increased over time? As noted, traditional economic doctrine is that wealth is accumulated through a slow process of saving and investment. And it is true that by saving steadily and investing wisely average people can build up a small nest egg for retirement. But the result is not wealth; it is, rather, the ability to live comfortably. There appear to be at least five strategies for wealth creation and expansion.

The first is windfall profit. In *Generating Inequality*, Lester Thurow argued that a newly valued asset generates a sudden, extraordinary return on an investment of time or money—what he called "windfall profit." Thurow phrased the hypothesis in the following way (1975, p. 149).

> *Large instantaneous fortunes are created when the financial markets capitalize new above average rate of return investments to yield average rate of return financial investments. It is this process of capitalizing disequilibrium*

returns that generates rapid fortunes. Patient saving and reinvestment have little or nothing to do with them. To become very rich one must generate or select a situation in which an above average rate of return is about to be capitalized.

In plainer language, the argument is that wealth is usually created suddenly, very suddenly. What happens is that a person possesses an asset whose value increases unexpectedly and exponentially, leading to what economists call capitalization: a high rate of investment.

A good example of what Thurow meant is provided by the (early years of the) Apple Computer Company. Steven Jobs and Stephen Wozniak produced the first microcomputer in a garage in 1976. A year later, they found a wealthy investor to underwrite their fledgling company. When Apple offered stock to the public in 1980, the value of the company ballooned. Their 37 percent share of the stock became worth $630 million. Thus two middle-class men parlayed genius, hard work, and a then peculiar asset into great wealth.

Thurow appeared to believe that windfall profits constitute the only means of generating great wealth. He argued, for example, that "the typical pattern is for a man to make a great fortune and then to settle down and earn the market rate of return on his existing [investment] portfolio" (1975, p. 153). But several additional methods of wealth accumulation exist, as shown by Michael Patrick Allen in *The Founding Fortunes* (1990, p. 218). In fact, he argued that the fortunes of the owner-rich are rarely created instantaneously, that they often take one or more generations to reach their zenith. This argument fits with the nineteenth century pattern described earlier: Inherited wealth is expanded over time.

A second strategy for wealth creation and expansion is to own a small company in a new field that becomes a growth industry. The Motorola Corporation provides an example. The Galvin brothers founded the predecessor of Motorola in 1928 with an investment of about $1,300. The company became the sole supplier of radios to the automobile industry, which expanded steadily over a half-century. By 1952, the Galvin family (including children and grandchildren) owned 31 percent of Motorola stock worth $21 million dollars. The company has continued to prosper, expanding into new areas of electronics, such as cellular phones, and the family's stake is now worth more than $550 million. The Johnson & Johnson Company provides another example. It sells medical equipment, supplies, and drugs to both hospitals and individuals. When Robert Johnson died in 1910 his estate, including shares in Johnson & Johnson, was worth only about $3 million. By the time the company went public in 1944, that same stock was worth $30 million. By 1971, the 34 percent of Johnson & Johnson stock held by the descendants of Robert Johnson was worth $2.2 billion. Note that both companies started small but were part of growth industries. Note also that in both cases the family fortunes continued increasing at a very high rate long after the founding entrepreneurs left the scene.

A third strategy for creating and expanding wealth is to own a corporation that radically increases its share of an important market. The Anheuser-Busch Company provides an example. Incorporated in 1875, it was for many years simply one of several hundred breweries supplying local markets around the country. As recently as 1952, Anheuser-Busch produced only 7 percent of the beer sold in the United States. At that time, the company had a market value of only about $100 million, which meant the 50 percent share held by the children and grandchildren of Adolphus Busch was worth only about $50 million. Since that time, however, the company has become the dominant brewery in the nation, producing about 37 percent of all beer sold. The Busch family, which now owns only 20 percent of the stock, is worth about $1.1 billion. Again, wealth expansion occurred long after the founder left the scene.

A fourth strategy for wealth creation and expansion is for inventors of new products to establish their own companies, which then grow in value over time. Thus, unlike the inventors of the personal computer (who found a wealthy investor to underwrite their company), Cyrus McCormick developed the mechanical reaper and, along with his brothers, founded McCormick Harvester Machine Company in order to sell it. The company eventually became International Harvester. Similarly, Charles Kettering invented a number of automotive devices, such as the self-starter, and founded Dayton Engineering Company to sell them. The company later merged with General Motors. A more recent example is Edwin Land. He founded the Polaroid Corporation in 1937 to sell polarizing filters he had invented. Other inventions followed, such as instant photography. By 1978, the 12 percent of Polaroid stock held by Land and his family was worth over $330 million. In these cases, the inventors are also entrepreneurs, creating fortunes through their own efforts and passing them on to their descendants.

A fifth strategy for the creation and expansion of individual wealth is for financiers to manipulate the assets and debt of companies while enriching themselves, a process that often results in corporate bankruptcy. The key to this strategy is the ability of companies to deduct interest payments on debt; otherwise credit would probably not be available. In simplified form, here is how such schemes work: Mitchell Milquetoast purchases the Widget Corporation for $100 million, 80 percent of which is borrowed. At Milquetoast's direction, the Widget Corporation, a profitable enterprise, then borrows $200 million by issuing high-interest (junk) bonds. He uses $100 million of this money to purchase more widget-making companies and the other $100 million to pay himself a dividend for his work. With his dividend, he pays off his personal debt of $80 million and pockets the remaining $20 million. In other words, he doubled his original investment. Overall widget sales go up, of course. Alas, even though profits rise as well, they are insufficient to pay the interest on the bonds, even given their deductibility. So the company is in financial trouble. Milquetoast sells out at a loss, taking a huge tax deduction for himself against his $20 million profit. In addition, the company no longer pays corporate income tax and may end up bankrupt. The latter will mean that several thousand ordinary people lose their jobs. Such mergers and acquisitions often do not carry any economic benefit, save for people like Milquetoast.[3]

---

[3]The vignette in this paragraph is designed to illustrate the impact of debt-leveraged corporate mergers and acquisitions that flourished during the 1980s. For a specific example, see Barlett and Steele (1994, pp. 148–55). On the lack of economic benefit, see Galbraith (1992, pp. 51–64).

Such destructive efforts, however, constitute an exception. In most cases, as the examples suggest, the members of rich families build their wealth over time, benefiting from hard work by others. To use a baseball analogy, these are (mostly) people who are born at third base and think they hit a triple. In saying this, I do not mean to denigrate the importance of hard work and ability in producing success. I do mean, however, to suggest that these characteristics do not distinguish those who become very rich from those who do not. What separates the wealthy from people in other social classes is, quite simply, luck. Many rich persons work hard, but then so do most people in all social classes. For the rich, however, the result is the possession of political resources (money) that can be used to protect their interests even though their numbers are relatively small.

Power and Wealth Inequality

One of the main indicators of the ability of the rich to protect their interests, even over the opposition of others, is tax law. Taxes have two purposes. One is to finance government activities that provide for the common good. These include national defense, highways, immunization programs, public aid for the indigent, and the like. The other is to redistribute income. Many people believe that taxes are too high; in fact, the rich always believe this no matter at what level they are set. In any case, as Barlett and Steele observed in *America: Who Really Pays the Taxes,* the real problem is not the size of the tax burden but its distribution (1994, p. 26). As they put it, taxes can be set so that the rich have enough money left to buy several houses and everyone in the middle and working classes can buy one house. Or taxes can be set so that the rich are left with enough money to buy many houses and a large number of working- and middle-class people cannot buy even one. Thus, as the house metaphor suggests, taxes can channel income up or down. This fact results in two dilemmas. The political dilemma is who benefits; that is, which class can keep most of its income. Do not be naive, fairness is never a choice—although it can be shown that progressive taxes are fair (Mitra & Ok, 1996). Although politicians often use the phrase "tax reform" when describing changes in tax law, such statements are really euphemisms for making someone else pay. The value dilemma is the common good; that is, should taxes be set so that everyone has plenty or so that some have plenty and others not enough? Over the past 30 years or so, these dilemmas have been resolved to the advantage of the rich, as tax rates declined and inequality increased.

Figure 7-2 suggests this result by displaying the top bracket for each year since the income tax was imposed in 1913. In considering these data, note the two periods in which the top tax bracket has been lowest: during the 1920s and 1980s. Now look back to Figure 7-1. Note the two periods when wealth inequality has been greatest: during the 1920s and 1980s. This correlation is not accidental.

It is achieved by establishing only a few brackets and having the highest set at a low income. Thus, from 1945 to 1964 there were 24 brackets, with the highest threshold set at various levels above 80 percent on income greater than $200,000 (CCH, 1994, p. 546). The impact of having so many brackets is that people at similar income levels

Tax Rate (percentage)

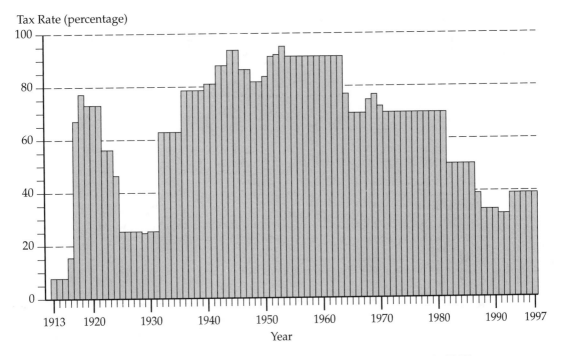

FIGURE 7-2   **Federal Individual Income Tax: Top Bracket Rates, 1913–1997**

Sources: USBC (1975, p. 1095); CCH (1993, p. 546); RIA (1998, p. 7751).

were treated similarly. In contrast, as of 1997 there were only five brackets, as listed below (RIA, 1998, p. 7752):

Income Bracket	Tax Rate
$0–41,200	15%
$41,200–99,600	28
$99,600–151,750	31
$151,750–271,050	36
Over $271,050	39

The impact of having only a few brackets is that people with different economic problems are treated as if they are the same (Barlett & Steele, 1994). Families with incomes of $42,000 and $95,000 face different economic obstacles. Families with incomes of $155,000 and $270,000 have different abilities to purchase a home and send their children to college. And families with incomes of $300,000, $1 million, or $5 million have vastly different lifestyles. The tax brackets allow more well-off families to retain more of their income. They channel income upward, creating more inequality.

You should remember, however, that the analysis above deals with tax brackets rather than actual tax rates. In a way, these brackets are symbolic because most people benefit from deductions and exclusions that reduce their tax obligations (explained in

Chapter 8). The rich, however, benefit the most (Allen & Campbell, 1994). For example, here are data on the number of persons with incomes greater than $200,000 who paid no income tax whatsoever in various years (Barlett & Steele, 1994, p. 40; IRS, 1998b):

Year	Number
1966	155
1974	244
1986	659
1989	1,081
1996	1,424

During this same period, Congress passed the four different "tax reform" acts. Despite "reforms," however, the enactment of various deductions and exclusions (tax expenditures) increased the ability of the rich to retain their income. This is why the overall level of wealth inequality also rose.

Since the rich comprise such a small percentage of the population, the trick is to persuade Congress to enact such laws against the interests of the majority of the population. As it turns out, Barlett and Steele observed, the arguments justifying low taxes on the rich have time-honored quality (1994, p. 63). Thus during the 1920s, Secretary of the Treasury (and one of the wealthiest men in the United States) Andrew Mellon asserted that low taxes on the rich would produce greater tax revenue and reduce tax evasion and avoidance. He added that high rates destroy business initiative and constitute a communist plot against the United States. These are precisely the same arguments used during the 1980s, recycled as supply-side economics. The only difference is that instead of a "communist plot," it was argued that high rates constitute an unfair form of "class warfare." Among many examples, Barlett and Steele cited former Senator Alphonse D'Amato's statement that there is something "very dangerous taking place in this nation. . . . It is class warfare under the theory of 'let's get the rich guy, the richest 1%.' So we set them up, target them; those are the people we are going to get" (1994, p. 93).

Whether fair or not, "class warfare" was being waged—by the rich—in order to secure more income for themselves. You should observe that in order to reduce the federal income tax, other taxes have increased: namely social security taxes and the entire array of state and local taxes. The overall tax structure now bears far more heavily on working- and middle-class people than it did only 30 years ago. These are the people who were set up, targeted, who now pay more taxes while the rich pay less. For example, the average actual federal income and social security tax rates of millionaires fell from 49 percent in 1953 to 27 percent in 1991. In comparison, for people in the middle-income brackets, the average actual combined tax rates rose from 11 percent to 18 percent during those same years (Barlett & Steele, 1994, pp. 22–25). Remember, this change reflects deliberate decisions. As the modified Kuznets hypothesis states, the level of inequality is now subject to negotiation.

It is worth thinking about whether this change adds to the common good. Please look back to Figure 7-2 and note the high tax brackets during the 1950s and 1960s.

Barlett and Steele argued, I believe correctly, that the income tax contributed decisively to both economic prosperity and the expansion of the middle class during that period (1994, p. 70).

> *The changes were evident in virtually every aspect of American life. The percentage of owner-occupied homes surged from 44% to 62%. Automobile registrations more than doubled, from 27 million to 62 million. The number of households with telephones more than doubled, from 37% to 78%. The number of college degrees awarded more than doubled from 217,000 to 477,000. All this at a time when population rose just 36%, from 133 million to 181 million. During these same years, average family income, produced largely by one wage earner, far outstripped inflation. And taxes were comparatively low. Except at the top.*

Now Barlett and Steele understood that other factors also contributed to the prosperity of these years. For example, mortgages from the Federal Housing Administration and Veterans Administration made home ownership (for whites) easier. In addition, the GI Bill helped millions (of whites) attend college. They simply argued that the highly progressive tax system "played a critical role."

The situation today is much different. Funding for a program to help students attend college (like the GI Bill) would be difficult if not impossible to pass in today's political climate. Corporate taxes, for example, constitute an indirect way of taxing the rich, since stocks and bonds issued by companies provide the basis of great wealth. Yet they have been reduced as well. Thus, while corporate taxes represented 33 percent of all federal tax revenues during the 1950s, they fell steadily over the years and now account for only 15 percent. Raising corporate rates would go far toward eliminating the upcoming deficit in Social Security revenues. Returning to 1950s rates on individuals would help eliminate the remainder—with no decline in benefits. Moreover, such increases would leave money available for the common good—schools and roads come to mind. Instead, we have chosen to allow the rich to retain their income. Their lifestyle is more opulent as a result.

Social Class and Lifestyle

In 1899, Thorstein Veblen published *The Theory of the Leisure Class,* a satirical look at the attempts by wealthy people in the late nineteenth century to appear sophisticated (1979). They did this by purchasing items that were both expensive and superfluous. In effect, the rich at this time were trying to express (and gain) social status by displaying the extent of their wealth. Veblen, a mordant critic, had a gift for descriptive phrases. Thus he portrayed a wealthy class engaged in "conspicuous consumption," "vicarious consumption," "conspicuous leisure," and "conspicuous waste." One of his many examples was the walking stick, a popular affectation in those days. Excluding the infirm, this item is entirely without purpose—for walking; its function was to demonstrate idleness based on wealth. Hence, walking sticks (as opposed to ordinary canes) were often very ornate. Such forlorn efforts still occur today, especially among the job-rich and people who are new to wealth. They seek out publicity and want the public to know about their glitzy lifestyle.

In contrast, as Michael Patrick Allen observed, most of the rich lead "intensely private lives" organized so as to make themselves as invisible as possible (1990, p. 2). This orientation reflects a desire to elude those searching for money, to enhance their personal security, and to avoid becoming a focus of political attention. The emphasis on privacy means that consumption tends to be inconspicuous.

Privacy combined with wealth brings much more personal autonomy than the rest of the population has. Although they are concerned with many political issues, especially those (such as tax law) that are related to the preservation of their wealth, many of the disputes that vex the public appear less important to the rich. Thus they tend to be uninvolved in issues like the abortion controversy. A wealthy woman wishing to terminate her pregnancy has always been able to do so, precisely because she possessed economic resources. Since Medicaid money cannot be used to pay for abortions, many poor women do not have a choice: They must bear children. Without medical insurance, many working-class women lack a choice as well (see Chapter 8). More generally, it seems to me, the fight over cultural values (for example, sex, abortion, and drugs) in the United States during the last several years provided useful political cover for the rich, who were able to increase their wealth without much reaction from ordinary people.

In addition, the combination of privacy and wealth also brings luxury that adds to the quality of life, such as larger homes, longer vacations, and more pleasant amenities. But these purchases tend to be designed to ensure their status within the upper class itself rather than to demonstrate it to ordinary (nonrich) people (Higley, 1995). Hence, rather than purchasing useless items, "the ideal expenditure [today] is one that represents a sound financial investment and that simultaneously enhances the social status and political influence of the family" (Allen, 1990, p. 248).

Here are several examples. First, a ranch in Montana not only provides a second home for vacations in a pristine location, it also serves as an income-producing asset. Second, an art collection not only demonstrates taste and brings pleasure, it also constitutes an investment. This result occurs because the prices paid for original works can multiply in a very short period (Keen, 1971). Thus paintings by Chagall increased in value by about 50 times between 1951 and 1969, while those by Picasso increased about 37 times during this same period. The impact of such appreciation can be seen with a hypothetical but plausible example. Suppose you buy a painting for, say, $50,000 and enjoy it for 20 years. Assuming it increases by 30 times, you then donate it to a museum at its new market price of $1,500,000 (30 × $50,000) and take a tax deduction in that amount. Third, owning race horses provides a certain cachet while also producing a profit or a tax deductible loss. In all these cases, the search for status combines with a financial investment.[4]

---

[4]According to the tax code, breeding race horses constitutes a farming business. So owners can deduct from their taxes the cost of food, housing, employees, insurance, transportation, state and local taxes, interest charges, depreciation (as horses age), stud fees, attending horse shows, and visiting (friends at other) horse farms (Barlett & Steele, 1994, p. 217). Thus horses provide the perfect expenditure in that a rich person's lifestyle is underwritten by the majority of taxpayers.

A similar process occurs with elite education, a topic on which I wish to elaborate. In order to place this issue in perspective, it is useful to recall the literature on mobility and status attainment reviewed in Chapter 3. This research shows that occupational status attainment reflects the impact of ascription and achievement, with the latter having greater impact over time. The dominant image in this literature is of an increasingly meritocratic society in which ability provides the key to occupational success.[5]

This image is consonant with the ideology of middle- and upper-middle-class parents, who see education as an investment in their children's occupational future and, hence, white-collar status. So it appears that much anguish occurs over getting their children into "gifted" programs, into select public high schools, and into good universities. For some, the latter translates into the state-supported Flagship University; for others, the goal is one of the elite private schools, especially in the Ivy League. Because the vehicles for admission are typically test scores and grades, middle-class parents see this process as based on merit. In comparing themselves to the poor and working class, they do not wish to recognize the impact of family background, with its advantages and disadvantages.

The rich are not so myopic. They know the meritocratic image is misleading, that family background is fundamental. In Chapter 3, I used a fictional vignette about the game of Monopoly to illustrate both the reproduction of the class structure as a whole and the existence of the rich, a group whose position in society does not depend on occupation but on source of income. Since their children's economic future is assured, education is designed to facilitate their children's entrance into the exclusive social circles of the upper class (Allen, 1990, p. 249). This process begins with attendance at one of the elite private prep schools.

The prep school has always served as means for inculcating upper-class values, preparing students for socially desirable universities (the Ivy League plus a few others), and building networks of friends and acquaintances who will become important in the future for both business and marriage (Baltzell, 1958, 1964). About 16 of these schools form the elite core; among them are Phillips Exeter Academy, Groton School, Kent School, Deerfield Academy, and Woodberry Forest School. All are located in the Northeast. Most are unknown to middle-class people, which constitutes another example of the ability of the rich to keep their lifestyles relatively private.

It should not surprise you that those attending such schools enjoy a decisive advantage over public school applicants in gaining admission to Ivy League universities (Persell & Cookson, 1985). Unlike public school advisors, college advisors at these prep schools typically have long-standing personal relationships with college admissions officers. During the spring, when decisions are made, prep school college advisors often sit-in on admissions committee meetings. In addition, some universities apparently make an effort to recognize applicants from elite prep schools; for example, by color coding their files. This process means that the public high school student from the Midwest with outstanding credentials who applies to Harvard is sometimes denied

---

[5]As indicated in Chapter 3, **achievement** refers to the use of performance-related criteria (such as grade point averages or test scores) that are equally imposed on all persons being evaluated. In contrast, **ascription** refers to the use of non-performance-related criteria (such as family background) in evaluating a person.

admission in favor of an undistinguished prep school applicant. When merit and pedigree clash, the latter often wins.

The result is the reproduction of the class structure over time. For example, graduates of elite prep schools are much more likely than nongraduates to rise in the hierarchy of Fortune 500 corporations (Persell & Cookson, 1985). Of course, as seen earlier, such graduates are also more likely to own or control stock in these corporations. Over the long run, then, the rich comprise a relatively well integrated network of people who know one another, marry one another, share similar experiences and values, and—most importantly—have access to resources that allow them to exercise political power.

Summary

The source of great wealth in the United States is ownership of capital, as indicated by the distribution of wealth. This chapter explored some of the implications of this fact. The rich are a relatively small proportion of the population. Income tax data, for example, show that only 3 percent of all returns have an adjusted gross income above $200,000, although this figure may understate the percent of rich persons in the United States (Table 7-1). The reliance of the wealthy on assets is shown by the fact that only 31 percent of the income from tax returns with an adjusted gross income above $1 million comes from wages and salaries; the remainder comes from capital.

Top wealthholders comprise about 3.4 million people (Table 7-2). The concentration of wealth is shown by the fact that the richest 1 percent of families own 35 percent of the nation's wealth. In fact, the richest 1 percent of families in the United States is worth more than the poorest 90 percent. The rich own most of the bonds, business assets, trust funds, and stock (Table 7-3). The table understates the concentration of wealth because it focuses on individuals rather than families.

The historical trend in the distribution of wealth in the United States shows that the Kuznets hypothesis of an upside-down U must be modified to take into account the huge increase in inequality since 1980 (Figure 7-1). Thus, it appears that wealth and income inequality increase with economic growth, stabilize, and then becomes subject to political negotiation.

Although most people think that great wealth results from hard work, this characteristic does not distinguish the rich from the nonrich. Rather, most rich people inherited their wealth. It is created or expanded by means of windfall profit, owning a small company in a growing industry, owning a company that increases its market share, or developing a new product and founding a company to market it. Other strategies probably exist.

Increasing inequality reflects the power of the rich, especially their ability to obtain reduced taxes while shifting the burden to middle- and working-class people (Figure 7-2). This change was justified by asserting that low taxes on the rich would produce greater tax revenue and reduce tax evasion and avoidance. In addition, it was argued that high taxes destroy business initiative and constitute a form of "class warfare" against the rich. Whether the common good is served by low taxes on the rich is questionable.

Finally, with some exceptions, the lifestyle of the rich reflects an attempt at preserving privacy. In this context, wealth allows for personal autonomy and considerable luxury. But in expressing their lifestyle, most people with a lot of money try to combine social status with sound financial investments. These can range from second homes that are working ranches to art that appreciates in value. Education in elite prep schools provides a vehicle for both preserving the lifestyle of the rich and access to power.

C h a p t e r 8

The Middle Class

The middle class has not always existed. The essence of middle-class life is to do nonmanual labor. Persons in white-collar jobs usually sit at desks, nearly always stay physically clean while they work, often supervise others, sometimes engage in entrepreneurial activity, and frequently have high incomes. More polemically, they do not "bend, lift, scrub, shovel, haul, or engage in other potentially damaging exertions for a living" (Ehrenreich, 1990, p. 233). They join fitness clubs instead. But this need of large numbers of people for physical activity as a respite from work is new in history.

In colonial times the structure of stratification did not include a middle class. Nearly everyone worked with their hands. A few people, however, were anomalies—pointing to the future. For example, in *Paul Revere's Ride,* the historian David Hackett Fischer observed that Revere saw himself as both an artisan (a silversmith) and a gentleman—without any sense of contradiction (1994). As a gentleman, he was part of the political elite of Massachusetts. He was not the loner described in the myth of "Paul Revere's Ride." Rather, he organized and directed resistance to the British in the Boston area during the 1770s. The ability of such a man to rise to the top suggests that the stratification structure was simple. Indeed, all societies prior to industrialization can be divided into two main classes: a small ruling class and the great mass of people (Marx & Engels, 1848; Lenski, 1967). Colonial America was no different; the vast majority of people worked the land while a small elite of landowners and entrepreneurs dominated the new society. The colonial stratification structure was unique in history, however, because it was relatively open. Hence, even though they lacked an aristocratic lineage, exceptional individuals like Revere could rise to the top and plausibly claim to be "gentlemen." But he worked with his hands. Indeed, Fischer showed that Revere was one of the finest silversmiths in the colonies. He was an artist. Today, the combination of artisanship and elite membership is unlikely; few silversmiths get elected to Congress or belong to the clubs of the rich. Revere's position was significant historically and sociologically because he was part of a very small group of "middling sorts," people who were highly skilled, relatively autonomous, earned a cash income, and on that basis had sufficient leisure time to be able to participate in the political life of the community.

Eventually, as Max Weber recognized, the stratification structure became more complex and a new term, *middle class,* came to be used to describe people who neither work with their hands nor possess wealth. According to Stuart Blumin in *The Emergence of the Middle Class,* this peculiar stratum arose over the course of the nineteenth century as the number of white-collar jobs increased (see Chapter 3), people in these jobs began being paid by salaries instead of hourly wages, and the spatial separation of blue- and white-collar jobs occurred (1989). In this context, Blumin showed, a unique **lifestyle** gradually developed that set the nascent middle class off from the working class. You should recall that the term refers to people's way of living as indicated by their consumption habits, use of leisure time, and fundamental choices and values. Thus, the greater income of the middle class allowed for larger homes filled with more elaborate furnishings. Patterns of housing segregation by class developed, and those doing white-collar work tended to live in one place, indicating that their jobs were stable. For example, in Boston during 1840 to 1850 only 36 percent of unskilled manual workers remained residentially stable for the entire decade, compared to 69 percent of white-collar workers (Archer & Blau, 1993). Although the emerging middle class was very small, its stability meant that people with similar characteristics began associating with one another in churches, clubs, and the like. They began keeping their children in school and even sending them to college. Young people with similar backgrounds and experiences began to marry one another. The spread of these characteristics over a period of years expressed a historically unique lifestyle, one that still exists today. It meant that the middle class crystallized as a more-or-less self-aware aggregate around the turn of the twentieth century.

Yet, surprisingly, intellectuals often disparage middle-class people because they are presumably unaware of their true interests. C. Wright Mills, for example, provided one of the most provocative accounts in *White Collar* (1951). Mills contrasted the "old middle class" of the nineteenth century, which he characterized (inaccurately) as independent, self-employed, and self-sufficient, with the "new middle class" of the present, which he depicted (also inaccurately) as mere employees who are politically impotent and alienated. In sociology, remember, the term **alienation** refers to people who feel powerless, so much so that dominant norms and values seem remote. While any book by Mills contains more interesting ideas than most sociological treatises, this one is fundamentally flawed by the fact that he has an intellectual's dislike for the "little people" who constitute his subject. They do not share his interest in ideas, his definition of freedom, or his fantasies about nineteenth century life. It is true that most middle-class people today are employees; for Mills, this fact indicates that they are essentially proletarians, such as those Marx described, and Mills condemned them as a result. Erik Olin Wright continued this tradition in *Classes* (1997). He argued that middle-class people occupy a "contradictory class location," meaning that they do not own capital yet have authority over working-class people—at least on the job. The implication is, once again, that middle-class people are really proletarians. Most middle-class people, however, do not share either Mills's or Wright's vision. They define themselves as representing what is best about the United States: hard work, economic and occupational success, and individual autonomy. Because these attitudes seem so central, so characteristic of this country, people who have them like to call themselves middle class. Thus, as shown in Chapter 2, the class identification question reveals that most people with white-collar jobs say they are middle class. And, along with the rich, they dominate the political process in the United States. In Chapter 1, Lenski proposed that power decisively affects the distribution of resources in the United States. Virtually all theorists describe **power,** the ability to achieve goals even if opposition occurs, as fundamental to understanding the structure of stratification. In covariance form, the Political Power Hypothesis presented in Chapter 1 was as follows:

> *The higher the social class, the greater the influence over the distribution of resources in the society.*

This chapter illustrates some of the ways the middle class protects its interests and affects the distribution of resources and public policy. I begin with job perquisites.

Social Class and Job Perquisites

Job perquisites consist of any protections, privileges, or benefits tied to one's employment status. They have a long history. For example, a 1913 Bureau of Labor Statistics study described 50 companies that provided employees with such perquisites as on-site eating facilities, pension plans, paid vacations, and the like (Mitchell, 1992). Although such benefits were the exception then, they are now more common. Today, the list of potential perquisites includes sick leave, personal leave, disability insurance, on-site child care, parental leave, free parking (very important in large cities), educational assistance, and much more. In addition to these sorts of "perks," many companies provide upper-echelon employees with rather special benefits, such as expense accounts, use of company-owned cars, membership in private clubs, entertainment, and stock options. Often called "fringe benefits," job perquisites are not fringe at all; rather, they are fundamental aspects of remuneration and constitute a significant element in the structure of stratification in the United States. Indeed, they are so central to middle-class people's lives that they cannot envision being without these benefits and privileges.

Employee job perquisites exaggerate the inequality resulting from class differences in income, to be described later (Pierce, 1998). Their pervasiveness reflects the power of middle-class people, who obtain resources that are usually limited to the working class and denied to the poor. Yet the importance of job perquisites is not well-known, mainly because they are difficult to measure. Nonetheless, people with higher incomes generally have the best protections, privileges, and benefits. This fact can be expressed by what I shall call the *Job Perquisite Hypothesis:*

The higher the social class, the greater the job perquisites.

Although the hypothesis is probably accurate, I do not describe the relationship as an empirical generalization because measurement problems exist and the research literature omits certain topics. For example, while considerable work has been done on the job perquisites available to ordinary workers, there is very little social scientific research on the additional perquisites enjoyed by top-level white-collar employees. Hence, the most conservative strategy is to pose a hypothesis and present what data do exist. The job perquisites I shall review in the following paragraphs are private pensions, health insurance, sick leave, disability insurance, vacation and personal leave time, and (more speculatively) top-level perquisites.

Private Pensions

Private pensions constitute earnings deferred until retirement. Pensions were unnecessary until recently because so few people lived into old age. In 1890, for example, only 4 percent of the population was over age 65 (USBC, 1975, p. 15). But that figure was an all-time high and apparently triggered the discovery of "old age" as a social problem and the need for pensions (Fischer, 1978). Thus, in 1903 Edward Everett Hale (himself more than 80 years old at the time) published an article titled "Old Age Pensions" in *Cosmopolitan.* He proposed that all workers should contribute $2.00 per year to a pension fund until they were 69. After that, they would receive an annuity of $100 for the remainder of their lives (Hale, 1903). This principle—contributions during people's working years (either by the employer, employee, or both) and yearly payments after retirement—remains the basis of all pension plans.

Although the principle remains the same, pension plans today can be divided into two types: defined benefit and defined contribution. Defined benefit plans provide annuities equal to a percentage of employees' preretirement earnings, usually calculated based on years of service to a company. In such plans, the employer invests the money and takes the risk. Defined contribution plans provide that an employer (and sometimes employees) will contribute a percentage of employees' wages to a pension fund each month; but there is no guarantee of a specific benefit on retirement. In this type of plan, the employee invests the money and takes the risk. Participation in pension plans is important, as people live longer now and the proportion of the population over age 65 has increased to 13 percent today. And this figure will rise to 20 percent or (probably) more during the next century (USBC, 1996b, pp. 2–3). Today, about 41 percent of all workers participate in employer- or union-sponsored retirement plans in addition to social security (USBC, 1997b, p. 434). This relatively low level of participation means that only about half of all retired families actually receive a pension (from any source: private or public) in addition to social security (USBC, 1997b, p. 374).

Participation in an employer-funded private pension plan varies by occupation, as shown in Table 8-1. Regardless of the size of the company or the type of plan, blue-collar workers are less likely to participate in pension plans. This is so even though the law requires that if a pension plan is offered to some employees, it must be offered to all. Companies find all sorts of ways around this requirement. These data are important because they mean that pension benefits and, hence, lifestyle after retirement reflect the preretirement class structure.

This fact is depicted in Table 8-2, which illustrates how private pension and social security benefits are distributed by income. The table uses two examples of final year's income, $35,000 and $65,000, which are typical of blue- and white-collar people. Column (4) shows that while blue-collar workers who have both a pension and social security receive about 66 percent of their preretirement income, it remains significantly less in dollars than that obtained by white-collar workers because of the latters' higher salaries. Columns (2) and (3) reveal an interesting insight: The impact of social security

TABLE 8-1   Participation in Employer Paid Private Pension Plans

(1)	Large- and Medium-Sized Firms		Small Firms	
	(2) Percentage with Defined Benefit	(3) Percentage with Defined Contribution	(4) Percentage with Defined Benefit	(5) Percentage with Defined Contribution
Occupation				
Professional and Technical	53%	67%	16%	45%
Clerical and Sales	53	64	16	39
All Blue Collar	50	45	15	26

Sources: USDL (1998a, p. 8; 1997, p. 4).

Note: Small firms are defined as those with fewer than 100 employees. Medium and large firms are defined as those with 100 to 250 or more employees.

TABLE 8-2   Examples of Retirement Income Available for Full-Time Employees in Private Sector Firms

(1) Final year's income	(2) Pension as percent of final year's earnings and as income	+	(3) Social Security as percent of final year's earnings and as income	=	(4) Total as percent of final year's earnings and as income
$35,000	34%	+	32%	=	66%
	$12,000	+	$11,244	=	$23,244
$65,000	39%	+	18%	=	57%
	$25,500	+	$11,976	=	$37,476

Source: Wiatrowski (1994).

is to reduce income inequality after retirement by providing lower-income people with a higher proportion of their preretirement income. This difference is one reason why many elderly people are not impoverished. Nonetheless, to repeat, those with higher preretirement incomes generally receive more cash benefits when they retire and, as a result, enjoy a nicer lifestyle in old age. You should remember that Table 8-2 is only illustrative of a general point:

The higher the preretirement income, the higher the postretirement income.

Thus, these data conform to the Job Perquisite Hypothesis.

Medical Insurance

Medical insurance pays for treatment when people become sick or injured. The earliest known coverage for medical treatment in this country occurred in 1798, with the establishment of the U.S. Marine Hospital Services (Scofea, 1994). Under this plan, seamen had deductions taken from their salaries in order to pay for hospital services. The first private insurance plans to pay for medical treatment were organized by mining, lumber, and railroad companies in the Far West in the 1870s and 1880s. Companies set up clinics and prepaid doctors to provide their employees with services. A movement advocating some form of nationwide medical insurance developed during the early years of this century, partly because most European nations had already enacted such plans. It was opposed in this country by unions (which thought they would be weakened), physicians (who assumed their salaries would be lower), and insurance companies (which wanted to retain a lucrative business for themselves) (Scofea, 1994).

This movement failed. Legislation mandating nationwide health insurance also failed in 1994. Thus, for most people today, about 70 percent of the population, medical insurance is tied to employment.

Insurance plans typically cover hospitalization, surgery, and medical treatment—although the way this process occurs varies. People become eligible to participate in these plans when they are hired and for as long as they continue employment with the sponsoring company. As with pensions, companies frequently pay most or all of the cost of medical insurance for employees, thereby helping them to pay lower income taxes. (I will illustrate what this means later.) Those who are laid off, fired, or quit for any reason lose insurance benefits—just when they are most needed. Some form of private or public medical insurance (Medicaid or Medicare) covers only about 85 percent of the population (USBC, 1997b, p. 120). I say "only" here because in other Western nations, the proportion is 100 percent. In this country, 15 percent of the population—42 million people—have no health insurance coverage. As with pensions, the coverage rate varies by social class. For example, the data below show the percentage of people not covered by medical insurance by family income (USBC, 1998d):

$75,000 or more	8%
$50,000–74,999	10%
$25,000–49,999	17%
Less than $25,000	24%

These data illustrate that individuals not participating in employer-based group medical insurance plans are disproportionately working class and poor, and nearly all of them do not participate because they cannot. Their employers do not give them a choice. Although Medicaid presumably aids poor persons without other means of obtaining medical treatment, Chapter 10 will show that coverage is inconsistent and a significant proportion of the poor are not eligible. Middle-class people, however, do not suffer from these problems and, hence, are relatively unconcerned. As with private pensions, the data on medical insurance conforms to the Job Perquisite Hypothesis.

Sick Leave

Sick leave constitutes protection against income loss for short periods of physical incapacity, usually providing full pay for several weeks. Columns (2) and (4) of Table 8-3 show the percentage of employees with employer paid sick leave by occupation in companies of varying size. Most white-collar workers (74 to 78 percent in large- and medium-sized firms, 61 to 69 percent in small firms) can stay at home and still get paid if they get the flu. Or, let's say, they have to undergo minor surgery; they can stay home and recuperate—and still get paid. In contrast, most blue-collar workers have a stark choice: work and get paid or stay home and do not get paid. Moreover, among those with sick leave, the number of days people can receive their wages varies by occupation, as shown in columns (3) and (5). After five years of employment with a large- or medium-sized company, white-collar professional worker receive three weeks or more of paid sick leave, while blue-collar workers receive less than two weeks. Small firms offer everyone a fewer number of sick leave days, and blue-collar workers still receive fewer days to recuperate than white-collar workers. Put differently, middle-class people, who are least likely to become sick or hurt, are most likely to have sick leave benefits and, when such perquisites are available, have more days in which to recuperate. Thus, as with the benefits considered previously, the data on sick leave agree with the Job Perquisite Hypothesis.

Disability Insurance

Disability insurance constitutes protection against income loss from long periods of physical incapacity. The first disability insurance policy was probably written in Massachusetts in 1850. For a premium of fifteen cents, a policyholder would be paid $200 in case of injury due to a railway or steamboat accident (Scofea, 1994). The nation's first group health policy was disability insurance purchased by Montgomery Ward and Co. in 1910. It provided benefits up to half of an employee's weekly salary. Benefits today are somewhat greater but participation in employer-paid long-term disability plans varies by occupation, as revealed in Table 8-4. Column (2) shows that in large- and medium-sized companies, 53 to 60 percent of white-collar employees have such coverage paid by the firm, compared to only 26 percent of blue-collar employees. The proportions are lower in small firms, as shown in column (4), but the pattern is the same. Once people get coverage, however, the proportion of their income replaced does not vary much (see columns (3) and (5)). Thus, given coverage, disability payments can be combined with social security disability, workers' compensation, and other government benefits such that total compensation provides a relatively high proportion of people's full pay for an extended period of time, which can be quite variable. Those working for companies not offering disability insurance must pay for it themselves, something middle-class people find easier to do, since they earn more than their working-class counterparts to begin with. Many of the latter simply go without.

TABLE 8-3   Employer Paid Sick Leave by Occupation

| (1) | Large- and Medium-Sized Firms | | Small Firms | |
| | (2) Percentage with Paid Sick Leave | (3) Average Number of Days | (4) Percentage with Paid Sick Leave | (5) Average Number of Days |
Occupation				
Professional and Technical	74%	22	69%	11
Clerical and Sales	78	17	61	10
All Blue Collar	39	13	36	9

Sources: USDL (1998b, pp. 7, 28; 1997, pp. 4, 25).

Note: The average number of days of paid sick leave used here occurs after five years of service with a firm. Small firms are defined as those with fewer than 100 employees. Medium and large firms are defined as those with 100 to 250 or more employees.

TABLE 8-4   Employer Paid Long-Term Disability Insurance by Occupation

| (1) | Large- and Medium-Sized Firms | | Small Firms | |
| | (2) Percentage with Paid Disability | (3) Percentage of Income Replaced | (4) Percentage with Paid Disability | (5) Percentage of Income Replaced |
Occupation				
Professional and Technical	60%	60%	36%	61%
Clerical and Sales	53	59	26	61
All Blue Collar	26	58	10	61

Sources: USDL (1998b, pp. 7, 35; 1997, pp. 4, 32).

Note: Small firms are defined as those with fewer than 100 employees. Medium and large firms are defined as those with 100 to 250 or more employees.

Hence, the data available on disability insurance also conforms to the Job Perquisite Hypothesis.

Vacation and Personal Leave Time

The perquisites discussed above consist of company-supplied income protection before and after retirement. Other job privileges exist, however, two of which are paid vacations and personal leave. Both reward employment and service to a company. Among large- and medium-sized firms, white-collar people usually receive longer vacations and are more likely to have personal leave time (USDL, 1998a, p. 7). Thus, on the average, professionals and administrators in such companies obtain about 16 days vacation after five years of service while blue-collar employees get 12 days or less. In these same companies, about 24 percent of professionals and administrators receive personal leave time while only 15 percent of blue-collar workers obtain paid leave. The pattern for smaller companies is similar. Thus, white-collar people have more opportunities to visit their children's school, go to the dentist, vote, or deal with any personal problem, without losing pay. Moreover, it should be emphasized that the above information about leave understates class differences because very few white-collar workers punch time clocks. Hence, their working hours are much less regulated. Even among the lowest prestige white-collar workers, informal norms often develop that allow for daily and situation-specific variations in established schedules. White-collar workers, in short, are much more capable of coming and going as they please, as long as their work gets done. These rewards go disproportionately to middle-class people, who see them as occupational rights. Once again, then, data on vacation and leave time conform to the Job Perquisite Hypothesis.

Top-Level Perquisites

Before leaving the issue of job perquisites, the issue of rewards to higher-echelon employees must be noted. Although data are sparse, one survey of 400 large companies shows that about 60 percent of them supply upper-level white-collar workers with company cars for their use, a source of tax-free income since recipients do not need to purchase their own car (Zane, 1995). At the extreme, members of the president's cabinet, other federal officials, and some corporate executives receive chauffeur-driven limousines as part of their remuneration. In addition, about 58 percent of these firms purchase memberships for high-ranking employees in country clubs, exclusive clubs (such as the Union League in Philadelphia or the University Club in New York City), or other private associations. There are lots of other "perks": expense accounts (another source of tax-free income), access to an executive dining room and other meal allowances, physical examinations, financial consulting, personal liability insurance, and home security systems, among many others. My guess is that companies provide many season tickets at professional sports events and sky boxes in stadiums for corporate officials and friends. Finally, upper-echelon employees often receive options to purchase stock at very favorable prices as part of their salary package. None of these perquisites are subject to federal income tax. The only limit to job perquisites for high-echelon people is the imagination. Although little research exists on the extensiveness of these benefits and privileges, when corporations provide such perquisites to employees in a tax-exempt fashion, they add to the level of inequality in a way that is hidden from view. I shall address this issue later when dealing with income transfers.

In sum, although the available data are more limited than I would like, it appears that the Job Perquisite Hypothesis accurately summarizes the relationship between social class and employee fringe benefits. If this is true, it suggests that middle-class people have a greater ability to protect their economic situation and lifestyle than do working-class people.

Power and Job Perquisites

The link between occupation and job perquisites increases inequality. The experience of Mary Mendez, a 40-year-old single mother, provides an example (Passell, 1998). She sorts apples in a packing house in Wenatchee, Washington, for $7.71 per hour. After a minor injury at work forced her to stay home for a few days to recover, her employer simply did not pay her for the time off. It is hard to imagine such harshness toward white-collar employees. Moreover, although the firm she works for offers medical insurance to employees, she must contribute $21 per month to cover her child. This on a budget that is only slightly above the poverty line. In contrast, the state takes care of all pension, medical, and disability needs in most Western European nations, which means that class differences are minimal. Hence, the millions of European citizens in jobs like that held by Mary Mendez have much more economic security than she does. This fact means there is less inequality in these nations. But this fact is irrelevant to most middle-class people in the United States because they have all the pension, health, and disability coverage they need. So they do not demand the development of government programs that might provide these benefits for everyone. Hence, those working-class and poor people who remain without adequate income protection are politically isolated and ineffective. Compared to the middle class, they lack power, especially (as shown in Chapter 7) voting power.

C. Wright Mills argued that white-collar people are politically impotent and alienated. Yet those who are powerless should not be able to garner for themselves higher pensions, better health insurance, more sick leave, and greater protection against disability. Moreover, these differences in perquisites indicate that middle-class employees have greater control over their lives, both on and off the job, than do working-class employees. So perhaps white-collar people are not as alienated as Mills suggested.

Social Class, Income Inequality, and Income Transfers

The job perks discussed above, while very important, are not the same as a pay check. Income makes a lifestyle possible, and it is lifestyle that separates the middle class from the working class.

Social Class and Income

The top row of Table 8-5 reveals that the median income for people working full-time all year long was $35,200 for males and $26,000 for females in 1997. As it turns out, the median highlights class differences, since most white-collar workers earn more than the median while most blue-collar workers earn less. Thus, the average male white-collar worker, an administrator of some sort or a professional worker, earns well over the median (for men), about $50,000. Similarly, the average female professional also earns well over the median (for women), about $35,000. Among men, the only white-collar job category in which people do not earn more than the median is administrative support. Among women, those in sales and administrative support usually do not earn above average wages. In general, then, most people in white-collar jobs find that their work pays off, not only in pleasure and prestige, but monetarily as well. In contrast, individuals in blue-collar jobs nearly always earn less than the median. The typical male machine operator earns about $27,900 each year, not much to live on, even with a spouse who is, say, a secretary. The only exception to this pattern is male precision production workers (such as skilled electricians, probably union members) who earn about $31,500 on average. More generally, however, as one looks down the table each occupational category includes a higher proportion of jobs with lower prestige and income. So work pays off for these people, but barely.

The income distribution shown in Table 8-5 reveals the importance of both spouses in maintaining family lifestyle—even though the table reveals that women earn less than men in every occupational category (recall Chapter 4). It is an empirical generalization that husbands and wives tend to be from the same social class; that is, white-collar men usually marry white-collar women, and blue-collar men marry blue-collar women (Eshleman, 1994). (The most prevalent cross-class marriage pattern is for blue-collar men to marry women in administrative support jobs.) This finding of class homogeneity can be used to suggest the implications family income has for class differences in lifestyle. For example, assume that a male physician is married to a female lawyer. Although not shown in the table, their incomes would usually be above the average for professional workers. Let us assume for a moment that the physician earns $150,000 and the lawyer $100,000. These plausible figures mean that their total

TABLE 8-5   Median Income by Occupation and Gender, 1997 (Year-Round, Full-Time Workers)

Occupation	Male	Female
All Workers	$35,200	$26,000
White Collar		
Executives and Managers	50,100	33,000
Professional Specialty	50,400	35,400
Technicians	37,700	27,600
Sales	35,700	21,400
Administrative Support	29,400	22,500
Blue Collar		
Precision Production	31,500	21,600
Machine Operators	27,000	17,700
Transportation	28,200	21,000
Handlers and Laborers	21,500	15,800
Service	22,300	16,000
Farming, Forestry, and Fishing	17,400	17,300

Source: USBC (1998f, p. 28).

income of $250,000 makes them rich—statistically, at least. In identification, however, they would undoubtedly see themselves as upper-middle class. A few years ago, they were called "Yuppies," young urban professionals, with unflattering connotations. In comparison, assume that a female nurse marries a male high school teacher. Again, both are professional workers. She earns, let us say, $45,000 per year, and he $40,000. Their combined income of $85,000 makes them solidly middle class, and they would undoubtedly identify as such. But their lifestyle is much restricted compared to the physician-lawyer couple. Finally, consider a male police officer married to a female secretary. Police officers are service workers, and they usually earn above the average for that category. Let's assume he earns $30,000 per year and she earns $28,000. Their combined income of $58,000 requires a more restricted lifestyle. That is to say: These three couples live in different neighborhoods, shop in different stores, take different vacations, and usually send their children to different colleges (although working-class youth are less likely to attend college). Such variations suggest what it means to be upper-middle, middle, and working class in the United States. All these people have been buffeted, although in different ways, by changes in the distribution of income over the past half-century.

Trends in Income Inequality

Whether the United States has become more unequal over time is a controversial topic, and not just among academics. During the quarter century after World War II, real incomes (adjusted for inflation) rose among all social classes (Levy & Murnane, 1992).

Hence, everyone could afford a better lifestyle. It is not accidental that rates of home ownership (among whites) expanded significantly during this period. But improvements in standard of living differ from changes in the degree of income inequality. For reasons that will become apparent, this discussion is divided into two parts: the period from 1950 to 1970 and from 1970 to the present.

Income Inequality, 1950–1970

Two alternative hypotheses describe income inequality during the years after World War II until about 1970: the Inequality Reduction Hypothesis and the Inequality Stability Hypothesis. The *Inequality Reduction Hypothesis* is as follows:

> *The lower the social class, the greater the benefit from income transfers and the lower the level of inequality from 1950 to 1970.*

The term **income transfers** in the hypothesis refers to government spending that provides money or benefits to individuals without obtaining goods or services in exchange, which means there is no increase in the gross national product (GNP). Thus, an income transfer occurs whenever money or an in-kind benefit, such as medical treatment, is simply given to recipients by the government with no expectation of receiving goods or services in return. Beginning in the mid-1930s, the federal government developed a variety of programs providing economic benefits to the population. Some of the most well known of these initiatives assist the poor: Temporary Assistance for Needy Families (TANF), Supplementary Security Income (SSI), Medicaid, and Food Stamps, among others (see Chapter 10). These programs are salient to the public and appear to reduce income inequality. After all, cash programs like TANF and SSI provide income, while noncash programs like Medicaid and Food Stamps provide economically valuable resources (Danziger et al., 1981). Additional programs benefit the aged: Social Security and Medicare, among others. You should recall Table 8-2 here: One impact of Social Security is to reduce income inequality among the aged. So the Inequality Reduction Hypothesis sounds like common sense.

It turns out, however, that the hypothesis suffers from three problems: First, the literature supporting it fails to include all cash income transfers to various population groups (Danziger et al., 1981; Danziger & Plotnick, 1977). To use only one example, the impact of farm price supports, which go mainly to the largest and richest farmers, is omitted (USDA, 1998a, p. 40). Second, this argument assumes that public assistance reduces poverty, ignoring the fact that recipients must remain poor in order to continue receiving benefits and that the cash goes to middle-class people (see Figure 10-3). The different impact of such programs as TANF and Social Security reflects the means test that characterizes the former but not the latter. Thus, precisely because it has no means test (that is, it does not require that recipients remain poor), the Social Security program reduces inequality among the aged. Third, the Inequality Reduction Hypothesis flies in the face of theoretical understanding. Gerhard Lenski, remember, found that power has determined the distribution of resources over most of human history (1966). Now theory can be refuted by evidence, of course, but those proposing the Inequality

TABLE 8-6   Income Inequality, 1950–1997

	1950	1960	1970	1980	1990	1997
Panel A: Percentage of Income Received by Each Quintile and Top 5%						
Poorest Fifth	5%	5%	5%	5%	4%	4%
Second Fifth	12	12	12	12	10	9
Third Fifth	17	18	18	18	16	15
Fourth Fifth	23	24	24	24	24	23
Richest Fifth	43	41	41	42	47	49
	100%	100%	100%	101%	101%	100%
Richest 5%	16%	16%	16%	15%	18%	19%
Panel B: Gini Coefficient of Income Inequality for Families and Households						
Families	.379	.364	.353	.365	.396	.426
Households			.394	.403	.428	.459

Source: USBC (1995c, p. xii; 1998f, p. xvii).

Note: Totals of 101% represent rounding error. The most recent Gini Coefficient for families (.426) is for 1994.

Reduction Hypothesis fail to address the issue. In sum, despite the redistributive effect of Social Security, the Inequality Reduction Hypothesis does not explain the facts.

Rather, the best explanation of the pattern of income inequality between World War II and about 1970 is the *Inequality Stability Hypothesis:*

> *The higher the social class, the greater the benefit from income transfers such that the overall distribution of income remained unchanged from 1950 to 1970.*

Table 8-6 illustrates the Inequality Stability Hypothesis in two ways. Please look first at Panel A for the years 1950 to 1970. These data show that the income distribution was relatively stable during this period. The poorest 20 percent of the population received about 5 percent of the total income, the second 20 percent about 12 percent, the third about 18 percent, the fourth about 24 percent, and the richest fifth about 41 percent. The top 5 percent of families (included in the "richest fifth") received about 15 percent of the total income. Now look at the Gini Coefficients displayed in Panel B for the years 1950 to 1970. The Gini Coefficient provides a more subtle measure of income inequality. It is a standard index in which the higher the number the greater the inequality.[1] Again, the data show that income inequality among families was rather stable (in fact, declining) during this period.

[1]A zero Gini Coefficient would mean complete equality (every family has the same income) and 1.00 would mean complete inequality (one family has all the income). This measure provides a way of suggesting how far an income distribution is from equality (USBC, 1996a, p. 1).

The reason for this stability lies in the impact of income transfers. The pattern shown in the left portion of Panels A and B is plausible because "income" includes cash received from virtually any source: not just earnings, but also unemployment and workers' compensation, social security and veterans' benefits, public aid, survivor and disability benefits, educational assistance, alimony and child support payments, and all other periodic cash income. Thus the impact of income transfers is included in the data. Moreover, the Inequality Stability Hypothesis makes sense theoretically, of course, because in most societies the more powerful classes make sure they obtain their "fair" share of the benefits from such programs. "Fair," of course, is defined as "more." Recall here the pie metaphor used in Chapter 5 to describe the different interests of racial and ethnic groups. Classes have different interests as well: They want a bigger piece of the pie.

Several studies have shown that the pattern displayed in Table 8-6 for the years 1950 to 1970 is accurate. Reynolds and Smolensky looked at the impact of governmental tax and spending policies in three years: 1950, 1961, and 1970 (1977). Their analysis included a wide array of income transfers plus some that clearly go to nonpoor individuals, such as "farm income" (apparently price supports) and "housing expenditures" (apparently housing subsidies). In addition, they also took into account governmental outlays for such public goods as "auto expenditures" (apparently roads), "estimated expenditure on higher education," and "children under age 18" (apparently public school outlays). The term **public goods** refers to government expenditures for goods and services that, presumably, anyone can take advantage of or use, such as lighthouses or airports. Reynolds and Smolensky's major finding is that the distribution of income after governmental taxing and spending decisions was unchanged between 1950 and 1970.

Benjamin Page came to a similar conclusion after looking at the impact of government spending on a wide range of public goods, such as expenditures for national defense, science and technology, the administration of justice, government operations, energy, the environment, community and regional development, revenue sharing, and interest on the national debt. He concluded that "over time, greatly increased government activity has not led to more income equality. There is little indication that the United States government has done much net redistributing of income" (1983, p. 144).

Finally, in *American Inequality: A Macroeconomic History,* Williamson and Lindert examined income inequality during years after World War II and came to an unequivocal conclusion (1980, p. 92).

> *By almost any yardstick inequality has changed little since the 1940s. . . . The data that yield this conclusion differ greatly from one another. Several series are available: the Statistics of Income reported by the Internal Revenue Service, the Survey of Consumer Finances, the Census Bureau's Current Population Survey, the income distributions of the Social Security Administration, and the benchmark consumer surveys of the Bureau of Labor Statistics. . . . One would expect such diversity to produce a variety in the estimates, but in fact none of the inequality measures exhibits any dramatic trend.*

So for the period between World War II and 1970, income inequality remained rather stable. Although income transfers to impoverished people became politically salient during these years as more programs benefiting the poor came into existence, the overall impact of transfers was to preserve the status quo. Two final points: First, I have made this discussion somewhat longer than it had to be in order to emphasize, once again, the importance of hypothesis testing in the social sciences. We proceed, very imperfectly, by conjecture and refutation, to get at truth. Second, I would like to remind you of Max Weber's aphorism cited in Chapter 1: The social sciences are granted eternal youth. The reason is that findings vary over time (and across societies). Thus, in the 1970s the pattern of income inequality changed.

Income Inequality Since 1970

This change was not fate. It did not "just happen." It reflects, rather, the impact of human decisions on the structure of stratification. Please look now at Panel A of Table 8-6 for the years 1970 to 1997. Data for this more recent period show that the income distribution became more unequal as the bottom quintiles began receiving less income and the richest fifth (and top 5 percent) began receiving more. Although the differences in percentage may not seem like much, the samples are so large that even small changes are significant. Just how significant can be seen by looking at the Gini Coefficients in Panel B. Although the level of inequality is greater for households than for families, that is not my concern for the moment. Note that regardless of which unit is used, the Gini rose from 1970 to 1997. The United States became more unequal (USBC, 1996a). Moreover, these data provide a practical measure of how much better the lifestyle at the top is today compared to a few years ago: The increase in income inequality between 1970 and 1997, as measured by the Gini, was 17 percent for families and 14 percent for households.

The reasons for this change are very straightforward (Levy & Murnane, 1992). First, the Baby Boomer generation graduated from college in precisely these years and, hence, the supply of people looking for white-collar jobs increased. Salaries fell as a result, especially for the lower-middle class. Second, the demand for people in blue-collar jobs fell with the decline in manufacturing and the rise of service industries. Third, the impact of so-called supply-side economic policies adopted during this period redistributed income to the rich. With regard to this last item, I now want to examine how certain elements of income tax policy contribute to income inequality.

Tax Expenditures and Income Inequality

Taxes are the source of income for government. But all governments use tax policy to influence behavior, stimulating some activities rather than others, profiting some citizens rather than others. So it follows that individuals and groups compete to see who can benefit from such policies.

The vehicle for such benefits is **tax expenditures.** They constitute the least well known type of income transfer. The term refers to provisions of the tax code that provide special or selective reductions in taxes for certain groups of citizens and corporations (JCT, 1997, p. 2). In effect, the government chooses not to collect money it would otherwise be due. According to the Congressional Budget Office, such tax relief constitutes an allocation of monetary resources and adds to the budget deficit by either allowing taxpayers to retain income or by not taxing certain in-kind benefits. Such "special income tax provisions are referred to as tax expenditures because they are considered to be analogous to direct outlay programs, and the two can be viewed as alternative means of accomplishing similar budget policy objectives" (JCT, 1997, p. 2). For example, if the goal is to insure that the population has adequate housing, one way to do this is to provide cash assistance or vouchers to people. Another more or less equivalent way is to allow people to deduct or exclude from their taxes certain aspects of the cost of obtaining housing. In addition, of course, housing policies also stimulate the economy and thereby provide people with jobs. Thus, both direct budget outlays and tax expenditures cost money and often serve similar goals. For such reasons, the cost of tax expenditures is routinely included in calculations of the federal budget (OMB, 1998a, p. 89).[2]

Table 8-7 displays the most significant tax expenditures by budget category. Individuals received about $496 billion in benefits during fiscal year 1999, many of which went to middle-class and rich people. The table has a (rough) orderliness to it. The items at the top (#1 through 6) refer to the value of some of the job perquisites discussed earlier. Of course, most of the remaining tax expenditures also benefit the middle class and rich. The exceptions are items #23 through 25 at the bottom of the table, which go mainly to the poor. I have selected two examples from the table to illustrate how these programs work.

1. The deductibility of mortgage interest on owner-occupied homes (item #7) provided individuals with $45 billion in 1999, more than twice the $20 billion spent on housing assistance for the poor (OMB, 1998b, p. 279). What these benefits mean on an individual level is that an upper-middle class or rich family in the 28 percent tax bracket that paid $20,000 in mortgage interest in one year received a $5,600 income transfer from the government. This amount is, of course, much more than a poor family receiving cash via the TANF program and food stamps. Moreover, the mortgage interest deduction is supplemented by other benefits to homeowners. For example, items #7 and 8 in the table provide an additional $62 billion to individuals. Again, most of them are middle class and rich. In addition, the deduction for state and local income and property taxes of $30.2 billion (item #15) also includes significant benefits for homeowners. These programs are not means tested. People qualify for them merely by having sufficient income to purchase a house and make their mortgage payments. The point to remember, however, is that these benefits provide people with real cash to spend on whatever they want, and there exists no expectation that they will provide goods or services in return.

2. The exclusion of employer contributions for medical insurance premiums (item #2) provided individuals with $55 billion in 1999 and other medical exclusions (item #13) gave them an additional $28 billion. What these programs mean for people can be

[2]This section is adapted from Beeghley and Dwyer, "Income Transfers and Income Inequality" (1989).

TABLE 8-7   Tax Expenditures by Budget Category, Fiscal Year 1999

Category	Amount (in billions)
Individuals	
1. Exclusion of employer-provided pension contributions	91.7
2. Exclusion of employer contributions for medical insurance	54.8
3. Exclusion of employer-provided life-disability insurance	2.1
4. Exclusion of employer-provided transportation	3.2
5. Exclusion of various employer-provided fringe benefits	13.8
6. Exclusion of employer-provided child care	1.0
7. Deductibility of mortgage interest on home	44.7
8. Deductibility of state and local property tax on home	17.3
9. Exclusion of capital gains on home sales	5.7
10. Deductibility of charitable contributions	17.0
11. Credit for child care expenses	2.8
12. Deductibility of medical expenses	4.9
13. Other medical exclusions	27.5
14. Tax credit for children less than age 17	19.3
15. Deductibility of state-local income and property taxes	30.2
16. Reduced rates on long-term capital gains	29.4
17. Exclusion of capital gains at death	19.2
18. Exclusion of interest on state-local bonds	3.5
19. Exclusion of workers' compensation benefits	3.9
20. Exclusion of social security benefits	28.2
21. Exclusion of veterans' benefits	2.3
22. Exclusion of interest on state-local debt	12.2
23. Exclusion of public assistance benefits	.5
24. Credit for elderly, disabled, and blind	2.2
25. Earned income tax credit	5.2
26. All other	53.3
Total	495.9
All Corporate Tax Expenditures	59.9
Grand Total	555.8

Source: JCT (1997, p. 17).

Note: Some budget categories have been combined for ease of presentation.

illustrated with a simple example from my own medical insurance plan (many of your parents have similar plans). My premium for family coverage is $5,643 per year, of which the University of Florida pays $4,351 (77 percent) and I pay $1,292. Because of the exclusion of employer contributions, I receive an income transfer of $1,218 (assuming a 28 percent tax bracket). In addition, because my share of the payment is taken out of pretax income, I also receive an additional $362 income transfer. The reason for this result is that if an employer pays the total premium directly to its employees (in my case $5,643), who then use it to purchase medical insurance, they will have to pay taxes on the income. While the amounts will vary, those who have medical insurance as a job perquisite save a great deal of money. Again, this is real cash that can be used to take a vacation cruise or for anything else my heart desires. Medicaid benefits to the poor constitute an analogous program. As will be pointed out in Chapter 10, however, since the poor do not have extra money to begin with, those who do not receive Medicaid benefits simply go without medical treatment. As before, the exclusion of employer contributions for medical insurance is not means tested; one member of a family must merely have a job with a group insurance plan. The $40 billion cost of medical exclusions is only about 40 percent of outlays for Medicaid, about $102 billion in fiscal 1999 (OMB, 1998b, p. 277). But note who gets the cash from the Medicaid program: physicians, nurses, hospitals, drug companies, and so forth. Thus, the poor receive (inferior) treatment while middle-class and rich persons receive the money.

The bottom of Table 8-7 shows tax expenditures to corporations, which cost $60 billion in 1999. These benefits, which are only a small part of the way the government caters to business interests, redound to those who own stock, to employees, and to customers, mostly middle-class and rich people. If the economic benefits individuals receive from these programs are taken into account, it becomes clear that most tax expenditures (and, of course, income transfers as a whole) go to the middle class and rich.

Table 8-8 illustrates the way tax expenditures distribute benefits across social class by examining five programs. The data are arrayed according to adjusted gross income. Thus most of the benefits of the earned income tax credit go to those with low incomes. Although Social Security benefits are spread throughout the class structure, most go to people in the middle-income brackets. Finally, the ability to deduct mortgage interest

TABLE 8-8   Distribution of Selected Tax Expenditures by Adjusted Gross Income, Fiscal Year 1999

(1)	(2)	(3)	(4)	(5)	(6)
Adjusted Gross Income	Exclusion of Earned Income Tax Credit	Exclusion of Social Security	Deductibility of Mortgage Interest	Deductibility of State and Local Property Taxes	Deductibility of Charitable Contributions
<$10,000	21%	0%	0%	0%	0%
$10,000–20,000	48	7	0	0	1
$20,000–30,000	25	20	1	0	2
$30,000–40,000	5	24	3	1	4
$40,000–50,000	1	23	5	3	5
$50,000–75,000	0	22	19	11	17
$75,000–100,000	0	2	23	16	15
$100,000–200,000	0	1	32	29	21
>$200,000	0	1	17	39	36
	100%	100%	100%	99%	101%

Source: JCT (1997, p. 29).

Note: Some totals do not add to 100% because of rounding.

payments, state and local property taxes, and charitable contributions mainly benefits high-income people. You should remember that "adjusted gross income" as used in the table is not people's total income; rather it is income for tax purposes, after various deductions. The pattern in the table is meant to be instructive: As one looks from left to right, from column (2) to (6), the benefits of tax expenditures go increasingly to middle-class and rich people. I mentioned earlier that job perquisites exaggerate income inequality. Tax expenditures constitute one way this process occurs. Middle-class and rich people have more money to spend on the good things in life.

A final note: Tables 8-7 and 8-8 do not take into account the benefits individuals receive from public goods purchased by the federal government. While public goods are presumably for everyone, they actually provide benefits for specific groups. For example, everyone can take advantage of harbor dredging, drawbridge erection, light-house construction, and buoy maintenance financed by the federal government so long as they own a sailboat. This amenity, of course, is mainly reserved for upper-middle-class and rich people. People with lower incomes are much less likely to take advantage of it. Similarly, everyone can use the government-financed commercial and general aviation facilities at airports so long as they are rich enough to fly commercially, own a private plane, or use corporate aircraft. Again, these amenities are primarily reserved for middle-class and rich people. About half of the federal budget goes for such public goods; for example, internal affairs, science and technology, natural resources, commerce, community development, education, the administration of justice, general government, fiscal assistance, and interest on the national debt. These general categories include hundreds of programs like those mentioned above. Although one could question whether such public goods are income transfers, many economists treat them as such (Page, 1983; Reynolds & Smolensky, 1977). Thus the impact of spending on public goods amplifies that of tax expenditures specifically and income transfers generally.

Power and Income Inequality

The benefits of income transfers, whether as budget outlays or tax expenditures, are legislatively enacted. Politics, the process of producing legislation in a democracy, is a competitive process in which the most powerful usually receive the most benefits. This is why laws rarely constitute the "best" solution to problems; rather, they reflect compromises among competing groups. So despite the public salience of transfers to the poor, the overall impact of transfers was to maintain income inequality for many years (1950 to 1970) and increase it since then.

This increase constitutes one of the great social experiments of our time. It was justified by "supply-side" economic theory, which argued that placing more money in the hands of the rich through reduced taxes would ultimately benefit everyone. This is because the rich invest (or supply) money, creating jobs and (presumably) increased tax revenues. Hence, the result of making the rich richer would "trickle down" to the rest of the population. Note what went on here: The majority of the population gave money to the upper-middle class and rich on the grounds that everyone would benefit. Regardless of your opinion about this experiment (mine is that we got snockered), these data imply a simple fact described in Chapter 1: Modern societies determine how much inequality exists, how much poverty exists, and the forms they take. Although international data on income distributions have not been presented yet, other Western industrial societies, such as Sweden and England, display a more equal distribution of income than does the United States (see Chapter 11). In addition, poverty in these other nations is significantly less. The social structure in each case reflects these choices.

Once again: Although C. Wright Mills claimed that middle-class people are politically impotent and alienated, the evidence suggests otherwise. Rather, as theory predicts, middle-class people appear to have sufficient political power to insure that they obtain the highest proportion of income transfers. Moreover, earlier sections of this chapter showed that middle-class people possess higher incomes and more job perquisites than do working-class people. The enjoyment of these benefits implies, therefore, that middle-class people are very much in control of their lives; they are not alienated.

I mentioned earlier that income makes lifestyle possible and that lifestyle separates the middle class and working class. The next section illustrates this phenomenon.

Social Class and Lifestyle

Lifestyle is often taken to refer to the stuff people surround themselves with, such as houses, cars, and paintings, and to the way in which people amuse themselves, such as their modes of entertainment or avocations. And these issues do indeed provide important indicators of social class. But lifestyle also refers to how people organize their lives at home. For example, prior to World War II, it was common for middle-class families to employ working-class women as servants, mainly nannies, cooks, and maids (Palmer, 1989). But over time they have been, as the new saying goes, outsourced. The nanny works for the day care center, often without job perquisites. The cook works at McDonalds or one of the food delivery outfits—again, without benefits. And the maid works for a janitorial or cleaning service—without perks. When middle-class families do employ a maid, the impression one gets is that many (most?) cheat her out of social security benefits. Think of it as a small way of keeping a bigger piece of the economic pie. Lifestyle and stratification are inherently connected.

This connection is also revealed in terms of people's moral choices, another aspect of lifestyle. Put bluntly: Middle-class families cannot maintain their lifestyle if they cannot control their fertility.[3]

Some background is necessary. As it developed during the nineteenth century, the middle class acquired some peculiar values regarding family life and gender roles that distinguished it from the working class. As the economy was being transformed, working-class families continued to need the income generated by children and wives. In an urban environment, children in the working class often brought in 30 to 40 percent of the total family income (Zelizer, 1985, p. 58). Hence, even though both parents may

---

[3]The remainder of this section is adapted from my *What Does Your Wife Do? Gender and the Transformation of Family Life* (Beeghley, 1996, pp, 51–85).

have been employed, many families' survival depended on their children's earnings. It is important to understand that I am referring to the wages of young people, aged six to fourteen years. Historically, such individuals had always labored on the farm. (They continued doing so in the late nineteenth century.) Urban living did not change this condition for working-class women and children. Thus, families in this situation continued the age-old practice of having many children.

The nascent middle class, however, found itself in a different situation and, hence, developed different interests. Upwardly mobile, often working in occupations that had not existed previously, by the second half of the nineteenth century husbands were earning a "family wage"; that is, they could support their wives and children without them having to work for pay. As always, most housework remained labor intensive and it was asserted that women, often with the help of servants from the working class, ought to take primary responsibility for it. In this context, middle-class people began wanting smaller families and the birth rate declined as a result. Thus, for every 1,000 white women of childbearing age, the birth rate fell from 275 in 1800 to 131 in 1900, with much of this reduction occurring among the middle class (USBC, 1975, p. 49). In this context, child rearing became central to the middle-class lifestyle, and norms about appropriate levels of care and attention became stricter. Childhood became a distinct stage of life, and women, it was said, ought to be the primary caretakers of children because men had to earn a living and lacked nurturing instincts. (This was, of course, an ideological stance.) Men's and women's roles, at least in the middle class at this time, became rather narrowly defined. It was during this period that what we now call **traditional gender norms** emerged. As described in Chapter 4, these rules specified that women and men ought to have separate spheres: Women should bear and raise children and take care of their husbands while men should provide for the family economically and dominate public life. Such norms grew widespread in the middle class during the latter part of the nineteenth century. They extended to the working class later.

But these norms became unstable over time. The reduction in the birth rate referred to above was achieved by use of birth control (condoms, douches) and abortion (Sanderson, 1979). The rising incidence of abortion among middle-class women ignited the first abortion controversy during the latter years of the nineteenth century (Luker, 1984). As a result, restrictions on access to abortion were enacted in every state around the turn of the century. They served as a legal buttress to traditional gender norms, since the inability to regulate fertility kept women, especially middle-class women, from pursuing occupations requiring long training or cumulative expertise. This is because pregnancy could occur at any time, changing the direction of a woman's life. The situation remained this way for many years. Eventually, however, gender norms began changing—albeit mainly in the middle class. One (not the only) expression of these changing norms was the desire to regulate fertility. And that goal meant, in turn, access to birth control and, if necessary, to an abortion. Thus, the second abortion controversy developed in the 1960s and continues today. Although the ability to control fertility is an issue affecting all women (and all couples) regardless of social class, middle-class people—especially women—have always been predominant among activists favoring abortion rights. They have interests to protect.

But abortion is a moral issue. All discussions of this topic revolve around the question of whether the developing embryo is a person or a potential person. If it is assumed to be a person, a baby, then it follows that abortion can never be morally right because it is murder. In contrast, if the developing embryo is assumed to be a potential person, a fetus, then abortion can be morally justified and the issue becomes women's right to control their fertility. You should observe that each moral stance reflects an unverifiable assumption about the nature of developing life. This suggests that an underlying social division exists.

Some perspective on this division can be obtained by looking at data. Here are international rates of abortion per 1,000 women aged 15 to 44 as of the mid-1990s (Henshaw et al., forthcoming):

United States	23
Sweden	19
United Kingdom	12
France	12
Germany	8
Netherlands	7

Abortion is legal in each of these nations. In each it is relatively unregulated early in the pregnancy with increasing restrictions over time. These data suggest that a solution exists to the "abortion problem," that we do not have to live with such a high rate. That solution is contraception. The low rate of abortion in other nations reflects an emphasis on preventing pregnancy. It is probable that encouraging contraceptive use in the United States would reduce the level of abortions by half or more, a result that would make our rate similar to that in Western European nations (Westoff, 1988).

In general, whenever relatively obvious solutions are rejected, you can be sure that hidden social divisions exist. In this case, the debate about abortion is not only about moral values; it is also—and perhaps more importantly—about the nature of the family and the centrality of motherhood in women's lives. It is, in short, about lifestyle. Those on each side of the abortion debate in the United States want to live in different worlds.

In a sense, they do live in different worlds, framed by their social class. In *Abortion and the Politics of Motherhood,* Kristin Luker described the pro-life activists she interviewed in the following way (1984, p. 197). They are in their forties. They married young, around age 17, and have borne three or more children. They have a high school education or some college. They are not employed. They are married to lower-level white-collar workers, with a family income around $40,000 per year. They are most often Catholic, frequently converts; but regardless of faith group, religion constitutes one of the most important parts of their lives. It follows that those opposed to legal abortions (not just activists) want women to place their reproductive roles at the center of their lives. From this point of view, biology remains (or ought to remain) destiny; women are designed to be and ought to be mothers. This value is central to their world.

Note, however, that this value reflects their social and economic position. These women generally cannot take advantage of occupational opportunities available to others, who are more educated and have fewer children. The underlying reason they oppose widespread availability of contraception is that if sex became more accessible, then a central part of the bargain they have made, an exchange of sexual access for economic and social support, would be threatened. Their marital relationships reflect traditional gender norms.

The pro-choice activists Luker interviewed are quite different. They are also in their forties. But they delayed marriage until age 22 or so and have had only one or two children. Their fathers were college graduates, and they have obtained education beyond the bachelor's degree. They are employed, often in careers that carry opportunities for upward mobility. Married to professional men, their family income is $60,000 or more per year. They are usually not religiously active. It follows that those who favor keeping abortions legal (again, not just activists) want women to be able to balance their reproductive and nonreproductive roles. For them, biology should not be destiny. Rather, the similarities between men and women are more important than their differences. They believe both genders can become occupationally successful, exercise political power, and the like. From this point of view, motherhood is valued, but it is only one of many things women want to do in their lives. These values are central to their world.

Note, once again, the correspondence between the moral stance and social and economic circumstances. These women are in a position to take advantage of occupational opportunity. Their family background, education, and marital relationships make this possible. They favor making contraception widely available because, for them, sex is primarily a means for intimacy; its procreative function remains secondary. Their marriages have become (a little) more egalitarian.

Here is a simple example, taken from Luker, that further illustrates how activists on each side differ (1984, p. 198). The pro-choice women she interviewed describe themselves trying to avoid unwanted pregnancies because, in their experience, the birth of a child transforms one's life. A single mistake over 40 years, they note, can alter the plans and ambitions of a lifetime. Their view of morality follows. They do not believe that anyone obtains an abortion casually, for convenience. The pro-life women argue, in contrast, that while a pregnancy may be a surprise, the baby that results is almost never unwanted; hence, in their experience, a woman and her family can always "make room for one more." And their view of morality follows. They believe that many people seek abortions casually, for convenience. "Convenience," in this case, refers to any reason that makes motherhood secondary to education, career, or other ambitions. Ultimately, then, activists on each side of the abortion issue are really protecting their lifestyles.

Not everyone, of course, is an activist. Yet abortion is often seen as a cornerstone of the feminist movement, a movement that is dominated by the interests of middle-class white women. There is some truth to this assertion. Phrased simply, restrictions on the possibility of abortion are taken by many (not all) middle-class people as a threat to their economic interests and lifestyles. At the same time, as mentioned, abortion is a moral dilemma. Most people try (albeit imperfectly) to live by their values. In this regard, most people find themselves in the middle—supporting women's right to an abortion with some ambivalence (Beeghley, 1996). Yet, as it turns out, people's moral positions often fit with their economic interests. So it is with abortion. This is because the conflict over abortion is one aspect of the larger conflict over fertility control. Both are, to some degree, class struggles.

Summary

The middle class originated in the nineteenth century as the number of white-collar jobs increased, people in these jobs began being paid by salaries, and blue- and white-collar jobs became spatially separated. As a result, middle-class people developed a unique lifestyle: They became residentially stable, lived near one another, and interacted with one another. By the end of the nineteenth century, the middle class had coalesced into a more-or-less self-aware aggregate. Following from theory, the political power hypothesis asserts that the middle class and the rich have greater influence over the distribution of resources than the other social classes.

The Job Perquisite Hypothesis specifies that middle-class people receive much more from job perquisites such as private pensions (Tables 8-1 and 8-2), medical insurance, sick leave (Table 8-3), disability insurance (Table 8-4), and vacations and personal leave. Although evidence about top-level perquisites is sparse, such phenomena as expense accounts, company cars, exclusive memberships, and the like are clearly valued forms of remuneration among high-ranking employees. Job perquisites add to the level of inequality in the United States, making middle-class and rich persons unwilling to demand government programs to provide such benefits to everyone. They illustrate the ability of middle-class people to influence the distribution of resources.

People in white-collar jobs nearly always earn more than those in blue-collar jobs (Table 8-5). Although the Inequality Reduction Hypothesis states that income transfers reduced income inequality between 1950 and 1970, this argument appears to be wrong. Rather, the Inequality Stability Hypothesis better explains the facts. That is, income transfers served to maintain the level of inequality for many years (Table 8-6). Since 1970, however, income inequality has risen, primarily because of (1) the increased supply of white-collar workers as the Baby Boom generation matured and (2) the reduced demand as a result of so-called "supply-side" economics. Tax expenditures are provisions of the tax code that allow reductions in taxes for selective groups of citizens and corporations. They constitute an important, if relatively unknown, form of income transfers. Tax expenditures are analogous to direct outlay programs, often attempting to achieve similar goals, such as providing housing or medical insurance for the population. Examining the array of tax expenditures by budget category suggests that some programs exist to benefit people at every class level (Table 8-7). Nonetheless, the benefits of tax expenditures appear to go primarily to middle-class and rich people (Table 8-8).

The last section of the chapter looked at how lifestyle reflects people's values by comparing activists on each side of the abortion issue. As it turns out, people's moral stance often corresponds to their economic interests. Pro-life activists tend to be working class and lower-middle class. In contrast, pro-choice activists tend to be upper-middle class. This difference suggests that the debate over abortion is, in part, class struggle.

Chapter *9*

The Working Class

Does the working class differ from the middle class? The Embourgeoisement Hypothesis suggests that it does not (DeFronzo, 1973). Although the word "embourgeoisement" is unwieldy, it stems from Karl Marx's work and attempts to account for the lack of working-class radicalism in the United States. To use his terminology for a moment, it asserts that the bourgeoisie have allowed proletarians to become sufficiently affluent that they are not very interested in political activity aiming at income redistribution, greater economic equality, or other forms of radical change. In plainer language, the hypothesis proposes that there has been long-term improvement in the occupational characteristics, income, and lifestyle of working-class people such that they now resemble middle-class persons, with the result that the members of the working class do not display distinctive political attributes.

If this argument is correct, then it should be observable. For example, researchers should find that the occupational settings of blue- and white-collar people are similar, that they have similar incomes, and that they have similar ways of living. Such findings would mean that a separate analysis of the working class, like that undertaken here, is unnecessary because most people in the United States, excluding the very rich and the poor, are reasonably affluent and middle class. I intend to show that this hypothesis is incorrect, that the working class differs from the middle class in fundamental ways.

I ought to mention that few social scientists think the embourgeoisement hypothesis accurately portrays the working-class situation because the evidence does not support it (van den Berg, 1993). Nonetheless, the argument is useful for my pedagogical purposes, since it shows how an interesting idea can be put forth and refuted empirically. Phrased formally, the *Embourgeoisement Hypothesis* is:

> *The more similarities in the occupational characteristics, income, and lifestyle between the working class and the middle class, then the less emphasis on radical political change by the working class.*

As stated, the hypothesis presupposes that middle- and working-class people are similar and uses this fact to explain why working-class people are not politically radical. Yet the presupposition may not be correct.

After all, previous chapters have shown some of the ways working-class and middle-class people differ. For example, as revealed in Chapter 2, people who have blue-collar jobs usually display lower occupational prestige than do their white-collar counterparts and their class identification is with the working class rather than middle class. Moreover, as described in Chapter 3, the division between blue- and white-collar work serves as a semipermeable barrier to mobility such that children of working-class parents usually end up in working-class jobs themselves. Finally, Chapter 8 revealed that working-class people have less income protection (pensions, medical insurance, sick leave, and disability insurance) and lower incomes than do middle-class people. Thus, the information already available casts doubt on the hypothesis: If working- and middle-class people differ so much, then the Embourgeoisement Hypothesis obviously cannot be correct.

In spite of these differences, however, other similarities are possible that have relevance for the Embourgeoisement Hypothesis. For example, perhaps the work settings of blue- and white-collar people do not differ so much as is thought. If so, that would be evidence for the argument. Or perhaps their level of job security is about the same. Although income is obviously vital, a secure income—even a low one—is fundamental to lifestyle. Or, finally, perhaps there are similarities in consumption habits, tastes, use of leisure time, or other elements of lifestyle. If it can be shown that middle- and working-class people resemble each other along these dimensions, then the plausibility of the Embourgeoisement Hypothesis would be greater.

Social Class and Occupation

Like the middle class, the working class has not always existed. As Daniel Bell put it in his book, *The Coming of Post-Industrial Society,* in preindustrial societies work was "a game against nature" as people used human and animal muscle power to obtain necessities for living (1976). For nearly all of human history, most people lived a rural life, struggling with the soil for subsistence (Lenski, 1966). In such contexts, a working class did not exist. In comparison, beginning in the nineteenth century, work increasingly became "a game against things" as people linked new forms of energy, mainly steam and fossil fuel, with machines, and productivity rose greatly. As a result of industrialization, the class structure changed dramatically. Increasing numbers of people became urban and labored at new kinds of jobs in which the tasks were routinized, systematic, and mechanical—not to mention dangerous to health and safety. These are the people Marx called proletarians in the 1840s. They coalesced as a recognizable working class over the remainder of that century.

Working-Class and Middle-Class Occupations

Today, as you may recall from Chapter 2, about 45 percent of the population answers the class identification question by saying they are working class. This answer correlates with the occupational distribution, as shown in Table 9-1. Column (2) reveals that about 41 percent of the population does blue-collar work. Table 9-1 also displays racial and ethnic variations in occupation in columns (3) through (7). These data show that, with the exception of Asian Americans, half to two-thirds of all minority groups do blue-collar work. The "Asian American exception" is partially, but not totally, due to the fact that the sample used in the table is somewhat older (see the note at the bottom of the table). These different occupational distributions suggest that while most working-class people are white (since they are the largest group by far), a higher proportion of minority group people are working class—which has important implications for life chances and life styles.

The millions of people referred to in the lower portion of Table 9-1 wear some form of work clothes on the job. This is so they can do manual labor, the essence of working-class life. These are the people who fix, haul, lift, scrub, shovel, help, and otherwise engage in potentially damaging exertions for a living. Hence, one gets the impression that working-class people are less likely to join fitness clubs. Their jobs are exhaustive enough. And often dirty.

In *Families on the Fault Line,* one of Lillian Rubin's respondents talks about the implications of getting dirty on the job: "I used to work in an upholstery factory. . . . The only thing I wanted to do when I got home was take a bath" (1994, p. 41). But there is more. The clean-dirty divide is a metaphor for the division between the middle class and working class. This same respondent now works as a word processor, making slightly less money. And the job characteristics differ:

> *You're a real person. . . . If you want to stop a minute and go talk to the other girls, nobody says anything. Or you can go to the bathroom and grab a smoke,*

TABLE 9-1   Occupational Distribution by Race and Ethnicity

(1) Occupation	(2) All 1997	(3) Whites 1997	(4) African Americans 1997	(5) Hispanics 1996	(6) Asian Americans 1996	(7) Native Americans 1990
White Collar						
Executives and Managers	14%	15%	10%	⎰15%	15%	9%
Professional Specialty	15	15	11	⎱	22	10
Technicians	3	3	3		6	3
Sales	12	13	10	⎰24	11	9
Administrative Support	<u>15</u>	<u>14</u>	<u>17</u>	⎱—	<u>14</u>	<u>15</u>
Total White Collar	59%	60%	51%	39%	68%	46%
Blue Collar						
Precision Production	11%	11%	8%	13%	9%	14%
Machine Operators	6	6	8		8	8
Transportation	4	4	6	⎰23	2	5
Handlers and Laborers	4	4	5	⎱	2	6
Service	13	12	22	22	10	18
Farming, Forestry, Fishing	<u>3</u>	<u>3</u>	<u>1</u>	<u>6</u>	<u>1</u>	<u>3</u>
Total Blue Collar	41%	40%	50%	62%	32%	54%

Sources: USDL (1998b, p. 29); USBC (1998a, table 2; 1998b, table 11; 1998e, table 9:1).

Note: Data for all, whites, African Americans, Hispanics, and Native Americans are for persons aged 16 and older; data for Asian Americans are for persons 25 years and older. Some totals do not add to 100% because of rounding.

> *and it's no big deal. I mean, they expect you to work, but they know you can't do it every minute. If it got slow in the factory, you got laid off. But in this job, they don't just dump you if there's a couple of slow days.*

Being laid off is always a threat if you are working class. Nonetheless, as Rubin commented, there is a sense in which working-class people provide the wheels and services that make the nation turn (1994, p. 26). Someone—almost half the population—has to fix, haul, and scrub. And they often do so in rather difficult contexts.

Social Class and Job Setting

Recall that the Embourgeoisement Hypothesis presupposes that middle- and working-class people are fundamentally alike. But, as the quotation suggests, the environment within which middle- and working-class people must labor is fundamentally different and logically incompatible with the hypothesis. Working-class job settings are frequently unpleasant and dangerous, closely supervised with petty work rules, and characterized by intense production pressures.

Unpleasant and Dangerous Working Conditions

Americans are much more likely to be killed and injured on the job than by a crime. But job-related deaths and injuries occur most often in the working class, simply because the work settings are not only more disagreeable they are also more dangerous. And this is true at all skill levels. Those who work inside frequently operate machines that are very hazardous if unreliable or handled incorrectly. In addition, they must often face high noise levels as machines clatter and grind, a great deal of noxious dust and dirt, toxic odors that are poorly ventilated, inadequate lighting, and extreme temperature variations because work stations have too little heat or air conditioning. All of these factors can lead to long-term health problems and physical deterioration. For example, miners and textile workers must inhale toxic fumes and dust while doing their jobs (Reardon, 1993). Similarly, forge and hammer operators must endure the tremendous heat and cacophony of sound created by their own and others' machines. Those who work outside must face the weather, the seasons of the year. Garbage collectors, mail carriers, and soft-drink drivers must work in the rain and the snow and the heat and the cold (Personick & Harthun, 1992). Electricians and telephone line repairers must work in the middle of storms, in the middle of the night, no matter what the temperature, with equipment that is often dangerous. Bricklayers and carpenters usually cannot wear gloves and still do their jobs. So if it is cold, they just suffer. And if it is hot, they just suffer. And if they fall, they simply go to the hospital. Thus, indoors or out, even if the tasks inherent to blue-collar work involve some degree of autonomy and satisfaction, which is sometimes the case, the environment within which they are accomplished is often very unpleasant as well as conducive to ill-health, injury—even death.

Rick Slusack, a 29-year-old laborer, lived in Steven's Point, Wisconsin, near a branch of the University of Wisconsin. He was married with one child. Each working day, he was supposed to load large plastic bags filled with bark chips and wood shavings into tractor trailers. These bags end up at suburban shopping malls and garden stores, where they are sold as mulch to middle-class people. One morning the forklift he was operating skidded on gravel, overturned, and pinned him underneath. He was dead within the hour. That same day, a 42-year-old iron worker named Dereck Hubbard was locking roof panels into place when he fell to his death in Muscle Shoals, Alabama. A wife and two children survive him. Similarly, Danny Newman, 46, married with three children, was an oil rigger in southeastern New Mexico who died when a mechanical failure caused a piece of equipment to crush him. Finally, an electrician named Lynda Gertner, a 31-year-old married woman with one child, died when a chemical explosion ripped through the plant where she was working and spread poisonous fumes throughout.[1]

Although events like these are extraordinary tragedies for the families of those who died, they are such an ordinary part of daily life for working-class people that they rarely make the news. Every day, about 17 people die in work-related accidents, more than 6,200 each year (BLS, 1998b, p. 1). Most of them are working class, as a look at the distribution of fatalities at work by occupation shows (BLS, 1998b, p. 7):

---

[1]These vignettes are constructed from many true examples cited in an analysis of the death toll on the job (Nordheimer, 1996).

Executives and Administrators	7%
Professionals	4
Technicians	3
Sales	7
Administrative Support	2
Precision Production	18
Operators and Laborers	35
Service	8
Farmers, Foresters, and Fishers	15
Military	1

These data reveal that 76 percent of all fatal work-related injuries occur to people in working-class jobs, mostly people who operate or come into contact with heavy equipment. Another way of seeing this fact is to look at the manner in which workplace fatalities occurred (BLS, 1998b, p. 5):

Transportation Accidents	42%
Assaults and Violent Acts	18
Contact with Objects and Equipment	17
Falls	11
Exposure to Harmful Substances	9
Fires and Explosions	3

The most common source of injury leading to death is connected to operating a vehicle. Some white-collar workers, such as those in sales, use cars regularly. But even more blue-collar workers must do so as they go from work site to work site, or operate moving equipment—such as forklifts. Ignoring homicides, a high proportion of deaths on the job reflects its inherent dangerousness: operating machinery or tools, the impact of structures on which people work, environmental conditions, toxic liquids, and the like.

I have focused on fatalities on the job because they are the ultimate price. But nearly two million work-related injuries occur every year that require people to stay at home for one or more days (BLS, 1998a). Nearly all of them occur in the working class; the occupations most prone to injuries are truck drivers, nonconstruction laborers, nursing aides and orderlies, janitors, assemblers, construction laborers, carpenters, stock handlers, cashiers, and cooks. About 40 percent of all injuries are sprains and strains, most often involving the back. Journals like *Monthly Labor Review* and *Compensation and Working Conditions* often carry articles with titles like "Workplace Injuries and Illness in the Extractive Industries" (McDermott, 1997). There are virtually no titles like "Workplace Injuries in the Office Suite." Apart from injuries due to repetitive motions at the keyboard (that is, carpel tunnel syndrome), I cannot think of any way in which white-collar work compares to the dangerousness of blue-collar work. And no one dies from carpel tunnel. This difference in degree of dangerousness is why working-class people lose an estimated 32 percent more days from work each year than do middle-class people (Hamermesh, 1998). Of course, when they become injured, working-class people are less likely to have health insurance, sick leave, or other job perquisites that protect their income (recall Chapter 8).

Middle-class jobs are different. Even in menial white-collar occupations, work stations are relatively quiet, reasonably clean, without offensive odors, and maintained at a constant temperature. In addition, it is common for office workers, even the lowest paid, to have cubicles in which they can surround themselves with flowers and pictures on the walls. Those who think, administer, sell, and push pencils or type keys for a living are, quite simply, subjected to fewer health hazards and, hence, injuries. Thus, even if the tasks that white-collar workers must do are routinized, the environment within which they are accomplished is, most of the time, reasonably pleasant and safe. I conclude that working-class jobs are much more dangerous than middle-class jobs.

Close Supervision and Petty Work Rules

Close supervision and petty work rules distinguish many working-class job settings. The pervasive time clock, at which people punch-in when they arrive to work and punch-out when they leave, suggests immediately how closely supervised blue-collar workers are. Along with supervision, of course, come rules to enforce. Working-class jobs are often characterized by work rules that resemble those in elementary school or, perhaps, boot camp. There are rules against talking, against going to the bathroom without authorization, against pausing for a moment to stretch tired muscles, against everything that would make a job more pleasant or enjoyable. The enforcers of these rules are the foreperson and line-level white-collar managers. Although the power of these supervisors is somewhat circumscribed in union plants, the millions of nonunion workers face a simple choice: do what they are told, toe the line, or be fired. Workers report that this kind of supervision makes them feel as though they are being treated like machines instead of human beings. This is a metaphorical way of describing what it means to feel powerless or, in the jargon, alienated.

Most middle-class jobs are rather different. For one thing, time clocks rarely exist; most people are paid annual salaries rather than hourly wages, which means punching in and out is viewed as less necessary. In addition, while nearly everyone has a supervisor or boss, the nature and quality of the supervision is often quite different. For example, it is hard to imagine college professors, engineers, computer programmers, salespersons, or even clerical workers having to justify going to the bathroom or a few moments on the telephone talking to their spouse. (Recall the quotation from the word processor a few pages ago.) To propose such rules is to propose an absurdity. Yet blue-collar workers live by them every day. In most middle-class jobs, getting the task done is the important issue, and this is accomplished with far less direct supervision and far fewer work rules.

Intense Production Pressures

By the phrase "intense production pressures," I mean the attempt at regulating the rate and rhythm of work. This characteristic is especially true of assembly line occupations, but it is also pervasive at any job where products are produced and some in which services are provided. What happens is that employers measure the amount of time it takes a competent person to perform a task and then set the pace of work accordingly.

And it does not matter if a person has a sprained hand or was up last night with a sick child. In addition, there tend to be persistent efforts at increasing the rate of production. Working-class people generally resist such attempts because their experience is that the reward for working harder and producing more is to be asked to work still harder and produce still more, in a never-ending cycle, with no increase in pay. As above, the effort at regulating the pace of work results in a high degree of alienation.

Most middle-class jobs are different, mainly because the "products" being produced are ideas, sales, blue prints, computer programs, and other things that cannot be standardized. As a result, there is much less attempt at regulating the pace and rhythm of work.

This emphasis on production pressure and close supervision reflects a specific managerial approach that is peculiarly American. In *Fat and Mean: The Corporate Squeeze of Working Americans and the Myth of Managerial "Downsizing,"* David Gordon argued that U.S. companies rarely emphasize raises, bonuses, and other "carrots" as mechanisms to motivate workers (1996). Rather, compared to other nations, U.S. companies typically develop rather large bureaucracies that emphasize a "stick strategy": arbitrary commands and threats of loss of job for failure to obey. This "fat" bureaucracy and "mean" management style is supposed to lead to greater productivity. It probably lowers productivity, however, as most people respond better to positive reinforcers ("carrots") than negative ("sticks"). Gordon argued that one—not the only—reason for rising inequality in this country (recall Table 8-6) is the existence of bloated bureaucracies in U.S. corporations whose personnel require income that might otherwise go to blue-collar workers. So working-class people toil harder, with less job security, just to stay in place. From this angle, the presupposition underlying the Embourgeoisement Hypothesis is incorrect.

Social Class and Job Security

I mentioned earlier that working-class men and women provide the wheels and services that make this nation turn—by fixing, hauling, lifting, shoveling, and helping. Although one might think that people employed in these sorts of jobs would be paid rather well for the extra danger and other difficulties, the income and job security of working-class people are less today than in the past. This fact is illustrated in Table 8-5 (see page 185), which shows median income by occupation for men and women. Please pause and look back at the table now. These data reveal that, despite the Embourgeoisement Hypothesis, reality for most working-class individuals and families is that they are not affluent; they are, rather, economically insecure. Nonetheless, popular stereotypes abound of the plumber, the teamster, and even the garbage collector as members of a new well-to-do working class. This perception reflects considerable misunderstanding because most people do not realize who gets the money when they employ skilled people, such as precision production workers. For example, when customers take their automobiles to be fixed, they are often charged $25 to $40 per hour for the job. While such figures seem like a high rate of pay for a "simple car repair" most of the money does not go to the mechanic; it goes, rather, to the owner of the dealership or repair shop to cover overhead and profit. Owners are classified as businesspersons, not blue-collar workers. The latter make $10 to $15 per hour ($21,000 to $31,000, if they work full-time all year long—many do not). This same point applies when people employ plumbers, electricians, and other skilled blue-collar people. Those who actually do the job often earn far less than the price paid by the customer and, as a result, are much less affluent and more economically insecure than white-collar employees.[2]

Although income is fundamental to families' economic circumstances, those who are assured a regular income, even if it is relatively low, can organize their lives to a greater degree than those for whom a steady income is more doubtful. Thus, if working-class people have job security similar to that of middle-class people, then this fact could be taken as evidence of embourgeoisement.

Unfortunately, job security, as indicated by the unemployment rate, is far less for those engaged in working-class occupations. Managerial downsizing, David Gordon argued, is a myth (1996). This fact is illustrated in Table 9-2. Column (3) of the table reveals that unemployment rates are much higher in all working-class occupations. For example, the unemployment rate among professional specialty workers was only 2 percent in 1998, compared to figures between 4 percent and 7 percent in most working-class occupations, up to 9 percent for those in handling and laboring occupations (a category I will return to in a few moments). These differences in likelihood of unemployment mean that of all those out of work at any time, most were previously in working-class jobs.

Moreover, most people who are unemployed do not leave their jobs voluntarily. Table 9-2 shows that the overall rate of unemployment was about 5 percent in 1998. This figure can be broken down in the following way (USDL, 1998c, p. 38).

44%	Lost job
13	Left job
35	Re-entering the job market
_8	Entering job market for the first time
100%	

Thus, very few of the unemployed are in that situation because they left their jobs by choice. Nearly all those without work, 79 percent (44 percent + 35 percent), either lost their jobs or, overcoming their discouragement, re-entered the job market. Discouragement, by the way, is a major issue in discussing the unemployment rate. This is because people are only classified as unemployed if they are looking for work. If they have become so demoralized that they have stopped looking, then they are no longer unemployed—at least officially. This paradoxical phenomenon is why you occasionally see newspaper articles describing hundreds or even thousands of applicants appearing when a new plant opens up. When jobs, real jobs, become available then people re-enter the labor market—another way of saying they become hopeful of actually finding work. I placed the number of unemployed people in column (2) of Table 9-2 in order to emphasize that millions of people are reflected in the percentages. You should

[2]Recall the vignette about William Meadows, the mechanic who owns a repair shop, from Chapter 2.

TABLE 9-2   Number Unemployed and Unemployment Rate by Occupation, 1998

(1) Occupation	(2) Number Unemployed	(3) Unemployment Rate
White Collar		
Executives and Managers	356,000	2%
Professional Specialty	523,000	3%
Technicians	76,000	2%
Sales	748,000	4%
Administrative Support	648,000	4%
Blue Collar		
Precision Production	606,000	4%
Machine Operators	415,000	5%
Transportation	269,000	5%
Handlers and Laborers	531,000	9%
Service	1,306,000	7%
Farming, Forestry, Fishing	162,000	4%
Overall	6,173,000	5%

Source: USDL (1998c, p. 36).

Note: Data refer to persons 16 years of age and older.

remember, however, that the figures in column (2) understate the number of unemployed and discouraged people: There are 15 million poor persons in this country (to be discussed in Chapter 10).

One last point: Although it is not shown in the table, the mean duration of unemployment across all social classes was 14 weeks in 1998 (USDL, 1998c, p. 39). This time has been fairly typical over the years, and it implies that a far higher proportion of the total work force, three to four times the overall rate, experience some unemployment in any specific year. The vast majority of these persons are working class, which is a typical situation, and many are poor for at least part of the time. Thus, the people who have the least job security, who have the most to fear from unemployment, are in working-class families. This finding is not consonant with the Embourgeoisement Hypothesis, since those who are economically insecure cannot be considered like the middle class.

The experience of unionized asbestos workers in New York City provides a good illustration of the economic problems and dangers many working-class people face (Passell, 1998). Recall from Table 8-5 that the median income of male handlers and laborers working full-time, all year round, was $21,500 in 1997. In addition, Table 9-2 reveals that handlers and laborers display the highest rate of unemployment of any occupational category. Asbestos is used in the mining and construction industries.

Further, anyone involved in the manufacture of insulation, fireproofing materials, cement products, and automobile brakes must work with asbestos. In many cases, they are classified as handlers and laborers. Members of unions, however, make considerably more than average, partly because they are organized and (in this case) partly because the substance they are handling is incredibly dangerous. Inhaling the dust leads to asbestosis—a progressive lung disease that kills the victim in a painful way. Respirators (which often function very imperfectly) are essential to prevent this result. The death toll among people doing this sort of work has always been high. During the early 1980s, unionized asbestos workers in New York City were earning about $31 per hour. Over the next few years, however, an influx of immigrants willing enough and desperate enough to do this work (often without the protection of either a union or a respirator) meant that wages fell to about $13.50 per hour during the early part of the 1990s. More recently, they have rebounded to about $19, as the union recruited many of these new workers. Although this wage is still not very high given the degree of danger involved, it is worth calculating what it means in practice. A person making $19 per hour who works 40 hours per week all year long will make $41,392 (before taxes). But if he (nearly all asbestos workers are men) is unemployed for part of the year—a likely possibility—income drops. Let us assume an average duration of unemployment, 14 weeks. This person's actual income (before taxes) becomes $30,248. Not many people can take a one-quarter drop in income without significant economic and familial consequences.

These consequences are more serious for racial and ethnic minorities. Their incomes are usually lower than whites at every occupational level (see Chapter 5). So they have fewer resources to begin with, on average, which means they are worse off when the axe falls. Table 9-3 compares the experiences of African Americans and whites with unemployment. It reveals that African American men are three times as likely to lose their jobs as whites and to be out of work for significantly longer when they do. The situation is not so bad for women (as these things go), since African American women are only twice as likely to lose their jobs as white women, although they also are unemployed for significantly longer than white women. Most of these job losses afflict working-class people.

As an editorial aside, economists often describe unemployment as "unpaid vacation," presuming, I guess, that people benefit from being thrown out of work because

TABLE 9-3   Unemployment Rate by Gender and Race, 1998

Race	Percentage Unemployed		Average Duration in Weeks	
	Men	Women	Men	Women
Whites	3%	4%	14	12
African Americans	9	9	17	15

Source: USDL (1998c, pp. 35, 40).

Note: Data refer to persons 16 years of age and older.

they have leisure time in which to enjoy themselves. I wish to comment on this image and those who use it.

Economists are usually employed in colleges and universities or come from an academic background—experiences that fundamentally influence their vision of reality. For example, college professors are generally employed on nine-month contracts and paid sufficiently well that they frequently view the summer as free time, as unpaid vacation. Those who publish often use the summer to do research, which means that (no matter how much they enjoy their jobs) they see themselves as giving up leisure time in order to work. Moreover, college professors have unpaid leave built into the academic year: at Thanksgiving, Christmas, and Spring Break. Once again, this time is often used for research, which involves giving up leisure. Thus, from economists' point of view, those who (like themselves) are sometimes unemployed have "unpaid vacation" and those who (like themselves) work anyway are particularly virtuous. It seems to me, in other words, that economists' rather privileged position in the society leads them to make inappropriate generalizations about those in other locations, such as working-class people.

This mistake illustrates a fundamental difficulty that is peculiar to social science research: How are observers to be objective about society even as they participate in it? This is the problem Max Weber alerted us to a long time ago. Alas, there remains no easy answer to the question, and those of us in sociology and economics rely on the disciplined skepticism of our colleagues to point out implicit bias in our work.

Reality, in fact, is far different from the image conveyed by the phrase "unpaid vacation": Any period without a job, especially long-term unemployment, is devastating to working-class families, often destroying their lifestyle completely and sometimes creating poverty where none had existed previously. This threat is a fundamental and pervasive source of stress among working-class people. It means they are not affluent, that the embourgeoisement thesis is incorrect. In the next section, I examine the human consequences of unemployment in more detail.

The Human Consequences of Unemployment

As will be explained in more detail in Chapter 10, a trade-off usually occurs between inflation and unemployment, and U.S. policy makers typically choose to allow unemployment to be higher than inflation. While this choice can be defended as one that benefits the nation as a whole (the argument is that "everyone is hurt by inflation"), poor and working-class people are hurt more by unemployment than by inflation. There is, however, surprisingly little research on the human consequences of unemployment. I am using the phrase "human consequences" to distinguish the suffering of individuals from the macroeconomic effects of unemployment: loss of productivity. Economists emphasize, correctly, that billions of dollars worth of goods and services are not produced when people, factories, and other resources stand idle.

The lack of research on the impact of losing one's job is important because a high rate of unemployment has far-reaching economic and noneconomic consequences for those who go through it—sometimes lasting long after the experience is over. Furthermore, it is possible that these results, nearly all of which are negative, redound (or spill over) into other arenas of society. This situation means that macroeconomic policies are made in relative ignorance, buttressed by stereotypes about unpaid vacations rather than social scientific evidence.

A Note on the Meaning of Work

Max Weber emphasized that in modern societies people's jobs have both economic and noneconomic implications (1920). Jobs not only provide a way to earn a living, but also affect people's identity. When unemployment occurs, this identity is threatened.

One indicator of this fact is that the vast majority of people would, if given a choice, continue working even if they had enough money to live comfortably (GSS, 1996). This is because many individuals view their jobs as relatively interesting and enjoyable, as a way of staying physically and mentally healthy, and as a means for justifying their existence and seeing themselves positively. Others, mainly those in less engaging and more physically arduous occupations, say they would keep working (although not always at the same job) because they do not want to be idle or bored, because their self-respect is tied to earning a living and providing for their families, and because they would "go crazy" if their work did not keep them occupied.

There are, however, class differences in the meaning work has for people. Those in middle-class occupations tend to emphasize that their jobs are interesting and carry a sense of accomplishment as well as a concern with self-respect and a desire not to be idle. It should be recognized that people in white-collar jobs are often in competitive environments where individual initiative can pay off, a fact that carries intrinsic interest. (Administrative support workers constitute an obvious exception to this generalization.) In contrast, working-class people tend to say that their jobs occupy their time, provide them with companionship, and give them a sense of earning an "honest living," which they define as working with their hands. This orientation leads to some harsh judgments. It appears that many working-class people see white-collar jobs as scams for avoiding "real work" (Ehrenreich, 1990, pp. 137–38). Moreover, from this angle the work middle-class professionals do often takes the form of harassing those below them—working-class people. Hence, they believe that working with your hands is more honorable than "shuffling paper" or "working with your mouth." Whatever one thinks of these judgments, they indicate how central employment is to the lives of working-class people. As E. E. LeMasters observed, "one of the best indicators of the importance of the job to these men is their discomfort when they cannot work" (1976, p. 26).

I mention men here because it appears that the specter of unemployment raises different issues for women and men, at least in the working class (Rubin, 1994, p. 104).

Ask a [working class] man for a statement of his identity, and he'll almost always respond by telling you first what he does for a living. The same question asked of a woman brings forth a less predictable, more varied response, one that's embedded in the web of relationships that are central to her life.

In the couples Lillian Rubin talked with, women tended to have multifaceted self-identities that include their roles as mother, wife, friend, daughter, and sister. So even for those women who were divorced and single mothers, their job only represented part of their sense of self. Hence, losing a job (or the potential for doing so) might be painful and anxiety producing, but it does not call their identity into question. For men, however, even though they also assume many roles (as husband, father, friend, son, and so forth), going to work is what they do. Their job is what they are, the core of their being. As will become clear, these differences in orientation affect the impact of unemployment on families.

Economic Deprivation

For young couples of any race or ethnic group, usually saddled with high debts and no savings, unemployment of either spouse is an immediate catastrophe. For families in the prime earning years, however, getting laid off usually does not result in poverty—at least not immediately. But it is a constant specter. In order to see why, I have sketched plausible income and expenses for a working-class Hispanic couple, whom I will name Margarita and Alberto Martinez. They have two teenage children and are active in their church. They are more or less a typical family. They are now doing pretty well economically because, after many years of struggle, Alberto, age 42, recently became a member of Local 78 of the Asbestos, Lead, and Hazardous Waste Laborers in New York City. Following from the discussion earlier, I am going to assume that he works full-time all year and earns $41,000. Margarita, 38, is a bank teller. She also works full-time all year and earns the average for clerical workers, $21,000 (see Table 8-5). Although their total gross income is well above average for blue-collar workers, I use it to illustrate the precariousness of lifestyle in the working class.

This uncertainty can be seen by looking at the breakdown of their gross income in Table 9-4. Following from the discussion of job perquisites in Chapter 8, I assumed certain pretax costs for medical insurance and retirement contribution. Because the Martinezes are unlikely to have many deductions (apart from mortgage interest), it is assumed they pay taxes on the remaining income at about 15 percent along with social security taxes. On that basis, they have a net monthly income of about $3,683. It is easy to manipulate the assumptions shown in the bottom portion of the table, raising some figures, perhaps, and lowering others. But as sketched in the table, Margarita and Alberto have relatively fixed expenses totaling almost two-thirds of their take home income, leaving about one-third ($1,333) for the periodic expenses that every family incurs. Note, for example, that this budget contains no provision for credit card debt, a new transmission for the car, dental work, or shoes for their son (endorsed by a popular athlete, of course), to name some obvious unallocated but plausible expenses. Nor does it take into account expenses for holidays, birthdays, or vacations. All in all, then, a family like this gets by. It is not poor. But, to repeat, the specter is always there: What happens if (or when) Alberto gets laid off? Because he has only recently joined the

TABLE 9-4   Income and Expenses for a Hypothetical Working-Class Family (Two Adults, Two Children)

Income

Gross income from husband's job	$41,000
Gross income from wife's job	21,000
Total gross income	$62,000

Minus Expenses Taken before Taxes

Employee share of cost of medical insurance	–1,200
Employee share of retirement contribution ($2,000 each)	–4,000
Total pre-tax income	$56,000

Minus Taxes

Income tax at 15%	–8,500
Social Security tax at 7.2%	–4,100
Net income	$44,200
Net Monthly Income (44,200 ÷ 12)	$3,683

Monthly Living Expenses

Total food (and other grocery supplies)	$800
Mortgage payment	$600
Property tax	150
Utilities (including telephone)	250
Transportation	150
Car insurance	100
Car payment	200
Church contribution	100
Nonallocated	1,333
Total nonfood	$2,883
Total Monthly Living Expenses (total food + total nonfood)	$3,683

union, Alberto has little seniority. Like many other minority persons, he will get the axe before others do.[3]

When this happens, the first task for Alberto and Margarita is to cut back on expenses. The family will retain medical insurance because they get it through Margarita's employer, but she will stop contributing to her retirement fund (as will Alberto, of course, since he is not working). Church contributions, holidays, entertainment, and optional purchases (dentist?) are eliminated. But if Alberto's unemployment persists (and unemployment tends to be of longer duration for minority persons), the

---

[3]The reason for the (somewhat ungainly) distinction between food and nonfood expenses in Table 9-4 will become clear in the next chapter when the poverty line is described. Table 9-4 is designed to be easily comparable to Table 10-1.

basic elements of the family's lifestyle will be affected: the car is sold, heat is set lower, and the like. The second task is to generate new resources. Alberto, as it turns out, is eligible for unemployment benefits (not everyone is). But his supplement is time limited and only covers a portion of lost pay. In addition, men like Alberto are resourceful, and he works off-the-books whenever possible. But such income is nearly always at or near the minimum wage. Moreover, the modest funds in Alberto's and Margarita's retirement funds can be tapped. Of course, that strategy means for a leaner old age. Finally, when they become truly desperate, they can obtain a small amout of financial help from kin or have one of the children leave high school and enter the labor force. Although none of these strategies will be effective for very long, they do tide families like the Martinezes over (remember, the sketch here is hypothetical). The single most important priority in cutting expenses and generating resources is to continue paying the mortgage. "We could be on the street"; it is the primordial fear that rises in working-class families when unemployment occurs (Rubin, 1994, p. 114).

If, however, the period without work is short-term—a few weeks or months (at most)—families like the Martinezes can often recover their lifestyle. If, however, it persists for very long, the consequences are catastrophic. Here is an empirical generalization that expresses the relationship between unemployment and economic deprivation:

> *The longer the duration of unemployment, the greater the economic depriva-*
> *tion and the more likely impoverishment.*

And homelessness.

Furthermore, remember that unemployment does not happen gradually. Rather, a person is suddenly laid off or fired, just before the mortgage payment is due, just before a holiday, just before something—there is no convenient time. And most unemployment, it will be recalled, occurs among working-class people, precisely those who have the least amount of money in savings, the least economic flexibility. The suffering that results can permanently erode people's sense of self-worth and confidence in the world, and often causes familial disruption.

Psychological Stress

Although, as indicated earlier, research on the human consequences of unemployment is rather sparse, some work has been done. For example, studies undertaken during and after the depression of the 1930s showed consistently that men who are thrown out of work—who are forced to be idle because no jobs are available—interpret this experience as a threat to their self-worth (Bakke, 1940; Komarovsky, 1940). More recent literature indicates that this remains the case (Glyptis, 1989; Feather, 1990; 1992). It shows that the economic deprivation, loss of social support, abrupt changes in daily routine, and the disruption of long-term financial plans that accompany unemployment lead individuals to suffer depression, anxiety, and physical ailments. Ethnographic studies of working-class families portray these results vividly (LeMasters, 1976; Rubin, 1994).

In effect, people without jobs feel small. They speak of their insignificance, their impotence, their boredom, their inability to control their own lives. As one of Thomas Cottle's respondents put it (1994, p. 78):

> *I've been lost in the general scheme of things. . . . I don't even know what I'm doing, you know? I'm just what they call "free falling." There's not plans or anything. I used to try to make plans; there's no concentration. I feel like I'm in a fog. I have been called a vegetable. I don't read the newspaper. I try. It's just that I can't really concentrate. I used to.*

"I can't really concentrate. . . ." This statement is a sign of depression, something that often accompanies unemployment (Rubin, 1994). What happens is that most people in the United States are socialized (or taught) by parents, teachers, and clergy that the work ethic is a fundamental value. (You should recall here the four principles of socialization presented in Chapter 1.) This value becomes part of their sense of self, of who and what they are. When people who have internalized the work ethic as part of their sense of self and who have been steadily employed all their lives suddenly find that they can no longer be active, productive members of the society, they lose confidence in themselves and display other indications of stress. This argument can be summarized as a simple empirical generalization:

> *Individuals who are or have been unemployed display more psychological stress than those who have not.*

One manifestation is depression. Another is excessive drug use, especially alcohol. These results can be long-lasting.

Familial Disruption

Although the available evidence is scant, it appears that individuals who experience unemployment also endure family disruption. By the phrase "family disruption," I refer not only to unhappiness and divorce but also spouse abuse and child abuse.

In a context where families are dealing with economic deprivation and the unemployed person is trying to cope with his or her own stress, disruption becomes likely. Both Rubin (1994) and LeMasters (1976), for example, reported that the blue-collar men they talked to not only had financial problems when they were unemployed, but also drank excessively and displayed more tense marital relationships. What happens, apparently, is that unemployed people—especially men—experience economic deprivation and stress, which leads them to become more irritable, tense, and hostile. Such feelings are acted out on those immediately around them: children and spouses. So the discipline of children becomes more arbitrary, punitive, and violent (Lenton, 1990; Elder et al., 1992). Marital relations also suffer, with spouse abuse and divorce more likely (Gelles, 1990; Sander, 1992; Rubin, 1994). This argument can be expressed as a simple, albeit hard to demonstrate, hypothesis:

Families in which one of the spouses is or has been unemployed have a higher probability of familial disruption than those who have not.

This hypothesis is hard to demonstrate because the relationship between unemployment and familial disruption is probably not a simple causal connection (Liker & Elder, 1983; Rubin, 1994). Thus, the overall strength of the marriage, the personality characteristics of the spouses, and previous experience with unemployment and income loss are all probably related to the degree of and form of familial disruption. For example, a couple in which the spouses are nurturing and supportive of one another and emotionally stable is probably going to have less familial disruption as it adjusts to economic deprivation and job loss than one in which the spouses are consistently critical of one another and display emotional instability. It is likely that these characteristics are class related.

In sum, one premise underlying the embourgeoisement hypothesis is that the working class is as affluent as the middle class. Unfortunately, those doing blue-collar work not only earn less money but also have less job security than those doing white-collar work. Their lifestyles are not secure.

Social Class and Lifestyle

The embourgeoisement hypothesis also presumes that working- and middle-class people have essentially similar lifestyles. **Lifestyle,** you might remember, refers to people's way of living, as indicated by their consumption habits, use of leisure, and fundamental choices and values. One easy indicator of how these characteristics differ by class is the kind of clothes people wear, both on the job (work clothes versus suits, for example) and at play. Paul Fussell identified many others in his witty *Class: A Guide Through the American Status System* (1983). For example, where people went to school, their furniture, the magazines they subscribe to, the mail order catalogues they buy from, even the sweetness of their drinks, all give fairly obvious clues about their social class and way of living. Moreover, there is an enormous amount of pretension inherent in lifestyle. And this is true at all class levels. One result of such hubris (or undue pride) is that people act to protect their way of life by discriminating against others whom they consider inferior or, at least, different (recall Chapter 2). I have chosen to focus on a single aspect of people's way of living, their housing, as a means of illustrating the differences in lifestyle displayed by the working and middle classes.

People's housing, whether a home or an apartment, is usually their biggest single expenditure. As such, it constitutes a fundamental cultural symbol and economic demarcation. It indicates people's stability, their ties to the community, and their status within the social order. If they own their home, it is usually the single most important economic asset they possess. Thus, if the embourgeoisement hypothesis is correct, then there should be few differences between the middle class and the working class in either the location or quality of their housing.

As described in Chapter 5, however, most U.S. cities are divided into neighborhoods by class, race, and ethnicity, and residents accurately perceive these differences (Harrison & Weinberg, 1992). When they are asked by researchers to identify how neighborhoods differ, most persons refer to the relative income characteristics of people living in different sections of town or, in suburban areas, entire communities. Thus, particular areas will be seen as poor, working class, middle class, or rich, by observing their housing characteristics and imputing income.

My suspicion, however, is that when respondents mention income to interviewers asking about housing location and neighborhood, it serves as a convenient proxy for invidious judgments they make but are reluctant to talk about openly and, sometimes, are only partly aware of. For example, my guess is that working-class neighborhoods are characterized by higher housing density, more garages converted into extra rooms, and more cars being repaired in driveways or on the street. While people recognize these differences, they are not the first thoughts that come to mind when asked to compare neighborhoods. In addition, I would be willing to bet even more subtle but meaningful characteristics distinguish working- and middle-class areas: for example, house color, lawn decorations, patterns of interaction, number of pets running loose, and many other external features. Moreover, as Fussell suggested, the interior of people's houses provides countless clues to the occupants' class identity and, hence, their lifestyle. For example, it appears that the television often occupies the central place in working-class living rooms (Rubin, 1994). All of these differences, of course, reflect taste and skill combined with economic necessity. My point here is that people become familiar with and develop an emotional affinity for a particular kind of neighborhood, and they make negative judgments of other areas in terms such as these. For example, I noted above that patterns of interaction probably differ in working- and middle-class neighborhoods. My impression is that working-class persons often evaluate middle-class neighborhoods as too impersonal, since people nearby do not interact much or even know one another. Conversely, middle-class people are often suspicious of working-class neighborhoods precisely because there is so much street life. These alternative value judgments reflect the lifestyle of each class.

But housing also differs in quality. In order to illustrate some of these differences, I have selected a few easily quantifiable measures. Table 9-5 compares families having incomes at three different levels: That between $40,000 and $59,000 is typical of a working-class household (note that it is just below that of the hypothetical Martinez family), while the other two are typical middle-class income levels (see Table 8-5).

Table 9-5 displays data for households who own their homes. It shows that working-class families usually live in older houses, which means that repair costs are higher. At some point, the roof begins leaking; the water heater stops functioning. Newer homes are less likely to have these problems. Given different income levels, it follows that working-class people own homes that are less expensive than those of middle-class people. But in order to obtain housing, working-class people must pay a higher proportion of their income for it. Thus, families with incomes around $50,000 who own their homes spend about 18 percent of their incomes for housing, compared to 14 percent and 11 percent for families with higher incomes. Although data for renters is not shown, the pattern displayed in Table 9-5 is the same. Hence, these differences can be expressed as an empirical generalization that applies to both:

The lower the social class, then the older the housing, the lower the value of the housing, and the higher the proportion of income spent on housing.

This empirical generalization has important implications that suggest, once again, how different are the lifestyles of working- and middle-class people. The high proportion of income spent on housing means there is less money available to working-class families for other things that bring pleasure and express lifestyle: going bowling or to the opera, buying a pickup truck or a car, contributing to a church or a political campaign. It also means that since the value of their house is often relatively less, when working-class people sell late in life, as at retirement, they have less money (and, hence, fewer choices) to take them through old age. Finally, the houses themselves have fewer amenities and, perhaps, depending on one's point of view, do not look as nice.

The bottom portion of Table 9-5 displays selected differences in housing amenities, another way of assessing the quality of housing. Some things people do to their homes indicate their taste: color of paint, level of yard maintenance, kind of yard decorations, and the like. Class differences in things like this reflect varying values as well as relative economic situation. In the table, however, I am using some big buck amenities, fundamental choices people make in purchasing and renting their homes, and in each case, working-class houses are significantly less "well off." Thus, on the average, families with lower incomes have significantly fewer rooms available to them: an average of 6.3 in the working-class home, compared to 7.0 and 7.8 in the middle-class home. Similarly, only 55 percent of owners in the $50,000 range have homes with two

TABLE 9-5   Social Class and Housing: Owner Occupied Units

Housing Characteristics	Household Income		
	$40,000–59,000	$80,000–99,000	$120,000+
Housing Age			
Median Year Built	1970	1974	1975
Housing Cost			
Median Value of Home	$94,000	$140,000	$214,000
Monthly Costs as % of Income	18%	14%	11%
Housing Amenities			
Median Number of Rooms	6.3	7.0	7.8
Percent with 2+ Baths	55%	66%	82%

Source: USBC (1995a, pp. 142–45).

or more baths, compared to 66 percent and 82 percent at higher income levels. Again, the pattern is the same for renters, although the percentages are lower in each case. Such variations are expressed in the following empirical generalization:

The lower the social class, the fewer amenities built into housing.

Items like those used in the table are significant because they indicate families' level of physical comfort and convenience. Not shown in the table are differences in the availability of air conditioning, quality of insulation, and other factors that decisively influence comfort and convenience. More generally, however, I submit that one could pick almost any indicator of lifestyle, type of car (or truck) owned or leisure time activities for example, and discover significant differences by social class. But the numbers of rooms and bathrooms are important in another way as well, for they indicate the degree of crowding that occurs. Part of this is "just" daily hassle: getting into and out of the bathroom each morning as family members prepare for work and school is much easier if more bathrooms are available. In addition, however, crowding has more serious implications. Smaller houses (or apartments) make daily life more difficult because people have less privacy. A couple's sex life is more restricted, there is less space for children to do homework, and there is less ability to get away from each other when someone is angry, among many other problems. Recall that unemployment leads to stress and family disruption; crowded living conditions exacerbate these problems. Ultimately, it does not matter whether these variations in amenities reflect comparative cost, which means in every case that the working class is less well off, or simply taste. As Max Weber emphasized, people make subjective invidious judgments of others based on their sense of sharing a common way of life. The working class is different from the middle class.

On the Working Class

The embourgeoisement hypothesis does not accurately describe the condition of the working class in the United States. As you may recall, I have used this argument as a pedagogical device, an example of hypothesis testing in the social sciences. Thus, the available evidence shows that working-class people labor at inferior occupational settings that carry with them lower incomes and less job security. Furthermore, the lifestyles of the working and middle classes differ. Thus, based on the empirical data, the embourgeoisement hypothesis should be rejected because its premise is incorrect.

For contemporary Marxists, however, the embourgeoisement hypothesis implies a rather different kind of analysis. Karl Marx saw capitalist society as divided into two great classes: the bourgeoisie, consisting of a small group of capitalists who own the means of production, and the proletariat, consisting of the vast majority of people who own nothing and must sell their labor power to survive. The relationship between the two was inherently exploitive, Marx believed, and he predicted that over the long run an impoverished proletariat would rebel and usher in a new society. The problem for contemporary Marxists is to explain why this scenario has not occurred.[4]

For this reason, the size, composition, and political orientation of the working class is a matter of some controversy (van den Berg, 1993). Although the circumlocutions (or excessive words) become very complex in Marxist writings, a typical strategy is to downplay the differences between the working and middle class and argue, in some form or another, that the vast majority of people are still essentially proletarians who have been temporarily bought off by the bourgeoisie. Thus, it is asserted, engineers, real estate sellers, electricians, and police officers are "really" proletarians because they possess few assets and have nothing to sell but their labor power (Wright, 1997). Ultimately, as Gagliani observed, contemporary Marxists are still presuming that all those who do not own capital will eventually disregard their middle- or working-class location, recognize their true interests, unite, and overthrow a repressive regime (1981). The embourgeoisement hypothesis implies this type of analysis. Thus, contemporary Marxists remain committed to an evolutionary interpretation of history: A communist revolution and the destruction of capitalism are historically inevitable. This position is as much a leap of faith today as it was in 1848, when the *Communist Manifesto* was published.

Yet even if a Marxist explanation is rejected, the question remains: Why are working-class people in the United States not politically radical? In Western Europe, working-class persons have organized socialist and labor political parties, some of which are quite radical, to represent their interests. This has not happened in the United States. Part of the reason, as shown in Chapter 6, is that working-class persons in the United States do not have political resources comparable to those of their counterparts in Western Europe and participate in politics at a much lower rate than do middle-class and rich persons. Furthermore, people in the United States consistently say they do not want economic equality (Hochschild, 1981; GSS, 1996).

While the reasons for these attitudes are unclear, a few suggestions can be made (Lipset, 1977). The transformative impact of the Protestant Reformation (especially Puritanism) was much greater in the United States than in other nations, mainly because of the absence of a feudal tradition in the New World. Moreover, the existence of the Frontier probably served as a sort of safety valve, diluting class conflict and allowing opportunity (F. J. Turner, 1920). Further, as seen in Chapter 3, the very real possibility of upward mobility over the past century has buttressed the dream of success through hard work. The result is a unique emphasis on individual rather than collective action. Finally, the half-century conflict between the former Soviet Union and the United States made the "American dream" with its emphasis on individual responsibility into an ideology, relatively impervious to contradictory facts. While the impact of these phenomena cannot be demonstrated empirically, they constitute plausible reasons for the lack of working-class radicalism in the United States.

---

[4]Marxist theories are not tested by observation and refuted. Rather, they are evaluated in light of how people act (or do not act) and then readjusted in light of changing historical circumstances (Appelbaum, 1978). For a critique of this point of view, see Turner, Beeghley, and Powers (1998).

Summary

This chapter used the Embourgeoisement Hypothesis as a pedagogical vehicle for sketching some of the characteristics of the working class in the United States. About 41 percent of the population does blue-collar work, with somewhat higher percentages among minorities (Table 9-1). Coupled with the class identification question in Chapter 2, this figure provides an approximate estimate of the size of the working class in the United States.

The occupational setting in which working-class people labor is often unpleasant due to heat and cold, noise, noxious and toxic fumes, dangerous machines, and other factors. It is also dangerous, as data on work-related fatalities reveal. Working-class people typically endure very close supervision, petty work rules, and intense production pressures as employers attempt to regulate the rate and rhythm of work.

As shown previously, working-class people have lower incomes, on the average, than do middle-class people and less job security (Table 9-2). Minority people (both men and women) have higher unemployment rates than do whites, as illustrated by the experiences of African Americans (Table 9-3). Most people without jobs do not leave them voluntarily. The human consequences of unemployment include economic deprivation (Table 9-4), lowered self-concept, and increased familial disruption.

The lifestyles of working- and middle-class people are quite different. I argued that this is true for a wide range of indicators and used housing as an example (Table 9-5). Working-class persons own houses at lower rates, own less expensive houses, and spend a higher proportion of their incomes paying for housing than do middle-class people. Furthermore, the houses working-class people live in have fewer amenities, such as extra bedrooms and bathrooms. The chapter concluded by describing some possible reasons why the working class in the United States is not radical.

The Poor

Concluding Comments

We are two nations. One of them is familiar. It comprises the majority of working-class and middle-class people who earn a decent living and enjoy the fruits of their labor. Although their level of affluence varies considerably, previous chapters have shown that they usually possess the resources necessary to deal with personal crises. Thus, when faced with a failed marriage, a pregnant daughter, or any of the other tribulations of modern life, they have a range of effective choices. The other nation is unfamiliar. Yet hand-lettered signs, "Will work for food," announce it. So does being accosted by a panhandler: "Can you spare some change?" So do those who walk the street: the drunk, the mentally ill, those possessed by their peculiar demons. Such behavior suggests they have become so poor and so desperate that they are willing to debase themselves in public. This response is inexplicable to most people. But not every member of this unfamiliar nation displays extreme behavior. Many work, often full-time. Many are aged. Many are children. All live poorly in America. Hence, the structure of stratification means they have few choices and find it hard to solve their personal dilemmas. Coping is often the best they can do.

Sometimes the results are heartbreaking (Klass, 1992). Maria Sanchez telephoned the emergency room at Boston's City Hospital. Her nine-month-old baby had diarrhea. A doctor told her to go to the pharmacy and buy Pedialyte, water with electrolytes added. She went to the pharmacy but did not have enough money for the medicine. It costs about $6.00 per bottle (!). Medicaid will pay for it in her state (most would not), but only with a written prescription. Instead of going to the hospital immediately, Ms. Sanchez took the child home. The little boy became worse. She brought him to the emergency room 36 hours later, moribund. He eventually died.[1]

This example, although extreme, illustrates the dilemmas the poor face and how difficult it is to cope. Ms. Sanchez had a medical emergency and no money. (I know it is hard to imagine not having $6.00, but that is reality for millions of people.) More affluent persons faced with the same problem would simply pay for the medicine, however overpriced. If short of cash, they would use credit cards. This was not a choice for Ms. Sanchez. Rebuffed at the pharmacy, she had no car and no money to pay for transportation. Also, she spoke little English. Hospital bureaucracies are hard to deal with, even for well-educated, reasonably affluent, English-speaking persons with insur-

---

[1]This vignette captures many of the deficiencies in the U.S. system of medical treatment: the lack of primary care, the high cost of medicine, and the lack of outreach to the poor (see Beeghley, 1999).

ance. For the poor, such organizations are even more intimidating. So, given these limitations, Maria Sanchez tried to care for the baby herself.

It is easy to view this decision harshly. And the harshness with which the nonpoor judge the poor ought to alert you to the fact that they inhabit an unfamiliar nation. In fact, Ms. Sanchez's decision does not appear irrational—given the difficulty in which she found herself. While the result was tragic, such events are rather common among the poor, who frequently find themselves in extreme situations. For them, coping with problems often requires a degree of wisdom and heroism that few possess.

The example also illustrates the dilemma faced by those who would help the poor. When physicians diagnose an illness, they confront not only a medical problem but also poverty. When teachers send work home or want a conference with parents, they confront not only lack of education but also poverty. When counselors deal with a drug abuser, they confront not only self-destructive behavior but also poverty. It affects every dimension of life. If the physician who talked to Ms. Sanchez on the telephone had told her to come for a prescription prior to going to the pharmacy, the baby's death might have been avoided. The physician, although well-meaning, did not understand the difficulties Ms. Sanchez faced. When would-be helpers are unfamiliar with the reality of poverty, they fail to recognize its connection to the problem at hand.

In order to consider such connections, a definition is necessary. The one used here is extrapolated from the government's official poverty line (to be discussed later). This is the threshold most familiar to the public: **Poverty** refers to a minimum income level below which individuals or families find it difficult to subsist. The word subsist should be taken literally. It is hard for poor people to obtain food, shelter, and medical treatment. Maria Sanchez provides an example of the last dilemma.

Dimensions of Poverty

An initial step toward making the poor seem more familiar is to count them. How much poverty exists? And just how poor are they? It turns out, however, that counting the poor requires a series of subjective decisions in order to produce a realistic figure.

Poverty in the United States

Standards of living change over time, which makes assessing the long-term trend in the poverty rate tricky (Fisher, 1997). In 1900, only 1 percent of all families owned an automobile, which meant it had no impact on people's economic circumstances because social life was organized without requiring ownership of high speed transportation (USBC, 1975, p. 717). Today, those without a car find it difficult (sometimes impossible) to get to and from work. Similarly, only 12 percent of the population had running water in their homes at the turn of the century, which meant that most people used outhouses to relieve themselves. Although this practice exposed people to disease and, hence, had negative health consequences, it was free. Today, it is impossible to use an outhouse in any city, where most people now live. The poor must pay—with cash—for water, heat, electricity, and all other items necessary for living.

One way to resolve the problem of changes in the standard of living is to ask a simple question that stems from the definition offered earlier: What proportion of the population has difficulty subsisting? The answer provides an estimate that takes into account the changes mentioned above. These data are presented in Figure 10-1.

The figure shows that about 45 percent of the population was poor during the latter part of the nineteenth century. This percentage, however, is squishy. In *America's Struggle Against Poverty, 1900–1985,* James T. Patterson reviewed the estimates for this period and showed that they range between 40 percent and 60 percent (1986). Hence, by selecting a relatively low estimate in this range, I have chosen to avoid overstating the level of impoverishment during the late 1800s. The poverty rate appar-

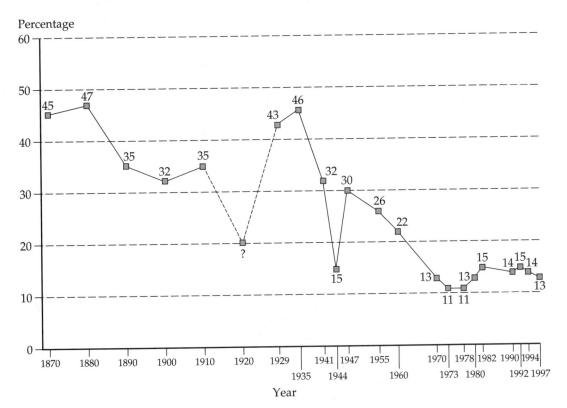

FIGURE 10-1   Poverty Estimates in the United States, Selected Years, 1870–1997

Sources: For 1870–1910 (Hartley, 1969, p. 19; 1998a, p. vi); for 1929–1944 (Ornati, 1966, p. 158); for 1947–1955 (CEA, 1969, p. 154); for 1960–1997 (USBC, 1998a, p. vi).

Note: There are no data for the World War I period (but see Plotnick et al, 1998). I have used dotted lines to suggest that the poverty rate probably fell during this period.

ently dropped around the turn of the century, primarily because of industrialization.[2] In assessing the long-term trend, ignore the spikes caused by World Wars I and II, and the Depression. Immediately after World War II, the poverty rate probably stood around 30 percent, with a much narrower range of error. By 1960, it had declined to about 22 percent, then to 11 to 12 percent during the 1970s. This is the lowest level ever attained, at least in the United States. The poverty rate rose during the 1980s to about 14 to 15 percent and remained at that level until recently. During the last few years, the poverty rate has declined to about 13 percent. It is too soon to know if this change represents a trend (I doubt it). Note that the data for the last 30 years reflect the official poverty line adopted by the government. They comprise the most accurate information available—assuming you agree that the poverty line provides a realistic measure.

The historical data presented in Figure 10-1 reveal that a long-term decline in poverty occurred in the United States prior to the recent upsurge. These data, however, need to be supplemented with information from other nations in order to place the U.S. poverty problem in perspective.

Poverty in Other Nations

Yet such data are difficult to obtain because no international standards exist for measuring poverty. Of the Western nations usually compared in this book, only the United States and United Kingdom have "official" measures. Hence, the most useful strategy, shown next, is to look at the percentage of the population earning less than 40 percent of the median income because the result provides comparable data (Smeeding, 1996).

	Population with Income Less Than 40% of Median
United States	13%
United Kingdom	7
Canada	7
Germany	5
France	4
Netherlands	4
Sweden	4

Although poverty declined in the United States over the past century, these international data show that it declined much further in comparable Western European nations. Moreover, because these nations provide more in-kind (noncash) benefits for all citizens, regardless of ability to pay, being poor is not nearly so onerous as in the United

---

[2]More recently, Plotnick and his colleagues have estimated poverty rates back to 1914 (1998). They show a pattern similar to that in Figure 10-1, but the percentages are higher: 70 percent prior to World War I, more than 30 percent after World War II. As they suggest, the former seems unreasonably high. What you should learn is that such estimates are tricky and involve a large amount of guessing and a large error term.

States. These differences imply that the level of poverty reflects political choices. Public policies can be devised which place fewer people in situations like Maria Sanchez. The United States, however, chooses to maintain a rather large impoverished population and to live with the consequences.

But is the poverty line realistic? Do 13 percent of the U.S. population find it hard to subsist? The answer to such questions inevitably involves issues of measurement.

The Measurement of Poverty

The official poverty line for a family of four in 1997 was $16,400 (USBC, 1998g, p. 1). Because most people still think in terms of the stereotypical family of four, this figure is the most commonly recognized poverty threshold. The cut-off varies, however, by family size, being lower for a two-person family and higher for a six- to seven-person family. The line also varies depending on the age of the head of the household, being slightly lower if the head is over 65 and higher if less than 65. The poverty threshold does not vary by region or rural-urban residence because the Census Bureau has determined that the methodological problems in making such distinctions are too great. Taking all these permutations into account, about 13 percent of the United States population lived in poverty in 1997: 36 million people. Of this total, approximately 14 million were children. Thus, more than one in five young persons in the United States lives in poverty. It would be wise to consider the long-term consequences, both for them and the society.

Right now, however, my interest is with the logic underlying the poverty line. Developed in the 1960s, the poverty line embodies a series of arbitrary decisions (Citro & Michael, 1995; Fisher, 1998). The first involves the criterion for need. Food was chosen, primarily because it is easily measured and understood in comparison to other indicators. Second, a standard market basket of goods had to be chosen so that the cost of food could be determined. The U.S. Department of Agriculture's Thrifty Food Plan is currently used. Although it does not provide a nutritionally adequate diet over the long term, this fact is ignored in setting the poverty line. Third, the ratio between food and nonfood costs had to be picked. The ratio selected assumes that poor persons spend one-third of their income on food and two-thirds on everything else (rent, utilities, medical treatment, and so forth). Yet this ratio is inaccurate. As will become clear in a few moments, it is probable that the poor spend a much higher proportion of their income on food. Fourth, an index had to be adopted so that the threshold could be adjusted each year in light of changing prices. The poverty line uses the Consumer Price Index (CPI). Although the CPI is often criticized, all indexes are imperfect measures of living costs (CBO, 1981). Finally, a definition of income had to be determined. The poverty line refers to cash income from any source: a job, alimony, social security, or public aid, for example. It does not include the value of in-kind benefits, such as Medicaid or food stamps. Again, all of these decisions are arbitrary. By changing them, one could define a smaller or larger population as poor.

One cannot, however, develop a scientifically accurate poverty line (Beeghley, 1984). Recall for a moment the limits of the social sciences discussed in Chapter 1 (in the section on Max Weber's work). These disciplines can discover the facts, explain them, and describe the implications that follow. For example, research can show that if the poverty line is defined as it is now, 36 million people are counted as poor and they have certain characteristics (to be described later). If it were defined differently, however, by—say—counting in-kind income (such as the value of food stamps) as real income, then fewer people would be labeled poor and their characteristics might differ from those currently labeled poor. Alternatively, if the ratio between food and nonfood costs was changed to reflect the actual percentage of income spent on food, then more people would be labeled poor and, again, their characteristics might differ. Neither result, however, would be a "more accurate" or "more scientific" poverty line.[3]

This fact is important because the search for a "more accurate measure of impoverishment" is a perennial siren song for social scientists (Focus, 1998c, p. 3). Moreover, this deceptive allure often involves illogic. For example, it is argued that the benefits of various public assistance programs lift people out of poverty.[4] Thus, food stamps allow (some) poor people to purchase more food than they could otherwise. Medicaid allows (some) of the poor to obtain medical treatment. Housing subsidies allow (some) of the poor to rent apartments. And cash programs, such as Temporary Assistance for Needy Families (TANF) and the Earned Income Tax Credit provide extra cash for (some) poor families. Impoverished people who receive such benefits are indeed better off as a result. But they remain poor. This assertion is correct substantively, as an analysis of their budget will show. It is also correct logically. Because these programs are means tested, people must become poor in order to be eligible for them and stay poor in order to keep receiving benefits. It is an illusion to think that a family so destitute that it receives TANF or food stamps or a housing subsidy or Medicaid is not poor (Beeghley, 1984).

Are the Poor Really Poor?

In order to illustrate the difficulties impoverished people face, I have constructed a budget for a hypothetical family of four living at the poverty line. Before doing so, however, you should understand that any family (or household) used as a point of reference is inevitably arbitrary. For example, the needs of a family composed of two parents and two small children will differ from the needs of a family composed of one parent and two teenagers. Also, families will have different needs depending on where they live. For example, the cost of living in Alaska and Hawaii is significantly higher than in the 48 contiguous states. So in considering the vignette that follows, make mental adjustments for families with different characteristics and situations. I would like to suggest, however, that no matter what variations are considered, any analysis of family budgets at the poverty line will show they have limited lifestyles and life chances compared to other citizens. They are poor.

---

[3]The Census Bureau, in fact, provides estimates of how the poverty line would change if different definitions were used (USBC, 1998g, p. xiii).

[4]These arguments have a long history, beginning in the early 1980s (Smeeding, 1982). More recent work includes Citro and Michael (1995), Focus (1998a; 1998b; 1998c), Short et al. (1998), Corbett (1998), and Wolfe (1998).

Please recall the Smith family. Since we last saw them in Chapter 3, Edward Smith lost his job because the food-processing plant in which he worked closed. He now stays home to care for the two children and maintain the household. Jane Smith continues working 40 hours a week, 52 weeks per year in the textile mill. Contrary to commonsense assumptions, there are no two-week paid vacations or holidays at this economic level. Those who do not show up for work do not get paid. As shown in Table 10-1, Ms. Smith has worked at the mill for many years and earns $7.75 per hour or $16,120 annually. This places the family just below the poverty threshold of $16,400. While her income is high for the kind of work she does, setting it at the minimum wage would leave the family far below the poverty line. The income and expenses shown in the table involve several assumptions. It is assumed, for the moment, that Edward Smith earns no money informally and that Jane Smith is employed on the books and must have Social Security taken from her pay check. But she is smart and has no income tax withheld. The Smiths are eligible for the Earned Income Tax Credit but, for now, the table assumes they do not receive that or any other form of public aid. Finally, it is assumed that, as posited by the poverty line, the Smiths spend one-third of their income on food and the remainder on everything else. For purposes of comparison, the format of Table 10-1 makes it easy to compare the Smith's budget with that of the Martinez family described in Chapter 9 (Table 9-4). Such a comparison will suggest how constricted the lifestyle of a poor family is compared to a working-class family.

The food budget of $412 translates into $3.43 per person per day, assuming a 30-day month. The amount will be slightly more in February (because it has only 28 days) and the Smiths will fast one day in each month that has 31 days. This last is sarcasm, of course, but with a serious message: The Smiths cannot obtain a nutritionally adequate diet on $3.43 per day. (Actually, you cannot even go to Burger King and get a Whopper meal on that amount.) Moreover, poor persons nearly always pay more for food because nearby markets are either mom-and-pop operations or franchised small stores. (Large supermarkets rarely serve impoverished areas.) Hence, it is hard for the Smiths to remain within their food budget. They are, however, eligible for food stamps. At their income level, they are eligible to receive approximately $150 per month in coupons, an additional $1.25 per person each day. Assuming they actually obtain the coupons, they now have $4.68 per person per day to spend on food. (They can afford a Whopper Meal.) But even with this supplement, the Smiths are like most poor families: They spend more than one-third of their income on food, which means they must use part of their nonfood budget in order to eat.

A sidebar: Assuming the Smiths receive food stamps (many poor families do not) their total value (at their income level in the state of Florida) would be $1,800 per year. If the coupons are seen as like money, their "income" is above the poverty line. Does it make sense to argue, either substantively or logically, that this family is no longer poor? Since the program is means tested (requiring low income and few resources as a condition for receiving benefits), is it not more accurate to say that their poverty makes them eligible for aid?

The Smith's nonfood budget is not adequate to cover their living costs, even if none of it is used for food. Table 10-1 shows a nonfood budget of $835 per month to cover the cost of rent, utilities, automobile use and maintenance, insurance, medical and

**TABLE 10-1   Income and Expenses for a Hypothetical Poor
Family Living Just Below the Poverty Line
(Two Adults, Two Children)**

Income

Gross income from husband's job	$ 0
Gross income from wife's job ($7.75 per hour)	16,120
Total Gross Income	16,120
Minus Expenses Taken before Taxes	
Employee share of cost of medical insurance	– 0
Employee share of retirement contribution	– 0
Total Pretax Income	$16,120
Minus Taxes	
Income tax at 15%	– 0
Social Security tax at 7.2%	– 1,161
Net Income	$14,959
Net Monthly Income (14,959 ÷ 12)	$ 1,247

Monthly Living Expenses

Total food (and other grocery supplies)	$ 412
Rent (not mortgage)	$ 350
Property tax	0
Utilities (including gas, electricity, and telephone)	200
Transportation	100
Car insurance	50
Car payment	0
Church contribution	0
Nonallocated	135
Total nonfood	$ 835
Total Monthly Living Expenses (total food + total nonfood)	$ 1,247

Assumptions: (1) The husband receives no off-the-books income. (2) The family
receives no public aid. (3) The family spends one-third of its income on food. The
reasons for these assumptions are explained in the text, as are the way changes in them
(e.g., receipt of public aid) modify the family's lifestyle.

dental bills, clothing, educational expenses, entertainment, and everything else necessary for living in the United States. Although dividing this sum up is difficult, the table
makes a few simple assumptions about the Smith's expenses. The figure for rent, $350
a month, is low in many cases. Impoverished people spend an average of 44 percent of
their income on shelter (Citro & Michael, 1995, p. 197), which is much more than the
28 percent allocated in the table ($350 is 28 percent of $1,247). Utility expenses refer to
the price of gas, electricity, and a telephone. The assumed cost, $200 a month, is low,
since many poor families pay higher utility bills than the nonpoor because their homes
are so badly insulated. Finally, transportation costs $100. This figure is only adequate if
Ms. Smith walks to work. It may not be enough even if members of a family use public
transportation regularly. And it is not sufficient if gasoline and auto maintenance must

be purchased. The amount given for auto insurance, $50 per month ($600 per year) is for cut-rate insurance. They better not have an accident. The Smith's budget now has $135 left each month to pay for medical and dental bills, clothing, purchases necessary for a school-age child, entertainment, and everything else. Even purchasing birth control pills is difficult. And if Jane becomes pregnant, the family's finances fall apart completely. Although none of these amounts is very high and much variation occurs from one location and family to another, no matter how these numbers are manipulated, it is clear that the Smiths probably cannot stay within the nonfood budget for very long. New and unexpected expenses always occur. Yet, as noted above, this family also has great difficulty staying within its food budget as well.

The income and expenses shown in Table 10-1 reveal that families like the Smiths face a conundrum: They must often choose between paying for utilities and food, or housing and food, or medical treatment and food (Frank et al., 1992). It should not be surprising, then, that hunger and homelessness occur among the poor. Remember, the example used here has been for a family living just below the poverty line. About 13 percent of the population lived below it in 1997. The average poor family had a cash income $5,735 below the cutoff (USBC, 1998g, p. 21). Put differently, imagine the problems a household of four would have with an income of $10,665. Yet millions of people did just that. Thus, it seems reasonable to assert that the 36 million persons living below the poverty line, of which 14 million are children, were really poor and that the official threshold provides a realistic indicator of the extent of poverty in the United States today.

Another sidebar: A temporary and partial solution to this conundrum exists. The Smiths filed federal income tax forms and received an Earned Income Tax (EIT) Credit of $2,184 (after taxes). Let us say that they used the money to pay two months' back rent of $700 and old medical bills of $500. They also spent $300 on new clothes and shoes for the children and themselves, and $180 on tires for the car. The remaining $504 they set aside for emergencies. As the analysis of the income and expenses shown in Table 10-1 reveals, these are perfectly plausible uses of this money. And as that analysis also reveals, the set aside will not last very long. The Smiths simply do not have enough money to meet their expenses. Now let's add the value of food stamps and the EIT to the Smiths' net earned income:

Net Income	$14,959
Food Stamps	1,800
EIT	2,184
	$16,973

Based on this amount, it can be argued that the Smiths are no longer poor. After all, their "income" is above the poverty line. But once again: Does this argument make sense, either substantively or logically? Since both public assistance programs are means tested, is it not more accurate to say that their poverty makes them eligible for aid?

As the situation in which the Smiths find themselves illustrates, the millions of families living at the poverty line are not simply short of cash, a problem everyone has sometimes. Such families are desperate. They do not, on their own, have enough money to meet the basic expenses necessary for living in a modern economy. This fact can be summarized by the Class Structure Hypothesis presented in Chapter 1:

> *The lower the social class, the fewer choices people have and the less effective they are in solving personal problems.*

People who have few options often must turn to public assistance in order to survive.

Public Assistance and Poverty

Because people are poor, public assistance alleviates some of the problems inherent to living poorly but does not change people's station in life. In fact, it can be argued that public assistance programs provide as many (if not more) benefits to those who are not poor as to those who are poor. In order to see why this paradox is possible, it is necessary to understand how the programs are organized and what actually happens to the money.

Characteristics of Public Assistance Programs

There are two types of public assistance programs: those providing cash to recipients, such as Temporary Assistance to Needy Families (TANF) and Supplementary Security Income (SSI), and those providing noncash benefits, such as food stamps and Medicaid. These are the four programs reviewed here.

Temporary Assistance to Needy Families

This program originated with passage of the Personal Responsibility and Work Opportunity Reconciliation Act of 1996. All states were required to replace Aid to Families with Dependent Children (AFDC) with TANF by July 1, 1997. TANF is financed by block grants from the federal government to the states and by state-appropriated funds. States have a great deal of discretion in how they use federal money to implement the goals of the program.

Although the details of the new program are devilishly complex, among its most important elements are the following: All "needy" families with children are eligible to receive aid, but each state determines the definition of "needy." A parent (typically a woman) must assist in identifying the other parent (typically a man) and sign over child and spousal support to the state. There is a five-year lifetime limit on eligibility, regardless of work effort or earned income. Parents must "work" after two years of receiving aid, but states can choose to require "work" prior to that time (even immediately). "Work" is defined as having a job, obtaining on-the-job-training, actively looking for a job, being in a vocational training program, attending school, or engaged in community service. Under complicated criteria, states can exempt certain parents from the work requirement. Nonetheless, states must encourage employment by disregarding some earnings in calculating benefits. How this goal is accomplished, however, is left to their discretion. At state option, limits can be set on receipt of Medicaid during the "transition" from public assistance to work. States must subsidize childcare, but have discretion as to the amount and duration. States may allow recipients to establish "individual development accounts" in order to save money. Finally, states must set a minimum level of resources a family may possess (the value of everything they own) and benefit levels. This resource limit combined with income constitutes the means test.

As implied by these requirements, the primary goal of TANF is to reduce the number of people receiving assistance by encouraging them to work. Indeed, the Department of Health and Human Services claims that the nation has "made dramatic progress [over the past few years] on the critical goal of moving families from welfare to work" (USDHHS, 1998b, p. 1). Nationwide, those receiving public aid declined by 40 percent between 1995 and 1998, to about 3 million families or 8.4 million persons (USDHHS, 1998b). But considerable variation occurred by state. For example, the number of recipients plunged 85 percent in Wisconsin and 80 percent in Idaho. Such declines suggest that many people are being pushed off the rolls. But leaving (or being pushed off) public assistance is not the same as getting out of poverty. It is possible, of course, that some unknown number of these people obtained jobs and are no longer poor. Thus, it can be argued that the strength of the economy (as indicated by the relatively low level of unemployment in recent years) has led to the slight decline in the poverty rate shown in Figure 10-1. The available data, however, suggest that many, if not most, of those who have left (or been pushed off) the rolls do not do very well. In Wisconsin, for example, about two-thirds of former recipients had lower incomes after losing public assistance. In Milwaukee (Wisconsin's largest city), 86 percent of those who lost public assistance had incomes below the poverty line (CDF, 1998a; 1998b). The Children's Defense Fund (CDF) data show that the major barriers to work are lack of child care and transportation. They show further that the major barriers to above poverty-level wages are low skills and the lack of available jobs (Weisbrot, 1998). I will argue in a few moments that the structure of the economy makes it unlikely that enough jobs will exist for former public aid recipients.

For those receiving TANF benefits, the program regulates their lives (and lifestyles) in rather detailed ways. As mentioned, each state has a great deal of latitude in setting requirements. Table 10-2 illustrates how the program might operate for a family of three.

Panel A of Table 10-2 displays some program provisions that recipients must satisfy. Recall that these will vary considerably by state. I have selected some common requirements for the table. Thus, in this illustration the family can have assets worth no more than $2,000. This amount refers to the value of pans, chairs, beds, clothing, and jewelry, as well as bank accounts and other financial resources. The applicant must begin working immediately—in the sense noted (employed, in school, looking for a job, and so forth). The only exemption would be if the applicant has an infant less than one year old. Although states can exempt others from work, there are funding penalties if they do so too often. In this example, the reward for employment is that the state will allow a family to retain 50 percent of the TANF grant for every dollar earned. In a fit of fantasy, the state in this example will allow recipients to save some money—in this case for educational purposes. It is unclear how the family will find any money to save.

During the first year of employment, the state will provide both Medicaid coverage and a child care subsidy. After that time, however, the family is on its own. This fact is important because, in the example, the family is at the end of its first year on the program.

Panel B of Table 10-2 illustrates the benefits from TANF and other programs that a family of three might receive at various income levels. As indicated in the notes to the table, I am using TANF benefits from the state of Pennsylvania in this example. As a point of comparison, the poverty line for a three-person family was $12,802 in 1997. In Example (1), the family resources of $7,600 are only 59 percent of the poverty line. It is hard to survive on this amount of money. Example (2) shows how employment is encouraged, since the family gets to keep half of its TANF grant as well as the Earned Income Tax credit. Hence, the available benefits (assuming food stamps are counted as

TABLE 10-2   Temporary Assistance to Needy Families (TANF): Illustrative Program Provisions and Public Aid Benefits at Three Earnings Levels for a Family of Three

Panel A: Illustrative TANF Program Provisions

Assets allowed:	$2,000 (excluding a car)
Must begin working:	Immediately on receiving TANF
Work exemption:	If child is less than 12 months old
Earnings disregard:	50%
Medicaid:	Yes, for 12 months
Child care subsidy	Yes, 20% of earnings for 12 months
Individual development account:	Yes, for education only; no dollar limit
Five-year lifetime limit:	Applicant at end of year one

Panel B: Illustrative Public Aid Benefits at Three Earnings Levels, Family of Three

Earnings (+ Benefits, – Taxes)	Example (1)	Example (2)	Example (3)
Earnings	$ 0	$7,000	$11,000
+ Earned Income Tax (EIT)	0	2,800	3,600
+ TANF	5,600	3,500	1,800
+ Food stamps	2,500	2,000	1,600
– Social Security taxes	0	500	800
	$7,600	$14,800	$17,200

Source: USDHHS (1998b).

Notes: Program provisions in Panel A are common among states. Receipt of EIT (shown in Panel B) is not automatic. I calculated the EIT in (2) and (3) and found that it was not easy to do. In (1) I used TANF and Food Stamp benefits from the state of Pennsylvania. The TANF benefit in (2) was obtained as shown below. The amount in (3) was obtained in a similar manner.

$7,000 (earnings)	$5,600 (maximum TANF)
–3,500 (50% earnings disregard)	– 2,100 (net earnings)
–1,400 (20% child care subsidy)	$3,500 (TANF benefit)
$2,100 (net earnings)	

cash) push the family above the poverty line, but barely. Note, however, that Medicaid benefits and the child care subsidy are expiring. It is not clear how the mother will be able to continue working under these conditions. Example (3) is most interesting. It posits that a recipient worked for nearly a year at the minimum wage and still retains part of the family's TANF benefits plus those from other programs. Observers arguing that public aid programs get people out of poverty, point to people in categories like this one. In this case, the family's income and benefits place them about $5,000 above the poverty line. Substantively, of course, the family remains poor, as a budget calculation will show. Logically, since the programs require that the family continues to have almost no assets, it must stay poor to remain eligible. Finally, the unstable job market for those earning the minimum wage combined with their limited resources mean that the odds are low of a family staying above the poverty line as Medicaid and child care subsidies are withdrawn. What will happen to this family if it hits the lifetime limit?

In thinking about the implications of this example, note that the TANF benefits it posits are above average for the nation as a whole. Nationwide, the average for a family of three is $4,572, well below that used in the example. Moreover, there is great variability by state, as shown in Table 10-3. At the lowest are the southern twins, Mississippi and Alabama, with maximum TANF benefits of $1,440 and $1,968 yearly. At the other end, Wisconsin and Vermont seem positively generous, with maximum benefits of $8,026 and $7,668 yearly. These data suggest that the lifestyle (and life chances) of an impoverished family receiving assistance varies a great deal depending on where they live.

Supplementary Security Income

Unlike TANF, which is administered by the states and displays considerable variability in benefit levels as a result, Supplementary Security Income (SSI) provides a minimum monthly income for poor aged, blind, and disabled persons that is relatively uniform

TABLE 10-3   Maximum Yearly TANF Benefit Levels in Least Generous and Most Generous States

Least Generous		Most Generous	
State	Yearly Maximum	State	Yearly Maximum
Mississippi	$1,440	Wisconsin	$8,026
Alabama	1,968	Vermont	7,668
Tennessee	2,220	Connecticut	7,632
Texas	2,256	Massachusetts	6,948
Louisiana	2,280	New York	6,924
Arkansas	2,248	California	6,780
Nationwide Average:	$4,572		

Source: USDHHS (1998b, Table 9:1).

Note: "Most generous" refers only to the continental United States. Both Alaska and Hawaii have significantly higher benefit levels because of the very high cost of living.

throughout the nation. There were about 6.6 million recipients in 1998. They received a maximum benefit of $5,808 yearly if they were single and living independently and $8,702 yearly if they were a couple (CWM, 1998, p. 278). As the title of the program suggests, recipients can have a small income from other sources, such as Social Security or wages, and use SSI benefits to supplement it. In addition, 23 states provide small additional stipends to the basic SSI grant. The result, however, still leaves most people below the poverty line. Apart from being aged, blind, or disabled, eligibility requirements for SSI dictate that recipients must satisfy a means test; they must become destitute and stay that way. Thus, their assets (again, everything they own) must be less than $2,000 for single persons and $3,000 for couples, excluding a car (CWM, 1998, p. 269). Like TANF, then, recipients must become poor and stay that way to remain eligible for SSI.

Food Stamps

As with all other public assistance programs, eligibility for food stamps requires that recipients satisfy a means test; that is, they must use up all their assets and earn little or no income. Thus, while TANF and SSI recipients are automatically eligible for food stamps, all other persons receiving them can retain material goods and resources worth less than $2,000, not counting a car (USDA, 1998b). All adults without dependent children must "work" (defined, more or less, the same way as in the TANF program). But whether employed or not, benefit levels are very low. For example, as shown in Table 10-2, a family of three with no income living in Pennsylvania receives only $2,500 in coupons. If they are treated as a form of cash and combined with TANF benefits, the total of $7,600 is only about 59 percent of the poverty line. Nationwide, food stamps provide an average benefit of $71.00 per person per month, about $2.37 per day (USDA, 1998b). But a significant proportion of those who are eligible for food stamps do not receive them. Although about 21.4 million people received coupons in 1997 (a sharp decline since 1995), about 36 million people were officially impoverished in that year and, presumably, eligible (USDA, 1998b). As will be discussed in a few moments, this fact implies that many people go hungry—at least sometimes.

Medicaid

Many also go without medical treatment. The Medicaid program pays for treatment for only about 45 percent of the poor. Among the poor, those covered vary by age, as shown below (CWM, 1998, p. 957):

Age	% of Poor with Medicaid
0–5	71%
6–10	64
11–18	50
19–44	33
45–64	33
65 +	30
Average	45%

Those not covered are left to fend for themselves, which usually means not obtaining treatment or begging for it at an emergency room. Among those covered, states are required to offer the following services: hospital (inpatient and outpatient), laboratory and x-ray, family planning (including supplies), physician and nursing treatment, and what is called "early and periodic screening, diagnosis, and treatment" for children (CWM, 1998, p. 956). This last is the only form of preventive treatment paid for by Medicaid. Beyond this minimum, the scope of health problems covered varies sharply from state to state (CWM, 1998, p. 988). For example, 11 states pay for optometrists' services and 12 pay for eyeglasses. Prescribed drugs are paid for in 14 states and psychologists' services in 6. Although TANF recipients are not automatically eligible for Medicaid coverage, most states provide it, usually for one year. Although impoverished persons who do not receive TANF qualify for the program, many do not receive benefits.

The Paradox of Public Assistance

Recognizing that public aid programs provide help while requiring that the poor remain poor reveals their paradoxical impact. On the one hand, they help the poor with income support and in-kind benefits. The result alleviates some of the problems they face. The word "alleviate" is important; it means to relieve pain, to make suffering more bearable. This is what public aid programs do by reducing the level of deprivation. It is all they do. For, on the other hand, public assistance maintains the economic status quo because people must remain poor in order to stay eligible for benefits. The mechanism for achieving this result is the means test, which stipulates that if recipients obtain additional income or assets above specified levels they become ineligible for public assistance. What happens is that recipients receive aid and the money is immediately returned to the taxpayers, either by the beneficiaries themselves when they use TANF and SSI to pay bills or purchase necessities, or by the government when it reimburses providers of noncash benefits.

As an aside, I do not wish to imply that there is anything wrong with using a means test or asking people to remain poor in order to continue receiving benefits. I do wish to suggest, however, that grandiose notions about America's generosity toward the poor are misbegotten. The cycle of poverty and public assistance programs shown in Figure 10-2 suggests this fact.

Box (1) of the figure anticipates the discussion in the next section by showing that the main causes of a family's entry on to the public assistance rolls are lack of a job, low wages, or marital dissolution. Job loss is always a potential problem for working-class people, whose employment responds to economic fluctuations (see Chapter 9). Thus, when a factory closes down or reduces its work force, the persons laid off first and for the longest time are those in blue-collar occupations. Further, for many intact families, their receipt of public aid—especially food stamps and Medicaid (where it is available)—reflects low wages rather than lack of work. As indicated previously, a family in which the head earns the minimum wage, $5.15 per hour (nationally, it varies somewhat by state), lives well below the poverty line. Millions of jobs pay at or near this level.

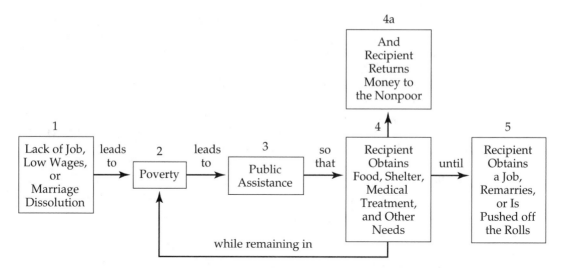

FIGURE 10-2   A Model of the Cycle of Poverty and Public Assistance

Finally, for many women with children, marital dissolution because of divorce or separation forces them to turn to public assistance.

Boxes (2) to (4) depict the obvious functions of public assistance. They describe what happens to recipients each month they receive aid: For reasons noted above, they become (2) poor enough to satisfy the means test, which leads (3) to the use of public assistance, so that (4) they obtain needed benefits. As indicated by the feedback loop, this sequence repeats itself each month while they remain in poverty. In this way, then, public assistance helps the poor to survive by alleviating some of their problems. The sequence does not stop until, as indicated in Box (5), recipients obtain an adequately paying job, remarry (in the case of women), or exceed the five-year lifetime limit and are kicked off the rolls.

Box (4a) depicts the nonobvious functions of public assistance. It describes what happens to the money recipients receive each month: They return it to the nonpoor and the economic status quo is maintained as a result. Middle-class people, of course, use this money to support themselves or to invest and better their lifestyles. In my *Living Poorly in America,* I described this process as the "trickle-up effect" in order to denote its artificial character (1983). In the physical world, water trickles down as a natural result of the force of gravity. In the social world, the trickle-down effect rarely occurs, despite claims by some economists (see Chapters 6 and 7). Thus, simply because money is appropriated to help the poor, does not mean they get to keep it or that income has been redistributed by the nonpoor to the poor. Just as governments can construct elaborate pumping stations and aqueducts in order to make water flow upward, so they can (far more easily) insure that money appropriated to help the poor is not permanently redistributed to them. The means test is the key to understanding this paradox. It insures that public assistance programs do not reduce the rate of poverty while, at the same time, guaranteeing that those who are impoverished obtain help to alleviate some of their problems. Thus, while the poor endure less deprivation, they remain impoverished.

Before leaving this topic, it is important to resolve the paradox. It seems to me that neither conspiracies nor accidents happen very often in social life. Most of the time, there are relatively straightforward explanations for social arrangements, if observers care to look. Put simply, the paradox of public assistance results from who has power in this country. As the *Political Power Hypothesis* suggests:

The higher the social class, the greater the influence over access to valued resources.

The nonpoor, who dominate the political process in the United States, make public aid programs. This fact means that the organization of these programs reflects the economic interests of the nonpoor. It is why the means test insures that only the very poor receive assistance and that the money is returned immediately to the nonpoor. The significance of the means test can be seen in its selective use. The many income transfer programs for the middle class and rich are never called public assistance (or welfare), and none include a means test as a condition for aid (see Chapter 7). Another problem remains: If public assistance requires people to remain poor and a large class of impoverished people persists, who benefits? And what implications follow?

The Benefits of Poverty

I would like to suggest that the nonpoor, such as readers of this book, benefit from the misery and deprivation of others. Moreover, I would also like to suggest that whenever harmful conditions persist over time, it usually means that some segment of the population is benefiting.[5]

First, poverty benefits the nonpoor by making available a class of low-skill workers who can and will perform vital tasks that others do not wish to do. Such jobs come easily to mind: making cloth and clothes, picking and cooking food, cleaning buildings and streets, and all the other dirty, menial, dangerous, low-paying, and short-term occupations that must be performed in an industrial society. Thus, the persistence of a high rate of poverty ensures that many people in the United States have so few options that they must fill positions no one else wants. This situation benefits the nonpoor.

An unexpected implication of this point of view is a recognition of the dual impact of the public schools mentioned in Chapter 3. On the one hand, schools facilitate

[5]The source of my remarks in the paragraphs below is an article by Herbert Gans, "The Positive Functions of Poverty" (1972). More recently, John Kenneth Galbraith made some of the same points in his description of the "functional underclass" (1992).

achievement. On the other hand, they also weed out a sufficient number of individuals who become available for dead-end jobs. Thus, even though education can be a vehicle for upward mobility on the part of some individuals, by systematically failing to educate a certain proportion of students, the schools help to create and perpetuate a class of poor people who make up the cadre of low-skill workers our society needs. The irony here is that this process really is unintended, for it occurs despite the efforts of dedicated teachers.

Second, poverty benefits the nonpoor by keeping prices down. Because the poor have no alternative to working for low wages, the existence of an indigent class subsidizes the consumption activities of the more affluent. Thus, clothes are cheaper, food is less expensive, mortgages are reduced, and taxes are kept low. What this interpretation means is that the lifestyle of the middle class and rich in U.S. society is dependent on the existence of a low-paid work force.

The unexpected implication of this point of view is that nonpoor people have an economic stake in preventing the majority of hardworking poor persons—whose jobs include picking produce in the hot sun, making clothes in sweat shops, and picking up garbage in the streets—from obtaining education or job skills and thereby earning higher wages. It is easy to dismiss such people as low-skill workers and, hence, deserving of low wages. But they perform vital tasks, and if they were paid decent wages, the lifestyle of nonpoor people would suffer.

Third, poverty benefits the nonpoor by creating jobs and income for persons who would regulate, serve, or exploit those who are less fortunate. For example, people who cannot obtain work sometimes resort to illegal drugs and street crime to sustain themselves, thereby guaranteeing jobs for police officers, lawyers, judges, probation officers, and everyone else connected with the criminal justice system. By the way, this fact is not an apologia, merely a recognition that such illegal activities benefit the nonpoor population (which is least victimized). In addition, dependence on public aid guarantees jobs for social workers, clerks, and administrators employed in social service departments of government at all levels. This is because people who publicly declare their inability to provide for themselves and thereby receive aid from the state must be regulated by the nonpoor (Piven & Cloward, 1971). Less obviously, but just as importantly, the existence of a class of poor persons provides work for grocers, clerks, liquor store dealers, pawn shop owners, doctors, nurses, pharmacists, and many other individuals. Finally, there exist academicians who get huge grants to study the poor, write books about them, obtain tenure, and make money thanks to mass poverty. Thus, the jobs of millions of affluent people are dependent directly or indirectly on the existence of a high rate of poverty.

An unexpected implication of the fact that poverty creates jobs and income for the nonpoor is the existence of the trickle-up effect associated with public assistance. As indicated earlier, this process occurs in two ways. On the one hand, public assistance programs require hordes of bureaucrats to administer them, social workers to regulate the recipients, physicians to provide health care, pharmacists to supply medicine, computer programmers to keep track of the funds, and so forth. Thus, the government gives public assistance money directly to middle-class people. On the other hand, the trickle-up effect occurs as poor persons spend their "welfare" checks and stamp allotments. This money also ends up in the hands of the nonpoor: grocers, gasoline station operators, utility companies, landlords, and so forth.

Fourth, poverty benefits the nonpoor because destitute persons purchase goods and services more affluent people do not want. Indigents have so few alternatives that they must buy deteriorating or ill-constructed merchandise, patronize secondhand stores and thereby give new life to old products, and provide a market for stolen goods of all sorts (if they wish any amenities of modern life). In addition, poverty forces people to obtain services from badly trained or malevolent professionals who cannot make a living from middle-class customers. It should be emphasized that this argument is not just a repetition of the assertion above that poverty creates jobs and income; rather, the point here is that the poor are exploited more and have less legal protection than any other segment of the population.

The unexpected implication of a recognition that poor people purchase goods and services others do not want is that perverse consequences result when they try to plan ahead. Thus, by purchasing discount (that is, shoddy) or aging merchandise, indigent people are trying to save money, be frugal, and plan ahead for other expenses; they are, in short, trying to live by dominant values characteristic of the United States. And what they often learn from this attempt is that such efforts do not pay off, since what they buy is so frequently either useless or does not last. While it is easy to indict impoverished people for not being willing to plan ahead, to delay gratification, the experience of many low-income persons is that such strategies are fruitless. As a caveat, it should be recognized that some highly qualified persons do choose to serve or work for the poor, our most vulnerable citizens. Thus, the irony is that while impoverished people can be readily exploited, and this benefits the nonpoor, they also constitute an outlet for those with a more altruistic orientation, and this also benefits the nonpoor.

Although there are other ways in which the nonpoor benefit from poverty, the last one I want to mention here is that the poor are made to absorb the costs of economic policies. For example, whenever inflation has been high over the past 25 years, the federal government pursued fiscal and monetary policies that produced increasing unemployment. Such policies did reduce inflation, but at terrible cost to those who, through no fault of their own, were thrown out of work. Similarly, when reducing the federal budget deficit became an issue during the 1980s, the programs that suffered the greatest cuts were those designed to aid the poor. Put bluntly, this interpretation means that the existence of mass poverty provides a class of people who can be exploited by the rest of the population—at least so long as they do not protest in some way.

The unexpected implication of this point of view is the possibility that the political system in the United States is not really open to everyone, especially the poor. As consistent losers, perhaps they are kept from participating, except by disruptive or unruly behavior (recall Chapter 6). For now, however, I want to discuss the causes of poverty from two different angles, each of which provides a different kind of information. Thus, one way to understand the causes of poverty is to ask why individuals (like the Smiths) become poor. This line of analysis applies a basic sociological orientation to understanding impoverishment: Individuals act on and react to the situations in which they find themselves. In addition, another way to understand the causes of poverty is to ask how the social structure produces a class of impoverished persons.

This question applies the notion that the social structure decisively influences rates of events to the study of poverty. Taken together, these angles of vision lower the possibility for self-deception and provide a clear, if cynical, view of U.S. society. They make the unfamiliar familiar.

The Individual and Poverty

Poor persons in the United States are unfamiliar because they live on the margin in a land of plenty. They do not share in its material abundance. Given the exposition here and in previous chapters, the characteristics of those who are poor are just those you might expect.

Age
Children and aged persons are more likely to be poor than people in other age categories of the population. Thus, the relationship between age and poverty is curvilinear in the form, roughly, of a bowl with one side higher than the other (USBC, 1998g, p. vii):

Age	% Poor
< 18	20%
18–24	18
25–34	12
35–44	10
45–54	7
55–59	9
60–64	11
65 +	11

One reason so many children are poor is that they are born of children and young adults, persons who have not acquired education or job skills. As people mature into adulthood and obtain job skills, the probability of poverty declines. Thus, it is usually unwise, most of the time, for young persons to marry or establish households independently of their parents. One factor leading to this decision is pregnancy. Yet the United States makes it relatively difficult for young persons to obtain contraception and, thereby, prevent pregnancy (Luker, 1996). This difficulty affects the poor most of all. Sadly, sometimes girls become sexually active and pregnant as a reaction to an abusive home life or other deprivations (Dash, 1989). In effect, they respond by confusing sexual intercourse with love and by conceiving a child as evidence of their humanity, their adulthood. Boys from impoverished backgrounds often react in similar ways. They make someone pregnant under the delusion that this result indicates their manhood (Marsiglio, 1993). Another factor leading young persons to establish their own household is the desire to escape an impoverished home life (Rubin, 1994). Hence, young persons make unwise decisions in specific contexts in which their choices are limited and their experiences teach them (often falsely) that they will be better off forming their own families.

Race and Ethnicity
Whites are less likely to be poor than any other racial or ethnic group (USBC, 1998a, table 2; 1998g, p. vii).

Native Americans	31%
African Americans	27%
Hispanic Americans	27%
Asian Americans	14%
White Americans	9%

You should note, however, that the pattern differs when absolute numbers are shown. The percentages refer to about 16 million white Americans, nine million African Americans, 8 million Hispanic Americans, one million Asian Americans, and a few hundred thousand Native Americans. Hence, more whites are poor than any other group. The reason a higher proportion of minorities endure poverty is discrimination (recall Chapter 5).

Family Characteristics
Divorce, separation, or abandonment often lead to poverty for mothers and children: *Female-headed families are more likely to be poor than two-parent families*: 32 percent versus 5 percent (USBC, 1998g, p. vii). Although there are so few male-headed families that data are difficult to obtain, it is plausible to hypothesize that their proportion is higher than that of two-parent families. I make this argument because the presence of only one earner increases the odds of poverty, whether male or female.

In considering the importance of a two-parent (hence, two-earner) family, I would like to return again to the Smiths. Recall from Chapter 3 that prior to Edward Smith's becoming unemployed, the family had a low but steady income, around $41,000 per year. They managed the stresses inherent to their economic situation. Since losing his job, however, Edward has battled feelings of meaninglessness and a sense of helplessness because he cannot provide for his family. Fights between Jane and Edward have increased. This is partly because Edward feels so bad and partly because money has become so tight. It will take courage for this family to remain together. Millions of couples find themselves in situations like this. Some break apart. And when this happens women usually get custody of the children (Beeghley, 1996). As a result, more than half of all poor families are headed by women (USBC, 1998g, p. vii).

Low-Wage Job Skills
The fewer the job skills people possess, the greater the likelihood of poverty. Thus, people with higher education—who write well, speak a foreign language, learn the law, and fill prescriptions—have job skills. They rarely become impoverished. People without higher education—who type, operate cash registers, and repair cars—also have job skills. But they are more prone to poverty. In modern societies, skills are traded for

wages. One of the most important indicators of skill is education. Listed below are poverty rates among individuals aged 25 years and older by educational attainment (USBC, 1997b, p. 479).

Less than High School Diploma	24%
High School Diploma	10%
College Diploma	2%

Work Experience
People who work less are more likely to be poor. Thus, among the poor population aged 25 to 54 (the prime earning years), 49 percent were not employed during the previous year. Some observers take this fact as indicating laziness. My own observation, however, is that some people get beaten down by poverty. I will elaborate on this idea later.

For now, I want to consider this finding in the context of the one above. Work experience often leaves people impoverished because their wages are so low. Put simply: A lot of employed people are poor. Jane Smith, for example, earns $7.75 per hour. This income places her family below the poverty line even though she works full-time all year long. Of course, the Smiths constitute a hypothetical example. But they represent millions of people. Among the poor population aged 25 to 54 years, 35 percent work part of the year and 16 percent work full-time all year long (USBC, 1998g, p. 7).

Poverty is thus a transformative event. In Chapter 1, I defined **socialization** as the life-long process by which individuals learn norms and values, internalize motivations and needs, develop intellectual and social skills, and enact roles as they participate in society. Children whose parents go through the experiences described here learn quickly that life is neither predictable nor controllable. Such events can be defining episodes in people's lives. Not all of them suffer hunger, but many do. Not all of them endure homelessness, but some do. Not all of them withdraw into drug abuse or join gangs and express their rage, but a few do. All of them, however, even those whose families remain stable, go through hardship and deprivation.

Now the usual, commonsense approach to understanding poverty is to blame individual deficiencies: If only they would work harder, it is said, they could escape impoverishment. And there is truth to this adage, albeit partial truth. Some economists adopt the commonsense approach by seeing poverty as resulting from lack of **human capital.** The term refers to job skills or education, which can be converted into skills that produce income (Becker, 1975). From this angle, people who are poor because they do not earn enough should simply augment their human capital so as to make their services more valuable and increase their income. At the very least, they should look for a job. And it is true, as common sense would have it, that individuals without a high school degree can often find a job if they look hard enough. Vacancies exist even in central cities, despite declining employment opportunities in these areas. Yet, if successful, this strategy will only solve an individual's problem. It will not reduce the high rate of poverty. The reason is simple: There are not enough jobs. Thus, if a large proportion of those out of work sought all the jobs available, they would overwhelm the vacancies at the lower skill levels (Kasarda, 1990). This means that advocating self-help strategies to eliminate poverty—whether as common sense or dressed up in academic jargon—is not very practical. Such proposals affirm dominant values without increasing understanding. The latter occurs when structural questions are asked.

Social Structure and Poverty

Throughout most of history, human beings lived at the mercy of nature. Productivity was low, based on muscle power. Nearly everyone scratched a living from the soil. The few amenities (goods that make life pleasant) were monopolized by an elite group. Life was short. Nearly everyone was poor. During the past century or two, however, this situation changed radically. Productivity is now high, based on nonliving sources of energy. Few people work the land. Amenities are spread throughout the population. Life is long. Relatively few people are poor. Today, nature lies at the mercy of human beings. Figure 10-1 revealed this transformation clearly. Poverty declined steadily over time, not only in the United States but also in every Western society. This fact suggests that common structural changes occurred in all of them. At the same time, data also reveal that the U.S. poverty rate is higher than in comparable nations. This suggests that our country chooses to maintain a larger population of impoverished persons. In this section, therefore, I deal with two issues. First, why did a long-term fall in the rate of poverty occur? Second, why is the U.S. level so much higher than that in other societies?

The Long-Term Fall in the Poverty Rate

Common sense, as mentioned earlier, suggests that people avoid poverty by working hard. Hard work, people are taught, produces success. Failure consists in giving up. From this point of view, it is easy for those who achieve some success to attribute it to their work ethic. After all, they sacrificed while training, found a job, and labored for years to advance. Their lives confirm the idea that hard work pays off. By extrapolation, then, the conventional explanation assumes that in "a social context where plenty of opportunity existed," those who worked hard have been successful and those who are poor must not have worked very hard.

Students, of course, employ a similar orientation. They have learned that a correlation exists between hard work and success, in the form of grades and college matriculation. Thus, those whose good grades (and family background) enable them to attend Outstanding Private University assume that anyone can get in if they work hard. Similarly, those whose good grades enable them to attend the state-supported Flagship University assume that anyone can get in if they work hard. Finally, those attending Community College assume that anyone can go if they work hard. Thus, in both everyday life and higher education, people assume that hard work explains their success.

But this explanation is too facile. I mentioned before that the conventional account assumes "a social context where plenty of opportunity existed." The phrase was placed in quotes to alert you to the structural question: What factors produced a context in which hard work could pay off? My answer, in the form of a hypothesis, is as follows:

> *The long-term fall in the poverty rate reflects (1) industrialization, (2) class differences in fertility rates, and (3) declining discrimination.*

Industrialization

You may recall from Chapter 3 that **industrialization** refers to the transformation of the economy as new forms of energy were substituted for muscle power, leading to advances in productivity. Now this definition, while accurate, is also rather narrow. Industrialization occurred in the context of other basic structural transformations: First, it is linked to the rise of **capitalism,** an economic system based on private ownership of the means of production—the machines and techniques used to produce goods and services (Berger, 1986). Ownership produces a concern with profit, one motivation for increasing productivity. Second, industrialization is also linked to the rise of **work-centered values.**[6] Such sentiments do not develop in individuals by accident. People are taught them—at home and at school. They emerged as unintended consequences of the Protestant Reformation (Weber, 1905). Third, industrialization is further linked to the value placed on personal freedom that arose in the West in the eighteenth century (Lenski, 1966). Free people choose for themselves what to produce and buy. Finally, industrialization is based on advances in scientific knowledge that occurred over the past 400 to 500 years. The terms *industrialization* and *industrial society,* then, are often used as shorthand ways of describing a historical watershed: the rise of new kinds of societies in the West over the last few centuries. So you should remember that the term *industrialization* implies more than merely a change in economic organization.

But precisely this change is of primary interest here. With industrialization, the proportion of white-collar jobs rose while farming jobs fell. Thus, as shown in Table 3-1 (in Chapter 3), the white-collar work force rose from 18 percent to 58 percent between 1900 and 1997. In contrast, the farm work force fell from 38 percent to 3 percent. The new job slots at the top of the class structure were, in effect, a vacuum that had to be filled. They "pulled" people upward, out of poverty. This is because an industrial society requires people in management positions. In addition, a host of new, highly skilled, white-collar occupations emerged in industrial societies. So people left farming and blue-collar jobs for better-paying, higher-prestige ones. Poverty fell as a result.

---

[6]The term **work-centered values** refers to ideals dictating that people should work hard, organize their lives methodically, delay immediate gratification, and earn money. In contrast, **leisure-centered values** dictate that people should pursue self-expression, enjoy pleasure, and consume goods and services. People usually act on these values in different contexts.

Class Differences in Fertility Rates

The **fertility rate** refers to the average number of children born to each woman. Although a two-century decline in fertility has occurred, the "baby boom" generation being the only exception, lower-class people have always displayed higher birth rates. This difference, greater in the past than today, meant that families in farming and blue-collar occupations had more children, on the average, than those in white-collar occupations. In the context of industrialization, in which the number of farming and blue-collar jobs was declining, these "excess" young persons were "pushed" upward in the occupational hierarchy by population pressure. The result was upward mobility and, hence, a decline in the rate of poverty.

Declining Discrimination

Discrimination refers to the unequal treatment of individuals and groups due to their personal characteristics, such as their race or gender.

In the past, the unequal treatment of racial and ethnic minorities was deliberate and overt, often legal. For example, the denial of civil rights kept racial and ethnic minorities from full citizenship. Other problems followed: unequal medical treatment, housing segregation, school segregation, and occupational discrimination, to name some obvious examples. Hence, whites enjoyed tremendous advantages in a context of industrialization and class differences in fertility rates. Yet, while discrimination continues in all these areas, Chapter 5 showed that significant improvement has occurred in each of them as well. African Americans, Hispanic Americans, Asian Americans, and Native Americans suffer less discrimination now than in the past. The result has been a lower rate of poverty.

The unequal treatment of women was similarly deliberate and overt, and also legal. For example, access to higher education and professional schools was restricted for women. Their ability to obtain credit in their own name was limited. **Traditional gender norms** dictated that women should remain home, bearing and raising children, and taking care of their husbands. Hence, males enjoyed tremendous advantages in seeking occupational and economic success over most of this century. Yet, while unequal treatment remains widespread, Chapter 4 showed that women suffer less discrimination today than in the past.

Now it remains true that, regardless of industrialization and class differences in fertility, people (usually white males) only succeeded by hard work. These structural variables are important, however, because they provided a historical context in which hard work could pay off. A little counterfactual thought experiment suggests their impact. A century ago, the vast majority of people worked either on the farm or in blue-collar jobs, using muscle power to produce goods. Most were poor. If the job structure had not changed, then these people and their descendants (most of you) would have remained hard-working farmers. In the real world, however, people's options changed. Although no one was forced to be upwardly mobile, both the jobs and the people to fill them existed. These facts had nothing to do with each individual's motives or abilities. In Emile Durkheim's phrase, they reflected a change "in the nature of society itself" (1895, p. 128). The result has been a decline in the proportion of poor people in all industrial nations, albeit more so in Western Europe than the United States.

The U.S. Poverty Rate Today

Despite the progress against poverty that has occurred throughout this century, the United States maintains a higher rate of poverty than other Western industrial societies. My hypothesis is that this difference can be accounted for in structural terms.[7]

The rate of poverty in the United States reflects (1) the reproduction of the class structure, (2) the vicious circle of poverty, (3) macroeconomic policy, (4) the structure of elections, (5) the structure of the economy, and (6) institutionalized discrimination.

The Reproduction of the Class Structure

In the United States, as in all societies, the class structure is stable over time. The main evidence for this stability comes from analyses of mobility reviewed in Chapter 3, which document that most people end up in the same class as their parents. Although authors of these studies usually emphasize how much movement occurs, the fact that most people remain in the same occupational category as their parents and go very short distances when mobility occurs means that the class structure is continually reproduced.

This stability exists because people at each level use their resources to protect their advantages and pass them on to their children (Weber, 1920). Thus, those who are most vulnerable to poverty, working-class families, tend to remain that way over time and across generations. Working-class individuals cannot alter the class structure into which they are born. It exists as a reality independently of them, limiting their choices. Thus, while a few near the top of the blue-collar hierarchy who work hard and have ability will move into white-collar jobs, most (including many who work just as hard and have just as much ability) will remain about where they began. Some of them will become impoverished during their lives. And, in turn, a small proportion of the poor become trapped.

The Vicious Circle of Poverty

Sometimes impoverishment that would ordinarily be temporary combines with other difficulties, like a vicious circle, to snare people into long-term poverty.

One way people become trapped is that their efforts at escape are thwarted and they become so discouraged they give up. Consider the Smiths, and remember they represent lots of families. As you may recall from Chapter 3, they live in Cedar Key, Florida, which has been a rural backwater for many years. It has always been a pleasant place to live. Although there is little crime (okay, a few locals run drugs up and down the coast), there are also very few (legal) jobs. But in the last few years it has become something of a tourist haven and a few artists have moved there. Hence, Edward decided to set up a kiosk next to the town dock and sell locally made "art" (junk, but the tourists don't know that). The result was transformative. He became clean shaven and stopped

---

[7]The argument in this section is revised and adapted from my "Individual versus Structural Explanations of Poverty" (1989).

drinking. He was bringing in an income. Alas, after protests to the police by the Chamber of Commerce, Edward was forced to stop because the law limits the number of street vendors. So Edward cleaned up his car and started using it as a jitney van, taking people staying in condominiums to the dock area at $1.00 per person. But after protests by the local Cab Company, he was again forced to stop. Edward knows the "American Rule": One is supposed to keep trying, to find work, and succeed over time. But this effort becomes hard after being repeatedly thwarted.

These illustrations are not exaggerated. Although some poor persons have so few job skills that years of training would be necessary for employment, many can operate small businesses. Lots of opportunities exist—cab drivers, jitney van operators, cosmetologists, and street vendors, to name a few—that do not require much capital or education. They require, instead, entrepreneurship. But such initiative is often restricted by local laws, in four ways (Mellor, 1996). First, limits are placed on the number of jobs in any one area. In New York City, for example, exactly 12,187 taxis, 4,000 food vendors, and 1,700 merchandise peddlers may operate—legally. Second, extensive training is required that has little relevance to public safety. In New York, one needs 900 hours of training to become a licensed cosmetologist, compared to 116 hours to become an emergency medical technician and 47 hours to become a security guard (with a gun). Third, outlawing certain jobs protects interest groups. Although jitney vans are in high demand in New York, the Transit Workers Union successfully lobbied the state Assembly and City Council to make such services illegal. Finally, bureaucratic sophistication is required, along with endless paperwork. In New York, the city's official directory contains 73 pages of directions about places to go and forms to fill out in order to get a license to repair videocassette recorders or open a parking lot. Thus, in New York as in other cities, thousands of bootstrap entrepreneurs operate illegally, on the economic margin, unable to expand their businesses. The long-term impact is to dull ambition and people become trapped.

These limits on ambition mean that some illegal capitalists also rely on public aid. They are, of course, guilty of welfare fraud if caught. Moreover, the penalties for obtaining legal jobs are severe. Let us suppose that one of Edward's friends works at a company where a janitorial position opens up and he gets the job (most jobs are obtained by word of mouth). He now earns $5.50 per hour, or $11,440 per year. (This assumes he works 40 hours per week for 52 weeks, including Christmas, and is never sick.) Alas, a major problem follows: The children have become ineligible for Medicaid because Edward and Mary's combined income of $27,400 is so high(!). The Smiths must choose between work and health insurance for their children. This is a *Catch-22* phenomenon (Heller, 1961). In the novel, if Youssarian was crazy he could get out of the military. But since he saw that the war itself was crazy, he was clearly sane. Hence, he could not get discharged. In the real world, people like Edward Smith sometimes choose not to accept employment. Is he lazy?

Assume for a moment that Edward turns down the job in order to maintain Medicaid coverage for the children. Their problems are not over. Young Samuel develops an earache. The nearest Medicaid provider is 90 miles away in Gainesville. Out-of-pocket expenses for gas and lunch while at the emergency room of the teaching hospital there will be at least $20. So the Smiths decide to wait and see if their son recovers. And he does. Although this is a reasonable strategy, since some medical problems improve over time without treatment, it can have unfortunate results. Sam had otitis medea, a common childhood ailment, easily diagnosed and treated. Left untreated, however, it can result in hearing loss, even deafness. Thus, this little child has a long-term disability, one that increases the odds of him doing poorly in school and ending up trapped in poverty himself as an adult. This is the social context in which the Smiths and millions of real people must act.

The Smith vignettes suggest how factors associated with poverty can sometimes form a vicious circle trapping people. Remember: Laws regulating small businesses and determining eligibility for welfare reflect policy choices made by middle-class and rich people. So do macroeconomic decisions.

Macroeconomic Policy

Macroeconomic policy refers to the way government regulates the economy, especially inflation and unemployment. Ideally, there would be minimal amounts of both. In practice, however, a trade-off usually occurs such that one is higher than the other (Heilbroner & Thurow, 1982).

In considering this issue, you should understand that all economic problems are political problems. There is no politically painless way to regulate the economy, to decide whether to emphasize low inflation or unemployment. No matter what choice is made, someone's interests must be harmed while others benefit. In general, unemployment hurts the poor more than inflation. For example, a 1 percent increase in the unemployment rate increases the poverty rate by an almost identical .97 percent. In comparison, a 1 percent increase in inflation increases the poverty rate by only .12 percent (Blank & Blinder, 1986, p. 187). Thus, unless the situation is atypical, when macroeconomic policy decisions are made, the poor benefit by keeping unemployment low.

Since World War II, however, U.S. policy has focused primarily on keeping inflation in check (Hibbs, 1977). It has sought (not always successfully) lower levels of inflation, 3 to 4 percent, in exchange for higher levels of unemployment, 5 to 6 percent. In contrast, most Western European governments have sought (again, not always successfully) to have higher levels of inflation, 5 to 6 percent, in exchange for lower levels of unemployment, 3 to 4 percent. These different choices have practical consequences: They influence the level of poverty. Put crudely, the United States chooses a higher and Western European nations a lower rate.

The U.S. emphasis on keeping inflation down reflects the political priorities of middle-class and rich persons. They generally do not worry about unemployment and do not suffer its consequences. Rather, they see the value of their salaries and their return on investments fall due to inflation, even if it is only moderate. Therefore, their representatives act to prevent it.

The Structure of Elections

The phrase "their representatives" is deliberately provocative. I mean to suggest that public officials usually make choices reflecting the interests of the most powerful segments of a society. The fact that public policy in the United States creates more poverty than in other nations indicates the dominance of middle-class and rich people. Quite simply, they participate in the political process at a much higher rate than the working class and poor.

This fact means, as shown in Chapter 6, that the working class and poor are relatively incapable of protecting their interests. Recall, for example, that holding elections on working days (rather than weekends or holidays) limits the ability of working-class and poor persons to vote. Those who overcome this handicap most easily have jobs that are less physically tiring, enjoy personal leave time as a job perquisite, have child care available, own a car, and live in safe neighborhoods. In addition, registration requirements limit the ability of the poor to vote. Those who overcome this handicap most easily are the middle class and rich, who are more aware of and able to deal with election laws. Finally, of course, people also participate by contributing money to campaigns. Rich persons always have an advantage here, and they gain access to decision makers as a result. It is not accidental that laws often favor their interests. As one example, macroeconomic and public aid policies reflect the interests of the nonpoor. In this context, the structure of the economy must also be recognized.

The Structure of the Economy

Hard work often does not prevent poverty, mainly because of the structure of the economy. The pay attached to many jobs is low, as indicated earlier by the fact that 16 percent of the poor population aged 25 to 34 work full-time all year long. Such persons, like Jane Smith, are motivated, responsible, and have jobs. What they do not have is an income high enough to live on.

But those with employment are lucky. They earn something. Recall that the Personal Responsibility and Work Opportunity Reconciliation Act posits that families will move "from welfare to work." This outcome is unlikely, given the structure of the economy. Projections of the availability of low-skill jobs indicate that former public aid recipients alone (that is, not counting impoverished persons who are not on the rolls) will outnumber the net new jobs by about two to one (Weisbrot, 1998). And the problem is worst in those states with the highest public aid caseloads. This phenomenon is not new. The number of job seekers (especially at the low-skill level) has always exceeded the number of jobs (Abraham, 1983). Thus, even though unemployment rates are currently low by historical standards, there are not enough jobs for former public aid recipients (or for the poor in general) to fill.

The phrase "low-skill jobs" in this discussion refers to occupations in such industries as cleaning and building service, food preparation, and textiles and apparel—jobs that require little formal education and limited on-the-job training. These jobs are not likely to carry high wages. It has been estimated that the odds of one of these low-skill jobs paying a poverty-level wage for a family of three are about 22 to one (Weisbrot, 1998). The odds of such a job paying a wage at 150 percent of the poverty line (roughly $18,000) are about 64 to one. And the odds of such a job paying a "livable wage" (arbitrarily but plausibly set at about $25,000) are about 97 to one. "These numbers probably represent the most realistic estimate of the odds that a typical target of welfare reform will escape poverty through employment" (Weisbrot, 1998, p. 8). These results are consistent with other studies (Danziger & Lehman, 1997; Meyer & Cancian, 1996; Burtless, 1998).

The structural problem, however, is not only the availability of any jobs at all, but also the location of those jobs that do exist. A mismatch exists between the location of jobs and people (Kasarda, 1990). In the past, cities were centers for the manufacture and distribution of goods. Hence, people without much formal education could find work. Since about 1970, however, cities have lost hundreds of thousands of manufacturing jobs. Many are now located in suburban areas (Kasarda, 1990). Getting to them requires a long and expensive commute, usually by car. This job mismatch has especially affected minority groups, who are less able to live in suburban areas because of housing discrimination. Observers can only speculate about why these jobs have moved. One reason is probably cheaper land and easier access to transportation (interstate highways and airports). Another possibility is corporate aversion to African American workers (Williams, 1987). Regardless of the reason, the result is massive unemployment in central cities, concentrated among minority people.

Thus, the structure of the economy insures that millions of people will be poor no matter how hard they work, no matter what their skills, no matter how much they try. This fact exists independently of their individual efforts. Institutionalized discrimination exacerbates this problem.

Institutionalized Discrimination

I mentioned earlier that members of minority groups suffered from overt and legal forms of institutionalized discrimination in the past. As a result, they were unfairly confined to low-wage blue-collar jobs. Thus, one cause of a high rate of poverty among minorities today is their historical class of origin, not current discrimination.

Yet, as discussed in Chapter 5, discrimination still exists, only now it is covert and illegal. In its institutionalized form, discrimination is sometimes not intended. For example, African Americans, Hispanics, Asians, Native Americans, and whites usually participate in different social networks. Thus, whites work at different jobs, their children go to different schools, they live in different neighborhoods, and they attend different churches. In effect, these forms of segregation identify the boundaries of the social networks in which members of each group participate. Such boundaries indicate how the class structure affects interaction patterns, housing choice, educational attainment, occupational attainment, and virtually every other aspect of life. The fact of segregation, of participating in different social networks, often produces discrimination, even when no discrimination is intended. One result is a higher rate of poverty among minority groups.

I also noted earlier that traditional gender norms meant, until recently, that women were systematically denied the opportunity to work outside the home, prevented from competing with men when they did, and kept economically, politically, and psychologically dependent on men. Although this situation has improved considerably in recent years, Chapter 4 shows that many people still govern their lives by such rules. Moreover, they teach their children, male and female, that such norms still provide guides for living. One result is that women are less successful occupationally, economically, and politically.

We are two nations: one poor, one nonpoor. In my experience, when presented with ethnographic accounts of poverty or the details of poor people's lives in some other way, nonpoor persons react with sympathy and understanding. When discussing "the poor," however, without specifics, these same persons revert to stereotypes about "deservedness." The structural analysis presented here should alert you to the fact that poor individuals acting in their own self-interest cannot reduce the level of poverty. No amount of moralizing about the importance of self-reliance and individual initiative will change that blunt fact.

Concluding Comments

Some individuals believe that suffering brings purification, that through suffering people achieve nobility. I have never observed this phenomenon. Rather, suffering often mutilates people. It twists the spirit, sometimes breaking it. As stress piles on stress, some people lose hope. In sociological jargon, they become **alienated.** That is, they believe they have little control over their lives. For people living in poverty, this perception is often very realistic. It is easy to convince ourselves that we would behave differently, heroically, if placed in the situations in which the poor find themselves. Reality is usually far different. In order to illustrate this fact, I want to describe the impact of poverty by focusing on hunger, homelessness, and violence. All are unfamiliar to the nonpoor.

Although the United States does not display starvation like that occurring in some third world nations, many people go hungry for significant periods of time. By the term **hunger,** I mean the chronic underconsumption of nutrients. The most reasonable estimate is that 20 to 30 million people suffer from hunger in this country (Brown, 1992). This figure makes sense in light of the family budget described earlier. For some, hunger occurs at the end of the month when food stamps run out and the cupboards are empty. For others, unable to obtain coupons, it is a pervasive, everyday affair. The presence of food distribution centers in every city suggests that the nutritional needs of many people go unmet. According to one study, such centers fed 26 million people in 1997 (SH, 1997, p. 8). Of those fed, 21 percent of adults are employed, 37 percent unemployed, 12 percent aged, and 31 percent disabled. About 38 percent of the recipients of food are children. These data suggest that hunger is widespread.

The long-term consequences of hunger are catastrophic, especially for children. Underfed children display slow growth and mental deficiencies as a result of hunger. A six-year-old can look (and act) three years old. Many children, hence, become stupid because they have not had enough food to eat during the first years of life. They do not recover. Ever. Lack of nourishment makes people more susceptible to disease and less capable of recovering. This is important because many common illnesses have a long-term impact. For example, if strep throat, a typical childhood disease, is not treated with antibiotics it leads to heart and kidney damage. The result is a sickly adult who cannot be a productive person. A nutritious diet can help prevent strep. Forcing people to choose between rent and food does not bring nobility. It does, however, provide a practical example of alienation. Moreover, the long-term impact redounds (overflows) to affect the entire society.

So does **homelessness.** By the term, I mean lack of access to a conventional dwelling: a house, apartment, mobile home, or rented room. Those without housing sleep in places not intended for these activities: cars, scrap-metal shacks, and public areas (such as bus stations or heat grates outside buildings). Some also sleep in shelters. The current estimate is that about 760,000 people are homeless on any given night (NCH, 1998). It appears that about 7 percent of the population (or 12 million people) have experienced homelessness at some point in their lives. As is often the case, these are SWAG's (Scientific Wild-Ass Guesses). By the flippant term, I merely want to suggest that precise counts are hard to obtain. Regardless of the exact number, the homeless are poor, extremely poor.

Former Secretary of Housing Henry Cisneros decided to see for himself who these impoverished people are (DeParle, 1993). Leaving the Department of Housing one night in January, he found "an African American woman, eight months pregnant, sleeping on the lawn of the Justice Department." He also found "five veterans, sleeping on a heat grate for warmth." If he had gone to a shelter, he would have found people like 26-year-old Martha Harris and her two children (Bassuk, 1991). After an abusive childhood, she had married an abusive husband who beat her regularly. She eventually fled to a shelter. Her five-month-old daughter, Sara, is listless and underweight. She cannot hold down food or grasp a rattle. Her fifteen-month-old son, Mathew, does not speak, has trouble sleeping, and often refuses to eat. The Secretary's tour thus provides more examples of alienation. The poor lack choices enjoyed by the nonpoor.

The impact is most obvious in children. One study reported that 40 percent of homeless pregnant women received no prenatal care (Bassuk, 1991). So the odds of bearing low-birthweight babies, with all the human tragedy and costs they entail, become much higher. Children in shelters or on the streets are more likely to be abused or neglected. They display chronic medical and psychological problems. They do not attend school or do so irregularly. The McKinney Act, by the way, requires school districts to provide extra educational help for homeless children. The logic, of course, is that such assistance can avoid long-term problems, misery, and societal costs. It is my impression, however, that most districts really wish homeless children would just go away (Dohrn, 1992). And they do.

They live in grief and on grates. Such experiences do not produce nobility of soul. Without a home, they lack stability and nurturance. They lack friends, family, faith group, schools, and regular medical treatment. The consequences are catastrophic and, like hunger, redound to affect the entire society.

So does witnessing and enduring violence during childhood. Impoverished neighborhoods are often violent. One study shows that 45 percent of first and second graders in Washington, D.C., have witnessed a mugging, 31 percent a shooting, and 39 percent have seen a dead body in the street (APA, 1993). In some public housing complexes, every child has either observed or known a victim of homicide (Garbarino, 1992). These children do not need to make up monsters and parents do not need to worry about too much violence on television; their neighborhood streets provide the real thing. The title of Alex Kotlowitz's book reveals the impact of such experiences: *There Are No Children Here.* In the book, LaJoe Rivers says that her sons, Lafayette and Pharoah, have "seen too much to be children" (1991, p. x). Thus, when asked what he wanted to be, ten-year-old Lafayette replied: "If I grow up, I'd like to be a bus driver."

"If I grow up." The wounds that follow from exposure to violence (or hunger or homelessness) are rarely so obvious. They resemble "Snowden's Secret" in Joseph Heller's novel *Catch-22* (1961). Snowden, a bomber navigator, appears to suffer from a minor wound. But when Captain Yossarian opens Snowden's flak jacket, he discovers a hideous and, indeed, fatal injury. Similarly, the wounds of children, cheated of their childhood by violence, are deep and long-lasting. Often fatal. Lodged in the psyche, such wounds haunt children, destroying their adulthood. I shall describe the impact as opposite ends of a continuum. Although this strategy simplifies the situation, it provides a way to highlight the problems that follow from witnessing and enduring pervasive violence.

At one end, some people react to these experiences by withdrawing. They may abuse drugs. They may develop various forms of psychosis or clinical depression. By the last term, I do not mean simply feeling bad. Depressed persons become immobilized, unable to function. This is one reason why some poor parents neglect their children. Regardless of the form of withdrawal, it redounds to the entire society.

At the other end of the continuum, some people react to pervasive violence by becoming enraged and violent themselves. Impoverished areas of large cities are often dominated by such persons. Some belong to gangs who wage war on each other and anyone else who gets in the way. Others are free-lance predators. Their numbers are difficult to estimate, but thousands of them exist in every large city (Huff, 1991). Their impact on the daily life of impoverished areas is profound.

In an aptly titled book, *Do or Die*, Léon Bing talks to Faro, who is seventeen years old, illiterate, and homeless (1991, p. 40). His mother died from a drug overdose. His eight-year-old brother was killed during a holdup at a convenience store. Faro belongs to a gang.

> *"See them two dudes?" . . . "I'm gonna look crazy at 'em. You watch what they do." He turns away from me. . . . The driver, sensing that someone is looking at him, glances over at my car. His eyes connect with Faro's, widen for an instant. Then he breaks the contact, looks down, looks away. And there is no mistaking what I saw there in his eyes: It was fear. Whatever he saw in Faro's face, he wasn't about to mess with it.*
>
> *Faro giggles and turns back toward me. He looks the same as he did before: a skinny, slightly goofy-looking kid. . . . I ask Faro to "look crazy" for me. He simply narrows his eyes. That's all. He narrows his eyes, and he looks straight at me and everything about his face shifts and changes, as if by some trick of time-lapse photography. It becomes a nightmare face, and it is a scary thing to see. It tells you that if you return his stare, if you challenge this kid, you'd better be ready to stand your ground. His look tells you that he doesn't care about anything, not your life and not his.*

"Not your life and not his." Such youths, raised in violence, provide still another example of alienation. They constitute our appalling, damaged, lost children. Yet, underlying the rage is an attempt to seek control and meaning in life. Where else, but in a gang, are children like Faro going to get love, attention, an income (through crime), and status. In a twisted, upside-down world, an anomic social structure, gang-related violence is a predictable consequence of widespread poverty. In a way, gang members are simply pursuing conventional goals in unconventional ways.[8]

Gang members are easy to write off: They are dangerous and often incorrigible. They seem alien, like some Incomprehensible Other. Yet I wonder. It can be argued, as one of Bing's respondents does, that a gang's code of loyalty, the bonds forged by violence, the fatalism, and the xenophobia (distrust of outsiders) resemble those that characterize the Marines or police officers. This interpretation suggests that their behavior is not so incomprehensible after all.

The high rate of poverty in the United States means that central cities, especially the largest ones, have the aesthetic flavor of some Third-World nations: Teems of homeless people wander around. Large areas are disorganized and dangerous. Drug abusers appear everywhere. People live amidst the rubble of empty buildings. An air of hopelessness pervades the streets. And this situation affects not only the unfortunate souls inhabiting these areas but everyone who is not poor as well. Yet it is not inevitable. As the international data show clearly, the level of poverty in this country could be far lower. If so, its negative consequences would be less severe. One has to wonder why it is allowed to continue.

If we wish to reduce the rate of poverty and endure fewer of its results, the direction public policy should take is clear: The United States needs to redistribute money, benefits, training, and—above all—jobs. By benefits, here, I refer to programs that prevent poverty over the long term. Access to birth control, for example, would allow poor women to regulate their fertility. Access to medical treatment would prevent illness from becoming chronic, especially if the emphasis is on prevention. Access to housing would help prevent trauma to children and family break-up. There are other types of programs that should be considered, but these suggest the direction this country should take if it wishes to cut the poverty rate. But such programs imply an expansion of what is sometimes called the "welfare state."

When confronted with this possibility, however, we tend to throw up our hands in despair. There exists a pervasive fear that government creates problems, it does not solve them. But this is self-deceptive. Middle-class and rich people do not hesitate to use government. They seek tax breaks, contracts, and services. They protest mightily, and often effectively, when these benefits are taken away. Only when the issue is sharing benefits with the poor do questions about the deservedness of the recipients arise. Only when the issue is protecting all our children does the public resist.

Now I am perfectly aware that reducing the rate of poverty will be difficult. Part of the reason for this difficulty is that people who have become alienated and learned to

---

[8]The term **anomie** refers to a disjunction between conventional values, such as economic success or political participation, and the legitimate means to achieve them (Merton, 1968). For many young people, raised in poverty and violence, often abused physically, typical venues for success—school, sports, jobs—simply do not exist. So they seek alternatives. In *Do or Die,* Sidewinder said, "I only feel comfortable in my 'hood. That's the only thing I'm connected to, that's my family. One big family, that's about it. . . . It ain't like a gang. It's more like a nation" (Bing, 1991, p. 49).

live poorly are hard to reach. Think about the examples used in this chapter: Maria Sanchez, Pharoah Rivers, Faro, and the fictional Smith family. One challenge is to move people like them into the mainstream of U.S. society. Given their background, people like the Smiths represent the simplest problem. Training, jobs, and access to child care would probably help them. Children like Pharoah need more, as Kotlowitz described (1991). But I can imagine a combination of government programs and devoted individuals who can rescue youths like him. But people like Maria Sanchez and Faro may, for quite different reasons, be lost. Perhaps all that can be done is to encourage and nurture them as much as possible, and jail them when necessary. Another challenge, then, is to avoid losing their children. As you can see, both challenges will be difficult.

But public resistance to such programs goes beyond a realistic pessimism about the odds of success. I noted earlier that a large population of impoverished persons provides benefits to the nonpoor. Yet explaining the opposition to so-called welfare state programs in this way seems incomplete, at least to me. There must be more going on than a simple desire to exploit others. I would like, rather tentatively, to suggest some additional reasons for the persistence of poverty in the United States.[9]

First, our federalist system and geographical size combine to prevent many programs that might aid the poor from being considered. A federalist system is a form of government in which power is divided between a central authority and its subunits, the states. The fear of a strong central government constitutes a recurrent theme in U.S. history. States protect their political turf and appeal to citizen distrust of "Washington" to justify this stance. Moreover, even when considered and passed, programs are not implemented in a uniform and well-organized manner. The way each state funds and administers programs ranging from public education to AFDC reflects their diversity. So the kind and level of benefits people get depend on where they live.

Second, ethnic and religious divisions make programs to aid the poor difficult to develop. Historically, various faith groups provided social services in communities. The purpose, of course, was to meet their own members' needs, not others. So a system of private, nonprofit agencies (partly government funded) exists. They also protect their turf. So the benefits people get depend on the groups to which they belong.

Third, the legacy of slavery imposed by whites on Africans haunts us still, preventing programs to aid the poor. I am inclined to think that whenever racial differences in a population exist and these differences are related to income and culture, the development of programs to provide universal benefits will be difficult. Buttressed by feelings of prejudice, any form of assistance seems to benefit "them," not "us." For this reason, whites do not support programs that appear to aid poor African Americans. Hence, not only have they gotten the fewest benefits of all, but programs to aid the poor generally have been hard to develop and implement.

Fourth, the middle-class ideology of individualism in the United States leads to the perception that the poor are lazy and undeserving. As most people use it, the term

---

[9]In so doing, I am drawing on Nathan Glazer's "The American Welfare State: Incomplete or Different?" (1988).

"individualism" refers to an amorphous yearning to be free of governmental rules, to be free to pursue one's economic and social goals. Remember, the United States is a society of immigrants who overcame great adversity to achieve success. In a self-deceptive way, they believe they "made it" without the help of government (without affirmative action programs, for example). Most people, Nathan Glazer remarked, will take government benefits readily. But they see such aid as buttressing their effort and, hence, deserved (1988, p. 189). Thus, they define Social Security as an insurance fund paid into by employed persons (it is not), and they see tax deductions for homeowners as assisting hard-working people. Regarding the poor: If they would just work harder . . .

Fifth, the existence of profit-making companies as benefit providers makes government programs difficult to consider and implement. Such outfits exist because the United States began to provide services to people later than most other nations. Perhaps I am unduly cynical, but *Tender Loving Greed*, the title of a study of abuses in the nursing home industry, seems to capture the spirit of some of these companies (Mendelson, 1974). Think about any issue that might help the poor. All of them run into profit-making companies that get most of their income from government. Thus, implementing a national health plan must accommodate insurance companies. Similarly, attempts at providing child care must accommodate child care companies. They resist government efforts to provide broad-based benefits to the entire population at low cost. I do not mean to suggest that government programs always work. In fact, I prefer market-oriented solutions whenever possible. My point here is that these companies serve as interest groups and, as such, contribute to the persistence of poverty.

This, then, is the context in which poverty persists: states, faith groups, racial and ethnic groups, the ideology of individualism, and profit-making companies. We are, hence, a divided country. In this situation, the search for solutions occurs. But politics involves finding policies with the most support and least opposition. Politics rarely involves finding the "best" policy. For the majority, the poor remain unfamiliar and, many believe, undeserving. They seem different from "us." Thus, I am pessimistic about plans to reduce the rate of poverty.

Summary

The poor remain unfamiliar to nonpoor persons. Poverty refers to a minimum income level below which individuals or families find it difficult to subsist.

Although living standards have changed considerably over time, it appears that at least 45 percent of the population was poor during the last part of the nineteenth century. Ignoring declines during World Wars I and II, and a huge increase during the Depression, a long-term decline in the poverty rate occurred (Figure 10-1). It dropped to a low of about 11 percent in the 1970s, jumped to 14 to 15 percent during the 1980s and 1990s, and has declined slightly since then. The level of poverty in the United States is significantly higher than in other Western societies. The measurement of poverty is an arbitrary process. The question is not whether a "scientifically accurate" measure exists, but whether the line is realistic or not. Preparing a budget for a family near the cut-off shows that those living below it are desperate (Table 10-1). They have difficulty obtaining food, shelter, medical treatment, and other necessities.

Public assistance programs alleviate some of the problems poor people face, but do not eliminate poverty. This is because the means test requires that people become poor and remain poor in order to stay eligible (Figure 10-2). TANF provides very low cash benefits (Table 10-2) that vary greatly by state (Table 10-3) to people who must not have any assets. SSI provides low cash benefits to poor aged, blind, and disabled people, who must also be devoid of all assets. Food stamps provide coupons for small amounts of food purchases, coupled with a means test. And Medicaid provides medical treatment for the poor, also coupled with a means test. Public assistance programs reflect the political priorities of the nonpoor population. It can be shown that the nonpoor benefit from a high rate of poverty: An impoverished population constitutes a class of low-skill workers who perform jobs others avoid. They subsidize consumption by the more affluent. They create jobs for nonpoor persons who regulate, serve, and exploit the less fortunate. They are exploited and have less legal protection than other segments of society. And they absorb the costs of change. These are practical examples of alienation, an inability to control one's own life.

Young and old persons display a greater likelihood of poverty. Whites are less likely to be poor than members of other racial and ethnic groups. Female-headed families are especially likely to be poor. Individuals with low-wage job skills are more likely to be poor, even if they are employed.

The long-term fall in the poverty rate reflects the impact of industrialization, class differences in fertility rates, and the decline of discrimination. Industrialization created job openings at the top of the class structure, while higher birth rates among the lower classes provided the people to fill those empty slots. Although discrimination continues, it has declined in every area.

The poverty rate today reflects the impact of the reproduction of the class structure, the vicious circle of poverty, macroeconomic policy, the structure of elections, the structure of the economy, and institutionalized discrimination. The reproduction of the class structure occurs because of the tendency for occupational inheritance. Poverty can be seen as a vicious circle that traps people, as indicated by the problems of obtaining work while on public aid and seeking medical treatment. Macroeconomic policy in the United States generally trades higher unemployment (hence, poverty) for lower inflation. The poor participate less in elections because elections are held on working days and require advanced registration. The economy does not provide enough high-wage jobs, located in areas the poor live. Finally, institutionalized discrimination continues to prevent women and minorities from achieving.

A major implication of poverty is that it twists the spirit; people become alienated. This response reflects people's experience with hunger, homelessness, and violence. Yet modern societies like the United States determine how much poverty exists. The chapter closed with a tentative analysis of the reasons why this country has not reduced its poverty rate.

Chapter 11

The United States in Global Context

Poverty and Inequality in the United States and Developing Nations

Inequality in the United States and Western Nations

Some Practical Strategies for Reducing Inequality

All societies display stratification. But the arrangement of classes and the level of inequality can vary a great deal. Consider the following societies:

In the first, everyone makes a living by fishing. People's incomes in this society will not be equal, of course, since some individuals are willing to work harder than others and some have more ability than others. Hence, over time a set of classes will develop and valued resources will be distributed unequally. In the process, however, the main criterion by which people are evaluated is achievement: how much fish they catch. Although people's life chances will vary by social class, it is likely that the level of inequality between the rich and poor will be low. In this context, most people will see the structure of stratification as fair. A nation like this one is likely to be democratic (in some form) and stable. There will probably be little need for the use of force (especially military force) to control the population.

In the second, everyone makes a living by gold prospecting. As above, people's incomes will not be equal, since a few will have discovered (or seized) mother lodes and become wealthy. Some may have found small deposits of ore and do reasonably well. Most, however, will not locate much and will end up with little to show for their efforts even though they work hard. As above, a set of classes will develop over time. In this case, however, distribution of valued resources will be very unequal and so will people's life chances. Of course, some of this inequality will reflect ability (since some individuals may have greater skill at spotting signs of gold) and some will be willing to spend more hours prospecting than others. For the most part, however, the stratification structure will reflect luck combined with rapaciousness. Over time, this result means that the main criterion by which people are evaluated will be ascription, non-performance-related characteristics. This is because no matter how much ability they have or how hard they work, most prospectors will end up poor. In this context, many people will see the structure of stratification as unfair. A nation like this one is likely to be undemocratic and, hence, it will sometimes be necessary to rely on force to control the population.[1]

These are, of course, hypothetical societies. They can seen be as ideal types, to use a phrase of Max Weber's, benchmarks against which our own and other (real) nations can be compared. Previous chapters have shown that inequality in the United States has increased over the past few years. The distribution of valued resources and the life chances that follow are more unequal than ever before. Thus, one can argue that the United States now resembles the gold-prospecting society more than the fishing society. And to the extent true, this result is cause for concern because, as mentioned in Chapter 6, people's dissatisfaction may erupt in violence or some other form of unruliness. But just how unequal is the United States compared to other (real) nations? Does the United States really resemble the gold-prospecting society? As it turns out, the answer to this question depends on the angle of vision from which it is asked.

In this chapter I deal with this question by looking at the structure of stratification in a global context. The focus will be on income inequality (although other points of comparison will be made as well), mainly because worldwide observations are available. But it turns out that such observations are difficult to compare for the following reasons: (1) The data are gathered in different years. This fact means they reflect different economic and social conditions—both within each nation and between them. (2) The definition of income varies. For example, it may be before or after taxes. The latter is a measure of disposable income (and, hence, probably better). In addition, "income" may include transfer payments. As should be clear from Chapters 8 (the middle class) and 10 (the poor), transfers can significantly alter people's lifestyles. (3) The reporting unit varies. It can refer to individuals, families, or households. If households constitute the unit of analysis, which is most common, then it is usually assumed that income sharing occurs. But this is not always so. (4) The purchasing power of money varies. And (5), translating local currencies into dollar values is a very imperfect business. These difficulties mean that complete comparability is not possible, even with countries like Canada and the United States or the United Kingdom and the United States. Nonetheless, comparability is a matter of degree, and it is possible to reach an acceptable and meaningful level. Scholars do what they can, knowing the pitfalls.

---

[1]The basis for this vignette came from an essay by Paul Krugman, titled "What the Public Doesn't Know Can't Hurt Us" (1995).

Poverty and Inequality in the United States and Developing Nations

I have selected four developing nations from around the world to compare with the United States: Brazil, India, Nigeria, and Guatemala. They are chosen arbitrarily, but not accidentally. Brazil and India represent what are called "semi-peripheral societies." That is, they display relatively diversified economies that may (or may not) become industrialized. See them as more or less in a middle stage of economic development. Nigeria and Guatemala represent what are called "peripheral societies." That is, they display a much lower level of economic development. See them as on the edge. The reason for these labels will become clear in a few moments.

As has been true throughout history, most of the world's population is poor—often desperately poor. Although data on global poverty are tricky to obtain and interpret, partly because the ability to consume nonmarket goods (especially food) varies and partly for the difficulties noted above, some international observations about poverty are available. One standard measure is the percentage of a nation's population living on less than $2.00 per day ($730 per year). Such data are presented next for the four nations being used as a continuing example in this section (WB, 1999, p. 196):

% Living on < $2.00 per day

Brazil (1990)	44%
India (1992)	89%
Nigeria (1993)	60%
Guatemala (1989)	48%

Although these nations are being used as examples here and much variability exists, a very high proportion of people living in developing nations are poor. And they are poorer than the poor in the United States. In comparison, the percentage of the population living on less than $2.00 per day in the United States and, indeed, in every Western nation, appears to be zero. The nation with the dubious honor of having the highest percentage of its population living on less than $2.00 per day is Guinea-Bissau, a small country on the west coast of Africa: 97 percent. The World Bank does not even include this item for these countries in its analysis of "world development indicators." Another indicator of how poor these nations are is the Gross National Product (GNP) per capita (WB, 1999, p. 190). This measure describes the value of all the goods produced in a society, as divided by the total population. It is $6,240 in Brazil, $1,650 in India, $880 in Nigeria, and $3,840 in Guatemala. The nation with the lowest GNP per capita in the world is Ethiopia: $510. By comparison, the U.S. rate is $28,740. All of these nations are extremely poor compared to the United States.

This high rate of poverty in developing nations translates into restricted life chances for their citizens. The infant mortality rate provides one indicator of just how restricted people's lives are because it reflects their overall living standards. You should recall from Chapter 3 that the infant mortality rate is defined as the number of live babies who die in the first year of life. The rate is 66 per 1,000 in Brazil, 69 in India, 70 in Nigeria, and 49 in Guatemala (USBC, 1997b, p. 833). The nation with the highest number of children dying during infancy is Malawi: 140 per 1,000. These rates are similar to those seen in the United States during the nineteenth century. The current U.S. rate is 7, and this is high by Western standards.

Their high level of poverty and restricted life chances imply that many developing nations exhibit a very unequal income distribution. And this is generally true, although some exceptions exist.

I shall begin with the "semi-peripheral" nations, Brazil and India. One overall way of assessing income inequality is to look at the Gini Coefficient. As you may recall from Chapter 8, the Gini Coefficient is a standard index in which zero would mean complete equality (every household has the same income) and 1.00 would mean complete inequality (one household has all the income). In the United States, for example, the distribution of household income produces a Gini Coefficient of .459, which (as shown in Chapter 8) is substantially higher than in the past. In comparison, the Gini for Brazil is .601, indicating greater inequality in the distribution of income, while in India it is .297, indicating less inequality. The main reason for these differences occurs at the extremes of the income distribution. Displayed below are the shares of income going to the poorest and richest 20 percent of the population in these three nations (WB, 1999, p. 198; USBC, 1998f, p. xvii):

	Income Share to the	
	Poorest 20%	*Richest 20%*
Brazil (1995)	3%	64%
India (1994)	9%	39%
United States (1997)	4%	49%

Thus, Brazil has a more unequal income distribution than the United States, mainly because the richest fifth of the population takes 64 percent of all the income. In comparison, India is less unequal than the United States, at least in terms of income distribution. The poorest fifth of Indian households receives about 9 percent of the nation's income, compared to 4 percent in the United States. A similar difference exists at the other end of the distribution: The richest fifth of all households receives 39 percent of the income in India, compared to 49 percent in the United States. But this relatively equal income distribution in India does not obviate the fact that it is a very poor nation: As pointed out earlier, nearly all its population subsists on less than $2.00 per day and 85 of every 1,000 of its children die at a young age.

The "peripheral" nations also vary a great deal in terms of income distribution. Guatemala, for example, displays a Gini Coefficient of .596, about the same as Brazil's. The most unequal nation in the world, by the way, is Sierra-Leone. In that sad nation, the poorest 20 percent of the population receives only 1 percent of the income and the Gini Coefficient is .629 (WB, 1999, p. 199). Nigeria, however, exhibits less income inequality. Its Gini Coefficient is .450, about the same as in the United States. But do not be fooled; Nigeria is a much poorer nation: Half its population subsists on less than $2.00 per day, and 70 of every 1,000 of its children do not see their first birthday.

Although these data may understate the degree of income inequality in some nations, such as India and Nigeria, some conclusions are nonetheless possible. First, most people in most developing nations are poorer than people in the United States. Second, many developing nations display both more poverty and more income inequality than the United States. Third, some developing nations display more poverty but similar or even less income inequality. This last point is revealing: It suggests the extent to which recent increases in inequality in the United States reflect political choice. In general, however, these comparisons imply that the United States resembles the fishing society more than the gold-prospecting society.

This conclusion, however, depends on the question asked. I would like to pause here for an excursus (digression) and ask a different question, one that goes beyond simply comparing poverty and inequality in developing nations and the United States: Why is there so much poverty and inequality around the world?

One way of answering this question requires a change in the unit of analysis such that the focus becomes the worldwide circumstances in which poverty and inequality occur. In sociological terms, the unit of analysis must change from the nation-state to a world system. This orientation is useful because developing nations today must confront the already developed nations, like the United States—which have interests to protect. Thus, it can be argued that economic and distributive processes that appear to be internal to them—to Brazil or Nigeria, let us say—are actually affected by their location in the world system. When this change in the unit of analysis takes place, then the United States and other Western nations are viewed in a different way.

In the world system, nations can be seen as like classes (Wallerstein, 1974; Chirot, 1986). Envision, if you will, a three-tiered global stratification structure.

The "core societies" are analogous to the rich: comprising the industrialized countries such as the United States, Sweden, Germany, France, and most of the other Western European nations. They control most of the world's wealth, military force, technology, and financial services. Their economies are diversified, with a focus on manufacturing and—increasingly—service industries. They do not export unfinished raw materials. These nations tend to be democratic, stable, and powerful.

The "semi-peripheral" societies are analogous to the middle class. Such nations are industrializing, or trying to. But achieving this goal is difficult because they are so dependent on the core societies. For example, developing nations often provide skilled labor to companies based in core nations, as when computer programmers and engineers from India work for U.S.-based corporations. Or, to take another example, developing nations are exploited due to their low labor costs: U.S.-based companies manufacture products or parts of products destined to be exported back to the United States and to other nations, such as when an automobile plant is located in Brazil. Although some of these societies are democratic, like Brazil and India, they remain unstable. They have little military power compared to the United States and other Western nations.

The "peripheral" societies are analogous to the poor. Like the poor, these nations are relatively "unskilled" in the sense that their economies are simple (and sometimes so disorganized that they are unable to take advantage of their resources). Hence, they depend on the "core" nations for financial aid, technology, and for markets for their raw materials (for example, coffee from Guatemala and oil from Nigeria). Economic development is difficult in this context because decisions are made in terms of the interests of corporations based in core nations and their governments. Moreover, elites in such societies (called compradors) are dependent for their wealth on these same foreign corporations and, hence, function as their agents against the nation's interests. Such nations are usually not democratic; they rely on military force (whose soldiers are often trained by core nations) to control their populations.

According to Immanuel Wallerstein in *The Modern World System,* the reason there is so much poverty and inequality in developing nations is because Western industrial nations like the United States exploit them (1974; see also Chirot, 1986). The "semi-peripheral" and "peripheral" societies provide the cheap labor and raw materials that enrich the rich nations. From this point of view, the Western industrial nations (the so-called "core societies") have an interest in keeping developing nations undeveloped; they have an interest in keeping them poor. In short, from this point of view, poverty and inequality around the world reflects the impact of Western imperialism.

This chapter opened with a comparison between a hypothetical fishing and gold-prospecting society. When nations of the world are compared in terms of this ideal type, then the United States appears to resemble the former more than the latter. But when the world system becomes the unit of analysis, the global stratification structure seems to resemble a single giant gold-prospecting society. From this point of view, the United States and other Western nations are the successful (and rapacious) prospectors.

Although Western exploitation provides one answer to the question of poverty and inequality around the world and it is useful, it is not the only answer. Another answer involves looking at the developing nations themselves. This angle of vision requires shifting the unit of analysis from the world system back to nation-states.

I mentioned earlier that most people in most developing societies are poor. But this is not always so. Some nations, such as Japan and South Korea, have successfully pursued economic development over the past half-century even though they were clearly economically and politically dependent on the United States. This fact has important implications, not only for understanding how development occurs but also for their levels of poverty and inequality.

Unlike Brazil and the other nations described earlier, there is very little poverty in either Japan or South Korea. As used before, one indicator of living standards is the infant mortality rate (USBC, 1997b, p. 833). It is 8 per 1,000 live births in South Korea and 4 in Japan—the lowest in the world. Japan, in fact, has become the healthiest nation in the world. The U.S. rate, you should recall, is 7. (Remember that the infant mortality rate is 69 per 1,000 in Brazil, 49 in Guatemala.) Another indicator of economic development and its impact on poverty and inequality is the Gross National Product per capita (WB, 1999, p. 190). In Japan, it is $23,400, while in South Korea it is $13,500. Although both are less than in the United States, $28,740, they resemble that in other Western nations: Sweden's is $19,030. And both are much higher than in Brazil, India, Guatemala, and Nigeria.

The overall level of inequality in Japan and Korea also resembles that displayed in Western nations, and is lower than in the United States. The Gini Coefficient summarizing the income distribution among households is .298 in Japan and .336 in South Korea

(Tabatabai, 1996, pp. 95, 126). The income distribution in these nations reflects this development, as shown below by the proportion going to the bottom and top 20 percent, respectively (Tabatabai, 1996, pp. 95, 126):

	Income Share to the	
	Poorest 20%	*Richest 20%*
Japan (1990)	8%	38%
South Korea (1988)	7%	42%

Yet both Japan and South Korea were devastated in the aftermath of war, World War II and the Korean War, respectively. It is hard to imagine two nations more dependent on the United States. But both pursued aggressive policies designed to produce economic development, with considerable success (Berger, 1986). The Kuznets Hypothesis describes what happened. As you may recall from Chapter 7, the argument is as follows:

Inequality of wealth and income increases during the early phases of economic growth when the transition from preindustrial to industrial society is most rapid, stabilizes for awhile, and then becomes subject to negotiation.

What apparently occurs is that the early stages of economic development require large-scale capital formation. Since only the (relatively few) who are rich have sufficient wealth to invest, they reap greater rewards initially and the level of inequality increases. Over time, however, as the economy is transformed the combination of demographic factors (the rich do not reproduce themselves) and government regulation of the market results in a reduced level of inequality, or at least the issue becomes open to political intervention. There is logic to this explanation. This is why I used the Kuznets Hypothesis in Chapter 7 to explain the historical pattern of inequality in the United States. The experience of both Japan and South Korea appears to conform to that predicted by the hypothesis. Today, neither would be called a developing nation.

According to Peter Berger in *The Capitalist Revolution,* there are lessons to be learned from the experiences of Japan and South Korea (1986, p. 138). As I understand it, what these nations did—in rather different ways—was to pursue an aggressive form of capitalism (what Berger described as "a growth-oriented private enterprise" strategy) with some attention to land ownership among the poor, attracting investment in labor-intensive projects that increased the wages of ordinary people and fostered industrialization, and removing legal and social barriers to opportunity. Obviously the specific form of this strategy would vary from one society to another. But over time, Berger hypothesized, *the more a developing nation is included in the world capitalist system* (by these and other strategies), *the greater its economic development.* And the impact of economic development will be, over the long run, to reduce poverty and inequality—as has happened in the West and in Japan and South Korea.

But nothing resembling this process has occurred in most countries around the world. To varying degrees, many developing nations can be described as "a Sweden superimposed on an India." That is, they display a relatively modern, technologically based, and (small) affluent sector of the population coexisting with masses who live in extreme poverty (Berger, 1986, p. 132). Those who have traveled to, say, Brazil know that deviating only a little way from a rather narrow range of airports, modern hotels, and tourist venues will lead a person into areas of abject poverty. Such experiences are even more common in other nations. From this angle of vision, then, perhaps wealthy elites and the governments they control are the problem in developing nations. They are like the lucky and rapacious gold prospectors in the hypothetical society described at the beginning of this chapter.

Apart from the metaphor, my guess is that any explanation of poverty and inequality in developing nations will have to take into account both a world system and a nation-state explanation. In other words, it is probably true that Western industrial nations have exploited developing nations and it is also probably true that many of these nations have adopted policies that mainly benefit their own elites (keeping the masses impoverished). But my overall interest in this book is somewhat different than that developed in the above excursus: an understanding of the structure of stratification in the United States. Even though the distribution of valued resources in the United States has become more unequal in recent years, it seems less harsh when compared to that in developing nations. The level of poverty in this country, bad as it is, is far less than in many nations in the world. And the consequences of poverty, in the form of infant mortality (other indicators could have been used) are less widespread. But whether such comparisons are meaningful is unclear. The economic, political, and cultural differences are so great that it is hard to know whether the contrasts are useful for understanding. People who are poor or working class in the United States do not compare their situations to people in Brazil or India. Hence, another perhaps more useful way to look at the structure of stratification in this country is to compare it to that among Western European nations. These nations are similar to the United States economically, politically, and culturally.

Inequality in the United States and Western Nations

The United States and other Western nations also display similar structures of stratification. In Chapter 2, for example, it was shown that an empirical generalization exists: *Hierarchies of occupational prestige are similar across all Western industrial nations.* This stable finding means that the social standing of the jobs people have is nearly the same in, say, the United Kingdom, France, and the United States. A physician and a lawyer, an automobile mechanic and a sales clerk, will all be similarly ranked. In Chapter 3, it was shown that, while some variability exists, all Western nations display high rates of occupational mobility. The U.S. levels of mobility are neither the highest nor the lowest. Finally, it was also shown in Chapter 3 that the variables affecting status attainment are similar in all these nations, a combination of ascribed factors (family background) and achieved factors (education), with increasing emphasis on the latter. These similarities suggest the degree to which all Western industrial societies resemble the fishing village described at the beginning of the chapter.

But there are differences as well, and they are significant. Chapter 6 showed that voting rates are much lower in this country. And these differences are class based: Those who participate at lower levels are primarily working class and poor. The middle class dominates voting. The rich dominate by contributing money to political campaigns, which allows them access to decision makers. Ultimately, it can be argued that these differences result in greater income inequality in the United States. One aspect of the overall income distribution is the greater number of poor persons in this country. Chapter 10 showed that the poverty rate in the United States is three times that in Sweden, Netherlands, and France, and more than twice that in the United Kingdom and Germany.

It follows that the United States displays much more inequality in the income distribution than does any other Western industrial nation. Gini Coefficients for the nations that have been compared to the United States in previous chapters are below (WB, 1999, p. 198; USBC, 1998f, p. xvii):

Sweden (1992)	.250
Germany (1989)	.281
Netherlands (1991)	.315
Canada (1994)	.315
United Kingdom (1986)	.326
France (1989)	.327
United States (1997)	.459

Nearly all the difference in the income distribution occurs at the bottom and top. For example, as mentioned previously, the bottom 20 percent of the U.S. population receives about 4 percent of the total income while the top 20 percent takes 49 percent. In comparison, in Sweden, the most egalitarian of these nations, the bottom 20 percent gets 10 percent and the top gets 35 percent. The other nations in the list are in between. By the way, there tends to be a division among Western European nations such that those in Southern Europe exhibit somewhat greater income inequality (Atkinson, 1996). Even so, none of these nations approach the level found in the United States.

The result is that people have more restricted life chances in this country, as indicated by the infant mortality rates (per 1,000 live births) shown below for 1997 (USBC, 1997b, p. 833):

Sweden	4.5
Netherlands	4.8
Germany	5.9
Canada	6.0
France	6.0
United Kingdom	6.3
United States	6.6

Taken together, these data suggest that when the angle of vision refers to other Western industrial societies then the United States is very unequal. It resembles the gold-prospecting society, in which a small elite has—by a combination of luck and rapaciousness—increased inequality for its own benefit. How can this situation be changed?

Some Practical Strategies for Reducing Inequality

Although some practical strategies exist, they will not be implemented easily. Partly because of the difficulties described at the end of Chapter 10 (our federalist system, racial and ethnic divisions, the legacy of slavery, the ideology of individualism, and the existence of private benefit providers), reducing inequality in the United States will not be easy. But for those who worry about how unequally the spoils are divided up in this country, here are some suggestions.

First, eliminate federal and state income taxes on the poorest one-third of the population. Increasing the number of tax brackets and enacting modest increases in taxes on the top third could make up the lost revenue. As described in Chapter 7, nearly all the changes in tax law over the last two decades have allowed the rich to keep more of their income.

Second, perhaps an alternative to the (very difficult) first, expand the earned income tax credit. This is a cumbersome way of redistributing income but it would work. And it has the advantage of being tied to employment.

Third, increase expenditures for communal services: day care (this would help poor and working-class people work), early childhood education, mass transit, even recreational opportunities. Policies like these would be one way of reducing the impact of income inequality and increasing people's opportunities for success.

Fourth, expand sex education and make birth control services free to young persons. Such policies would reduce the birth of unwanted children. They would also enable young adults to learn job skills and develop the ability to support themselves prior to making decisions about parenthood.

Fifth, develop some form of nationwide health insurance so that everyone can at least obtain medical treatment. Better yet, such an insurance program ought to emphasize preventive care. It is nearly always cheaper to prevent disease rather than to treat it.

Sixth, build lots of low-cost housing, preferably near jobs. Access to housing and jobs would do much to reduce the level of inequality in this country.

These changes are, however, unlikely. Even when the greater poverty and inequality in developing nations is taken into account, the United States appears to resemble the gold-prospecting society. Is this the direction we should be heading?

Summary

When the United States is compared to developing nations, such as Brazil, India, Nigeria, and Guatemala, it becomes clear that they are much poorer. Many developing nations, but not all, also display greater income inequality.

Two explanations for these differences were discussed. In the first, the world system becomes the unit of analysis, with various nations being seen as analogous to classes. The "core nations" are like the rich. The "semi-peripheral nations" are like the middle class. The "peripheral nations" are like the poor. The argument is that both "semi-peripheral" and "peripheral" nations are exploited and kept dependent by the "core" nations. The second explanation shifts the unit of analysis back to nation-states and focuses on the elites and governments in developing nations. Japan and South Korea constitute examples of how economic development can occur, thereby reducing poverty and inequality.

When the United States is compared to other Western nations, it becomes clear that all have similar structures of stratification. It also becomes clear that the U.S. exhibits much more inequality than any other economically developed country. There are, however, a number of practical strategies that can be used to reduce the level of inequality in this country—if we have the will.

Chapter *12*

Reflections on the Study
of Social Stratification

Objectivity in the Study of Stratification

Research Methods in the Study of Stratification

Paradox in the Study of Stratification

Sociology systematically attempts to see social life as clearly as possible, to understand its various dimensions and their interrelationships, and to do so without being swayed by personal hopes and fears.[1] This book has attempted to illustrate the possibilities inherent to sociology by focusing on a specific aspect of social life—the structure of stratification—explaining it on different levels (individual and structural), and presenting research results as fairly as possible. In this last chapter, I would like to reflect on some implications that follow from this orientation. Although my comments will emphasize the study of social stratification, the topics are of general significance to all areas of sociological inquiry. The first issue is the problem of objectivity, because it is required if sociologists are to see the world clearly. The second is the problem of research methods, because they provide the key to understanding the dimensions of social life. The final issue is the paradoxical nature of sociological analyses, because this characteristic highlights people's hopes and fears about the future.

[1]This definition paraphrases a line in Peter Berger's "Sociology and Freedom" (1977, p. vii). This essay provides the framework for my remarks in this chapter.

Objectivity in the Study of Stratification

In order to see clearly any aspect of social life, such as stratification, a specific orientation is necessary—one not required of ordinary persons: Bias must be eliminated as much as possible. This goal is far more difficult to achieve in the social sciences than in other disciplines because observers are embedded in their subject. Thus those interested in the study of stratification also occupy a specific location in the class structure; they earn an income, they have a job with its level of occupational prestige, they probably own property, they may be married, they may have children, and the like. These facts mean that a researcher's personal experiences, values, and economic interests can easily influence the analysis.

The reduction of bias requires that sociologists adhere to the norms of science, regardless of their personal experiences, values, or economic interests. These rules direct researchers to try to report findings without regard to their motives for undertaking the study. They require researchers to use the most systematic evidence available and to make logical deductions. And they adjure researchers to make their own values explicit so that others may assess whether bias enters the analysis. Such rules provide those studying stratification with a way of looking at the world that is decisively different from daily life. Moreover, two additional norms exist that influence the community of scholars who examine social scientific findings. Thus researchers are directed to critically evaluate others' work. This injunction also applies to students. It means, for example, that readers should ask themselves whether my personal values have distorted the presentation in earlier chapters. Finally, researchers are taught to try to refute previous work. When these efforts fail and findings are replicated, especially if different types of data or methods produce similar results, then the probability of their being accurate reflections of reality goes up. Over the long run, these norms insure that objective, scientific findings about the structure of stratification will be produced. They help us to see social life as clearly as possible.

This orientation is why I emphasized the importance of hypothesis testing throughout the book. Thus some intuitively plausible ideas, such as the job perquisite hypothesis (Chapter 8) or the Kuznets hypothesis (Chapters 7 and 11), must remain tentative statements because either adequate data do not exist or testing has not yet occurred. Such hesitance is useful because some very good ideas, like the embourgeoisement hypothesis (Chapter 9), turn out to be false when systematically examined. Moreover, even empirical generalizations must be continually evaluated and sometimes modified, as with the finding that the prestige hierarchy is similar across Western industrial societies (Chapter 2). But over the long run, empirical generalizations emerge. These stable research findings constitute statements of fact. Although they are not immutable, since times change, they do indicate how the benefits of a stress on objectivity and the elimination of bias lead to knowledge.

Research Methods in the Study of Stratification

Research methods, C. Wright Mills asserted in *The Sociological Imagination,* comprise the procedures sociologists use to apprehend social life in all its aspects (1959). No matter how objective research is—no matter how free of bias—if the procedures sociologists use do not take into account the various dimensions of stratification, then a full and accurate depiction of this topic becomes impossible. As it turns out, an understanding of each level of social life requires rather different procedures.

One dimension of social life involves the study of individuals and the way in which they act on and react to the situations in which they find themselves. As indicated in Chapter 1, most researchers, at least in the United States, are prone to focus on individuals when studying stratification. Thus a great deal of work exists that identifies the reasons why people move upward or downward occupationally, become poor, vote or participate in politics in other ways, and endure gender or racial inequality. The empirical generalizations summarizing these relationships are among the most significant results in sociology. Such studies typically involve survey data, statistical analyses, and quantitatively precise findings. An exclusive focus on individuals, however, is limiting because it omits the existence of other aspects of social life which, although less often studied, provide additional insight into stratification.

Yet sociologists in the United States tend to avoid asking any questions that cannot be answered in quantitative terms. In practice, this orientation means that "research" is usually defined as the analysis of survey data. Underlying this choice of methodology is a dominant value orientation shared by all U.S. citizens, regardless of class: a preference for seeing individuals as both cause of and solution to social problems. Sociologists are no different from other people. They believe in and benefit from individual initiative, competition, and the rewards that ensue. This background leads many of them to adopt a nominalist methodological stance, which means that society is considered to be nothing more than the sum of its parts—individuals (Bryant, 1985). If this were true, then quantitative analyses of survey data ought to identify the true causes of the high mobility rate, the poverty rate, the rate of political participation, and the level of gender and racial and ethnic inequality. In fact, however, they do not, primarily because such an orientation excludes the structural dimension of social life from consideration.

In public policy terms, this preference for focusing on individuals, is why the United States lost the war on poverty in the 1960s. Virtually all the antipoverty programs developed at that time emphasized job training and education so that poor individuals could better themselves. While there is nothing particularly wrong with such programs, they did not and could not reduce the poverty rate in this country because individual characteristics are not responsible for the large number of impoverished people. Rather, as shown in Chapter 10, the rate of poverty results from the reproduction of the class system, macroeconomic policy, and other structural factors. What is needed is a way of seeing the structural aspect of social life as clearly as possible. This alternative approach does not substitute for the study of individuals; rather, it complements such analysis and leads to greater insight into social stratification.

It was argued in Chapter 1 that the social structure determines rates of events and that this orientation can be seen in the work of sociologists as different as Marx, Durkheim, and Merton. The hypothesis offered there was that lower-class people have fewer and less effective choices in comparison to upper-class persons, with the result that rates of behavior are decisively affected. In subsequent chapters, this idea was applied to the analysis of mobility rates, poverty rates, political participation rates, levels of gender inequality, and levels of racial and ethnic inequality. Each account followed a similar pattern and, as Table 12-1 illustrates, none of the proposed explanatory factors dealt with individuals.

As can be seen in the table, in order to explain the rate of mobility, variables like industrialization, class differences in fertility rates, immigration, institutionalized gender discrimination, and institutionalized racial and ethnic discrimination are necessary. Note that the rate of mobility is accounted for in terms of other rates, not individual characteristics. Thanks to the explosion of research on status attainment over the past 25 years, it is clear in this case more than any of the others that the factors affecting

TABLE 12-1   Social Structure and Social Stratification

Structural Hypothesis	Proposed Explanatory Factors
Long-Term Social Mobility	Industrialization Class differences in fertility rates Immigration Affirmative action for white males
Decline of Gender Stratification	Industrialization Female labor force participation Advances in medical technology Legal changes Rise of feminism
Perpetuation of Gender Stratification	Traditional gender role norms Institutionalized discrimination
Historical Variations in Racial and Ethnic Group Mobility	Conditions of settlement Prejudice and discrimination Affirmative action
Racial and Ethnic Inequality Today	Reproduction of the class structure Institutionalized discrimination
Structure of Voting	Voting day Registration requirements Voting procedures Separation and frequency of elections
Long-Term Fall in Poverty	Industrialization Class differences in fertility rates Declining discrimination
U.S. Poverty Rate Today	Reproduction of the class structure Vicious circle of poverty Macroeconomic policies Structure of elections Structure of the economy Institutionalized discrimination

individual mobility (the status attainment process) are different than those influencing the rate of mobility. And the same conclusion follows when the other issues shown in Table 12-1 are considered.

An important but little recognized implication follows from the fact that rates of events must be explained by rates of other events. To use Durkheim's language, social facts (rates) are things, and they must be explained by other social facts (1895). Methodologically, this injunction usually means that survey research or other analogous modes of data analysis often cannot be used. Although the topics discussed in this book are amenable to quantitative methods in principle, the aggregate survey data needed for their analysis do not exist. Instead, it was necessary in each case to perform a mental experiment similar to Max Weber's in *The Protestant Ethic and the Spirit of Capitalism* (1905). Weber's research strategy involved the construction of a set of logically interrelated variables, which he called "ideal types," and the empirical assessment of how actual cases deviated from a purely logical formulation (see Turner, Beeghley, & Powers, 1998). The analyses in this book proceeded in a similar way, that is, by identifying a set of structural factors, such as the rate of mobility, poverty, and so forth, and hypothesizing the manner in which they are affected by other structural variables. In each case, an implicit counterfactual hypothesis posited that if the proposed explanatory variables had different configurations, then the rate of mobility and the like would be far different. My argument is that this methodological procedure provides observers with a way to confront many significant issues for which survey data cannot be used.

In practice, this research strategy reflects a process Willer and Webster (1970) called abduction; that is, it attempts to identify, based on theory and empirical observation, those variables affecting the phenomenon of interest. This procedure invites creativity, which is useful in any analysis. In this book, the process involved looking at how the major institutions—economy, family, education, and government—interact with the stratification structure. The resulting explanation did not identify new variables; it was, rather, synthetic: showing how well-known forces (many of which appear unrelated to one another) produce a high rate of some phenomenon, placing these factors into a coherent theoretical context, and systematically following through the implications of the analysis. In so doing, the way explanations focusing on individuals and structures complement one another became clear. For example, when the process of status attainment and the causes of a high rate of mobility are considered together, then much more is known about stratification in the United States than if either angle of vision is ignored. A similar conclusion applies to the other structural variables shown in Table 12-1.

Yet structural analyses such as those presented in this book appear unscientific to many sociologists because the results seem unmeasurable quantitatively and, hence, imprecise. The assumption that quantitative precision makes an analysis scientific constitutes a frequent mistake by researchers in the "soft" sciences. In all disciplines, significant questions exist that cannot be measured directly and, as indicated earlier, it becomes necessary to perform a mental experiment. In so doing, however, it is often convenient to think in multivariate statistical terms. Thus, in accounting for the level of impoverishment in the United States, the dependent variable (Y in a regression equation) is the rate of poverty, and the independent variables (the Xs in a regression equation) comprise a set of structural factors: the reproduction of the class system, macroeconomic policies, and so forth. The advantage of thinking in this way is that each of the variables must be clearly specified and related to one another. The major difference, of course, is that the data are manipulated logically rather than computationally. Now there is no special reason why mathematical values could not be assigned to each of the variables shown in Table 12-1 and numerical results produced. For example, armed with a set of plausible assumptions, one could show that if inflation averages X percent higher and unemployment X percent lower, then the rate of poverty will be reduced by Y percent. Having performed this exercise, however, the result would be neither more precise nor more scientific than before.

A similar judgment could be made about most econometric models, such as forecasts of next year's inflation rate; they constitute mental experiments in quantitative form and the numbers should be translated to mean "a lot" or "a little." So too with mental experiments in other disciplines. For example, Sagan and his colleagues calculated that 10,400 thermonuclear explosions with a total yield of 5,000 megatons of which 20 percent explode over cities may produce so much dust and soot in the atmosphere that the average July temperature at mid-latitudes would decline to –9 degrees Fahrenheit within a few weeks (1984). Subsequently, Thompson and Schneider, using a different model of the atmosphere and making somewhat different assumptions, found that the average temperature might decline to between 60 and 70 degrees Fahrenheit (1986). It is important to recognize that in both cases these rather precise numbers are illusions. In reality, the Sagan group showed that one result of a thermonuclear war might be that the temperature would decline "a lot" as a result of "nuclear winter," while Thompson and Schneider showed that the temperature might decline "a little" due to "nuclear fall." Now this research is imaginative and substantively important; it is good science. It is also a mental experiment, no different in logic from that occurring in many other fields, including those performed in this book. Of course, the effects of one variable on another should be empirically measured whenever possible. But observers should not let either a fetish for measurement or a shortsighted view of what science is get in the way of research. Economists do not. Physicists do not. Neither should sociologists.

Nonetheless, both the procedures described here and the results summarized in Table 12-1 often seem alien because they are so unfamiliar, especially in the United States.[2] The emphasis on individuals runs deep. But sociology, Emile Durkheim said, should cause people to see things in a different way than the ordinary, "for the purpose of any science is to make discoveries and all such discoveries more or less upset accepted opinions" (1895, p. 31). A structural approach such as that used in this book is one (but not the only) way of performing this task. The consequences, however, are paradoxical.

---

[2]It should be recognized that much more complex structural orientations exist, as shown by Turner (1984) and by the readings in Blau (1975), Blau and Merton (1981). Unfortunately, most of them are impractical for understanding such real-world issues as social mobility, poverty, political participation, gender inequality, or racial and ethnic inequality.

Paradox in the Study of Stratification

If sociologists are indeed able to see social life clearly and to understand its dimensions and their interrelationships, the results have implications for people's hopes and fears about the future. Paradox follows. Sociological analyses, including those presented in earlier chapters, often seem to be contradictory; they appear politically radical yet also conservative, liberating for the individual yet also constraining. This paradox, Peter Berger suggested, is inherent to sociological inquiry (1977).

On the one hand, almost any sound analysis of the topics covered in this book can suggest ways in which to improve our society or aspects of it. This fact constitutes people's hope for progress in the future. What happens is that knowledge liberates people by opening up the possibility for change. This is especially true of structural descriptions because they often reveal hidden or nonobvious facets of a phenomenon. As a result, those proposing radical departures from the status quo can point to alienation, exploitation, inequality, and inequity. Yet sociological analyses also show that improvement does not always follow from change, a fact that has conservative implications. Disorder, at least for a short time, often does. This fact makes people fear the future and constrains them. Thus, most individuals are enmeshed in structures of norms and roles with which they are both familiar and comfortable. Few persons dislike everything about their lives, which means they want to preserve what is good, maintain their traditions, and retain a sense of orderliness and continuity from one generation to another. This orientation militates against radical change.

The result of these contradictory impulses, as Berger commented, is that sociology often produces a paradoxical, but by no means irrational, stance on the part of its practitioners and others exposed to it: that of a person who thinks daringly but acts prudently. Put differently, there are no easy answers to the problems revealed in this book. All solutions carry with them both benefits and liabilities, and it is best to be as clear as possible about each.

Hypotheses Discussed in The Structure of Social Stratification in the United States

Chapter	Hypothesis Discussed	Tentative Empirical Status
1	The lower the social class, the fewer choices people have and the less effective they are in solving personal problems.	Possibly true
1	Women at every class level have fewer and less effective choices than do men.	Possibly true
1	Minority groups at every class level have fewer and less effective choices than do whites (non-Hispanic).	Possibly true
1	The higher the social class, the greater the influence over access to valued resources in the society.	Possibly true
2	Hierarchies of occupational prestige are similar over time within the same society.	Empirical generalization
2	Hierarchies of occupational prestige are similar across societies.	Probably false
2	Hierarchies of occupational prestige are similar across all Western Industrial Hypotheses.	Empirical generalization
2	Employed married women ignore their own jobs and education, and consider only their husbands' characteristics in deciding with which class to identify.	Probably false

Chapter	Hypothesis Discussed	Tentative Empirical Status
2	Employed married women take both their own and their husbands' characteristics into account in deciding with which class to identify.	Probably false
2	Employed married women who believe in traditional gender norms consider only their husbands' characteristics in deciding with which class to identify.	Possibly true
2	Employed married women who believe in egalitarian gender norms take both their own and their husbands' characteristics into account in deciding with which class to identify.	Possibly true
3	There is a great deal of occupational inheritance in the United States.	Empirical generalization
3	Social mobility is widespread in the United States.	Empirical generalization
3	Short-distance occupational movements exceed long-distance ones.	Empirical generalization
3	The rate of mobility in the United States reflects the impact of (1) industrialization, (2) class differences in fertility rates, (3) immigration rates, and (4) affirmative action for white males.	Possibly true
3	In every society, the greater the industrialization, the more equality of opportunity, upward mobility, and similarity in mobility rates.	False
3	When jobs decline in an industry, the less job security and fewer labor market boundaries, the greater the emphasis on individual resources in determining occupational mobility.	Possibly true
3	Father's education, father's occupation, mother's education, and family income are all highly correlated and each influences status attainment at all stages of a child's life.	Empirical generalization
3	Ability influences every subsequent stage of the status attainment process.	Empirical generalization
3	Academic performance directly influences subsequent status attainment: the level and kind of encouragement received from others, aspirations, and eventual educational and occupational attainment.	Empirical generalization
3	Significant others' encouragement affects aspirations and educational and occupational attainment.	Empirical generalization
3	Educational and occupational aspirations influence educational and occupational attainment.	Empirical generalization
3	Educational attainment strongly influences occupational attainment, both first job and main job.	Empirical generalization

Chapter	Hypothesis Discussed	Tentative Empirical Status
3	Among males in Western industrial societies, (1) family background exerts a weak but significant and direct impact on children's occupation, and (2) children's education exerts a strong and direct impact on their occupation.	Probably true
3	The higher the family income (especially in early childhood), the greater the achievement of children.	Probably true
3	The lower the family income, then the greater the economic pressures and the greater the stress between parents—which leads to harsher parent-child interaction.	Probably true
3	The harsher the parent-child interaction, the lower the children's self-confidence and the lower their achievement.	Probably true
3	The less knowledge and self-confidence parents have, the less likely they are to see themselves as the status equal of teachers.	Probably true
4	The higher the rate of women's labor force participation, the higher the rate of divorce.	Probably true
4	The higher the proportion of women in an occupation, the lower its occupational prestige.	Probably true
4	For both genders, the greater the skill level, the higher the income.	Empirical generalization
4	At every skill level, men earn significantly more than women.	Empirical generalization
4	The fewer the skills people acquire and the lower the priority employment has versus other activities, the lower their income.	Partially true
4	The long-term decline in gender inequality reflects the impact of (1) industrialization, (2) female labor force participation, (3) advances in medical technology, (4) legal changes, and (5) the rise of feminism.	Possibly true
4	The continuation of gender inequality reflects the impact of : (1) traditional gender norms and (2) institutionalized discrimination.	Possibly true
4	The lower the proportion of women in a work group, the greater the discrimination.	Possibly true
5	The less experience people from different groups have with one another, the more likely are members of the dominant group to display prejudice and discriminate.	Possibly true
5	The more people from different groups compete for scarce resources, the more likely are members of the dominant group to display prejudice and discriminate.	Possibly true
5	African Americans' relative lack of economic success in comparison to other immigrant groups reflects	

Chapter	Hypothesis Discussed	Tentative Empirical Status
	historical differences in (1) conditions of settlement, (2) prejudice and discrimination, and (3) affirmative action.	Possibly true
5	Historically, the greater the proportion of African Americans in an area, the less educational opportunity available to them.	Possibly true
5	Racial and ethnic stratification today reflects the impact of (1) the reproduction of the class structure and (2) institutionalized discrimination.	Possibly true
5	At each skill level, the more members of a minority group employed in an organization, then the greater the number of their job applicants and the greater the rate at which they will be hired.	Possibly true
6	The more money spent on a political campaign, the greater the odds of winning.	Empirical generalization
6	The rate of voting in the United States reflects the impact of (1) election day, (2) registration requirements, (3) voting requirements, and (4) separation and frequency of elections.	Possibly true
6	The sources of partisanship in the United States are (1) money, (2) family background, and (3) institutional location.	Possibly true
6	The higher the social class and the greater the campaign contribution, the greater the access to public officials.	Empirical generalization
7	The higher the income, the greater the reliance on capital as the source of income.	Empirical generalization
7	Inequality of wealth and income increases during the early phases of economic growth, stabilizes for awhile, then decreases.	Needs revision
7	Inequality of wealth and income increases during the early phases of economic growth, stabilizes for awhile, then becomes subject to negotiation (revision of above).	Partially true
7	The greater the wealth, the more likely is a person to have inherited rather than created it.	Possibly true
8	The higher the social class, the greater the job perquisites	Probably true
8	The higher the preretirement income, the higher the postretirement income.	Probably true
8	The lower the social class, the greater the benefit from income transfers and the lower the level of inequality from 1950–1970.	Probably false

Chapter	Hypothesis Discussed	Tentative Empirical Status
8	The higher the social class, the greater the benefit from income transfers such that the overall distribution of income remained unchanged from 1950–1970.	Probably true
9	The more similarities in the occupational characteristics, income, and lifestyle between the working class and the middle class, then the less emphasis on radical political change by the working class.	False
9	The longer the duration of unemployment, the greater the economic deprivation and the more likely impoverishment.	Empirical generalization
9	Individuals who are or have been unemployed display more psychological stress than those who have not.	Probably true
9	Families in which one of the spouses is or has been unemployed have a higher probability of familial disruption than those who have not.	Possibly true
9	The lower the social class, then the older the housing, the lower its value, and the higher the proportion of income spent on housing.	Empirical generalization
9	The lower the social class, the fewer the amenities built into housing.	Empirical generalization
10	Children and aged persons are more likely to be poor than people in other age categories.	Empirical generalization
10	Whites are less likely to be poor than any other racial or ethnic group.	Empirical generalization
10	Female-headed families are more likely to be poor than two-parent families.	Empirical generalization
10	The fewer the job skills people possess, the greater the likelihood of poverty.	Empirical generalization
10	People who work less are more likely to be poor.	Empirical generalization
10	The long-term fall in the poverty rate reflects the impact of (1) industrialization, (2) class differences in fertility rates, and (3) declining discrimination.	Possibly true
10	The U.S. poverty rate today reflects the impact of (1) the reproduction of the class structure, (2) the vicious circle of poverty, (3) macroeconomic policy, (4) the structure of elections, (5) the structure of the economy, and (6) institutionalized discrimination.	Possibly true
11	Inequality of income and wealth increases during the early phases of economic development, stabilizes for awhile, then becomes the subject of negotiation.	Partially true
11	The more a developing nation is included in the world capitalist system, the greater its economic development.	Partially true

References

Abraham, Katharine G. 1983. "Structural/Frictional vs. Demand Unemployment: Some New Evidence." *American Economic Review* 73:708–24.

Abramson, Jill. 1998. "The Business of Persuasion Thrives in Nation's Capital." *New York Times,* National Edition. September 29:1.

Acker, Joan. 1973. "Women and Social Stratification: A Case of Intellectual Sexism." *American Journal of Sociology* 78:936–46.

———. 1990. "Hierarchies, Jobs, Bodies: A Theory of Gendered Organizations." *Gender & Society* 4:139–58.

Aguirre, Adalberto, and Jonathan H. Turner. 1993. *American Ethnicity: The Dynamics and Consequences of Discrimination.* New York: McGraw-Hill.

Alexander, Karl L., Bruce K. Eckland, and Larry J. Griffin. 1975. "The Wisconsin Model of Socioeconomic Achievement: A Replication." *American Journal of Sociology* 81:324–42.

Allen, H. W., and K. W. Allen. 1981. "Vote Fraud and Data Validity." In J. M. Chubb, W. H. Flanigan, and N. H. Zingale (eds.), *Analyzing Electoral History* (pp. 153–93). Beverly Hills, CA: Sage.

Allen, Michael Patrick. 1990. *The Founding Fortunes: A New Anatomy of the Super-Rich Families in America.* New York: E. P. Dutton.

Allen, Michael Patrick, and John L. Campbell. 1994. "State Revenue Extraction from Different Income Groups: Variation in Tax Progressivity in the United States, 1916 to 1986." *American Sociological Review* 59:160–86.

Allport, Gordon W. 1954. *The Nature of Prejudice.* Cambridge, MA: Addison-Wesley.

Anderson, Elijah. 1990. *Streetwise: Race, Class, and Change in an Urban Community.* Chicago: University of Chicago Press.

Anker, Richard. 1998. *Gender and Jobs: Sex Segregation of Occupations in the World.* Geneva: International Labour Organization.

APA (American Psychological Association). 1993. *Violence & Youth: Psychology's Response.* New York: American Psychological Association.

Appelbaum, Richard. 1978. "Marx's Theory of the Falling Rate of Profit: Towards a Dialectical Analysis of Structural Change." *American Sociological Review* 43:73–92.

Archer, Melanie, and Judith R. Blau. 1993. "Class Formation in Nineteenth-Century America: The Case of the Middle Class." *Annual Review of Sociology* (vol. 19). New York: Annual Reviews.

Argersinger, Peter H. 1986. "New Perspectives on Election Fraud in the Gilded Age." *Political Science Quarterly* 100:669–89.

Atkinson, A. B. 1996. "Income Distribution in Europe and the United States." *Oxford Review of Economic Policy* 12:15–28.

Bakke, Edward W. 1940. *The Unemployed Worker.* New Haven, CT: Yale University Press.

Baltzell, E. Digby. 1958. *Philadelphia Gentlemen: The Making of a National Upper Class.* New York: Free Press.

———. 1964. *The Protestant Establishment: Aristocracy and Caste in America.* New York: Vintage.

Barlett, Donald L., and James B. Steele. 1994. *America: Who Really Pays the Taxes.* New York: Simon & Schuster.

Bassuk, Ellen L. 1991. "Homeless Families." *Scientific American* 265(December):66–74.

Becker, Gary S. 1975. *Human Capital: A Theoretical and Empirical Analysis.* New York: Columbia University Press.

Beeghley, Leonard. 1983. *Living Poorly in America.* New York: Praeger.

———. 1984. "Illusion and Reality in the Measurement of Poverty." *Social Problems* 31:312–24.

———. 1986. "Social Class and Political Participation: A Review and an Explanation." *Sociological Forum* 1:496–513.

———. 1989. "Individual versus Structural Explanations of Poverty." *Population Research and Policy Review* 8:201–22.

———. 1992. "Social Structure and Voting in the United States: A Historical and Comparative Analysis." *Perspectives on Social Problems* 3:265–87.

———. 1996. *What Does Your Wife Do: Gender and the Transformation of Family Life.* Boulder, CO: Westview.

———. 1999. *Angles of Vision: How to Understand Social Problems.* Boulder, CO: Westview.

Beeghley, Leonard, and Debra Van Ausdale. 1990. "The Status of Women Faculty in Graduate Departments of Sociology: 1973 and 1988." *Footnotes* 18(December):3–4.

Beeghley, Leonard, E., Wilbur Bock, and John C. Cochran. 1990. "Religious Change and Alcohol Use: An Application of Reference Group Theory." *Sociological Forum* 5:261–78.

Beeghley, Leonard, and John C. Cochran. 1988. "Class Identification and Gender Role Norms among Employed Married Women." *Journal of Marriage and Family* 50:719–29.

Beeghley, Leonard, and Denise Donnelly. 1989. "The Consequences of Family Crowding: A Theoretical Synthesis." *Lifestyles: Family and Economic Issues* 10:83–102.

Beeghley, Leonard, and Jeffrey W. Dwyer. 1989. "Income Transfers and Income Inequality." *Population Research and Policy Review* 8:119–42.

Beeghley, Leonard, Ellen Van Velsor, and E. Wilbur Bock. 1981. "The Correlates of Religiosity among Black and White Americans." *Sociological Quarterly* 22:403–12.

Bell, Daniel. 1976. *The Coming of Post-Industrial Society.* New York: Basic Books.

Bendix, Reinhard. 1974. "Inequality and Social Structure: A Comparison of Marx and Weber." *American Sociological Review* 38:149–61.

Berger, Peter L. 1977. "Sociology and Freedom." Pp. x–xix in P. L. Berger, *Facing Up to Modernity.* New York: Basic Books.

———. 1986. *The Capitalist Revolution.* New York: Basic Books.

Biblarz, Timothy, Vern L. Bengtson, and Alexander Bucur. 1996. "Social Mobility across Generations." *Journal of Marriage and the Family* 58:188–200.

Bielby, William T., and Denise B. Bielby. 1992. "I Will Follow Him: Family Ties, Gender-Role Beliefs, and Reluctance to Relocate for a Better Job." *American Journal of Sociology* 97:1241–67.

Bing, Léon. 1991. *Do or Die.* New York: Harper Collins.

Bird, Carolyn. 1968. *Born Female: The High Cost of Keeping Women Down.* New York: Van Rees Press.

Blair, Sampson L., and Daniel T. Lichter. 1991. "Measuring the Household Division of Labor." *Journal of Family Issues* 12:91–113.

Blanchard, Fletcher A., Teri Lilly, and Leigh Ann Vaughn. 1991. "Reducing the Expression of Racial Prejudice." *Psychological Science* 2:101–5.

Blank, Rebecca M., and Alan S. Blinder. 1986. "Macroeconomics, Income Distribution, and Poverty." In S. H. Danziger and D. H. Weinberg (eds.), *Fighting Poverty: What Works and What Doesn't* (pp. 180–208). Cambridge, MA: Harvard University Press.

Blau, Peter M. (ed.). 1975. *Approaches to the Study of Social Structure.* New York: Basic Books.

Blau, Peter M., Terry C. Blum, and Joseph E. Schwartz. 1982. "Heterogeneity and Intermarriage." *American Sociological Review* 47:45–67.

Blau, Peter M., and Otis Dudley Duncan. 1967. *The American Occupational Structure.* New York: Wiley.

Blau, Peter M., and Robert K. Merton. 1981. *Continuities in Structural Inquiry.* Beverly Hills, CA: Sage.

Blossfeld, H. P., and G. Rohwer (eds.). 1997. *Between Equalization and Marginalization: Part-Time Working Women in Europe and the United States.* New York: Oxford University Press.

BLS (Bureau of Labor Statistics). 1998a. "Lost-Worktime Injuries and Illnesses: Characteristics and Resulting Time Away from Work, 1996." http://stats.bls.gov.

———. 1998b. "National Census of Fatal Occupational Injuries, 1997." *News.* August 12:1–13.

Blumin, Stuart. 1989. *The Emergence of the Middle Class.* New York: Cambridge University Press.

Bowles, Samuel, and Herbert Gintis. 1976. *Schooling in Capitalist America.* New York: Basic Books.

Boyd, Richard W. 1981. "Decline of U.S. Voter Turnout: Structural Explanations." *American Politics Quarterly* 9:133–59.

Boyer, Debra, and David Fine. 1992. "Sexual Abuse as a Factor in Adolescent Pregnancy and Child Maltreatment." *Family Planning Perspectives* 24:4–11.

Bradley, Bill. 1997. "Foreward." In Chester Hartman (ed.), *Double Exposure: Poverty and Race in America* (pp. ix–xv). Armonk, NY: M.E. Sharpe.

Bridges, J. S. 1989. "Sex Differences in Occupational Values." *Sex Roles* 20:205–11.

Brim, Orville G. 1966. "Socialization Through the Life-Cycle." In O. G. Brim and S. Wheeler, *Socialization After Childhood* (pp. 1–49). New York: Wiley.

Brown, Larry. 1992. "Estimates of the number of Hungry Americans done for the House Select Committee on Hunger." Bedford, MA: Center on Hunger, Poverty, and Nutrition Policy, Tufts University.

Bryant, Christopher, G. A. 1985. *Positivism in Social Theory and Research.* New York: St. Martin's Press.

Burnham, Walter Dean. 1980. "The Disappearance of the American Voter." In Richard Rose (ed.), *Electoral Participation* (35–73). Beverly Hills, CA: Sage.

Burtless, Gary. 1998. "Can the Labor Market Absorb Three Million Welfare Recipients?" *Focus* 19 (Summer/Fall):1–6.

Case, Charles E., Andrew Greeley, and Stephan Fuchs. 1989. "Social Determinants of Racial Prejudice." *Sociological Perspectives* 32:469–83.

Catalyst. 1997. *The 1997 Catalyst Census of Women Corporate Officers and Top Earners.* New York: Catalyst.

Cavilli-Sforza, Luca, Paolo Menozzi, and Alberto Piazza. 1995. *The History and Geography of Human Genes.* Princeton, NJ: Princeton University Press.

CBO (Congressional Budget Office). 1981. *Indexing with the Consumer Price Index: Problems and Alternatives.* Washington, DC: U.S. Government Printing Office.

CCH (Commerce Clearing House). 1993. *Federal Tax Reporter.* Chicago: Commerce Clearing House.

CDF (Children's Defense Fund). 1998a. *"New Studies Look at the Status of Former Welfare Recipients."* Washington, DC: Children's Defense Fund.

———. 1998b. *Welfare to What: Early Findings on Family Hardship and Well-Being.* Washington, DC: Children's Defense Fund.

CEA (Council of Economic Advisors). 1969. *Economic Report of the President.* Washington, DC: U.S. Government Printing Office.

Centers, Richard. 1949. *The Psychology of Social Classes: A Study of Class Consciousness.* Princeton, NJ: Princeton University Press.

Cherlin, Andrew J. 1992. *Marriage, Divorce, and Remarriage*, Revised and Enlarged Edition. Cambridge, MA: Harvard University Press.

Chinhui, Juhn, and Kevin M. Murphy. 1997. "Wage Inequality and Family Labor Supply." *Journal of Labor Economics* 15:72–97.

Chirot, Daniel. 1986. *Social Change in the Modern Era.* New York: Harcourt Brace Jovanovich.

Churchill, Ward, and Glenn Morris. 1992. "Key Indian Laws and Cases." In M. Annette Jaimes (ed.), *The State of Native America: Genocide,*

Colonization, and Resistance (pp. 13–21). Boston: South End Press.

Citro, Constance F., and Robert T. Michael (eds.). 1995. *Measuring Poverty: A New Approach.* Washington, DC: National Academy Press.

Clines, Francis X. 1992. "Ex-Inmates Urge Return to Areas of Crime to Help." *New York Times,* National Edition. December 23:1.

Coleman, James S. et al. 1966. *Equality of Educational Opportunity.* Washington, DC: U.S. Government Printing Office.

Coles, F. S. 1986. "Forced to Quit: Sexual Harassment Complaints and Agency Response." *Sex Roles* 14:81–95.

Conger, Rand, Katherine Conger, and Glen Elder. 1997. "Family Economic Hardship and Adolescent Adjustment: Mediating and Moderating Processes." In G. Duncan and J. Brooks-Gunn (eds.), *Consequences of Growing Up Poor* (pp. 288–310). New York: Russell Sage.

Converse, Philip E. 1972. "Change in the American Electorate." In Angus Campbell and Philip E. Converse (eds.), *The Human Meaning of Social Change* (pp. 263–338). New York: Russell Sage.

Conway, M. Margaret. 1991. *Political Participation in the United States,* 2nd edition. Washington, DC: Congressional Quarterly Press.

Corbett, Thomas. 1998. "Working Around the Official Poverty Measure." *Focus* 19(Spring):21–24.

Corcoran, Mary, Linda Datcher, and Greg J. Duncan. 1980. "Most Workers Find Jobs Through Word of Mouth." *Monthly Labor Review* 103(August):33–36.

Coser, Lewis A. 1956. *The Functions of Social Conflict.* New York: Free Press.

———. 1967. "Some Social Functions of Violence." In his *Continuities in the Study of Social Conflict* (pp. 73–92). New York: Free Press.

Cott, Nancy. 1987. *The Grounding of Modern Feminism.* New Haven, CT: Yale University Press.

Cottle, Thomas J. 1994. "When You Stop, You Die: The Human Toll of Unemployment." In J. H. Skolnick and E. Currie (eds.), *Crisis in American Institutions,* Ninth Edition (pp. 75–82). New York: Harper Collins.

Crane, Jonathan. 1991. "The Epidemic Theory of Ghettos and Neighborhood Effects on Dropping Out and Teenage Childbearing." *American Journal of Sociology* 96:1226–59.

CRP (Center for Responsive Politics). 1998. *The Big Picture: Who Paid for the Last Election.* Washington, DC: CRP.

CWM (Committee on Ways and Means). 1998. *1998 Green Book: Background Material and Data on Programs within the Jurisdiction of the Committee on Ways and Means.* Washington, DC: U.S. Government Printing Office.

CWRIC (Commission on Wartime Relocation and Internment of Civilians). 1982. *Personal Justice Denied.* Washington, DC: U.S. Government Printing Office.

Dahl, Robert A. 1967. *Pluralist Democracy in the United States: Conflict and Consent.* Chicago: Rand McNally.

Dahrendorf, Ralf. 1959. *Class and Class Conflict in Industrial Society.* Stanford, CA: Stanford University Press.

Dansky, Bonnie. 1997. "The National Women's Study: Relationship of Victimization and Post-traumatic Stress Disorder to Bulimia Nervosa." *International Journal of Eating Disorders* 21:213–28.

Danziger, Sheldon, Robert Haveman, and Robert Plotnick. 1981. "How Income Transfer Programs Affect Work, Savings, and the Income Distribution." *Journal of Economic Literature* 19:975–1026.

Danziger, Sheldon, and Jeffrey Lehman. 1997. "How Will Welfare Recipients Fare in the Labor Markets." *Challenge* 39(March/April):8–15.

Danziger, Sheldon, and Robert Plotnick. 1977. "Demographic Change, Government Transfers, and Income Distribution." *Monthly Labor Review* 100(April):7–11.

Dash, Leon. 1989. *When Children Want Children: The Urban Crisis of Teenage Childbearing.* New York: William Morrow.

Davidson, James D. 1995. "Persistence and Change in the Protestant Establishment,1930–1992." *Social Forces* 74:159–78.

Davis, Kingsley, and Wilbert Moore. 1945. "Some Principles of Stratification." *American Sociological Review* 7:242–49.

Davis, Theodore J. 1995. "The Occupational Mobility of Black Males Revisited: Does Race Matter?" *Social Science Journal* 32:121–36.

Davis, Nancy J., and Robert V. Robinson. 1998. "Do Wives Matter? Class Identities of Wives and Husbands in the United States, 1974–1994." *Social Forces* 76:1063–86.

DeFronzo, James. 1973. "Embourgeoisement in Indianapolis?" *Social Problems* 21:269–83.

Degler, Carl N. 1980. *At Odds: Women and the Family in America from the Revolution to the Present.* New York: Oxford University Press.

de la Garza, Rodolfo. 1992. *Latino Voices: Mexican, Puerto Rican, and Cuban Perspectives on American Politics.* Boulder, CO: Westview Press.

Deloria, Vine, Jr. 1992. "Trouble in High Places: Erosion of American Indian Rights to Religious Freedom in the United States." In M. Annette Jaimes (ed.), *The State of Native America: Genocide, Colonization, and Resistance* (pp. 267–90). Boston: South End Press.

DeParle, Jason. 1993. "Secretary of Housing's Intentions on Homeless Raise Questions." *New York Times,* National Edition. January 30:1.

DiPrete, Thomas A., and K. Lynn Nonnemaker. 1997. "Structural Change, Labor Market Turbulence, and Labor Market Outcomes." *American Sociological Review* 62:386–404.

DiPrete, Thomas A., Paul M. de Graaf, Ruud Luijkx, Michael Tåhlin, and Hans-Peter Blossfeld. 1997. "Collectivist versus Individualist Mobility Regimes? Structural Change and Job Mobility in Four Countries." *American Journal of Sociology* 103:318–58.

Djilas, Milovan. 1965. *The New Class.* New York: Praeger.

Domhoff, G. William. 1970. *The Higher Circles.* New York: Random House.

———. 1974. *The Bohemian Grove and other Retreats.* New York: Harper.

Dohrn, Bernardine. 1992. "Chicago's Homeless Children and the Failure of Schools." *Poverty and Race.* 1:3–5. Washington, DC: Poverty and Race Research Action Council.

Dubois, Ellen. 1978. *Feminism and Suffrage: The Emergence of an Independent Women's Movement in America 1848–1869.* Ithaca, NY: Cornell University Press.

Duncan, Greg J., W. Jean Yeung, Jeanne Brooks-Gunn, and Judith R. Smith. 1998. "How Much Does Childhood Poverty Affect the Life Chances of Children?" *American Sociological Review* 63:406–23.

Durkheim, Emile. 1895. *The Rules of the Sociological Method.* New York: Free Press, 1982.

Dye, Thomas R. 1983. *Who's Running America*, 3rd Edition. Englewood Cliffs, NJ: Prentice-Hall.

Easton, Barbara. 1976. "Industrialization and Femininity: A Case Study of 19th Century New England." *Social Problems* 23:389–401.

Ehrenreich, Barbara. 1990. Fear of Falling: The Inner Life of the Middle Class. New York: Harper Collins.

Elder, Glen, Robert Conger, Elizabeth Foster, and Monica Ardelt. 1992. "Unemployment and Alcohol Disorder in 1910 and 1990: Drift vs. Social Causation." *Journal of Occupational and Organizational Psychology* 65:277–90.

Ellis, Joseph. 1997. *American Sphinx: The Character of Thomas Jefferson.* New York: Knopf.

Engelberg, Stephen, and Deborah Sontag. 1994. "Behind One Agency's Walls: Misbehaving and Moving Up." *New York Times*, National Edition. December 21:A1.

England, Paula. 1992a. *Comparable Worth: Theories and Evidence.* New York: Aldine de Gruyter.

———. 1992b. "From Status Attainment to Segregation and Devaluation." *Contemporary Sociology* 21:643–47.

Erikson, Robert, and John H. Goldthorpe. 1993. *The Constant Flux: A Study of Class Mobility in Industrial Societies.* New York: Oxford University Press.

Eshleman, J. Ross. 1994. *The Family: An Introduction,* 7th edition. Boston: Allyn & Bacon.

Eulau. Hans. 1966. "The Politics of Happiness." *Antioch Review* 16:259–65.

Feagin, Joe R. 1991. "The Continuing Significance of Race: Antiblack Discrimination in Public Places." *American Sociological Review* 56:101–16.

Feagin, Joe R., and Harlan H. Hahn. 1973. *Ghetto Revolts: The Politics of Violence.* New York: Macmillan.

Feather, Norman T. 1990. *The Psychological Impact of Unemployment.* Ann Arbor: Edwards Brothers.

———. 1992. "Expectancy-value Theory and Unemployment Effects." *Journal of Occupational and Organizational Psychology* 65:315–30.

Featherman, David L., and Robert M. Hauser. 1978. *Opportunity and Change.* New York: Academic Press.

Featherman, David L., F. Lancaster Jones, and R. M. Hauser. 1975. "Assumptions of Social Mobility Research in the U.S.: A Case of Occupational Status." *Social Science Research* 4:329–60.

Felson, Marcus, and David Knoke. 1974. "Social Status and the Married Woman." *Journal of Marriage and Family* 36:63–70.

Ferree, Myru Marx, and Beth B. Hess. 1985. *Controversy and Coalition: The New Feminist Movement.* Boston: Twayne.

Field, Simon, George Mair, Tom Rees, and Philip Stevens. 1981. *Ethnic Minorities in Britain: A Study of Trends in their Position Since 1961.* London: Her Majesty's Stationery Office.

Fischer, David Hackett. 1978. *Growing Old in America.* New York: Oxford University Press.

———. 1989. *Albion's Seed: Four British Folkways in America.* New York: Oxford University Press.

———. 1994. *Paul Revere's Ride.* New York: Oxford University Press.

Fisher, Gordon M. 1997. "Disseminating the Administrative Version and Explaining the Administrative and Statistical Versions of the Federal Poverty Measure." *Clinical Sociology Review* 15:163–82.

———. 1998. "Setting American Standards of Poverty: A Look Back." *Focus* 19(Spring): 47–53.

Fix, Michael, and Raymond J. Struyk. 1993. *Clear and Convincing Evidence: Measurement of Discrimination in America.* Washington, DC: Urban Institute Press.

———. 1998a. "Estimating the Value and Cost of Housing." *Focus* 19(Spring):31–35.

———. 1998b. "Measuring the Cost of Medical Care." *Focus* 19(Spring):25–28.

———. 1998c. "Revising the Poverty Measure." *Focus* 19(Spring):1–3.

Fosu, Augustin Kwasi. 1997. "Occupational Gains of Black Women since the 1964 Civil Rights Act: Long-term or Episodic?" *American Economic Review* 87:311–15.

Frank, D. A., M. Napoleone, A. Meyers, N. Roos, K. Peterson, and L. A. Cupples. 1992. "Seasonal Changes in Weight for Age in a Pediatric Emergency Room: A Heat or Eat Effect." Boston City Hospital Pediatric Nutrition Surveillance Study. Boston: Boston City Hospital.

Frank, Erica. 1998. "Prevalence and Correlates of Harassment among U.S. Women Physicians." *Archives of Internal Medicine* 158(February 23):352–58.

Franklin, Benjamin. 1961. *The Autobiography and Other Writings.* New York: New American Library.

Friedan, Betty. 1963. *The Feminine Mystique.* New York: Norton.

Fuchs, Stephen, and Charles E. Case. 1994. "A Grid-Group Theory of Prejudice." *Research in Race and Ethnic Relations* 7:37–54.

Fussell, Paul. 1983. *Class: A Guide Through the American Status System.* New York: Ballantine.

Gagliani, Giorgio. 1981. "How Many Working Classes?" *American Journal of Sociology* 87:259–85.

Galbraith, John Kenneth. 1992. *The Culture of Contentment.* New York: Houghton Mifflin.

Gallman, Robert E. 1969. "Trends in the Size Distribution of Wealth in the 19th Century." In Lee Soltow (ed.), *Six Papers on the Size Distribution of Wealth and Income.* New York: Columbia University Press.

Gamson, William A. 1975. *The Strategy of Protest.* Homewood, IL: Dorsey Press.

Gans, Herbert. 1972. "The Positive Functions of Poverty." *American Journal of Sociology* 78: 275–89.

Garbarino, James. 1992. *Children in Danger: Coping with the Consequences of Community Violence.* New York: Jossey-Bass.

Gelles, Richard. 1990. *Intimate Violence in Families.* Newbury Park, CA: Sage.

Glazer, Nathan. 1988. "The American Welfare State: Incomplete or Different?" In N. Glazer, *The Limits of Social Policy* (pp. 168–94). Cambridge, MA: Harvard University Press.

Glick, Peter. 1995. "Images of Occupations: Components of Gender and Status in Occupational Stereotypes." *Sex Roles* 32:565–83.

Glyptis, Sue. 1989. *Leisure and Unemployment.* Philadelphia: Open University Press.

Goldin, Claudia. 1990. *Understanding the Gender Gap: An Economic History of American Women.* New York: Oxford University Press.

Goode, William J. 1973. "Functionalism: The Empty Castle." In W. J. Goode, *Explorations in Social Theory* (pp. 64–96). New York: Oxford University Press.

Gordon, David M. 1996. *Fat and Mean: The Corporate Squeeze of Working Americans and the Myth of Managerial "Downsizing."* New York: Free Press.

Gordon-Reed, Annette. 1997. *Thomas Jefferson and Sally Hemings: An American Controversy.* Charlottesville, VA: University Press of Virginia.

GP (Gallup Poll). 1994. *The Gallup Poll: Public Opinion 1993.* Wilmington, DE: Scholarly Resources.

———. 1997a. Black/White Relations in the U.S. http://www.gallup.com.

———. 1997b. *The Gallup Poll: Public Releases of Gallup Poll Results.* http://www.gallup.com.

Graham, Lawrence Otis. 1995. *Member of the Club.* New York: Harper & Row.

Graybill, Wilson H., Clyde V. Kiser, and Pascal K. Whelpton. 1958. *The Fertility of American Women.* New York: Wiley.

Greider, William. 1992. *Who Will Tell the People.* New York: Simon & Schuster.

Greven, Philip. 1991. *Spare the Child: The Religious Roots of Punishment and the Psychological Impact of Physical Abuse.* New York: Knopf.

Grieco, Margaret. 1987. *Keeping It in the Family: Social Networks and Employment Chance.* New York: Tavistock Publications.

Grossman, James R. 1989. *Land of Hope: Chicago, Black Southerners, and the Great Migration.* Chicago: University of Chicago Press.

Grusky, David B., and Jesper B. Sørensen. 1998. "Can Class Analysis be Salvaged?" *American Journal of Sociology* 103:1187–1234.

GSS (General Social Survey). 1996. *Cumulative Codebook.* Chicago, IL: National Opinion Research Corporation.

Guest, Avery M., Nancy S. Landale, and James C. McCann. 1989. "Intergenerational Occupational Mobility in the Late 19th Century United States." *Social Forces* 68:351–78.

Hale, Edward Everett. 1903. "Old Age Pensions." *Cosmopolitan* 35:168–69.

Haller, Archibald, and David B. Bills. 1979. "Occu-pational Prestige Hierarchies: Theory and Evidence." *Contemporary Sociology* 8:721–34.

Hamermesh, Daniel S. 1998. "Changing Inequality in Markets for Workplace Amenities." *Working Paper 6515.* Cambridge, MA: National Bureau of Economic Research.

Harrison, Roderick J., and Daniel H. Weinberg. 1992. "Changes in Racial and Ethnic Residential Segregation, 1980–1990." Paper presented at the Annual Meeting of the American Statistical Association.

Hartley, William B. 1969. *Estimation of the Incidence of Poverty in the United States, 1870–1914.* Madison, WI: Unpublished Ph.D. Dissertation, Department of Economics, University of Wisconsin.

Hauser, Robert M. 1975. "Structural Changes in Occupational Mobility: Evidence for Men in the United States." *American Sociological Review* 40:585–98.

Haveman, Robert, and Barbar Wolfe. 1995. "The Determinants of Children's Attainments: A Review of Methods and Findings." *Journal of Economic Literature* 33:1829–78.

Hayghe, Howard V. 1997. "Developments in Women's Labor Force Participation." *Monthly Labor Review* 120(September):41–46.

Heilbroner, Robert L., and Lester C. Thurow. 1982. *Economics Explained.* Englewood Cliffs, NJ: Prentice-Hall.

Heller, Joseph. 1961. *Catch-22: A Novel.* New York: Simon & Schuster.

Henshaw, Stanley K., Susheela Singh, and Taylor Haas. Forthcoming. "Incidence of Abortion Worldwide." *International Family Planning Perspectives* 25(January):Table 2.

Herbert, Bob. 1998. "Mounting a War on Bias." *New York Times,* National Edition. January 18:A–21.

Herman, Judith Lewis. 1981. *Father-Daughter Incest.* Cambridge, MA: Harvard University Press.

———. 1989. "Wife Beating." *Harvard Mental Health Newsletter* 5(April):4–6.

———. 1992. *Trauma and Recovery.* New York: Basic Books.

Hibbs, Douglas A. 1977. "Political Parties and Macroeconomic Policy." *American Political Science Review* 71:1467–87.

Highton, Benjamin. 1997. "Easy Registration and Voter Turnout." *Journal of Politics* 59:564–75.

Higley, Stephen Richard. 1995. *Privilege, Power, and Place: The Geography of the American Upper Class.* Lanham, MD: Rowman & Littlefield.

Hochschild, Jennifer. 1981. *What's Fair? American Beliefs about Distributive Justice.* Cambridge, MA: Harvard University Press.

Horsfield, Margaret. 1998. *Biting the Dust: The Joys of Housework.* New York: St. Martin's Press.

Hout, Michael. 1988. "More Universalism, Less Structural Mobility: The American Occupational Structure in the 1980s." *American Journal of Sociology* 93:1358–1400.

Hout, Michael, and William R. Morgan. 1975. "Race and Sex Variations in the Causes of the Expected Attainments of High School Seniors." *American Journal of Sociology* 81:364–94.

Howard, Judith A., and Jocelyn Hollander. 1997. *Gendered Situations, Gendered Selves.* Thousand Oaks, CA: Sage.

Huff, C. Ronald. 1991. *Gangs in America.* Newbury Park, CA: Sage.

Hyman, Herbert. 1942. "The Psychology of Status." *Archives of Psychology*, No. 269.

ILO (International Labour Organization). 1997. *Breaking Through the Glass Ceiling: Women in Management.* Geneva: International Labour Organization.

Ingham, John. 1978. *The Iron Barons.* Chicago: University of Chicago Press.

Inniss, Leslie, and Joe R. Feagin. 1992. "The Black 'Underclass' Ideology in Race Relations Analysis." *Social Justice* 16:13–34.

IRS (Internal Revenue Service). 1998a. "Individual Income Tax Returns, 1995." *SOI Bulletin* 17(Spring):82.

———. 1998b. "Number of Individual Income Tax Returns, Income, Exemptions, and Deductions, by Size of Adjusted Gross Income, Tax Years 1994–1996. *SOI Bulletin* 17(Summer):86.

Jackman, Mary R., and Robert W. Jackman. 1983. *Class Awareness in the United States.* Berkeley, CA: University of California Press.

Jacobs, Janet Liebman. 1994. *Victimized Daughters: Incest and the Development of the Female Self.* New York: Routledge.

Jacobs, Jerry A. 1990. *Revolving Doors: Sex Segregation and Women's Careers.* Stanford, CA: Stanford University Press.

Jaffe, A. J. 1940. "Differential Fertility in the White Population in Early America." *Journal of Heredity* 31:407–11.

Jaynes, Gerald David, and Robin M. Williams. 1989. *A Common Destiny: Blacks and American Society.* Washington, DC: National Academy Press.

JCT (Joint Committee on Taxation). 1997. *Estimates of Federal Tax Expenditures for Fiscal Years 1998–2002.* Washington, DC: U.S. Government Printing Office.

Jencks, Christopher S. 1972. *Inequality: A Reassessment of the Effect of Family and Schooling in America.* New York: Basic Books.

Jencks, Christopher S. et al. 1979. *Who Gets Ahead: The Determinants of Economic Success in America.* New York: Basic Books.

Jewell, Michael E., and David M. Olson. 1978. *American State Political Parties and Elections.* Homewood, IL: Dorsey Press.

Johnson, Barry. 1998. "Personal Wealth, 1992–1995." *SOI Bulletin* 17(Spring):70–95.

Joshi, Heather (ed.). 1989. *The Changing Population of Britain.* London: Basil Blackwell.

Kanter, Rosabeth Moss. 1978. "Some Effects of Proportion on Group Life: Skewed Sex Ratios and Responses to Token Women." *American Journal of Sociology* 82:965–90.

Karnig, A. D., and B. O. Walter. 1977. "Municipal Elections: Registration, Incumbent Success, and Voter Participation." In *Municipal Yearbook* (pp. 41–85). Washington, DC: International City Management Association.

Kasarda, John D. 1990. "Structural Factors Affecting the Location and Timing of Urban Underclass Growth." *Urban Geography* 11:234–64.

Keen, Geraldine. 1971. *Money and Art: A Study Based on the Times-Sotheby Index.* New York: Putnam.

Kennedy, Stetson. 1995. *After Appomattox: How the South Won the War.* Gainesville, FL: University Press of Florida.

Kennickell, Arthur B. 1997. "Consistent Weight Design for the 1989, 1992, and 1995 SCFs, and the Distribution of Wealth." Washington, DC: Federal Reserve Board.

Kennickell, Arthur B., and R. Louise Woodburn. 1992. "Estimation of Household Net Worth Using Model-Based and Designed-Based Weights: Evidence from the 1989 Survey of Consumer

Finances." Washington, DC: Federal Reserve Board.

King, Mary C. 1992. "Occupational Segregation by Race and Sex, 1940–88." *Monthly Labor Review* 115(April):30–36.

Klass, Perry. 1992. "Tackling Problems We Thought We Solved." *New York Times Magazine,* December 12:54–64

Kohn, Melvin. 1987. "Cross-National Research as an Analytic Strategy." *American Sociological Review* 52:713–31.

Kolko, Gabriel. 1962. *Wealth and Power in America.* New York: Praeger.

Komarovsky, Mira. 1940. *The Unemployed Man and His Family.* New York: Octagon Books.

Konner, Melvin. 1991. *Childhood.* Boston: Little Brown.

Koss, Mary P. 1993. "Rape: Scope, Impact, Interventions, and Public Policy Responses." *American Psychologist* 38:1062–69.

Kotlowitz, Alex. 1991. *There Are No Children Here.* New York: Doubleday.

Krugman, Paul. 1995. "What the Public Doesn't Know Can't Hurt Us." *Washington Monthly* 27(October):8–12.

Krymkowski, Daniel H. 1991. "The Process of Status Attainment in Poland, the U.S., and West Germany." *American Sociological Review* 56:46–59.

Kurz, Demi. 1993. "Social Science Perspectives on Wife Abuse: Current Debates and Future Directions." In Pauline Bart and Eileen Gail Moran (eds.), *Violence Against Women: The Bloody Footprints* (pp. 252–69). Newbury Park, CA: Sage.

Kuznets, Simon. 1955. "Economic Growth and Income Inequality." *American Economic Review* 45:1–28.

Lareau, Annette. 1989. *Home Advantage: Social Class and Parental Education in Elementary Education.* Philadelphia: Falmer Press.

LeMasters, E. E. 1976. *Blue Collar Aristocrats.* Madison, WI: University of Wisconsin Press.

Lenski, Gerhard. 1966. *Power and Privilege.* New York: McGraw-Hill.

Lenton, Robert L. 1990. "Techniques of Child Discipline and Abuse by Parents." *Canadian Review of Sociology and Anthropology* 27:157–85.

Lersch, Kim M. 1993. "Current Trends in Police Brutality: An Analysis of Recent Newspaper

Accounts." Unpublished Master's Thesis, University of Florida, Gainesville, FL.

Levy, Frank, and Richard J. Murnane. 1992. "U.S. Earnings Levels and Earnings Inequality: A Review of Recent Trends and Proposed Explanations." *Journal of Economic Literature* 30:1333–81.

Lieberson, Stanley. 1980. *A Piece of the Pie: Blacks and White Immigrants Since 1880.* Berkeley, CA: University of California Press.

———. 1992. "Einstein, Renoir, and Greeley: Some Thoughts About Evidence in Sociology." *American Sociological Review* 57:1–15.

Liker, Jeffrey K., and Glen H. Elder, Jr. 1983. "Economic Hardship and Marital Relations in the 1930s." *American Sociological Review* 48:343–59.

Lipset, Seymour Martin. 1963. *The First New Nation: The United States in Historical and Comparative Perspective.* New York: Basic Books.

———. 1977. "Why No Socialism in the United States?" In S. Bialer and S. Sluzar (eds.), *Sources of Contemporary Radicalism* (pp. 31–149). New York: Westview Press.

Lipset, Seymour Martin, and Hans L. Zetterberg. 1959. "Social Mobility in Industrial Societies." In S. M. Lipset and R. Bendix (eds.), *Social Mobility in Industrial Society* (pp. 11–75). Berkeley, CA: University of California Press.

Lloyd, Susan. 1998. "Domestic Violence and Women's Employment." *NU Policy Research: An Electronic Journal of the Institute for Policy Research at Northwestern University.* <http:www.nwu.edu/ipr/publications> 3(Spring):1–10.

Luker, Kristin. 1984. *Abortion and the Politics of Motherhood.* Berkeley, CA: University of California Press.

———. 1996. *Dubious Conceptions: The Politics of Teenage Pregnancy.* Cambridge, MA: Harvard University Press.

MacKinnon, Neil J., and Tom Langford. 1994. "The Meaning of Occupational Prestige Scores." *Sociological Quarterly* 35:215–45.

Makinson, Larry, and Joshua Goldstein. 1994. *Open Secrets: The Encyclopedia of Congressional Money and Politics,* 3rd Edition. Washington, DC: Congressional Quarterly.

Marsiglio, William. 1993. "Adolescent Male's Orientation Toward Paternity and Contraception."

*Family Planning Perspective*s 25(January/February):22–31.

Martinez, Michael D., and David Hill. Forthcoming. "Did Motor Voter Work?" *American Politics Quarterly.*

Marx, Karl. 1843. "Contribution to the Critique of Hegel's Philosophy of Right." In R. C. Tucker (ed.), *The Marx-Engels Reader*, 2nd edition (pp. 16–26). New York: W. W. Norton, 1978.

———. 1867. *Capital.* New York: International, 1967.

———. 1875. "Critique of the Gotha Program." In Karl Marx and Friedrich Engels, *Selected Works*, Vol. III (pp. 9–30). Moscow: Progress Publishers, 1956.

Marx, Karl, and Friedrich Engels. 1848. "The Communist Manifesto." In Dirk Struik (ed.), *The Birth of the Communist Manifesto* (pp. 85–126). New York: International, 1967.

Massey, Douglas S., and Nancy A. Denton. 1993. *American Apartheid: Segregation and the Making of the Underclass.* Cambridge, MA: Harvard University Press.

McDermott, David. 1997. "Workplace Injuries and Illnesses in the Extractive Industries." *Compensation and Working Conditions* 3(Winter):57–61.

McPherson, Michael S., and Morton Owen Shapiro. 1998. *The Student Aid Game: Meeting Need and Rewarding Talent in American Higher Education.* Princeton, NJ: Princeton University Press.

Mellor, William H. 1996. "No Jobs, No Work: Local Restrictions Block the Exits from Welfare." *New York Times*, National Edition. August 31:A12.

Mendelson, Mary Adelaide. 1974. *Tender Loving Greed.* New York: Knopf.

Merton, Robert K. 1968. *Social Theory and Social Structure.* New York: Free Press.

Merton, Robert K., and Alice S. Rossi. 1968. "Contributions to the Theory of Reference Group Behavior." In R. K. Merton, *Social Theory and Social Structure* (pp. 279–334). New York: Free Press.

Meyer, D. R., and Maria Cancian. 1996. "The Economic Well-Being of Women and Children Following an Exit from AFDC." *Discussion Paper 1101-96.* Madison, WI: Institute for Research on Poverty.

Michels, Robert. 1911. *Political Parties.* New York: Dover, 1959.

Miller, S. M. 1960. "Comparative Social Mobility." *Current Sociology* 9:1–89.

Mills, C. Wright. 1951. *White Collar.* New York: Oxford University Press.

———. 1959. *The Sociological Imagination.* New York: Oxford University Press.

Mitchell, Alison. 1998. "A New Form of Lobbying Puts Public Face on Private Interest." *New York Times,* National Edition. September 30:1.

Mitchell, Daniel J. B. 1992. "'Employers' Welfare Work:' A 1913 BLS Report." *Monthly Labor Review* 115(February):52–55.

Mitra, Tapan, and Efe A. Ok. 1996. "Personal Income Taxation and the Principle of Equal Sacrifice Revisited." *International Economic Review* 37:925–48.

Morgan, Philip D. 1998. *Slave Counterpoint: Black Culture in the Eighteenth Century Chesepeake and Lowcountry.* Chapel Hill, NC: University of North Carolina Press.

Morris, Lydia. 1992. "The Social Segregation of the Long-Term Unemployed in Hartlepool." *Sociological Review* 40:344–69.

Murrell, A. J. 1991. "Aspiring to Careers in Male and Female Dominated Professions: A Study of Black and White College Women." *Psychology of Women Quarterly* 15:103–26.

NACCD (National Advisory Commission on Civil Disorders). 1968. *Report of the National Advisory Commission on Civil Disorders.* New York: Bantam.

Nakao, Keiko, and Judith Treas. 1994. "Updating Occupational Prestige and Socioeconomic Scores: How the New Measures Measure Up." In Peter V. Marsden (ed.), *Sociological Methodology* (pp. 1–72). Washington, DC: American Sociological Association.

NCH (National Coalition for the Homeless). 1998. "How Many People Experience Homelessness." http://www.nch.ari.net.

NCHS (National Center for Health Statistics). 1996. "Advance Report of Final Mortality Statistics, 1994." *Monthly Vital Statistics Report.* Hyattsville, MD: U.S. Department of Health and Human Services.

———. 1998a. "Infant Mortality Statistics from the 1996 Period Linked Birth/Infant Death Data

Set." *Monthly Vital Statistics Report*, 46, #12, Supplement, August 27. Hyattsville, MD: U.S. Department of Health and Human Services.

————. 1998b. Report of Final Natality Statistics, 1996." *Monthly Vital Statistics Report*, 46, #11, Supplement, June 30. Hyattsville, MD: U.S. Department of Health and Human Services.

Neibuhr, Gustave. 1998. "Southern Baptists Declare Wife Should 'Submit' to Her Husband." *New York Times*, National Edition. June 10, p. 1.

Neilsen, François, and Arthur S. Alderson. 1997. "The Kuznets Curve and the Great U-Turn: Income Inequality in U.S. Counties, 1970 to 1990." *American Sociological Review* 62:12–33.

Niemi, Richard. 1989. *Trends in Public Opinion: A Compendium of Survey Data*. New York: Greenwood Press.

Nisbet, Robert A. 1969. *Social Change and History*. New York: Oxford University Press.

Nordheimer, Jon. 1996. "One Day's Death Toll on the Job." *New York Times*, National Edition. December 22:3–1.

NRCCSA (National Resource Center on Child Sexual Abuse). 1992. *The Incidence and Prevalence of Child Sexual Abuse: No Easy Answer*. Huntsville, AL: NRCCSA.

NVC (National Victim Center). 1992. *Rape in America: A Report to the Nation*. Arlington, VA: National Victim Center.

Oakes, Jeannie. 1985. *Keeping Track: How Schools Structure Inequality*. New Haven, CT: Yale University Press.

OMB (Office of Management and Budget). 1998a. *Analytical Perspectives: Budget of the United States Government, Fiscal Year 1999*. Washington, DC: U.S. Government Printing Office.

————. 1998b. *Budget of the United States Government, Fiscal Year 1999*. Washington, DC: U.S. Government Printing Office.

O'Neill, William L. 1972. *Women at Work, Including "The Long Day: The Story of a New York Working Girl, by Dorothy Richardson."* Chicago, IL: Quadrangle Books.

ONS (Office for National Statistics). 1997. *Social Trends 27*. London: The Stationary Office.

Ornati, Oscar. 1966. *Poverty Amidst Affluence*. New York: Twentieth Century Fund.

Oshinsky, David M. 1996. *Worse than Slavery:*

Parchman Farm and the Ordeal of Jim Crow Justice. New York: Free Press.

Page, Benjamin I. 1983. *Who Gets What from Government*. Berkeley, CA: University of California Press.

Palmer, Phyllis M. 1989. *Domesticity and Dirt: Housewives and Domestic Servants in the United States, 1920–1945*. Philadelphia: Temple University Press.

Parsons, Talcott. 1951. *The Social System*. New York: Free Press.

————. 1954. "A Revised Analytical Approach to the Theory of Social Stratification." In T. Parsons, *Essays in Sociological Theory*, revised edition (pp. 386–439). New York: Free Press.

————. 1960. "The Distribution of Power in American Society." In T. Parsons, *Structure and Process in Modern Society* (pp. 199–225). New York: Free Press.

Passell, Peter. 1998. "Benefits Dwindle Along with Wages for the Unskilled." *New York Times*, National Edition. June 14:A-1.

Patterson, James T. 1986. *America's Struggle Against Poverty, 1900–85*. Cambridge, MA: Harvard University Press.

PC (Public Campaign). 1998. "Ouch! How Money in Politics Hurts You." www.publicampaign.org.

Perrin, Emily. 1904. "On the Contingency between Occupation in the Case of Fathers and Sons." *Biometrika* 3:467–69.

Persell, Caroline Hodges, and Peter W. Cookson, Jr. 1985. "Chartering and Bartering: Elite Education and Social Reproduction." *Social Problems* 33:114–29.

Personick, Martin E., and Laura A. Harthun. 1992. "Job Safety and Health in Soft Drink Manufacturing." *Monthly Labor Review* 15(April):12–18.

Pessen, Edward. 1971. "The Egalitarian Myth and American Social Reality: Wealth, Mobility, and Equality in the 'Era of the Common Man.'" *American Historical Review* 76:989–1034.

Pierce, Brooks. 1998. "Compensation Inequality." Washington, DC: Bureau of Labor Statistics.

Piven, Frances Fox, and Richard A. Cloward. 1971. *Regulating the Poor*. New York: Vintage Books.

————. 1977. *Poor People's Movements*. New York: Pantheon.

———. 1988. *Why Americans Don't Vote.* New York: Pantheon.

Plotnick, Robert D., Eugene Smolensky, Eirik Evenhouse, and Siobhan Reilly. 1998. "Inequality and Poverty in the United States: The Twentieth-Century Record." *Focus* 19:7–14.

Presser, Harriet B. 1994. "Employment Schedules among Dual-Earner Spouses and the Division of Household Labor by Gender." *American Sociological Review* 59:348–64.

Reardon, Jack. 1993. "Injuries and Illnesses among Bituminous and Lignite Coal Miners." *Monthly Labor Review* 115(October):49–55.

Reed, James. 1978. *From Private Vice to Public Virtue: The Birth Control Movement and American Society Since 1830.* New York: Basic Books.

Rees, P., D. Phillips, and D. Medway. 1995. "The Socioeconomic Geography of Ethnic Groups in Two Northern British Cities." *Environment and Planning A.* 27:557–91.

Reskin, Barbara, and Irene Padavic. 1994. *Women and Men at Work.* Thousand Oaks, CA: Pine Forge Press.

Reynolds, Morgan, and Eugene Smolensky. 1977. *Public Expenditures, Taxes, and the Distribution of Income: The United States, 1950, 1961, 1970.* New York: Academic Press.

RIA (Research Institute of America). 1998. *United States Tax Reporter.* New York: Research Institute of America.

Ritter, Kathleen, and Lowell L. Hargens. 1975. "Occupational Positions and Class Identification: A Test of the Asymmetry Hypothesis." *American Journal of Sociology* 80:934–48.

Rosenthal, Robert, and Lenore Jacobson. 1968. *Pygmalion in the Classroom: Teacher Expectations and Pupils' Intellectual Development.* New York: Holt, Rinehart, and Winston.

Rothman, Ellen K. 1984. *Hands and Hearts: A History of Courtship in America.* New York: Basic Books.

Rubin, Lillian. 1994. *Families on the Fault Line.* New York: HarperCollins.

Ruggles, Patricia. 1990. *Drawing the Line: Alternative Poverty Measures and Their Implications for Public Policy.* Washington, DC: Urban Institute Press.

Rusk, John G. 1970. "The Effect of the Australian Ballot Reform on Split Ticket Voting: 1876–1908." *American Political Science Review* 72:22–45.

Rytina, Nancy F., and Suzanne M. Bianchi. 1984. "Occupational Reclassification and Distribution by Gender." *Monthly Labor Review* 107 (March):11–17.

SA (Special Advisor to the Board of Police Commissioners on the Civil Disorders in Los Angeles). 1994. *City in Crisis.* Los Angeles: Special Advisor to the Board of Police Commissioners.

Sagan, Carl et al. 1984. "Nuclear War and Climatic Catastrophe." *Foreign Affairs* 62:257–92.

Sander, William. 1992. "Unemployment and Marital Status in Great Britain." *Social Biology* 39:299–305.

Sanderson, Warren. 1979. "Quantitative Aspects of Marriage, Fertility, and Family Limitation in Nineteenth-Century America." *Demography* 16:339–58.

Sawinski, Zbigniew, and Henryk Domanski. 1991. "Stability of Prestige Hierarchies in the Face of Social Changes: Poland, 1958–1987." *International Sociology* 6:227–42.

SC (Statiska Centralbyrån). 1996. Statistical Abstract of Sweden. Stockholm: Statiska Centralbyrån.

Schneider, Beth E. 1991. "Put Up and Shut Up: Workplace Sexual Assaults." *Gender & Society* 5:533–46.

Scofea, Laura A. 1994. "The Development and Growth of Employer-Provided Health Insurance." *Monthly Labor Review* 117(March):3–10.

Searles, Patricia, and Ronald J. Berger (eds.). 1995. *Rape and Society.* Boulder, CO: Westview Press.

Sewell, William H., Archibald O. Haller, and George W. Ohlendorf. 1970. "The Educational and Early Occupational Attainment Process: Replication and Revisions." *American Sociological Review* 35:1014–27.

Sewell, William H., and Vimal P. Shah. 1968a. "Parent's Education and Children's Educational Aspirations and Achievements." *American Sociological Review* 35:1014–27.

———. 1968b. "Social Class, Parental Encouragement, and Educational Aspirations." *American Journal of Sociology* 73:559–72.

SH (Second Harvest). 1997. *Hunger 1997: The Faces & Facts.* Chicago, IL: Second Harvest.

Shakespeare, William. 1989. *Romeo and Juliet.* London: Metheun Drama.

———. 1991. *Measure for Measure.* New York: Cambridge University Press.

Shaw, George Bernard. 1957. *Pygmalion.* New York: Penguin.

Shipler, David. 1993. "Jefferson Is America—And America Is Jefferson." *New York Times,* National Edition. April 12, A-12.

Short, Kathleen, Martina Shea, David Johnson, and Thesia I. Garner. 1998. "Putting the Experimental Poverty Measure into Practice." *Focus* 19(Spring):16–20.

Sibley, Elbridge. 1942. "Some Demographic Clues to Stratification." *American Sociological Review* 7:315–25.

Simmel, Georg. 1908. "The Significance of Numbers in Social Life." In Georg Simmel, *The Sociology of Georg Simmel* (pp. 87–180). New York: Free Press, 1954.

Sixma, H., and Ultee, W. C. 1984. "An Occupational Scale for the Netherlands in the Eighties." In B. F. Bakker (ed.), *Social Stratification and Mobility in the Netherlands* (pp. 101–15). Amsterdam: SISWO.

Sly, Frances, Tim Thair, and Andrew Risdon. 1998. "Labour Market Participation of Ethnic Groups." *Labour Market Trends* 106(December):1–18. London: Office of National Statistics.

Smeeding, Timothy. 1982. *Alternative Methods for Valuing Selected In-Kind Transfer Benefits and Measuring Their Effect on Poverty.* Washington, DC: U.S. Government Printing Office.

———. 1996. "America's Income Inequality: Where Do We Stand?" *Challenge* 39:45–54.

Smith, J. Owens. 1987. *The Politics of Racial Inequality.* New York: Greenwood Press.

Solon, Gary. 1992. "Intergenerational Income Mobility in the United States." *American Economic Review* 82:393–408.

Soltow, Lee. 1975. "The Wealth, Income, and Social Class of Men in Large Northern Cities of the United States in 1860." In James D. Smith (ed.), *The Personal Distribution of Income and Wealth* (pp. 233–76). New York: National Bureau of Economic Research.

Sorokin, Pitirim. 1927. *Social and Cultural Mobility.* New York: Free Press, 1959.

Staples, Brent. 1994. "Just Walk on By: A Black Man Ponders His Power to Alter Public Space." In Donald M. McQuade and Robert Atwan (eds.), *The Writer's Presence* (pp. 130–33). Boston, MA: St. Martin's Press.

Starr, Paul. 1982. *The Transformation of American Medicine.* New York: Basic Books.

Stock, Jacqueline L. 1997. "Adolescent Pregnancy and Sexual Risk-Taking Among Sexually Abused Girls." *Family Planning Perspectives* 29:200–203.

Sullivan, Harry Stack. 1940. *Conceptions of Modern Psychiatry.* Washington, DC: William A, White Foundation.

Tabatabai, Hamid. 1996. *Statistics on Poverty and Income Distribution.* Geneva: International Labour Office.

Takaki, Ronald. 1989. *Strangers from a Different Shore: A History of Asian Americans.* New York: Penguin Books.

TBA (Television Bureau of Advertising). 1991. *Trends in Viewing.* New York: Television Bureau of Advertising.

Teixeira, Ruy A. 1992. *The Disappearing American Voter.* Washington, DC: Brookings Institution.

Thompson, Starley, and Stephen H. Schneider. 1986. "Nuclear Winter Reappraised." *Foreign Affairs* 64:981–1005.

Thurow, Lester C. 1975. *Generating Inequality: Mechanisms of Distribution in the U.S. Economy.* New York: Basic Books.

Timpone, Richard J. 1998. "Structure, Behavior, and Voter Turnout in the United States." *American Political Science Review* 92:145–58.

Tocqueville, Alexis de. 1835. *Democracy in America.* New York: New American Library, 1954.

Treiman, Donald J. 1977. *Occupational Prestige in Comparative Perspective.* New York: Academic Press.

Treiman, Donald J., and Harry B. G. Ganzeboom. 1990. "Cross-National Status Attainment Research." *Research in Social Stratification and Mobility* 9:105–130.

Treiman, Donald J., and Kam-Bor Yip. 1989. "Educational and Occupational Attainment in 21 Countries." In M. L. Kohn (ed.), *Cross-National Research in Sociology* (pp. 373–94). Newbury Park, CA: Sage.

Turner, Frederick Jackson. 1920. *The Significance of the Frontier in American History.* New York: Henry Holt.

Turner, Jonathan H. 1984. *Societal Stratification.* New York: Columbia University Press.

———. 1998. *The Structure of Sociological Theory*, Sixth Ed. Belmont, CA: Wadsworth.

Turner, Jonathan H., Leonard Beeghley, and Charles Powers. 1998. *The Emergence of Sociological Theory*, Fourth Ed. Belmont, CA: Wadsworth.

UN (United Nations). 1989. *1989 Report on the World Social Situation.* New York: United Nations.

———. 1997. *Trends in Europe and North America, 1996/97.* New York: United Nations.

USBC (United States Bureau of the Census). 1974. *Statistical Abstract of the United States.* Washington, DC: U.S. Government Printing Office.

———. 1975. *Historical Statistics of the U.S.: Colonial Times to 1970.* Washington, DC: U.S. Government Printing Office.

———. 1995a. "American Housing Survey for the United States in 1995." *Current Population Reports,* H150/95RV. Washington, DC: U.S. Government Printing Office.

———. 1995b. "Child Support for Custodial Mothers and Fathers, 1991." *Current Population Reports,* P60–187. Washington, DC: U.S. Government Printing Office.

———. 1995c. "Income, Poverty, and Valuation of Noncash Benefits, 1993." *Current Population Reports,* P60–188. Washington, DC: U.S. Government Printing Office.

———. 1996a. "A Brief Look at Postwar U.S. Income Inequality." *Current Population Reports,* P60–191. Washington, DC: U.S. Government Printing Office.

———. 1996b. "65+ in the United States." *Current Population Reports,* P23–190. Washington, DC: U.S. Government Printing Office.

———. 1997a. "Money Income in the United States, 1996." *Current Population Reports,* P60–197. Washington, DC: U.S. Government Printing Office.

———. 1997b. *Statistical Abstract of the United States.* Washington, DC: U.S. Government Printing Office.

———. 1998a. "American Indian and Alaska Native Populations." *<http://www.census.gov/population>*

———. 1998b. "Asian and Pacific Islander Population in the United States: March, 1996." *Current Population Reports,* P20–503. Washington, DC: U.S. Government Printing Office.

———. 1998c. "Black Population in the United States: March, 1997." *Current Population Reports,* P20–508. Washington, DC: U.S. Government Printing Office.

———. 1998d. "Health Insurance Coverage: 1996." *<http://www.census.gov/hhes/hlthins/cover96/c96tabb.html>*

———. 1998e. "Hispanic Population in the United States: March, 1997." *Current Population Reports,* P20–511. Washington, DC: U.S. Government Printing Office.

———. 1998f. "Money Income in the United States: 1997." *Current Population Reports,* P60–200. Washington, DC: U.S. Government Printing Office.

———. 1998g. "Poverty in the United States: 1997." *Current Population Reports,* P60–201. Washington, DC: U.S. Government Printing Office.

———. 1998h. "Voting and Registration in the Election of November, 1996." *Current Population Reports,* P20–504. Washington, DC: U.S. Government Printing Office.

USDA (United States Department of Agriculture). 1998a. *Agriculture Fact Book.* Washington, DC: U.S. Government Printing Office.

———. 1998b. "Introduction to the Food Stamp Program." *<www.usda.gov>*

USDHHS (United States Department of Health and Human Services). 1998a. "Change in Welfare Caseloads." *<www.acf.dhhs.gov>*

———. 1998b. *Temporary Assistance for Needy Families.* Washington, DC: U.S. Government Printing Office.

USDJ (United States Department of Justice). 1998. *Violence by Intimates.* Washington, DC: U.S. Government Printing Office.

USDL (United States Department of Labor). 1997. *Employee Benefits in Small Private Establishments, 1994.* Bulletin 2475. Washington, DC: U.S. Government Printing Office.

———. 1998a. *Employee Benefits in Medium and Large Private Establishments, 1995*, Bulletin 2496. Washington, DC: U.S. Government Printing Office.

———. 1998b. *Employment & Earnings* 45(January). Washington, DC: U.S. Government Printing Office.

————. 1998c. *Employment & Earnings* 45(September). Washington, DC: U.S. Government Printing Office.

Valian, Virginia. 1998. *Why So Slow? The Advancement of Women.* Cambridge, MA: The MIT Press.

van den Berg, Axel. 1993. "Creeping Embourgeoisement? Some Comments on the Marxist Discovery of the New Middle Class." *Research in Stratification* 12:295–328.

Van Velsor, Ellen, and Leonard Beeghley. 1979. "Class Identification Among Employed Married Women." *Journal of Marriage and the Family* 41:771–79.

Vanneman, Reeve, and Fred C. Pampel. 1977. "The American Perception of Class and Status." *American Sociological Review* 42:422–37.

Veblen, Thorstein. 1899. *The Theory of the Leisure Class.* New York: Penguin Books, 1979.

Vernon, Amelia Wallace. 1993. *African Americans at Mars Bluff, South Carolina.* Baton Rouge, LA: Louisiana State University Press.

Voslenski, Michael. 1985. *Nomenklatura: The Soviet Ruling Class.* Garden City, NY: Doubleday.

Wagner, Ellen J. 1992. *Sexual Harassment in the Workplace.* New York: AMACOM.

Wallace, James. 1993. *Hard Drive: Bill Gates and the Making of the Microsoft Empire.* New York: HarperCollins.

Wallace, Michael. 1997. "Revisiting Broom and Cushing's 'Modest Test of an Immodest Theory,'" In *Research in Social Stratification and Mobility* 17:239–54.

Wallerstein, Immanuel. 1974. *The Modern World System.* New York: Academic Press.

WB (World Bank). 1999. *World Development Report.* New York: Oxford University Press.

Weber, Max. 1904. "'Objectivity' in Social Science and Social Policy." In Weber, *The Methodology of the Social Sciences* (pp. 50–112). New York: Free Press, 1949.

————. 1905. *The Protestant Ethic and the Spirit of Capitalism.* New York: Scribners, 1958.

————. 1913. *Religion of China.* New York: Free Press, 1951.

————. 1917. *Religion of India.* New York: Free Press, 1952.

————. 1918. "Science as a Vocation." In Hans Gerth and C. Wright Mills (eds), *From Max Weber: Essays in Sociology* (pp. 129–58). New York: Oxford University Press, 1947.

————. 1920. *Economy and Society.* Totowa, NJ: Bedminster Press, 1968.

Weed, James. 1980. *National Estimates of Marital Dissolution and Survivorship: United States.* Washington, DC: U.S. Department of Health and Human Services.

Weisbrot, Mark. 1998. *Welfare Reform: The Jobs Aren't There.* Washington, DC: Preamble Center for Public Policy.

Weitzman, Lenore. 1985. *The Divorce Revolution.* New York: Free Press.

Weitzman, Lenore, and Mavis MacLean (eds.). 1992. *Economic Consequences of Divorce.* Oxford: Clarendon Press.

Westoff, Charles F. 1988. "Contraceptive Paths Toward a Reduction of Unintended Pregnancy and Abortion." *Family Planning Perspectives* 20:4–13.

Whelpton, Pascal K. 1928. "Industrial Development and Population Growth." *Social Forces* 6:458–67.

Wiatrowski, William J. 1994. "On the Disparity between Private and Public Pensions." *Monthly Labor Review* 117(April):3–9.

Wilcox, Clyde. 1998. *Preliminary Report: 1996 Congressional Campaign Finance Survey.* Chicago: Joyce Foundation.

Willer, David, and Murray Webster. 1970. "Theoretical Concepts and Observables." *American Sociological Review* 35:748–56.

Williams, Bruce B. 1987. *Black Workers in an Industrial Suburb: The Struggle Against Discrimination.* New Brunswick, NJ: Rutgers University Press.

Williams, Robin. 1977. *Mutual Accommodation: Ethnic Conflict and Cooperation.* Minneapolis, MN: University of Minnesota Press.

Williamson, Jeffrey G., and Peter H. Lindert. 1980. *American Inequality: A Macroeconomic History.* New York: Academic Press.

Wilson, William J. 1996. *When Work Disappears: The World of the New Urban Poor.* New York: Knopf.

Winkler, Anne E. 1998. "Earnings of Husbands and Wives in Dual-Earner Families." *Monthly Labor Review* 121(April):42–48.

Winship, Christopher. 1992. "Race, Poverty, and

'The American Occupational Structure.'" *Contemporary Sociology* 21:639–43.

Wolfe, Barbara. 1998. "Incorporating Health Care Needs into a Measure of Poverty: An Exploratory Proposal." *Focus* 19(Spring):29–30.

Wolfe, Alan. 1998. "Climbing the Mountain: The Second Volume of Taylor Branch's Study of Martin Luther King Jr. Runs from the March on Washington to Selma." *New York Times Book Review,* January 18:12.

Wolffe, Edward N. 1995. *Top Heavy: The Increasing Inequality of Wealth in America and What Can Be Done about It.* New York: Twentieth Century Fund.

Wolfinger, Raymond E., and Steven J. Rosenstone. 1980. *Who Votes?* New Haven: Yale University Press.

Woodward, C. Vann. 1966. *The Strange Career of Jim Crow.* New York: Oxford University Press.

Wright, Erik Olin. 1997. *Classes.* New York: Verso.

Wu, Xu, and Ann Leffler. 1992. "Gender and Race Effects on Occupational Prestige, Segregation, and Earnings." *Gender & Society* 6:376–392.

Zane, Peter. 1995. "Company Perks: Ego Is Out, Safety Is In." *New York Times,* National Edition. August 20:F–9.

Zelizer, Viviana A. 1985. *Pricing the Priceless Child: The Changing Social Value of Children.* New York: Basic.

———. 1994. *The Social Meaning of Money.* New York: Basic.

Index